TELLING PACIFIC LIVES

PRISMS OF PROCESS

TELLING PACIFIC LIVES

PRISMS OF PROCESS

Published by ANU E Press
The Australian National University
Canberra ACT 0200, Australia
Email: anuepress@anu.edu.au
This title is also available online at: http://epress.anu.edu.au/tpl_citation.html

National Library of Australia
Cataloguing-in-Publication entry

Title:	Telling Pacific lives : prisms of process / editors, Vicki Luker ; Brij V. Lal.
ISBN:	9781921313813 (pbk.) 9781921313820 (pdf)
Notes:	Includes index.
Subjects:	Islands of the Pacific--Biography.
	Islands of the Pacific--Anecdotes.
	Islands of the Pacific--Civilization.
	Islands of the Pacific--Social life and customs.
Other Authors/Contributors:	
	Luker, Vicki.
	Lal, Brij.
Dewey Number:	990.0099

All rights reserved. No part of this publication may be reproduced, stored in a retrieval system or transmitted in any form or by any means, electronic, mechanical, photocopying or otherwise, without the prior permission of the publisher.

Cover design by Teresa Prowse

Cover image: Choris, Louis, 1795-1828. Iles Radak [picture] [Paris : s.n., [1827] 1 print : lithograph, hand col.; 20.5 x 26 cm. nla.pic-an10412525 National Library of Australia

This edition © 2008 ANU E Press

Table of Contents

Preface	vii
1. Telling Pacific Lives: From Archetype to Icon, *Niel Gunson*	1
2. The Kila Wari Stories: Framing a Life and Preserving a Cosmology, *Deborah Van Heekeren*	15
3. From 'My Story' to 'The Story of Myself'—Colonial Transformations of Personal Narratives among the Motu-Koita of Papua New Guinea, *Michael Goddard*	35
4. Mobility, Modernisation and Agency: The Life Story of John Kikang from Papua New Guinea, *Wolfgang Kempf*	51
5. Surrogacy and the Simulacra of Desire in Heian Japanese Women's Life Writing, *Christina Houen*	69
6. 'The Story that Came to Me': Gender, Power and Life History Narratives—Reflections on the Ethics of Ethnography in Fiji, *Pauline McKenzie Aucoin*	85
7. A Tartan Clan in Fiji: Narrating the Coloniser 'Within' the Colonised, *Lucy de Bruce*	93
8. Telling Lives in Tuvalu, *Michael Goldsmith*	107
9. My History: My Calling, *Alaima Talu*	117
10. Researching, (W)riting, Releasing, and Responses to a Biography of Queen Salote of Tonga, *Elizabeth Wood-Ellem*	139
11. On Being a Participant Biographer: The Search for J.W. Davidson, *Doug Munro*	149
12. 'You Did What, Mr President!?!?' Trying to Write a Biography of Tosiwo Nakayama, *David Hanlon*	165
13. Telling the Life of A.D. Patel, *Brij V. Lal*	177
14. On Writing a Biography of William Pritchard, *Andrew E. Robson*	195
15. Writing the Colony: Walter Edward Gudgeon in the Cook Islands, 1898 to 1909, *Graeme Whimp*	205
16. An Accidental Biographer? On Encountering, Yet Again, the Ideas and Actions of J.W. Burton, *Christine Weir*	215
17. E.W.P. Chinnery: A Self-Made Anthropologist, *Geoffrey Gray*	227
18. Lives Told: Australians in Papua and New Guinea, *Hank Nelson*	243
19. Biography of a Nation: Compiling a Historical Dictionary of the Solomon Islands, *Clive Moore*	277
Notes on Contributors	293
Index	295

Preface

Make bare the poor dead secrets of the heart
Strip the stark-naked soul
       Swinburne

The great poet's words, of an era long gone, speak to continuing biographical conventions and aspirations. Even those who believe that life writing, as a genre, is more easily handled than other forms of historical and creative writing concede the complexities and uncertainties involved in constructing a life—whether another's or one's own. This volume of essays is an exploration of the way in which scholars from different disciplines, standpoints and theoretical orientations attempt to write life stories in the Pacific. It is the product of a conference organised by the Division of Pacific and Asian History at The Australian National University in December 2005.

The aim of the conference was to explore ways in which Pacific lives are read and constructed through a variety of media—films, fiction, 'faction', history—under four overarching themes. The first, *Framing Lives*, sought to explore various ways of constructing a life—from a classic western perspective of birth, formation, experiences and death of an individual to other ways, for example, life as secondary to a longer genealogical entity, life as a symbol of collective experience, individual lives captured and fragmented in a mosaic of others, lives made meaningful by their implication in a particular historical or cultural web, the underlying values and world views that inform one or another approach to framing a life. The second theme, the *Stuff of Life*, looked at materials, methods and collaborative arrangements with which the biographer, autobiographer and recorder work, their objectives, constraints, inspirations, challenges and tricks. The third section, *Story Lines*, focused on formats and genres such as edited diaries, collections of writings, voice recordings, genres of biography, autobiography, truth and fiction (verse, dance, novels) and the varieties and different advantages of narrative shapes that crystallise the telling of a life. The final section, *Telling Lives/Changing Lives*, focused on biography/autobiography and the consciousness of identity, history, purpose, lives as witness and windows, telling lives as change for those involved in the tale, the telling, the listening. The overall aim was to bring out both the generic or universal challenges of 'telling lives' as well as to highlight the particular tendencies and trends in the Pacific.

Yet these four themes, which seemed analytically promising at the outset, proved in practice difficult to disentangle from the presentations at the workshop. Instead, another pattern of difference began to emerge, anchored in apparent contrasts between the literate and oral cultures of the Pacific. On the one hand were 'life tellers' operating with what could be called Western concepts of the individual, time and history—or at least with people or texts which harmonised with these. For the subjects of these life stories and their tellers, literacy was a crucial element of their existence that in fundamental ways could be taken for granted. On the other hand were 'life tellers' dealing with people and evidence influenced by a different matrix: by traditional Pacific cultures which are oral. Here personhood is defined largely by relations with kin, alive and dead—Western concepts of the individual, together with the consciousness of the self on which 'biography' and 'autobiography' in important Western senses depend, are alien and, some would argue, inconceivable. In these cultures, time is imagined, ultimately, as cyclical rather than linear; and the past is palpably immanent in the present. Niel Gunson's comprehensive keynote address to the workshop, which as chapter one serves as an introduction to this volume as a whole, adumbrates this cultural divide. Though it can be overstated and several of the 'lives told' here, and their tellers, in different ways bridge or question it, nevertheless this divide remains fundamental to the collection and poses particular challenges for those 'tellers' who work across it.

Anthropologists Deborah Van Heekeren, Michael Goddard and Wolfgang Kempf, more searchingly than any other contributors, explicitly address the cultural foundations of biography and autobiography. They deal with lives rooted in traditional Pacific cultures or with lives lived, and represented, in the midst of great cultural change, including a shift towards literacy. Each of these authors poses a difficult question.

Deborah Van Heekeren meditates upon the stories which the Vula'a people of coastal Papua New Guinea tell of a fabled warrior, Kila Wari, who lived between 1820 and 1860. She asks: why do the Vula'a tell these stories? The question is all the more arresting because the informant who pressed her to record stories about Kila Wari—and indeed wanted a film to be made of Kila Wari's life—appears to reject so much that his ancestor, Kila Wari, embodies. Whereas Kila Wari was a great killer of men and a pagan, his descendant is a fulltime Christian evangelist. Deborah concludes that these stories serve two purposes: first, they establish relationships between the tellers and Kila Wari that can advantage the tellers in local disputes over land and politics; second, these stories preserve and provide access to a pre-Christian Vula'a existence. Kila Wari's stories do not constitute biography in the sense indicated by Swinburne—'making bare the poor dead secrets' of the subject's inner heart: rather, they constitute identity for their tellers and have an important collective function in protecting, through the tales of Kila Wari, a traditional worldview and way of life.

Michael Goddard reflects on the autobiographical writings of Bobby Gaigo, from the village of Tatana in PNG's capital, Port Moresby. Bobby Gaigo's autobiographical writings, unlike the majority of Melanesian 'autobiographies', were written entirely by himself, without a European collaborator or mentor. For Goddard, the question is: how did Bobby Gaigo develop the autobiographical self-consciousness necessary for such writing? Goddard argues that in the traditional culture from which Gaigo sprang, the concepts of 'self' and 'history' that are necessary preconditions for autobiography were nonexistent. To support this argument, Goddard describes traditional concepts of self and time among Bobby Gaigo's people and draws analogies from other Melanesian cultures. Goddard also finds supporting evidence in certain so-called 'autobiographies' which have resulted from collaboration between a Melanesian 'teller' and a European mentor-cum-editor. These particular 'autobiographies', on scrutiny, reveal how the teller's concepts of personhood and time were often radically at odds with those of his or her collaborator. Goddard notes the thesis that among the traditional cultures of the Pacific, 'autobiographical consciousness' has been fostered by Islanders' interaction with Christianity and capitalism, which promotes concepts of the 'individual'. However, he rejects this thesis in the case of Bobby Gaigo. Instead, he proposes that Gaigo's long participation in land-claims for his people against the colonial administration led to an appreciation of the value Europeans placed on documentary evidence and history in the Western sense. Gaigo thereby developed the 'autobiographical self-consciousness' from which to write 'The Story of Myself'.

Finally, Wolfgang Kempf writes from his experience as a collaborator-cum-editor, co-constructing the life story of John Kikang, a man from PNG's Madang hinterland. John Kikang was of an earlier generation than Bobby Gaigo's, but like him grew up in a traditional oral society, though with less formal schooling. As a youth, Kikang left home to work for the whites, participating in the colonial economy and engaging with Christianity. On returning to his home village, Kikang was an energetic promoter of agricultural projects and Roman Catholicism, working closely with administrators and missionaries.

Kempf's question is: how best can he put John Kikang's life on paper? He uses John Kikang's own writings: a journal and a 'holy book', both unsettling and thought-provoking texts; and recordings of John Kikang's narratives and conversations with his collaborator. Kempf has thought about the processes by which Kikang tried to make sense of the world and change his corner of it. He also respects Kikang's projections of himself as a mediator between his 'backward' home and the spiritual and material realms of the whites. Further, Kempf sees commonalities in the processes—characterised by Kempf as 'mimetic'—by which he, as collaborator, tries to understand and reproduce Kikang's writings and narratives and by which Kikang understands and represents his own life. Kempf's resolve to honour these processes result in plans for a 'life story' that will graphically distinguish the different materials used, Kikang's and Kempf's respective efforts, and the dynamics of co-creation. It will look unlike 'biography' or 'autobiography' in the conventional Western format.

Several other chapters can be savoured within the problematic suggested by contrasts between traditional/oral and Western (alternatively modern)/literate approaches to the telling of Pacific lives. Thus in his efforts to write a biography of Tosiwo Nakayama, David Hanlon is keenly sensitive to the cultural differences between biographer and biographee, including Nakayama's fundamental ambivalence about texts. Pauline MacKenzie Aucoin is left with unanswered and perhaps unanswerable questions of what to do with the life story imparted to her by a Fijian village woman, one day as they sewed together and the rain fell. Though Michael Goldsmith, in his survey of Tuvaluan life stories, challenges schematic contrasts between 'traditional' and 'Western' concepts of the self (and reader take note: treat the dichotomies drawn in this preface with suspicion!), in the chapter that follows his, the autobiographical reflections of Tuvalu-born Alaima Talu at one level record a painful process of individuation through which she separated from her parents, their wishes and their church.

Christina Houen's contribution on Heian Japanese women's life writing may appear out of place in a collection on the Pacific. But it is the methodology rather than the subject matter that is of interest. Houen is concerned with the way *The Tale of Genji* speaks pleasurably to a certain kind of woman of which Houen presents herself as an exemplar. 'It is a mirror to my own life', she remarks. The genres which Heian women developed, in poetic diary and prose romance, with their themes of loss, longing, exclusion, separation, loneliness and repressed desire for emotional security and artistic freedom, find resonance in her own life. Alaima Talu, too, reads other attempts at life writing—by Mahatma Gandhi, Sidney Poitier and Sheila Graham—for inspiration and guidance before writing down her own life. Aucoin is a similarly autobiographical contributor, in that she dramatises the ethical issues posed to her—as a woman and an anthropologist—by the question whether and how to interpret the story told to her. Lucy de Bruce embeds her family history in a kind of autobiographical essay—the kind that postulates the author as typical of a social category. The *kailoma* story (and her own) is that of moving from silent invisibility to articulate visibility through self-narration.

The contributions by historians Wood-Ellem, Munro and Lal are about the process of research and discovery, chance encounters with revealing bits of information, about the role of contingency in scholarship: a stray letter here and a piece of paper there which throw interesting light on the subject, such as Lord Dening's letter to Lal about A.D. Patel's critical arbitration into Fiji's sugar industry and Davidson's letter to his musical friend about sleeping with him. The contributions by Hanlon and Moore and, to some extent, Wood-Ellem are about biographical projects aligned with the project of nation-building in situations where centrifugal dynamics render the task perilous. Hanlon notes and accepts Tosiwo Nakayama's stated motives and intentions. Moore is more explicit: he intends his dictionary as an impetus towards nationhood in the Solomon Islands.

There are many similarities in the way historians and anthropologists approach the task of life writing, but there are important differences as well. Historians sometimes seem less interested in questions about the role of culture in the formation of ideas, attitudes and values in the life of the individuals about whom they are writing. Whereas anthropologists tend to expose western models of life telling, historians generally work within their broad strictures. They often focus on the unique particularities of a lived life. The concerns of most historian-biographers in this volume are the explication and illumination of individual lives caught in a particular set of specific historical, cultural and political circumstances. The telling of these lives can indeed throw light on the complexities of circumstances and larger patterns of change. In telling the life of Walter Edward Gudgeon in the Cook Islands, Graeme Whimp aims to use biography for insights into the multifaceted, labile and ambivalent dynamics of the colonial world—characteristics that several scholars of recent decades have stressed against visions of a monolithic and omnipotent 'colonialism'. Similarly, Christine Weir, musing on the possibilities of writing a life of John Wear Burton, foreshadows a project that would reveal little of the inner or private man, but much about the intellectual, political and religious milieu of a liberal Christian committed to 'native development' through the work of governments, international organisations and Christian missions.

Telling the life of another person is often necessarily an obtrusive act. The teller or writer is taken into confidence, and allowed to enter spaces of a life unseen by others. The act of writing or recording is never neutral or innocent. A subtle mutual manipulation is an integral part of the process, as several contributors remind us. David Hanlon's experience of interviewing Toshio Nakayama will be familiar to many biographers. He talks to the first President of the Federated States of Micronesia at the end of a distinguished career, his life slowly coming to an end on the island of Oahu. Hanlon's interviews reveal many hitherto hidden aspects of Nakayama's life, but many remain shrouded in mystery about which Nakagama is not forthcoming. 'To be honest', says Hanlon, 'I think Nakayama was also careful, selective and even evasive at times in these interviews'. How the biographer finds his or her way through the deliberately hidden tracts of a private life becomes a challenge that will be recognised by many.

Several contributions allude to the complexities of telling or recording lives in cross-cultural situations. But the difficulties are not cross-cultural alone. Similar problems arise when story tellers attempt to uncover lives largely absent from the records, from family ephemera and memorabilia, or when there is a reluctance to tell the story. How does one write about a past where memory is not properly archived, when verifiable facts are bare? Official archives may hold little promise of revealing much to the aspiring life teller, but fortunately, as Hank Nelson reminds us, there are other rich sources to exploit, most notably memoirs. Papua New Guinea has been particularly lucky in this regard. Once, writing memoirs was largely male domain, recording achievements and savouring satisfaction of a job well done, whether in the field of missions or plantations or ordinary life. But in recent years, women have published their own accounts of their time. Often these are not about moments of grandeur: 'they are the memories of nights spent on pitching small boats, clinging to small children, chucking up over the side, and accepting the impossibility of using the only toilet, a bucket…or trying to explain to a 16-year-old son why he could not ride a motor bike exuberantly in front of a group of Highlanders who once would have been entertained but were now enraged because this was an arrogant display of what they did not have and could not do in their own country'. Such finely-grained detailed accounts of everyday life, unnoticed by officials and unrecorded in official archives, provide historical story tellers a valuable mine of material.

Telling lives, focusing on the specific and the particular, can act as valuable corrective to 'generalisations and stereotypes spawned by older, positivist historical schools of thought and more recent theory-based postcolonial approaches', writes Andrew Robson. His own account of William Pritchard destroys the conventional wisdom about Pritchard's role in mid-19th century Fijian politics as an imperialistic, unfeeling meddler in the islands' affairs. Lal's account of Fiji leader A.D. Patel in mid-20th century shows him as a man ahead of his times, reviled by his critics in public but respected in private, who made significant if at the time unheralded contribution to Fiji politics, especially in its march to independence. Geoffrey Gray in his contribution rescues the government anthropologist E.P. Chinnery from the confusion and misunderstanding about the influences which shaped his work in Papua.

'Luck and serendipity are just as crucial, although good researchers will often make their own luck', Doug Munro writes. '[B]umpy rides are frequently enough the biographer's lot, something I wish that I had known earlier because it might have given a measure of grim comfort'. Lal shares that sentiment although he did not encounter as many setbacks as Munro in his researches into the lives of A.D. Patel. He was however worried about writing a book without seeing the enormous archives in London. He was relieved when he did consult the London archives several years after he had published his book, that the story he had told was substantially supported. David Hanlon searches in archival and oral testimony for clues into the life and motivation of Tosio Nakayama believing that his life 'offers a critical focal lens through which to examine a host of key themes that link Micronesia to the larger Pacific region and beyond'.

Clive Moore is the only contributor to this volume who takes the challenge of life writing to a national scale in creating a dictionary of biography as well as a historical encyclopaedia of events for the Solomon Islands. This is a mammoth task requiring meticulous planning and coordination, involving scores of contributors from all walks of life, many of whom may not have written biographical entries before. The emphasis in such projects is not on a carefully nuanced account, properly contextualised and documented. Its purpose, rather, is more utilitarian: to make basic, reliable, information about individuals and institutions accessible to the larger public and which could in the process contribute to the creation of a national identity. The task in the Pacific is not easy where documentation on individual lives outside official circles is sparse and where, in some cases, there may be actual resistance to making such information available. Moore's project has counterparts in other parts of the Pacific, notably Papua New Guinea and Fiji, but lack of financial resources and local expertise—in contrast to the national dictionary of projects in Australia and New Zealand—have prevented them from reaching fruition.

Among historians at the workshop, animated discussion took place about the purpose of the historical enterprise and the role of biographical writing in it. All the old arguments were rehearsed, but no conclusion reached. Later, Doug Munro sent Lal an excerpt of a piece written by the Australian historian Geoffrey Serle. It captures the way many historians conceive of history. 'After the fundamentals of truth-seeking and honesty, the first requirement for history is that it should be literature', Serle wrote.[1] 'My main purpose in writing general history is to tell a story (a 'true' story) and to reflect, however inadequately, the nobility and grandeur and the squalor and misery involved in man's striving. The great secondary task of the scholar is to communicate.' He noted the advances the profession had made in developing the techniques of scholarship, regretting the loss of the 'mass reading public there was for history in the nineteenth century'. In particular, he regretted that historians had 'banished the individual to some remote limbo and forgotten how to tell a story'. The need to 'preserve the story, to retain the biographical element, to write for a literate public': these are as much a part of our discipline, as urgent a concern now as they were in the past.

To end, we return to the beginning. 'Telling Lives' is an intricate and contested exercise. As several of our contributors remind us, entering the life world of another person is problematic even at the best of times. Some matters always remain beyond the reach of reason and rational research. The problem is especially fraught in cross-cultural and non-literate contexts where notions of time, space, history, myth, the role and obligations of individuals in society differ greatly and where, moreover, historical memory is not archived. How, in these situations, do we construct lives? This volume shows that the answer varies enormously depending on the teller's discipline as well as the subject's circumstance and context. If 'making bare the poor dead secrets of the heart' is the task, it is not easy, never was.

Finally, some words of thanks. First to the Division of Pacific and Asian History in the Research School of Pacific and Asian Studies at The Australian National University which sponsored the workshop and provided administrative assistance. Oanh Collins prepared the manuscript for publication with her characteristic efficiency. Second, we are truly grateful to all the contributors who waited patiently to see their work in print.

B.V.L. and V.L.

ENDNOTES

[1] See Geoffrey Serle, 'Recreating an Era: Victoria in the '50s and '80s,' in David Duffy, Grant Harman and Keith Swan (eds), *Historians at Work: investigating and recreating the past* (Sydney 1973), 52-54.

Chapter 1

Telling Pacific Lives: From Archetype to Icon

Niel Gunson

If historians aim at presenting what can only be an approximation of the past, biographers, for their part, attempt an approximation of a life. Usually a good biographer goes beyond the life, and attempts to illustrate the age in which his or her subject lived. Authors may think their own autobiographies achieve a more exact approximation of their lives but the historian is not always convinced. Autobiography is a doubtful primary source for writing biography, usually being less reliable than letters, diaries, vital statistics and archival files. Apart from the tricks of undocumented memory, the writer of autobiography is often subject to self-delusion, polemic and, in the pejorative sense, romance. We shall later consider this in the Pacific context.

Because writing biography and autobiography is a fairly recent development in the history of the Pacific Islands we might first look at the way Islanders themselves, and no doubt the preliterate ancestors of humankind in general, first commemorated the individual life.

When I first knew the anthropologist Derek Freeman he was in the habit of explaining everything in terms of kinship.[1] At every history seminar he attended, he was never satisfied until the whole hour's historical analysis had been reduced to a formula using kinship terms. One scholar was even reduced to tears because she had not introduced kinship into her otherwise immaculate presentation. Certainly kinship provides the basic framework for identifying the individual life. In some societies, there never seems to have been a real sense of history. The basic kinship structure was so set in the ethnographic present that it simply repeated itself as the generations passed away. There were a limited number of personal names that could be used in particular preordained relationships and these names were re-used, or rather, embodied in a child born into an identical relationship.[2] To an outside observer such a society could appear static. The sense of self was identified with a particular role. Something of this survives in the way Pacific title-holders readily identify with their 'past incarnations', that is, the previous title-holders, and can speak in the first person of having been present at certain events in distant historical time.[3] This can be very confusing when a narrator uses the personal name of a title-holder instead of the title in what we would regard as an anachronistic context.

Closely related to the concept of the perpetuation of the ethnographic present was the circular view of time based largely on the recurring seasons, and on other cycles in nature, particularly the rising and setting of the Pleiades. The physicists Isham and Savvidou recently voiced the obvious: 'If time is represented mathematically by a circle then it is clear that no real concept of history can be developed. For if an event lies in the future of a present one, then it also lies in its past'.[4]

In those societies where the shaman regulated social and artistic ritual the whole drama of human existence was transformed into an epic cycle. Every event in the cycle such as a flood, a hurricane, a war or a famine drew on all floods, hurricanes, wars and famines, every new experience adding to the detail of the repertoire when the cycle was either performed or recited. There was no room for individuals and in so far as there were characters they were archetypes—trickster, shaman or king and warrior. In the Pacific, song cycles were as developed as in India, Greece and Finland, all regions with circular views of time, some of the longest and best known song cycles being in Polynesia.[5]

We might ask to what extent the archetypes represent real lives. What do the cycles of the great culture hero Maui tell us about real people? I have argued elsewhere that the historical Maui is more likely to have been a shaman than an actual voyager, though the composite character undoubtedly draws on stories of the ancestral voyagers.[6] I have also suggested that Maui represents the more common shaman, the trickster noted for shape-changing and cunning as opposed to Tafaki, the high initiate who manipulates knowledge. But everywhere that one finds Maui, he has been localised. He has numerous birthplaces, different partners, even different mothers. He has been merged with other tricksters and soul travellers such as Rupe, Kura and Kisikisi and it is not always easy to know how recently Maui has supplanted an earlier culture figure.[7]

The distribution of the Maui myths seems to emanate from Tonga and the Western Polynesian triangle, one main route leading direct to Hawaii and the other main route leading direct to New Zealand, particularly the South Island. These routes are supported by tradition if not by current theories of migration to the Islands. We owe much to Katharine Luomala for her delightful study of Maui, but it is doubtful if the Maui myths were as widespread as she suggests.[8] In the 1950s I was told that her search for Maui in the Gilbert Islands was rewarded by indigenous story-tellers only too happy to recast their own tricksters as the Polynesian demigod in exchange for American cigarettes.

While I shall settle for Maui as archetype there may well have been a Tongan figure for whom we could resurrect a life. Just to outdo Gavin Menzies[9] and send a shiver down the spines of my prehistory colleagues, I offer Crown Prince Maui, a genuine historical figure and last of the Silla dynasty of Korea, exiled in 936, not that long before the Tuʻi Tonga dynasty was allegedly established on Tongatapu.[10] I might add that the Silla royal burial mounds closely resemble the royal burial *langi* of Tonga, and there were interesting shamanic parallels in the royal lineages including the veneration of snakes and eels. But when all is said and done the historian has no life story to tell. I am reminded of Peter Sellers as Sir Eric Goodness being interviewed on the life of a 13th century mystic Fazab El Barashadam Hashid, known as Smith, and his 'endeavour to bring to the common man the portrait of a man [who was culturally significant but] about whom we know practically nothing'.[11]

We are on safer ground in telling Pacific lives when we have a large corpus of traditional stories supported by archaeology. Even then some historical figures can be as elusive as Smith. Chris Ballard, in his current research in Vanuatu, may be able to date the remains of Roimata/Loimata and his minions to the 16th century but will he be able to embody and authenticate the historical life of the legendary figure? Fortunately, in some Pacific countries, particularly in Hawaii and Tonga, the existence of parallel inter-island and inter-family traditions enable the biographer to check and countercheck the genealogical and chronological sources. Using such sources scholars such as Augustin Krämer and Penny Schoeffel-Meleisea have attempted to piece together the life of Salamāsina, the first Samoan *Tafaifā* (holder of all four paramount titles) and, as I would argue, the first Tongan *Tamahā* (the most sacred female chief).[12] I shall briefly look at another important female figure in Tongan history, the high chiefess Taʻemoemimi, whose name, if translated for a children's story, would be rendered Princess Pooh and Piddle. A respected senior Tongan colleague thought the name was so disgusting that he assumed the missionaries who recorded it had been the victims of irreverent leg pulling. But the traditional sources taken together with the evidence of archaeology, ethnology and the methods of historical revisionism reveal that Taʻemoemimi was a person of great consequence.[13]

The sanitised records of the 19th century and the rewritten or censored records of the Tupou dynasty have reduced Taʻemoemimi and her full brother to children who died in infancy, but these are flawed sources.[14] More convincing is the vast *langi* of Taʻemoemimi in Vavaʻu and the fact that genealogies kept in Vavaʻu and related traditions name Taʻemoemimi as a Tuʻi Tonga Fefine, the most influential female figure in the Tongan Islands who bore the title Sinaitakala. We also learn from fragments of song that her full brother, like several dynastic heirs before and after, was installed as co-regent during his father's lifetime.[15] This may have been done to allow the son to marry his *moheofo* or Great Royal Wife. The junior Tuʻi Tonga died before his father presumably without issue and his *moheofo*, known as Tupou Moheofo, then married one of her husband's younger half brothers, the warrior Pau, who was, at various times, a contender for the *hau*ship (or position of political king) of Tonga.

Pau and Tupou Moheofo were to produce a family of four daughters, the male heir probably being the son of a secondary wife of the *moheofo*'s lineage. When the first daughter was born it was probably the Tu'i Tonga Fefine's privilege to name the child.

One can only guess, but I think with cultural insight, how Ta'emoemimi acquired her mucky moniker. The name is a title for the *matāpule* (or chief's attendant) whose responsibility it was to attend to the royal toilet needs and wrap and bury the royal stool. A baby was likely to mess or wet a chief or chiefess who held it and it was not unknown for a chiefly person to kill rather than cuddle such a messy child. One supposes that the Tu'i Tonga Fefine was so delighted with her baby niece that she looked after her toilet needs and took the *matāpule* name for herself in exchange for her own title, Sinaitakala'i Fekitetele, which became the child's name and was no longer a title, a puzzle for those who correctly believed Pau's eldest daughter never succeeded as Tu'i Tonga Fefine.

Ta'emoemimi was an important figure and no doubt when her father died she selected Pau as his successor particularly as he was already married to the *moheofo*. When Ta'emoemimi died she was succeeded as Tu'i Tonga Fefine by Pau's older half sister Nanasipau'u who lived into the 1790s. Elizabeth Bott believed there was no way of finding out why the succession of Pau was 'irregular' but by telling or reconstructing the life of Ta'emoemimi we are able to show that it was not altogether irregular.[16]

With the advent of Europeans in the Pacific the amount of primary material for writing lives should have made the biographer's task easier but most of us know that reconciling voyage narratives with recorded traditions and orally transmitted accounts is one of the most difficult exercises for the historian. In the case of Tonga, just when scholars were beginning to agree about the identity of high ranking Tongans who met the British and French explorers, the appearance of new translations of Malaspina's visit to Vava'u has raised many questions.[17] Certain characters remain particularly elusive such as Cook's Fīnau. The biographer, particularly the brief biographer, could get the identification horribly wrong.

With the advent of Europeans we also find the writings of beachcombers and missionaries. In 1964 Harry Maude listed all the then known writings of beachcombers.[18] Since then other accounts have been found, one of the most recent being that of Joseph Barsden, known in Tahiti as 'Joe the beachcomber', who played a major role in the transition from paganism to Christianity.[19] That

Barsden has surfaced after nearly two centuries highlights the constant need for revision and research and also the element of chance in telling Pacific lives.

For missionaries, chance was replaced by a providential view of history, an elaboration of the linear concept of history, supposedly rooted in Judaeo-Christian theology. Time was defined as the linear ordering of events between the creation of the world and its 'final apocalyptic consummation'. Although much missionary literature was objective and even scientific, it was also pious and didactic. The natural mode of missionary biography was hagiography. Missionaries sometimes complained that they were the instruments of 'pious fraud' and nowhere was this more blatant than in telling the lives of Pacific missionaries. Many a missionary confessed in his diary that the published life of a colleague was very different from the reality. The apotheosis of the renowned Protestant missionary John Williams was a case in point and his colleagues were only too glad to point out he had feet of clay.[20] While Williams was undoubtedly a great pioneer figure, Congregational historians in particular have turned him into a sanctified blacksmith-carpenter who built ships single-handedly apparently with little help from the faceless and virtual slave labour put at his disposal by compliant chiefs. One of his first biographers, the minister of his own church, the Reverend Dr John Campbell, was quick to point out Williams' personal limitations but until the 20th century the sanctified image remained largely unchallenged.[21]

Hagiography lends itself to visual images. Williams' life was mirrored in the oil prints by George Baxter, and several of Baxter's missionary prints are highly idealised such as the death and martyrdom of Williams, where he is attacked by brutish looking New Hebrideans, and the Reverend John Waterhouse superintending the landing of Wesleyan missionaries at Taranaki in 1844.[22] With these in mind we leap forward to a modern idealistic painting by the New Zealand artist Piera McArthur showing Bishop Pompallier after disputing with Henry Williams, in which the great Catholic missionary bishop is shown levitating, a fine example of the hagiographic image.[23]

Until well into the 20th century missionaries remained in charge of the telling and representation of their own lives. With the development of Freudian analysis and advances in forensic science the telling of missionary lives became more the function of social and largely secular historians. Father Damien de Veuster, now beatified by his Church as the Blessed Damien of Molokai, has been the subject of numerous biographies. Although traduced by Protestant critics, particularly the Presbyterian Dr Hyde, Father Damien was ably defended by Robert Louis Stevenson,[24] yet it is clear that, like John Williams, he was not the plaster saint of the pious monographs. Two biographical studies of modern times have done much to reveal the essential character of the leper saint as an inspirational if flawed human being. Gavan Daws, in 1973, provided a sympathetic portrait in *Holy Man*, drawing on the new techniques of psychohistory and analysing his subject in terms of sibling rivalry. Richard Stewart, a professor of medicine in Wisconsin, has produced the most recent biography in which much new information is used in conjunction with a medical analysis of the disease and of Damien himself.[25] These studies reveal, in the words of one commentator, that 'even his detractors could not deny that he was almost single-handedly responsible for tremendous improvements to Kalaupapa [leprosy settlement] in the face of overwhelming odds having taught himself the practice of medicine and the skill of a master builder of chapels, churches and houses'.[26]

In telling Pacific lives through psychohistory Gavan Daws was able to help us understand historical processes that might otherwise have eluded us. Just as forensic science convinces us who it is that committed a crime, so the clinical study of the biographical subject enables the historian to understand the workings of the subject's mind and prompts him or her to ask particular questions and look for particular signs. The historian becomes a profiler. The method was particularly useful for understanding missionaries usually partly concealed in pious propaganda. Apart from Father Damien, Daws treated at least three other missionaries, John Williams, Father Laval of the Gambiers and Walter Murray Gibson of Hawaii.[27] I recall that Barrie Macdonald once commented that he could learn as much from my essay on John Williams and his ship as from the Daws analysis, but he was forgetting that the Daws analysis, because it was clinically sound, had a scientific finality about it. My own reservations about the Daws psychohistory methodology are that the clinical analysis is converted into literary prose when I would prefer it to be presented in clinical terms like a forensic analysis. Of Gavan Daws' missionary portraits, the one I found most enthralling was that of Father Laval when it was presented as a clinical case rather than as a finished portrait. That even the portrait was never published suggests that sometimes the dark places of the mind can be unnerving, something we are aware of in his portrait of Melville.

In his fascinating notes on writing biography in the Pacific, Daws touches on another controversial missionary, Shirley Waldemar Baker, sometime premier of Tonga. Noel Rutherford in his excellent study of Baker and the King of Tonga had some doubts about Baker's antecedents, contrasting the missionary's apparent lack of education and polish with the relationships he claimed. Daws took the contrast further, arguing that 'Baker's shame about obscure origins was counter-balanced by strong drives to aristocratic status, prestige and power, and he mediated all this through family romance'.[28]

But is this the correct analysis? Were Baker's origins as obscure as the scant records suggest? Geoff Cummins, himself the author of a very insightful life of Baker's rival, the Reverend J.E. Moulton,[29] discovered that Baker's father was who he claimed him to be, the Reverend George Baker, an Anglican priest who died on 28 December 1869. As Noel Rutherford attests, Baker's maternal Wesleyan connections with the Woolmers and the Parkers were highly respectable. But there are hints that it was not obscure origins that Baker was escaping from. Baker's clergyman father died in the Marylebone Workhouse of chronic cerebral disease and paralysis, a common euphemism for death from alcoholism and syphilis. Shirley Waldemar Baker was probably escaping from his heredity and also possible neglect, causing him to run away from home at an early age. Madness was almost certainly inherited in Baker's family and his first given name, the surname Shirley, points to a great Methodist dynasty which produced the Countess of Huntingdon and several Evangelical divines. This was a family who were literally 'mad as hatters' as they suffered from transmissible mercury poisoning and inherited syphilis. When the head of the Shirley family, Lord Ferrers, was tried and hanged for murdering his steward, the Reverend Walter Shirley and his brothers testified to the madness in their family. Any reassessment of Baker is likely to find that a fresh clinical analysis is called for and this may explain Baker's fierce spirit of independence in breaking with the parent Methodist body and also his eventual return to the church of his father.

There are, of course, many ways to write biography. I sometimes think that the well-tried 'life and letters' method is a good way to capture the essential nature of the life subject. This method has been well utilised in the Pacific in religious, literary and anthropological circles; to a lesser extent in the other sciences. Another valuable approach is the group biography. Many of us have drawn on the lives of particular groups of men and women in the Pacific to illustrate missionary, commercial and general historical themes. Diane Langmore was a pioneer in setting out to write a group biography of missionaries in Papua New Guinea.[30] The group biography has the advantage of showing complexity and variety, an excellent corrective both to hagiography and the literary or popular stereotype. What Langmore has done for Papua New Guinea could also be done for other areas and other social groups. Caroline Ralston and Ian Campbell have both worked on beachcombers and transculturists but most of their findings are based on general primary sources rather than on collecting and analysing individual lives.[31] By tagging and asking questions of the individuals we are likely to produce a group biography which will give us a fresh perspective on transculturists. Islander missionaries and teachers are another group who would benefit from the techniques of the group biographer.

This brings us to another related topic, the suitability of the biographer. Is an Islander the best person to write the lives of other Islanders? I would like to think that this whole issue has been put to bed. As Oskar Spate believed in 1978, Island-born and trained historians from Fiji or Tonga, for instance 'should [be able to] tackle John Wesley as well as the Lotu Weseli na Viti; be able and willing to consider Sir Basil Thomson as a political figure in England, not only as the supplanter of Shirley Baker'.[32] It must be admitted, however, that some Pacific Islanders are going to be more suitable than most non-Islanders to tackle indigenous biography. Growing up in a community is the best qualification for understanding others brought up the same way and knowing the language and culture is half the battle. But one can make wrong assumptions based on environmental influences. Anyone who knew that at the age of seven I recited a piece of verse from the Victorian School Paper—

> Little Jika Jika, all the darkies like her
> In her dainty dress and pinny

—and was not aware of the influence of home and church, might conclude I was already an incipient redneck racist.

The late Jim Davidson had strong views about the suitability of prospective historians, and especially biographers. Preferably they should have a similar background to the subject, or at least have a common thought-world and he believed it desirable if they had abandoned or at least questioned these common values. I remember that he was apprehensive that Norman Douglas was proposing to study the Mormons in the Pacific as their religion was foreign to him and Douglas was an amused outsider.[33] Certainly the best work on Mormons has been done by ex-Mormons such as Fawn Brodie. Historians who tackle unknown or unfamiliar psychological territory can come to grief. Perry Miller was a great historian of Puritanism but the dark conflicts of the Puritan mind eroded his own mental stability.[34]

The biographer from outside is often tempted to ignore or dismiss facets of a subject's life that appear alien or irrelevant to him or her. I recall attending a seminar on the Victorian Premier Alfred Deakin by the late John La Nauze when he almost boasted that Deakin had possessed an extensive library of theosophical literature but he, La Nauze, could see no point in reading it. I was therefore not surprised when a Sydney historian produced a book which gave significance to Deakin's interest and which complemented La Nauze's excellent political biography.[35] Pacific historians would be similarly unwise to neglect the input of both traditional and introduced religious values when writing the biographies of Pacific Islanders.

Biography is usually not a main preoccupation of historians but something which emerges from a period study or thematic analysis. Most historians have had the experience of immersing themselves in the sources they are using for a wider project and realising that excellent material exists for the biography of an important representative individual. At one stage, I started to work on a biography of the maverick London Missionary Society missionary John Muggridge Orsmond as the archival material was so rich. I even had my title, Chaplain to Venus. The only thing that stopped me from continuing was the knowledge that the greater part of Orsmond's writing has not surfaced. Many volumes of history, letters, journals and lexicons in his handwriting were known to exist in the early 20th century and may well do so in France, Sweden, California and even in the Society Islands. Perhaps one should not be put off by this. After all there are many lives of buccaneer William Dampier and they all ignore the missing years which I am told on good authority are fully documented in the Dutch Archives. On the other hand, ANU historian Barry Smith was savaged by one reviewer because he did not know of a huge cache of Florence Nightingale papers she was editing.[36]

There are, of course, biographers who tackle major subjects. In the area of 'big biography' it is almost inevitable that there will be competition. There appears to be no end to lives of James Cook. Each new life is forced to proclaim something new to justify the exercise. Multiple biographies exist for voyagers such as Bougainville and La Pérouse. Next are probably the lives of artists and literary figures such as Gauguin, Melville and Stevenson. Missionary lives abound for John Williams, Father Damien, and James Chalmers. There are also multiple lives for the Society Islands celebrity Mai (called Omai), and Will Mariner of Tonga. Islands royalty much written about include Kamehameha of Hawaii and Queen Sālote of Tonga.

In the field of 'big biography' the academic lives tend to be definitive, towering above their subject competition such as Di Langmore's life of Chalmers and Elizabeth Wood-Ellem's biography of Queen Sālote.[37] I myself am a big-biographer manqué. Sir Keith Hancock suggested in the 1950s that I should write a life of Chalmers. 'He was eaten, wasn't he', said Hancock. As we had been discussing the education of missionaries, I assured him that Chalmers did not go to a public school. For most Pacific figures there has been scope for only one serious biographer though some of the political figures, such as Rabuka, have several books written about them. Some of these figures belong in the category of 'big biography' such as Deryck Scarr's lives of Thurston and Ratu Sukuna.[38] Many of those with single biographies may not be known so well outside the Pacific.

Jim Davidson's life of Peter Dillon is a representative biography which was seen by its author as a spin-off project which provided relief from more demanding projects. Dillon was a romantic alter-ego and Jim found great pleasure in piecing together small snippets of Dillon material culled from obscure places. He intended to name the volume Pita, the name by which Dillon was known in the Islands. When Jim died the chapters were in various stages of completion. Oskar Spate, who took on editing the manuscript, found one set of chapters and set about completing the text. I remember discussing Dillon's charges against the missionary John Thomas with Oskar and did not realise he was using an old draft. When the book was published[39] I checked it to find the dates for Dillon's visit to Vavaʻu, and was dismayed to find there was no mention of the visit, especially as I had discussed the visit with Jim. Some time later when we were moving some of Jim's papers to the archives I was amazed to find Jim's more complete versions of several chapters.

I might now return to autobiography as a way of telling Pacific lives. I have already suggested that autobiography is a doubtful source for writing biography and that the writer of autobiography is often subject to self-delusion, polemic and, in the pejorative sense, romance. Certainly we can be badly deceived by some alleged life histories. The Swiss adventurer Henri Louis Grin, known more familiarly as Louis de Rougemont, invented fanciful adventures searching for pearls and gold in New Guinea and living with a tribe of Aboriginals in Australia.[40] These were serialised in *Wide World Magazine* from August 1898 and, on examination, deceived members of the Royal Geographical Society and the British Association for the Advancement of Science. But if de Rougemont was perhaps the most blatant Pacific fictional adventurer he was not alone. From the 18th century to the present there have been adventurers who have been happy to hoodwink the public with fictional lives. One or two writers simply cannibalised the writings of others and it is difficult to establish whether or not they actually visited real islands. More convincing are the writings of authors such as Louis Becke and Frank Bullen who actually sailed in the Pacific and wrote from experience. Bullen wrote with knowledge about whaling and life at sea though sometimes his islands were changed about, a device also used by Arthur Grimble in his popular books.

More genuine autobiographies should be treated like any other source used in biography. An aging person's memory is notoriously unreliable. As an early diary keeper, I am frequently surprised to find that events that I imagined happened over three years actually all happened in one year as confirmed by my diary. Many of the story-tellers' techniques used in the dim past of cyclic history still apply. The story-teller starts with a complex historical situation which is meaningful to those involved. Next time the story is told the audience may not be able to appreciate the fine detail so the setting is simplified or changed slightly. Still later the story-teller relates the story back to the original scene but incorrectly surmises where it took place so we have a new variant. By the time a remembered event is recorded in memoirs it often differs considerably from an account which may have been recorded in a contemporary diary or letter.

Another problem with autobiography in the Pacific is that it is sometimes ghost-written so that one is never sure whether the original information or text has been tailored to fit the outlook and prejudices of the ghost-writer. Missionaries automatically edited the published writings of their indigenous colleagues though texts such as the Cook Islander missionary Taunga's narrative constitute an autobiography relatively free of interference.[41]

The autobiography is often seen as a key to the essential nature of the writer, but this is not always the case. Peter Hempenstall, himself an experienced biographer, stated in his review of Robert Langdon's autobiography, *Every Goose a Swan*, that it did not tell the reader much about the inner man. But with Bob what you saw was what you got. His stoical approach to life was far removed from the self-discovery that frequently accompanies puberty and sometimes leads to religious experience. Bob admitted that he never had such feelings. Not for him the Great Yea and the Great Nay of Carlyle's questioning.[42] We learn from this that we cannot impose our own experience on another's. In telling Pacific lives we need autobiography but we can only use it properly if we understand 'where it is coming from' and its limitations.

Finally, we might consider the biographical collections, one of the oldest historical forms in the linear tradition, exemplified in classical times by the Romans Plutarch and Suetonius and in early Christian times in the Lives of the Saints. The British Lives of the Saints tell us more about individual Celtic lives than any other source from that time. Byzantine historiography was largely centred on the lives of court officials. The Western world has a long tradition of biographical dictionaries and collected lives. In the Pacific, the earliest attempts at collecting lives were the necrologies of Island teachers and missionaries sometimes published in the missionary magazines. William Gill published lives of teachers in *Gems from the Coral Islands* and A.W. Murray assembled more lives in his *Martyrs of Polynesia*.[43] Most serious work on collections dates from the mid-20th century, notably the regional biographical dictionaries and bio-bibliographies of Father Patrick O'Reilly for Tahiti, New Caledonia and the New Hebrides. These excellent compilations contain indigenous entries but most relate to persons of European origin. *Pacific Islands Portraits* edited by Jim Davidson and Deryck Scarr initiated short studies of important or representative Pacific personalities.[44] Potted Pacific lives can be found in earlier editions of the *Pacific Islands Yearbook*. Various Hawaiian biographical series appeared in the course of the 20th century. John Dunmore's *Who's Who in Pacific Navigation*[45] covers the voyagers while the Marists have published a necrology for their missionaries. Multiple Pacific lives appear in collections such as the *Australian Dictionary of Biography* and other general collections. There have also been more recent attempts to compile regional or modern biographical dictionaries of the Pacific.

Dictionary projects are highly desirable not only in providing essential vital data for those working in general areas of history but also to commemorate the lives of important or representative individuals. There are dangers, of course, in arbitrary selection as sometimes undue importance is given to those included at the expense of those excluded. Any good dictionary system should have a revision policy. I have been impressed by the new material in the new English *Dictionary of National Biography*, especially many new entries that did not appear in *The Dictionary of National Biography Missing Persons* volume. I was also disappointed that some of these entries were written by people who had no background knowledge, obviously members of the dictionary staff. Also, there are still important omissions.

The telling of Pacific lives has moved from the mythical archetypes of early settlement in the Islands through the ruling families of traditional Island cultures to the representatives and icons of modern times. Our increased knowledge and new professional techniques help us to better understand the lives of those who lived many centuries ago as well as the lives of contemporary men and women. We may soon be able to reconstruct the life of a man such as Roimata who presently, apart from a few myths, is in the words of Peter Sellers' Sir Eric Goodness, 'a man about whom we know practically nothing'.

Acknowledgements

I would like to thank Hugh Laracy for introducing me to Piera McArthur's painting of Bishop Pompallier, Masato Karashima for explaining Korean characters and Gillian Scott and Oanh Collins for preparing the text.

ENDNOTES

[1] As most of the references to past colleagues are drawn from my own reminiscences, observations and personal communications, annotation has been restricted to documenting printed sources and elucidatory comments.

[2] This was common in many traditional Australian Aboriginal societies.

[3] For a Samoan example see Robert J. Maxwell, 'Anthropological perspectives', in Henri Yuker, Humphry Osmond and Frances Cheek (eds), *The Future of Time* (London 1972), 55-6.

[4] Christopher J. Isham and Konstantina Savvidou, 'Time and modern physics', in Katinka Ridderbos (ed.), *Time: the Darwin College Lectures* [no. 14] (Cambridge 2002), 8.

[5] See Niel Gunson, 'Shamanistic story and song cycles in Polynesia', in Tae-gon Kim and Mihály Hoppál (eds), *Shamanism in Performing Arts* [Bibliotheca Shamanistica, vol. 1], (Budapest 1995), 213-24.

[6] Ibid., 214-15; see also Niel Gunson, 'Understanding Polynesian traditional history', *Journal of Pacific History*, 28: 2 (1993), 147, 151; and 'Great families of Polynesia: inter-island links and marriage patterns', *Journal of Pacific History*, 32: 2 (1997), 142.

[7] The merging of characters in association with the circular view of history was present in medieval romance as both Merlin and King Arthur were composite characters. Despite assumptions that the Judaeo-Christian view of history was linear it was not always so. Graham Phillips, *The Moses Legacy: in search of the origins of God* (London 2002), has made a good case for the scriptural Moses being based on two persons of the name and even the historical Jesus was recast in a composite mould.

[8] Katharine Luomala, *Maui-of-a-Thousand Tricks: his Oceanic and European biographers* [Bulletin 198] (Honolulu 1949). See also Luomala, *Voices on the Wind: Polynesian myths and chants* (Honolulu 1955/rev. ed. 1986). For a Jungian view of Maui see Rita Knipe, *The Water of Life: a Jungian journey through Hawaiian myth* (Honolulu 1989), 59-76.

[9] Gavin Menzies in his provocative *1421: the year China discovered the world* (London 2002) clutches at every unusual piece of information to support his thesis. His chapter on the Pacific is particularly weak and the story of the emerald ring which he accepts as evidence for a Chinese presence has already been shown by Robert Langdon to be based on a faulty translation.

[10] For Prince Ma-ui see Edward B. Adams, *Korea's Kyongju: cultural spirit of Silla in Korea* (Seoul 1979/86), [354] and appended genealogical table of Silla Kings.

[11] '"Smith"—an interview with Sir Eric Goodness', recorded by Peter Sellers on high fidelity stereo recording, *Peter and Sophia*, produced by George Martin in London and Rome.

[12] Augustin Krämer, *Salamasina: Bilder aus altsamoanischer Kultur und Geschichte: Lebens- und Kulturbilder aus ehemaligen deutschen Kolonie Samoa* (Stuttgart 1925). Translated by Brother Hermann as *Salamasina: scenes from ancient Samoan culture and history* (Pago Pago 1949/1959). Penelope Schoeffel, 'Rank, gender and politics in ancient Samoa: the genealogy of Salamāsina O Le Tafaifā', *Journal of Pacific History*, 22:4 (October 1987), 174-93. For a popular biography see Glen Wright, *Salamasina, Queen of Love: romantic mystery of the Samoan Islands* (Hawaii 1982).

[13] A genealogy that I collected in Vava'u lists her correctly as a Tu'i Tonga Fefine. For her *langi* see Pesi and Mary Fonua, *A Walking Tour of Neiafu, Vava'u* (Tonga 1981), 13.

[14] See, for instance, the genealogy of the Tu'i Tonga collected by E.W. Gifford in the Bernice P. Bishop Museum Library, Honolulu, and other genealogies approved by Queen Sālote.

[15] 'On the death of the Tui Tonga' in E.E.V. Collocott, *Tales and Poems of Tonga* [Bulletin 46] (Honolulu 1928), 79, 139.

[16] Elizabeth Bott with the assistance of Tavi, *Tongan Society at the Time of Captain Cook's Visits: discussions with Her Majesty Queen Sālote Tupou* [Memoir no. 44], (Wellington 1982), 100.

[17] After Queen Sālote had edited Tongan traditions to accommodate what she read in the Mitchell Library, Robert Langdon publicised the visit of Malaspina to Vava'u in *Pacific Islands Monthly*. Although Karl R. Wernhart drew on Malaspina's account in *Fatafée Paulaho, der 36. Tui Tonga (1740-1784) ...* (Horn-Wien 1977), Malaspina has only recently become available in English translation (3 vols, Hakluyt Society).

[18] See the list appended to H.E. Maude, 'Beachcombers and Castaways', *Journal of the Polynesian Society*, 73: 3 (1964), 254-93.

[19] See Grant Rodwell and John Ramsland, 'The maritime adventures of Joseph Barsden, according to his own account, 1799-1816', *The Great Circle*, 21:1 (1999), 16-45. Barsden's journal has since been deposited in the Mitchell Library, Sydney.

[20] See Niel Gunson, 'John Williams and his ship: the bourgeois aspirations of a missionary family', in D. P. Crook (ed.), *Questioning the Past: a selection of papers in history and government* (St Lucia, Qld 1972), 73-95.

[21] John Campbell, *The Martyr of Eromanga: or the philosophy of missions, illustrated from the labours, death and character of the late Rev. John Williams* (3rd edn, London 1843), 194 ff provides a 'warts and all' portrait. 'On nearly all subjects, except that of Missions, his views were narrow and superficial', 197.

[22] For Baxter's prints see C.T. Courtney Lewis, *George Baxter, Colour Printer, His Life and Work: a manual for collectors* (London 1972) and Max E. Mitzvah, *George Baxter and the Baxter Prints* (Newton Abbot 1978). For commentary see Bernard Smith, *European Vision and the South Pacific* (2nd edn, Melbourne 1989), 320-21.

[23] Piera McArthur, ['Pompallier levitating'], untitled, in series 'The Holy Ghost among the Fantails', 2005. Exhibition Auckland, Studio of Contemporary Art, November 2005. Painting in private collection.

[24] Hyde's letter and Stevenson's response have been reproduced in various lives of Damien; see, for instance, Omer Englebert (trans. by Benjamin T. Crawford), *The Hero of Molokai: Father Damien, Apostle of the Lepers* (Homebush, NSW 1954), 263-82 (The testimony of Robert Louis Stevenson).

[25] Gavan Daws, *Holy Man: Father Damien of Molokai* (New York 1973) (numerous printings and translations); Richard Stewart, *Leper Priest of Molokai: the Father Damien story* (Honolulu 2000).

[26] Synopsis of *Leper Priest of Molokai* (www.booklineshawaii.com/book/bhh/ 823222.html).

[27] Gavan Daws, *A Dream of Islands: voyages of self-discovery in the South Seas: John Williams; Herman Melville; Walter Murray Gibson; Robert Louis Stevenson; Paul Gaugin* (New York/Milton, Qld 1980). The clinical analysis of Laval was presented in a seminar.

[28] Gavan Daws, '"All the horrors of the half known life": some notes on the writing of biography in the Pacific' in Niel Gunson (ed.), *The Changing Pacific: essays in honour of H.E. Maude* (Melbourne 1978), 305. For Baker see Noel Rutherford, *Shirley Baker and the King of Tonga* (Melbourne 1971).

[29] H.G. Cummins, 'Missionary Chieftain: James Egan Moulton and Tongan Society 1865-1909', PhD thesis, Australian National University (Canberra 1980).

[30] Diane Langmore, *Missionary Lives: Papua, 1874-1914* (Honolulu 1989).

[31] Caroline Ralston, *Grass Huts and Warehouses: Pacific beach communities of the nineteenth century* (Canberra 1977); Ian Christopher Campbell, 'European transculturists in Polynesia 1789-ca. 1840', PhD thesis, University of Adelaide (Adelaide 1977).

[32] O.H.K. Spate, 'The Pacific as an artefact' in Gunson, *The Changing Pacific*, 44.

[33] Douglas produced an excellent thesis but as a complete outsider he had a number of difficulties, and publication was made almost impossible. Similarly, another outsider, the Irish biographer Rex Taylor, faced legal opposition in his attempts to publish his biography of John Williams. On the other hand Fawn M. Brodie successfully launched *No Man Knows My History: the life of Joseph Smith, the Mormon prophet* (New York and London 1963), and became a prominent psycho-biographer.

[34] Professor Perry G. Miller of Harvard, who died in 1963, was regarded as America's greatest interpreter of the Puritan mind and 'the master of American intellectual history'. He wrote lives of Roger Williams and Jonathan Edwards. There was an inevitable tension between his acknowledged atheism and his sensitivity to the complex religious issues of Puritanism.

[35] J.A. La Nauze, *Alfred Deakin: a biography*, 2 vols (Carlton 1965, 2nd edn 1979); Alfred J. Gabay, *The Mystic Life of Alfred Deakin* (Cambridge 1992).

[36] Lynn McDonald, 'An unscrupulous liar? Florence Nightingale revealed in her own writings', *The Times Literary Supplement* (8 Dec. 2000).

[37] Diane Langmore, *Tamate—a King: James Chalmers in New Guinea, 1877-1901* (Melbourne 1974); Elizabeth Wood-Ellem, *Queen Sālote of Tonga: the story of an era 1900-1965* (Auckland 1999).

[38] Deryck Scarr, *The Majesty of Colour: a Life of Sir John Bates Thurston*, vol. 1, *The Very Bayonet* (Canberra 1973), vol. 2, *Viceroy of the Pacific* (Canberra 1980); *Ratu Sukuna: soldier, statesman, man of two worlds* (London 1980).

[39] J.W. Davidson, *Peter Dillon of Vanikoro: chevalier of the South Seas*, ed. O.H.K. Spate (Melbourne 1975).

[40] For a recent biography see Rod Howard, *The Fabulist: the incredible story of Louis De Rougemont* (Milsons Point, NSW 2006).

[41] R.G. and Marjorie Crocombe (eds), *The Works of Ta'unga: records of a Polynesian traveller in the South Seas, 1833-1896* (Canberra 1968).

[42] *ANU Reporter* (Canberra 1996). Thomas Carlyle's great spiritual autobiography *Sartor Resartus* (1833/34) is a useful reminder to the biographer of self-awareness and the subjective nature of intellectual scepticism.

[43] William Gill, *Gems from the Coral Islands; or, Incidents of Contrast between Savage and Christian Life of the South Sea Islanders*, 2 vols (London 1856); Archibald Wright Murray, *The Martyrs of Polynesia: memorials of missionaries, native evangelists, and native converts, who have died by the hand of violence, from 1799 to 1871* (London 1885).

[44] See J.W. Davidson and Deryck Scarr (eds), *Pacific Islands Portraits* (Canberra 1970); Deryck Scarr (ed.), *More Pacific Islands Portraits* (Canberra 1979).

[45] John Dunmore's *Who's Who in Pacific Navigation* (Melbourne 1992).

Chapter 2

The Kila Wari Stories: Framing a Life and Preserving a Cosmology

Deborah Van Heekeren

This chapter is a sketch drawn from a work in progress about the way a collection of stories which together frame the life of a single heroic figure engender the identity of the Vula'a, a coastal people of Papua New Guinea. I conducted fieldwork in the Vula'a village of Irupara in 2001 as part of my doctoral research, and made a return visit in 2005. My doctoral research was concerned with Melanesian Christianity, particularly women's experiences of the United Church. During the first visit I did not anticipate the project that would be initiated by my male interlocutors. From the outset, the men were eager to tell me about Kila Wari, the great warrior of Alewai. At first I paid little attention to their stories, dismissing Kila Wari for his apparent lack of relevance to my research. Yet I came to realise that the Kila Wari stories were contributing to my historical and cultural understanding, as they have much to say about Vula'a religion and cosmology.

My investigation of these stories speaks to a number of theoretical concerns which arise in the interstices of the transition from an oral tradition to a written one. These include the relationship between myth and history and the influence of Christianity, the possibility of biography in light of relational theories of Melanesian personhood, and, consequently, the significance of genealogy and place in the constitution of identity. My perspective is both anthropological and phenomenological insofar as my focus is on the particularity of Vula'a story-telling—its context, intent and existential significance. I recognise, though, the richness of the narrations themselves and so present them as fully as space allows as an invitation to further analysis. Phenomenologically it is important to know who our story-tellers are and to whom their stories are told and why. This edict provides the framework for my discussion in which some similarities as well as differences in Vula'a and Western story-telling traditions may be discerned.

The Vula'a occupy six villages on the southeastern coast of Papua New Guinea, four of which are located on the western side of Hood Bay and two on the eastern side. Including those now living in the National Capital District, they constitute a population of more than 4,000. The largest of the Vula'a villages is known as

Hula, a term which also describes the language and which has been widely used to refer to the people. Nevertheless, the so-called Hula people call themselves Vula'a and I follow their convention. Traditionally a maritime people, the Vula'a settled in the Hood Point area at the beginning of the 19th century, having migrated from the Marshall Lagoon area, further east. By the beginning of the colonial period they had established themselves as expert fishermen and traders. The Vula'a first encountered Christianity in the early contact period of the London Missionary Society (LMS) during the 1870s. And it has been claimed that they were the first people in the LMS sphere of influence to enthusiastically adopt Christianity.[1] Further, by the end of World War II the LMS is said to have consolidated its position in Hula village with almost all social activities being undertaken in the name of the Church.[2]

The Hula language forms part of what is sometimes called the 'Austronesian One' group which is mainly found in two language patches in the southeast, one in Milne Bay and the other in Central District.[3] Today the Vula'a use the *Tok Pisin* term *stori* when referring to a range of story-telling activities, from anecdotes and local gossip to events of historical importance. Vula'a enjoyment of *stori* is noteworthy, as is the fact that conversation is given a high social value. Generally, social interaction begins with the chewing of betelnut, is followed by *stori* and, on some occasions, concludes with the sharing of food. There is another Hula term, *rikwana*, that may also be translated as story, but has almost fallen from use. This term was originally translated from the Hula language by Lillian M. Short in the 1930s as 'story of olden times; folklore'.[4] It is usefully compared with Malinowski's translation of the Boyowan (Trobriand) word *libogwo*, a general term for 'old talk' which, he suggests, includes historical accounts and myths, or *lili'u*.[5]

The stories of the past most frequently told in the Vula'a villages of Irupara and Alewai recall the important events of the life and death of the great warrior Kila Wari. In the past, the Kila Wari stories would have been classified locally as *rikwana*. In Western terms they most closely resemble our classification, 'legends', and this is how English-speaking Vula'a would translate *rikwana* today. Most importantly, these stories traverse the divide between myth and history. They are not strictly 'myths' in the conventional sense because they do not have the quality of timelessness which characterised the old stories. They have now been fixed in time—historicised. They do, however, retain other mythic qualities. As myth, they are experiential and demonstrate a tangible connection between place, teller and ancestor. This is aptly demonstrated in the convention of introducing the stories with the teller's genealogy. And although they are now often invoked in the context of local land claims, the Kila Wari stories have come to serve a quite different Vula'a concern—the preservation of pre-Christian language, tradition and cosmology in the face of a growing sense of cultural loss.

Even though they focus on the life and death of a local hero, a uniquely identified individual—the Kila Wari stories both are and are not biography. While a number of Vula'a and non-Vula'a people know the Kila Wari story, each of them tells their own inherited version. Together these are complementary rather than contradictory and it is only when they are organised by the researcher that we see a resemblance to Western biography. For the Vula'a, though, they are 'biographical' in a different sense and this is related to their ontology—the particular way in which they experience their existence. From this perspective, the biography is not that of Kila Wari, the warrior, but, rather, that of the Vula'a themselves. For it encapsulates their collective identity as a people and preserves the possibility of a mode of existence which belonged to their ancestors and so is also theirs. Those who tell the story of Kila Wari are also telling the story of themselves. In short, the stories are 'biographical' because that is how we read them but phenomenologically, they are not biography in the conventional sense because their intention is not to reveal the life of a single individual. They are a representation of cultural identity. They are existential. This makes sense for a people who, it has been argued, value relation over and above individualism.[6]

Genealogy as Wealth and Preface

It is important to recognise that the distinction between an oral tradition and a written one has become blurred in this part of Papua New Guinea. While oral conventions continue to operate insofar as the flow of certain types of knowledge is controlled through rights of inheritance, a significant amount of information is written down. This is not to say that it becomes public, though. In Irupara the 'traditional wealth' or 'customary treasure' of a lineage is passed from generation to generation in the form of the *poni poni*. The term refers to a small woven basket which actually, or symbolically, contains the treasured items. It was explained to me as follows:

> A string bag (*bilum*) can hold many purse-like *bilums* inside. There could be several. For example, a mini bag for betel nuts, another for cigars and the other for gas lighter parts etc. in different mini bags all in one shoulder-to-waist-*bilum*. Of all these, one is the sacred *poni poni*.

Such treasure may include remedies for certain types of sickness, incantations for abundant food, the tooth of an ancestor, special gingers for successful fishing, the rights to land, or it may simply consist of the passing of a 'genealogical book' which has replaced the remembered relationships or *gulu ai* (lit. generation counting) of former times.

The purpose of the genealogical book was explained to me by Wala Iga, a senior man who holds a *poni poni*, as *maino* (peace). Its keeper is the designated mediator in matters of conflict. For instance, if there is a dispute between two men, the holder of the genealogical book will use it to link the men to a single ancestor and say 'You are not foreigners [strangers] but brothers. Why then are you fighting?'

As an anthropological tool, genealogies have the capacity to verify certain types of information, such as the approximate dates of settlements and battles. They help us to situate individuals and, therefore, events in time and place. For the Vula'a, genealogy attests to identity and endorses a person's authority or right to tell a story by claiming a connection to ancestor and place.

In the 1960s, Nigel Oram commented on the fullness of Vula'a genealogies. He wrote that 'not only wives' names and origins are known but the shifts in descent group allegiances of various individuals are remembered'.[7] Vula'a genealogies do not trace blood-lines. Rather, they are mnemonic indicators of the obligations and entitlements constituted in human relationships. They are, in a sense, stories in themselves. Vula'a genealogies *gather*. They gather person to ancestor and ancestor to place. It is to village founders that origins are traced. Genealogies may thus be invoked to explain such things as an inter-village alliance, a person's entitlement to land, or their claim to certain types of knowledge. And so it is that each and every story which constitutes the legend of Kila Wari may be, and generally is, represented by its teller in terms of a genealogical relationship. It we wish to translate the Vula'a convention into our own we might aptly say that the relationship story serves as a preface.

The accounts of Kila Wari's exploits, like those of many legendary heroes, have taken on mythic proportions, but there is no doubt that he actually existed. He was the fourth-born son of the founder of Alewai village, a fact which is easily demonstrated in the genealogies I collected. Alewai village was settled at the beginning of the 19th century by Kila Wari's father, Warinumani Lui, and Vula'a oral traditions which present the period between about 1820 and 1860 as one of intense warfare along this section of the coast comfortably accommodate Kila Wari's life span.

The complex of stories that constitute the legend of Kila Wari is thus clarified diagrammatically. The kinship diagram shown in figure 1 identifies the founders of the western Vula'a villages. It also illustrates that an important connection between Warinumani Lui, the founder of Alewai village, and Kana Vali, one of the founding brothers of Irupara, was established during the early period of settlement. It happened that Kwamala Wari, Warinumani's third-born son, married the daughter of Kana Vali. Her name was Kopi Kila Kana and Irupara people say that regardless of the custom of patrilocality she persuaded Kwamala Wari to settle in Irupara because it was still a young village and there was a lot of work to be done there. The people of Alewai village claim that Kwamala Wari went to Irupara to oversee land there that had been given in compensation for the death of Kila Wari.

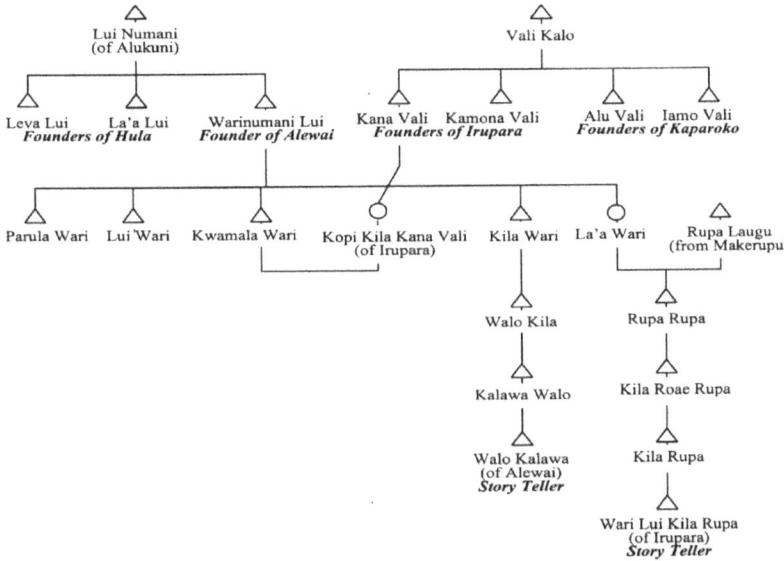

Fig. 1. The founding fathers of the western Vula'a villages (following original migration from Alukuni), and genealogical links to two story tellers cited in the text.

Meeting Kila Wari

My introduction to Kila Wari came from Wari Lui Kila Rupa of Irupara. Wari Lui was, at the time of my fieldwork, a man in his mid-30s whose self-stated occupation was 'Christian evangelist'. As such he had devoted himself to spreading the gospel and was not often to be found in his home village. Our meeting was fortuitous. Wari Lui told me that he and a brother had wanted to film a documentary about the life of Kila Wari which was to be titled 'Shark Warrior' but the demands of his work did not allow the time to pursue this goal. He anticipated my assistance and consequently shared with me his accumulated knowledge of local history—his 'family treasure'—most of which had been gathered by his father during his long employment as a magistrate in the land courts.

Wari Lui's family treasure includes a genealogical book such as that described above as a *poni poni*. His underlying motives for sharing his family treasure with me are partly obscured by a complex intertwining of local politics and Christianity. Nevertheless, his evangelical employment suggests that he is well placed to recognise the power of a good story. To Wari Lui's credit, then, *The Shark Warrior of Alewai* will be the title of my book. He is not, though, the only story-teller of note in this collection. We will encounter a cast of other narrators as well, all of whom are important contributors, and discover that the telling of the legend of Kila Wari does not entail the construction of a single 'true' story or a fixed chronicle of events.

I will begin with Wari Lui and note that his genealogical relationship to the great warrior is of the utmost importance.[8] His brief, written account of the Kila Wari story is prefaced by a genealogy which links him to the warrior's sister, La'a, who married one of the chiefs of a neighbouring inland village in order to secure land for the people of Alewai. Having family links to that village, Makerupu, as well as Irupara, Wari Lui describes himself as being of 'mixed-blood' (see figure 1). He explains that:

> Wari Lui's (the founder of Alewai) daughter, La'a Wari, Kila Wari's sister was given to the chief of Makerupu's son in exchange for land and peace. She was eventually forced to return to Alewai with her children. She had two sons and two daughters. Her first born daughter married land lords of Irupara.[9] Her second born son married the daughter of Irupara land lords. From this alliance came my grandfather Kila Rupa. His son, who was also called Kila Rupa had seven children. Among them I am the sixth born named after the forefather and founder of Alewai village.

Before I relate Wari Lui's story of Kila Wari, I want to draw attention to an aspect of its narration. James Clifford, commenting on the characteristics of myth in Melanesia, has written that the mood of a story is recreated as its teller re-enters the space-time of the occurrence.[10] This was borne out in the transformation which Wari Lui's person underwent as he recounted the greatness of Kila Wari. Drawing on every aspect of his ancestral connections, he appeared as the embodiment of the legendary figure. For instance, Wari Lui did not merely describe Kila Wari's spear throwing ability, he lived it out. His expression changed. His eyes were seemingly focused on another reality as he demonstrated the action the warrior used. The persuasiveness of his engagement with the subject—his familiarity with the minutiae of the events described—was captivating. Ancestor, place and story-teller became a single mythic identity in that moment.

What follows then is Wari Lui's verbal description of Kila Wari.

> Wari Lui, the father and founder of Alewai village, had ten children. Kila Wari was the fourth born son. One day the father took his sons out to the reef to fish. At low tide the father sighted a small shark in a reef pond. He challenged his sons saying, 'The one who catches the shark will become a great warrior'. The brothers rushed to the pond. Although Kila Wari was the youngest among his brothers, he caught the shark and held it up by the tail. From that day onward, he was to live like a

warrior—fasting, eating only certain foods and sleeping lightly. He was not to touch any woman but to sleep in the company of men.

As a young warrior, Kila Wari underwent extensive training and had to pass many tests. Wari Lui elaborates:

> Kouagolo, near Kwaipo[11] village, was known as a mountain of power and mystery. It had been said that no one ever returned alive from this mountain. Kila Wari was the first warrior from the coast to receive its special powers and return unharmed. He procured a powerful ginger called *lavi rakava* [bad, or spoiled evening] which made him a fierce and great battle warrior. The Kwaipo war chief gave him special gingers and spells for protection and extra strength. His final test, which he passed, was to jump into many spears.[12] Kila Wari became known as a great spear-thrower. He could kill his enemies from 50 metres away. Enemy spears were beaten aside by a wooden club. In his left hand other spears were caught and thrown back at the enemy with accuracy, never missing their targets. He would move four to five metres ahead of his fighting men with his armoury bearers following behind him with dozens of spears. His eyes were fixed and forecast on the enemy. Spears were placed one by one in Kila Wari's hand as he charged forward without fear. He could throw them from 30 to 50 metres ahead. His head dress was unique and colourful. He fought his battles as far away as Kapa Kapa, Kila Kila, Manumanu and on to Kerema.

Walo Kalawa of Alewai is a direct descendant of Kila Wari. I will say more about him later. Here I include his description of Kila Wari's visit to Kwaipo.

> One day Kila, wanting to get some *mula'a* (power from some plants or other sources) went to Kwaipo, further inland from Kalo village. Upon meeting the Kwaipo chief, Mapakulu, they tested him making him jump from the treetop and onto the ground where sharp sticks were planted pointing upwards. This he achieved without injuring himself. And so to him was given an *ivoa* (ginger) called *lavi rakava*.

The special powers that Kila Wari received from the mountain near Kwaipo village are part of a system that is conceptualised by the Vula'a as *waka*. Generally speaking, *waka* is a form of ritual preparation which is based on a period of fasting and sexual abstinence. *Ani waka* (lit. food abstinence) is that part of the preparation which relates specifically to fasting. It includes restrictions on the type of food eaten as well as the way it is cooked and usually consists of so-called 'burnt' vegetables, the emphasis being on dryness. *Waka* abstinence aimed to eliminate moisture and hence softness from the body. For example, fish and meat were to be avoided and smoked banana was acceptable. The aim of the practice is to become like the ancestors, who are perceived to be dry and light. It is used today in preparation for sporting events.

Traditionally *waka* aimed to develop a relationship with the ancestral spirits—to gain their favour, and protection against malevolent forces. The more difficult the task to be undertaken the more intense must be the *waka*. In the case of warfare, there is a sense in which the battle is fought by invisible forces as well as visible ones. Certain types of hunting and fishing are approached in the same way. Battles undertaken by war chiefs required an intense *waka* which also included social restrictions such as periods of seclusion, and the chewing of powerful gingers. To be in breach of these requirements was to invite death. Wari Lui told me that Kila Wari returned from Kouagolo Mountain, where he had gone for his *waka,* via the village of Makerupu. He was in such a wild state that he was yelling and screaming. During this 'uncontainable' outburst he is said to have killed a pregnant woman.

Chewing special gingers during *waka* heats the body, providing courage and power. Both the terms 'heat' and 'power' are translated as *iavu* in the Hula language. When a successful *waka* has been performed the practitioner is said to be in a state of *vea'a*. In Christian times *vea'a* is translated as holy. Ultimately, the success of a war chief was perceived to be determined by his *iavu* but, as we have seen, Kila Wari was appointed over his brothers because he exhibited chiefly qualities. Much of Wari Lui's description focuses on Kila Wari's physical prowess. The kinds of skills required of such a great war chief are consistent with the legends of other areas of the Pacific. The Hawaiian story of 'Lono and Kaikilani', for example, in which we are told that 'Early in life Lono exhibited remarkable intelligence, and as he grew to manhood, after the death of his father, in athletic and warlike exercises and other manly accomplishments, he had not a peer in Hawaii'.[13]

Telling the Battles of Kila Wari with Some Contributions from Western History

It is said that Kila Wari's reputation extended from Mailu in the east to Kerema in the west. He had established friendly connections with the war leaders, Mea Gure and Gure Gure, two brothers from Paugolo (the neighbouring inland village which is now known as Babaka). In their own village the brothers are known as Mega Velapo and Gure Velapo. The war leaders had assisted Kila Wari and his war party when they fought with Mailu in the southeast and in the battle of Kila Kila. (Apart from the battle at Babaka in which Kila Wari finally met his death, he is most often remembered for the burning of the Koita village of Kila Kila which is also called Kira Kira.) While the Gure brothers had been Kila Wari's allies in this task, accompanying his war party when they travelled down the coast in their war canoes, they were later instrumental in bringing about his death.

The Koita or Koitapu as they are sometimes called have been described as the 'uncompromising enemy' of the Vula'a.[14] Oram sheds some light on the rivalry explaining that 'The western group of Vulaa villages, who traded with the Western Motu, were hostile to the Koita because they thought that the Koita caused wrecks and loss of sago [their main cargo] through sorcery'.[15] When he visited the Papuan coast in 1885 Lindt observed that 'The charred ruins of old Kapa Kapa [Gaba Gaba] were still discernible away to the east of the ship. This village had been destroyed about two years ago by the Hula natives, who, sparing women and children, massacred three of the men'.[16] Eleven people were also wounded in this battle which Oram has suggested was probably the last traditional war to take place on the Port Moresby coast.[17] He gives the following explanation for the incident:

> A Hula man returning from Hanuabada with two women in a canoe laden with pots was enticed on shore by some Gaba Gaba people who speared him. According to one account, an inland man speared him. In those days there were two Gaba Gaba villages and in retaliation the Hula in their war canoes burned the Eastern village.[18]

Sometime before the burning of Gaba Gaba, the Vula'a are reported to have burned a Kila Kila site on the hill of Varimakana. Evidence suggests that Kila Wari was dead by the time of the destruction of Gaba Gaba but he led the expedition that was responsible for the burning of Kila Kila. Oral testimony cited by Oram claims that the Vula'a destroyed the Koita villages of Kila Kila and Roku. More recent Vula'a accounts focus on the role Kila Wari played in both battles.[19]

Through a number of conversations with Wari Lui, I learned the details of the events that led to the burning of Varimakana village.

> The chief from Kila Kila would invite other chiefs who were known for their victories and bravery to his village for friendly visits and assassinate them. One day he and his warriors visited Kila Wari at Alewai. Kila Wari had invited them to a great feast. On their way they had killed a chief from another village, removed his necklace and hidden it in their canoe. While Kila Wari was entertaining his guests his servants were cleaning the Kila Kila chief's canoe. There they found Kini Olo chief's lime pot and necklace hidden in the inner section. Meanwhile, Kila Wari had agreed to go and talk with the Kila Kila chief in his village and they set a date. At that time days, weeks, and months were counted on tied knots. Kila Wari tied knots in a string and gave it to the Kila Kila chief along with his necklace, string bag and lime pot. He was to hang them as a sign outside his house. When the chief left the servants took the necklace and lime pot to Kila Wari. He became furious and vowed that on the arranged date he would challenge the Kila Kila chief. Tied knots were

untied. Days, weeks, months passed until only a few knots remained. As the days grew closer to the meeting with the Kila Kila chief Kila Wari gathered his fighting men. They paddled their canoes to the host camp under cover of darkness. By sunrise they had sunk the canoes in the mangroves and marched to Sabama and surrounded the mountain village. They beat their drums so the Kila Kila chief knew there was going to be a battle. He put on his armour and waited. Kila Wari made his way to the chief's house. 'Who has come to fight with me?' asked the surprised chief. 'Don't they know I am the mighty warrior of Kila Kila?' Kila Wari answered, 'I have come to kill you'. The Kila Kila chief threw his spear and missed. As he rushed back into his house for his weapons, Kila Wari thrust his spear through his chest killing him instantly. The Alewai warriors killed men, women and children and burnt the village to the ground. The site of the battle was given the name Kila Kila which means 'talk' because Kila Wari had promised the chief he would talk when they met at the feast.

Walo Kalawa also tells the story of the battle of Kila Kila. Importantly, he recalls that they sang a song to mark the event of the death of the Kila Kila chief. He explains that 'after killing Iovauna, the Kila Kila war chief, and burning the village they sang this *lekwai*':[20]

Kira Kira ati vanuga rage rage
Kila Wari na mora geana
Iovauna venena kouta koutalia
Kwamala Wari ama kini veatona
Lekwai, lekwai.

Although Kila Wari had named the battle site Kila Kila it is also known as Kira Kira which the Vula'a translate as humiliated, destroyed, or trampled flat. The shore of a small bay near Kila Kila is known by the Vula'a and the Motu as Taikone, which means 'beach of tears'. It was so named because of the destruction of Kila Kila.[21]

The Death of Kila Wari

The death of Kila Wari is the centrepiece of the legend. It exemplifies the warrior's bravery and enforces important cosmological precepts.

Wari Lui explains that some time after the burning of Kila Kila, Kila Wari and his warriors killed a man from Paugolo (Babaka). This man had two sisters who walked up and down the streets[22] of the village crying over their brother's death. After this went on for a number of weeks, Mea Gure and Gure Gure began to feel sorry for them. They prepared themselves and their weapons to take revenge on Kila Wari and his party. When everything was in order the two brothers went early one morning to Alewai village.

According to Wari Lui, on the day Kila Wari was killed he was visiting his uncles in Hula village. The point is significant because, as we know, it was usual before a battle to undergo *waka*—a rigorous regime of preparation and fasting. But on this day Kila Wari had eaten fish with his relatives. (The point attests to the strategic timing of his enemies.) It was at Hula that Kila Wari received the news that Babaka warriors were at Alewai, which is adjacent to Hula on the western side. 'He got his string bag and his spear and rushed to the battle zone', explained Wari Lui.

The most detailed account of the ensuing events is provided by an Alewai resident, Kila Kaile Igawai, who at the time of telling was aged in his early 70s.

> The brothers [Gure and Mea] went down to the beach as they regularly did. They called the name 'Kila Wari' and said 'say goodbye to your family and follow us'. Kila Wari heard them and went after them and his brother, Parula Wari, followed him to Paugolo. However, Kila Wari was not afraid of Mea and Gure's tricks because he knew they could not take him by surprise. He followed them to the entrance of the village where the battle began.

Wari Lui recalls that: 'When Kila Wari reached the battle zone he was pushing the enemy back'. He goes on to explain that a man from Riwali village, who was fighting with the Babaka forces, had been instructed to aim for Kila Wari at close range with a poison spear—this would ensure his death. Attacking from the rear, he speared Kila Wari in his right leg.

Igawai's account states that it was one of the Gure brothers who speared Kila Wari and that it was his left leg that was hit. According to Igawai:

> Mea Gure speared Kila Wari in the left leg and called out '*ah, kea kino kolovana*'. Kila Wari struggled through the bushes with the spear in his leg until he reached the site where the present church station is. Then Kila Wari fell down and the war party threw spears at his body. At that time La'a Wari (Kila Wari's sister) ran to her brother and threw herself on top of him. The fight stopped. Later, Parula Wari and others took the body back to Alewai for burial.

Again, Wari Lui adds to the description of Kila Wari's death. He explains that after he was speared and 'as spears landed on him like rain' he instructed his brother to run for his life. His body was then taken to the village for public display and for Babaka warriors to use for target practice. As we know, Kila Wari's sister, La'a was at that time living at Makerupu. Hearing of the incident, La'a ran to her dead brother and took off her grass skirt and placed it over his body. The violence to her brother's body ceased immediately. The reasons for this remain unclear, although I am confident they will be found in further investigation of the cosmological system.[23] What is known is that Kila Wari's head would have been removed if La'a had not acted as she did. The head of a warrior was a valued trophy. Alewai warriors then took the body home, intact, for burial. Later they joined forces with Riwali and Kaparoko in a revenge battle in which they killed the Babaka chief.

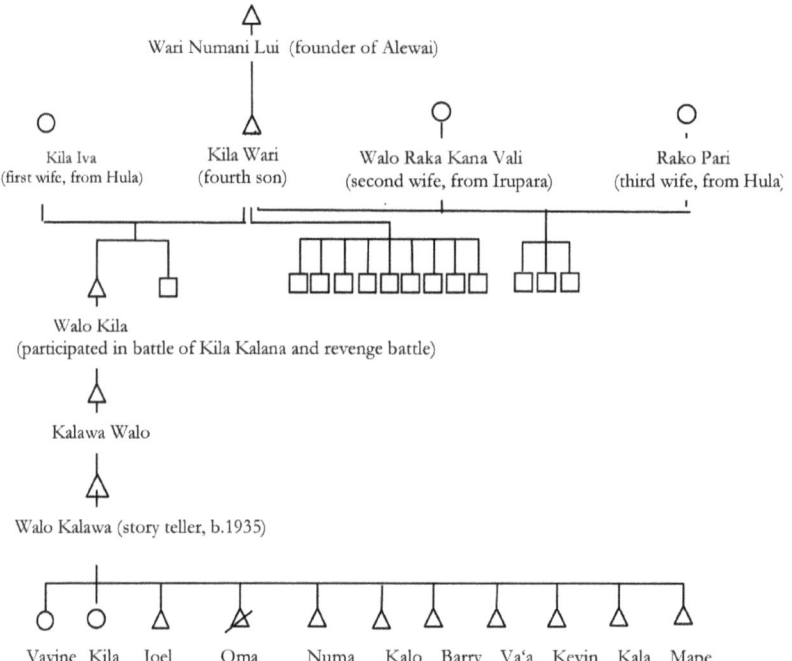

Fig. 2. Patrilineal relationship of a story teller, Walo Kalawa, to Kila Wari. Other relatives are included as named and/or described by narrator.

As I have said, Walo Kalawa is a direct descendant of Kila Wari. His genealogical story (see figure 2) reveals that Kila Wari had three wives and many descendants. Here is Walo Kalawa's version of Kila Wari's death. He begins with the assumption that Kila Wari is at Hula village when Alewai is attacked:

> Kila Wari although absent sensed defeat and joined his warriors to wage a full scale war. They fought almost as far as Babaka village when Gure Velapo, the Babaka chief, speared Kila Wari on the ankle above the heel. Walo Kila, his son, realising his father was struggling and in agony, raced to help his father to maintain his standing to give courage to the warriors. By then Kila Wari, going weak with heavy loss of blood, pleaded for his son's safety and said '*magulimu on avua* (run for your life)'. His warriors then retreated with a broken heart and left him. Babaka then took their trophy—Kila Wari—alive and lined him up for target practising. La'a Wari was at her husband's village when news arrived that Kila Wari was captured and the warriors were spearing him at Babaka. La'a Wari

was devastated and ran all the way sobbing to the spearing place. There she untied her grass skirt and covered her brother's body. Seeing the nakedness of a woman the warriors broke up and left quickly without chopping off the head. Kila Wari's body was brought back by his people to Alewai for burial and the people mourned for some time.

The place where Kila Wari was speared to death is called Kila Kalana, now the place where Babaka United Church is. Previously it was called Iome Kalana—a place where a poor old lady was buried.

Kila Wari's spear was made into a *warimo* (long-tom[garfish]) spear for fishing which my grandfather, Walo Kila, used.

The View from the Other Side: A Babaka Story

I went to Babaka village to hear the story of Kila Wari's death from a descendant of a war chief of the enemy side, Numa Nama Gure. Numa Nama's knowledge and authority in this matter are located in the genealogy which relates him to the war chief who fought Kila Wari (see figure 3). Numa Nama was born at Babaka in 1927. His father was Gure Kila, Gure's father was Kila Mega, Kila's father—Numa's great grandfather—was Mega Velapo, who, alongside his brother, Gure Velapo, had been involved in the killing of Kila Wari. Before Mega Velapo came Velapo Vanua, Vanua Kila and Kila Keina. In figure 3, I compare Numa Nama's genealogy with that of Walo Kalawa. It shows that Numa Nama's great grandfather was a contemporary of Kila Wari and, because Numa Nama's is the lineage of Babaka village war chiefs, it is reasonable to conclude that his ancestor was involved in the battle in which Kila Wari was killed. It is interesting, in light of the ancestry illustrated here, to note that Numa Nama is a deacon in Babaka United Church and that Walo Kalawa is also a retired United Church deacon.

In the course of my meeting with Numa Nama I was shown the place where Kila Wari received the fatal blow and also the place where he died. The distance between was significant, attesting to the warrior's endurance. Numa Nama's version of Kila Wari's death provides some additional details and clarifies some points that have already been made. Most importantly, he claims that it was Gure Velapo, or Gure Gure as he is known in Alewai, who actually wounded Kila Wari in the leg with the first spear.[24] He begins:

> Kila Wari was a great warrior. One day he killed someone from Babaka (name unknown) so...He had two sisters. When this man was killed by Kila Wari his sisters wept so much for him and wished for someone from Babaka to kill him for doing that. While this was going on, two brothers, Gure Velapo and Mega Velapo, my great grandfathers, sent some people over to remove the dead man's necklace and to comfort them. When the two had gone over to remove the neckwear the sisters stopped them

saying, 'Whoever thinks they are strong enough to kill Kila Wari can come and remove the neckwear. There is also food there that we will give in return for the killing of Kila Wari'. The men became scared because Kila Wari was such a great warrior.

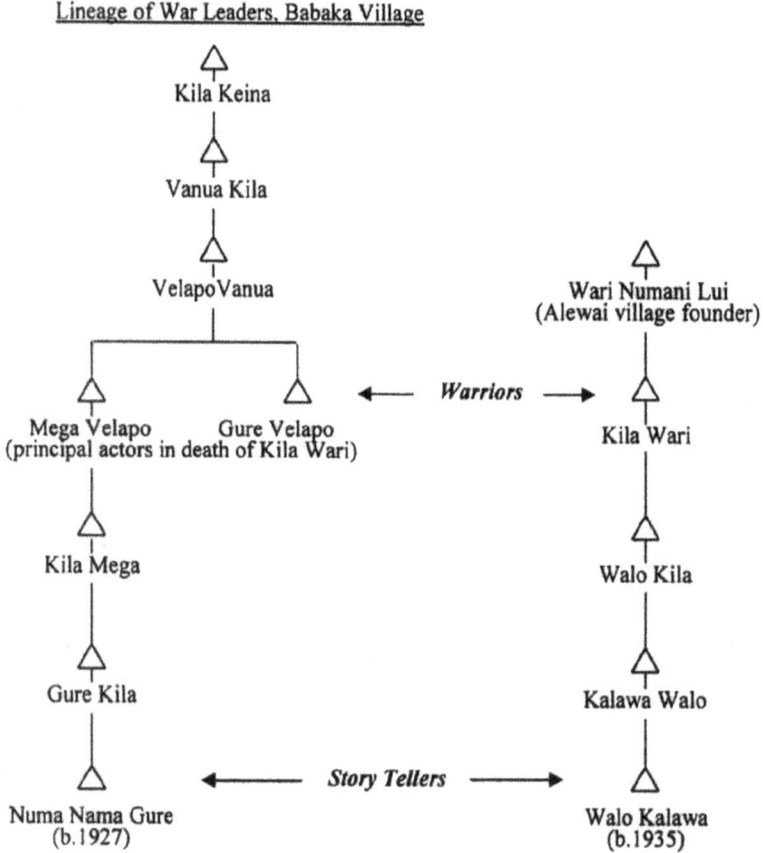

Fig. 3. Patrilineal relationships of two narrators to principal figures in the Kila Wari stories.

Seeing this, the two brothers, Gure and Velapo, spoke to each other. After some time the younger, Gure, went over and removed the neckwear. Later they discussed tactics and began intensive exercise and training—not only the brothers but all the warriors in the village. They practised until it came to the time when they thought they should avenge their loss. They sent word to Kila Wari. They didn't send messengers. They went themselves. Arriving in the early hours of the morning at Alewai beach they called out to Kila Wari (his house was over the sea),

'Kila Wari Oh! Kila Wari Oh!' (the houses were built some 200 metres off shore).

Then Kila Wari appeared from his house and said 'Who are you? You think you can just call my name like that? Wait, I'm coming over'. Hearing all this Kila Wari's warriors got their weapons and the fighting began. But it had been carefully planned. They fought their way inland and just before reaching the village (Rilo),[25] fresh men in large numbers joined the Velapos but Kila Wari's dignity did not allow him to withdraw. Then suddenly Gure Velapo speared him on the leg just above the heel. As Kila Wari jumped up, Gure called to him, 'Eagle where will you go? You are going to die'. Then Kila Wari's brother came and fought beside him while Kila Wari, still throwing spears, was struggling to kick off the spear in his heel. [During the course of the interview it was mooted that the spear had barbs that would prevent it from coming out.]

By now Kila Wari had tired so he spoke to his brother, Parula, who had been trying to help him safely home while fighting at the same time, 'I've been hit. It's no use, I'm dying so leave me here. But please go back or else you will end up dead like me'. It was here that they left him and his enemies killed him. This place is called Kila Kalana (Kila's grave). Because Kila Wari was a war chief the Velapos wanted to cut off his head (this was the custom). But the ladies from Babaka rushed over and covered Kila Wari, who was speared again and again (the ladies' names are unknown). So they did not cut off his head. He had a fishbone tattoo from jaw to mouth on both sides. They did however remove his chiefly neckwear.

Numa Nama concludes by saying that because the two women had now avenged their brother's death and because some other women had covered the body, nothing more could be done with it so his villagers carried him back. He says that nobody knows the exact spot where the death took place because there was no village there then, although 'it was a busy place'. The general vicinity is now the grounds of the United Church pastor's house and it is marked on local maps as Kila Kalana (Kila's grave).

Collectively, these accounts of the death of Kila Wari are rich in detail. We notice, though, that they present a number of contradictions. For instance, that three different men inflicted the mortal wound—an unknown warrior from Riwali and each of the Gure brothers. Such claims are not contested, however. It is evident from the multiple versions presented here that those who tell the story of Kila Wari are telling the story of their own ancestors. That Kila Wari is at the centre of these stories is coincidental. So, when Numa Nama was questioned about the revenge battle that inevitably followed the battle in which Kila Wari was killed his response was to suggest that we should speak to Kila Wari's descendants about the matter. The inference was that the revenge battle was not a story told by his family.

The point Numa Nama did make was that when his ancestor, Gure, was killed his body was badly mutilated, unlike the death of Kila Wari when 'they didn't spoil his body or cut off his head'. This Christian descendant of a war leader finds himself on familiar ground with regard to the importance of taking the head of a dead warrior. Numa Nama explains, 'Chopping off the head was important. It signifies something. Think about David and Goliath. David chopped off Goliath's head to prove he killed him'.

We return, then, to the Vula'a villages for the story of the battle that was to avenge the death of Kila Wari. First, we have an account from Wari Lui:

> Riwali and Babaka people were invited to 'bring and buy'[26] [this was a common form of trade] at Kaparoko [the westernmost of the Vula'a villages]. Alewai warriors chose to go fishing on this particular day. Riwali and Kaparoko chiefs together with Hula and Alewai warriors had made a plan to kill the Babaka chief. After the 'bring and buy' the Babaka chief was making his way home. The Alewai warriors hid in the bush waiting for him to come their way. They had placed a large human excrement on the road where he would pass (to signal the impending death). When the Babaka chief saw the human waste he knew something was wrong. Minutes later he was ambushed and taken alive. His ears were cut off and he was told that he was going to die because they had killed Kila Wari. After they killed him they cut off his head and rolled the body from Irupara to Alewai. The head was taken to Alukuni and sold for pigs' tusks and arm shells.

Walo Kalawa also gives us an account of the revenge battle.

> Then came a time when Babaka and Riwali agreed to a *raiwa* [trade]. Traditionally a knot was tied to mark the day and month of the *raiwa*. Just days before the *voi/raiwa* [27] a Riwali man broke the news of the *voi* to Kila Wari's brothers who were still mourning the death so an ambush was planned by Wari's brothers. Very early on the morning of the *raiwa* Babakas made their way to Kaparoko through the bush (it was so early that the birds were up and about trying to catch the first worm and the people's presence caused a commotion). Gure's warriors were cautious of the natural warnings but Gure reassured them saying '*auna paga vagia*' (we killed him [Kila Wari]). After a while they found a human waste. Gure realised someone had gone before them. Just then someone shouted '*poika amana era*' (now you are finished) and a battle erupted. Surrounded and seeing his men die, Gure ran for his life with Walo Kila, who was holding a *kora* [net], and Lui Wari in pursuit. Finally he was

caught by Lui Wari and pleaded for his life, '*Koa Kila govagi kona era?*' (Koa Kila—brother of the dead man—are you killing me now?). And was answered, '*Arimai poro va magulia, paga na va magulimu*' (Should you spare our brother's life, we would…[spare yours]). Then they pushed all the rubbish including the morning leaves into his mouth and killed him. The man who chopped his head off was Pala Pika (the head chopper). Gure's head was then rolled all the way back while spearing it. At Hula it was given to Vele Kopi for transportation to Keapara [on the other side of Hood Bay, adjacent to Alukuni]. The place where Gure died was called Gure Kalana (Gure's grave) and is now commonly known as Gurika—just after you leave Kone Kone creek towards Kaparoko.

It is said that after this battle Alewai village was given land *maino pakunai* (for the sake of peace) between the coastal villages and their inland neighbours.

Relations between the Vula'a and Babaka people have remained relatively friendly. Intermarriage is common and the presence of the United Church has created greater opportunities for a shared sociality. As we might expect, though, it is considered unwise to raise the topic of Kila Wari when both Babaka people and Vula'a people are present. More problematic today is that the people of two Vula'a villages, Irupara and Alewai, who describe themselves as 'one family' and, as such, share 'the same story' dispute its legitimacy in the determination of land claims. The question is a simple one: what *was* Kila Wari fighting for? Some say land, others disagree. The purpose of this chapter has not been to find answers to these questions, however.

Myth, History, and Existence: Some Concluding Remarks

It was Wari Lui's intention that the story of the life of the Shark Warrior be told to an audience beyond the southeast coast of Papua New Guinea. His request has been met. Clearly, though, this collection of stories has a significance far beyond the documenting of the life of a great warrior. For myself as researcher, the Kila Wari stories have provided a focal point for examining many aspects of Vula'a history, culture and cosmology. For instance, the practice of *waka* which emerges as an important theme in the narratives can be linked to similar concepts—the themes of other Vula'a narratives—which together provide a glimpse of a more complete cosmological system.

We have also seen that each and every story which constitutes the legend of Kila Wari is represented in terms of a genealogical relationship. These *treasured* relationships connect people to their ancestors in a most immediate sense. They also serve as a form of logic[28] that maps people *into*—because it is an experiential conjunction—the locations of emplaced events. Although differently conceived, genealogies are maps for the Vula'a and for the anthropologist. As maps they offer a unique opportunity for translation.

For the Vula'a, the Kila Wari stories embody identity. Although they are not widely known among the younger generations, they are held in trust by those who know their value. And while the application of this knowledge is occasionally invoked in the context of local politics, the Kila Wari stories serve a broader purpose. They are a repository for 'traditional' knowledge in a climate where the practices of the past have been significantly eroded by Christianity. Most importantly, they are reminders of an alternative way of life—a possibility of Being that is available, at least in the imagination, should people choose to engage it.

We have seen the weight that Wari Lui attributes to his genealogical connection to Kila Wari and glimpsed his mythic enactment of the warrior's life. Similarly, when Numa Nama Gure speaks of the chiefly lineage to which he belongs, he is not merely commemorating the past. Rather, he is acknowledging a possible present—a present in which he may be called upon to enact the duties of his forebears. And he remembers the actions of his ancestors largely in terms of the landscape in which they are embedded. The Kila Wari stories speak of history but they are also mythic. They tell of the life of a great man but they also tell of what it is to engage with such a life—story-teller, ancestor and place participate in a shared identity that is aptly described as mythic.[29] Western philosophy makes the existential point that human existence in the world is the primary concern of historical reflection.[30] Although the Kila Wari stories are profoundly existential, they are more than the reflection of historical subjectivity. They encourage mythic Being in the face of social change and feelings of loss. Nevertheless, there is a common ground that transcends distinctions usually made between myth and history. The motivation for 'telling lives' stems from the need to reproduce identity—our sense of 'self' in whatever way that is conceived.

Acknowledgements

This chapter would not have been possible without the assistance of the Rupa family of Irupara village, especially Gerre Rupa, who provided much of the translation. I am also indebted to Wari Lui, Numa Nama Gure, Wala Iga, Vela Kila, and everyone who shared their stories with me. My thanks go also to my good friends Kila Viri Rupa and his wife Elizabeth, Tani, Meena and Mape, and the many other men and women whose kindness and companionship made my work in Irupara so rewarding. Michael Goddard has patiently endured many readings of earlier drafts and offered helpful comments and discussion. Finally, I am grateful to Brij Lal and Vicki Luker for organising 'Telling Pacific Lives'.

ENDNOTES

[1] N.D. Oram, 'Culture change, economic development and migration among the Hula', *Oceania*, 36:4 (1968), 254.

[2] Ibid., 259.

[3] J. Kolia, *The History of the Balawaia* (Port Moresby 1977), 21-22.

[4] L. Short, *The Phonetics and Grammar of the Hula Language with Vocabulary and Translation and Notes of Other Dialects of the Hood Bay District* (Adelaide 1963 [originally MA thesis, University of Adelaide (Adelaide 1939)]), 68.

[5] B. Malinowski, *Argonauts of the Western Pacific* (New York 1961), 299.

[6] See Goddard this volume; D. Van Heekeren, '"Don't tell the crocodile': an existential view of Melanesian myth', *Critique of Anthropology*, 24:4 (2004), 430-454; Van Heekeren, 'Feeding relationship: uncovering cosmology in Christian women's fellowship in Papua New Guinea', *Oceania*, 75:2 (2004), 89-108; J. Robbins, *Becoming Sinners: Christianity and moral torment in a Papua New Guinea society* (Berkeley 2004); M. Jolly, 'Epilogue', *Oceania*, 74:1-2 (2003), 134-147; M. Strathern, *The Gender of the Gift: problems with women and problems with society in Melanesia* (Berkeley 1988).

[7] N.D. Oram, Papers, Nigel Oram Collection, Box 4, Folder 23, MS9436, National Library of Australia, Canberra.

[8] Some of the narrations that follow were given to me in written form, others are transcriptions of taped interviews. The tapes were translated by Gerre Rupa who also collected some of the written accounts. As much of the material was prepared for an audience unfamiliar with its details, it occasionally has an explanatory tone. The narrator's explanations appear in the text in round brackets and where I have felt it necessary to include further elaboration for the sake of coherence I have used square brackets.

[9] Wari Lui's use of the term 'land lords' should be taken as referring to the lineage head, or other designated individual who is responsible for overseeing family land. I have also heard the term used to refer to the ancestral spirits that have guardianship of garden land. I see little difference in the two examples, however, as the ancestral lineage is the significant aspect.

[10] J. Clifford, *Person and Myth: Maurice Leenhardt in the Melanesian world* (Berkeley 1982), 253, note 27.

[11] In a paper published in 1898 R.E. Guise describes 'Kwaipo' as 'a much dreaded village', 207. He offers no explanation but it is reasonable to assume that it is due to its reputation for powerful magic.

[12] Wari Lui is referring particularly to the ability to pass through a shower of spears without being hit.

[13] D. Kalakaua, *The Legends and Myths of Hawai'i: the fables and folk-lore of a strange people,* ed. R. M. Daggett (Honolulu 1990), 321.

[14] J.W. Lindt, *Picturesque New Guinea* (London 1887), 113.

[15] Oram, 'Pots for sago: the *hiri* trading network', in Tom Dutton (ed.), *The Hiri in History: further aspects of the long distance Motu trade in Central Papua* (Canberra 1982), 9.

[16] Lindt, *Picturesque New Guinea*, 60.

[17] Oram, 'The history of the Motu-speaking and Koita-speaking peoples according to their own traditions', in D. Denoon and R. Lacey (eds), *Oral Traditions in Melanesia* (Port Moresby 1981), 220-221.

[18] Ibid.

[19] Oram, 'Pots for Sago', 9.

[20] *Lekwai* is an archaic song form which had a commemorative purpose. There is no accurate translation of this song because the language is archaic. Nevertheless, it is evident that the actions of the protagonists, Kila Wari, the Kila Kila chief, Iovanu and Kila Wari's older brother, Kwamala are celebrated.

[21] Oram, 'The Hula in Port Moresby', *Oceania*, 39:1 (1968), 7.

[22] This is not merely a modern interpretation. Early European visitors found that the houses in the agricultural villages of this area were built in rows creating 'streets'. The Vula'a villages were built mainly over the water until after World War II. Their houses were also built in neat lines.

[23] In Maria Lepowsky's account of women's roles in warfare on the island of Vanatinai (Milne Bay District) she explains that the removal of an outer skirt expressed the woman's protection or, according to context, signalled an attack. Leposky, *Fruit of the Motherland: gender in an egalitarian society* (New York 1993), 62.

[24] A leg wound is the equivalent of a fatal blow. The victim can no longer jump to avoid further spears, or run at sufficient speed to escape. When the infamous Papuan Karo was hanged for murder by the colonial government many stories were told by the Papuans who witnessed it of the wounds inflicted by his white killers. One of these claims that when the body was taken away from the gallows there was a knife wound in its side and both Achilles tendons had been cut. Amirah Inglis, *Karo: the life and fate of a Papuan* (Canberra 1982), 119.

[25] At the time of Kila Wari's death Babaka village was located further east near the present site of Rilo school. It was then known as Paugolo (the name the people call themselves) until the move took place around the end of the 19th century.

[26] Here Wari Lui used the contemporary term for a gathering where food is prepared by one village and sold to another, usually to raise money for church projects, rather than elaborate the more traditional form of exchange of goods which was locally known as *raiwa*.

[27] '*Voi*' is a general term for trade as compared to '*raiwa*' which refers to a more 'social' exchange which included feasting.

[28] I use the phrase 'form of logic' here because I do not wish to suggest an abstract framework. Rather, I want to emphasise that genealogies are a concrete reality intrinsic to identity.

[29] Van Heekeren, '"Don't tell the crocodile"'.

[30] M. Heidegger, *Being and Time*, trans. J. Macquarrie and E. Robinson (London 1962), 433.

Chapter 3

From 'My Story' to 'The Story of Myself' — Colonial Transformations of Personal Narratives among the Motu-Koita of Papua New Guinea

Michael Goddard

Since the late colonial period, there have been a significant number of publications which could be roughly classified as Melanesian autobiography.[1] The majority of these have, in fact, been encouraged and commonly written down, edited and substantively organised, by European acquaintances of the subjects. The observation that the phenomenon of Melanesian autobiography is a product of the colonial encounter is a statement of the obvious. Further, as autobiography is an account of the development of a self-conscious individual during a period of historical time, the existence of the individual at its narrative core invites consideration in terms of currently popular critiques of the development of individualism in Melanesia. Problematising the traditional Melanesian person as non-individualist,[2] critical considerations of nascent Melanesian individual-ism contextualise its development particularly in the encounter with Christianity and capitalism, which are commonly seen as the major historical determinants of individualism in the West.[3]

Other aspects of the Melanesian experience of colonialism, however, may have influenced discursive representations of the self in the form of autobiography. In what follows, I use an example of a brief autobiography which itself was produced with no direct encouragement from a European mentor. Rather, its generation can be understood in terms of the development of a historical consciousness through the praxis of its writer, who was a prominent advocate in his village's legal claims to land around Port Moresby, Papua New Guinea, in the late colonial period. The advent of unsolicited autobiography in the society to which he belonged, the Motu-Koita, demonstrates a significant shift from the traditional role of a story's narrator, for in the mythopoeic, and therefore non-historical, worldview of the Motu-Koita an autobiographical individual could not exist.

I begin with a brief discussion of the Motu-Koita, their traditional mythopoeic worldview, and two examples of mentored narratives indicating a lack of autobiographical consciousness in the mid-colonial period. I then turn to the case of Bobby Gaigo, who represented Tatana, a Motu-Koita village, in land claims in the late colonial period and wrote a number of historical documents, including an autobiographical account. Finally I offer some comments on the development of a historical consciousness, in relation to autobiography.

Motu-Koita Mythopoeia

The land on which the city of Port Moresby, Papua New Guinea, has developed was traditionally the territory of two intermarried peoples now often collectively called the Motu-Koita, or Motu-Koitabu. The Koita spoke a non-Austronesian language, closely related to that of a group further inland, known as the Koiari, of which they may once have been a part.[4] The implication of linguistic evidence, oral tradition, and archaeological investigation is that at some stage in the distant past they moved, or were driven by the Koiari, toward the coast.[5] There they settled, and began to intermarry with the Western Motu. The latter spoke an Austronesian language, and built their houses at the edge of the sea, or sometimes offshore. The Western Motu migrated into the area from places both inland and on the coast[6] and when Europeans arrived they were settled in a number of villages along about 50 kilometres of the coast, separated from their coastal enemies, the Eastern Motu, by an inlet.[7]

A number of Koita groups became allied with the Motu villages known as Hanuabada, Tanobada, Tatana, Vabukori and Pari close to where Port Moresby would develop and friendly relations were maintained between the two peoples, though the Motu regarded the Koita as prone to sorcery. Both the Motu and Koita were fearful of the Koiari, whom they regarded as barbaric and possessed of great sorcery skills. Of the seven Motu villages established when Europeans arrived in the 1870s, two—Vabukori and Tatana—claimed different origins from the rest, despite sharing with them a common language and social organisation. Both the Motu and the Koita villages were divided into residential groups with a patrilineal idiom. These groups were, and are, called *iduhu*, a term popularly translated as 'clan', contrary to the caution of anthropologists.[8]

Traditionally, the Motu-Koita comprehension of their world was mythopoeic. That is, mythic narratives disclosed extra-ordinary potencies beyond what we might regard as commonsense explanations of everyday experience. Here I take Motu-Koita mythopoeia to be an intellectual activity similar to that which dominated ancient Greek thought before myth in that society was largely displaced by philosophy. Hatab suggests that for the Greeks myth was not a 'detached account', but a spoken correlate of an acted rite, or a thing done: 'Myth is therefore non-theoretical in the sense that it is not detached from *praxis*;

it is originally a *lived* reality'.[9] This phenomenological interpretation is particularly apt in respect of traditional Motu-Koita society, and in talking of mythopoeia in the Melanesian context I follow an exemplary and succinct formulation by Mimica, to mean a 'mode of activity of consciousness instrumental in the structuring of experience of the world in which humans are situated'.[10]

As a brief example of Motu-Koita mythopoeic consciousness, we can consider a figure known as Buasi, the founding ancestor of Tubumaga *iduhu*, who lived eight generations before the Motu culture hero Kevau Dagora. Archaeological investigation and the comparative examination of oral history suggest Kevau Dagora himself was active about 250 years before the present,[11] and core male members of the *iduhu* now known as Idibana Taulamiri in Pari village (near Port Moresby) trace their descent patrilineally to Kevau, and hence to Buasi. Beyond his human lifespan, Buasi continued his existence in serpentine form within a fissure in the rock of the hill called Taurama, overlooking a section of the local coastline. Crews of passing canoes paid obedience to Buasi and fell silent, lest their canoes capsized. The story of Buasi continued to be told through the colonial era, although it is largely forgotten nowadays.[12] We note the conflation of the past and present in the mythopoeic apprehension of Buasi's potency. The ancestor was present and efficacious, transcending the mundane abilities of the canoe paddlers, who depended on his benevolence as they negotiated what a foreigner might observe to be a relatively unhazardous stretch of water.

The immanence of ancestors meant that the past was not conceived historically in relationship to the present, but was experienced as part of a lived-present. Moreover, the relationship between members of a mortal community and ancestors could be enhanced by *siahu*, which can be glossed in English as 'heat'. Heat was an important constitutive concept in traditional Motu cosmology. Ancestors could be ritually approximated through the creation of conditions of heat, dryness and lightness. One way of achieving this was by intensifying a fire at an *irutahuna*, a potent central space in, for example, a house, which facilitated enhanced communication between a living assemblage and the phalanx of their ancestors. Men or women could also increase their *siahu* by chewing ginger in combination with other foods recognised as generating lightness and dryness. Such dietary regimes were instrumental in achieving a state of potency known as *helaga*, in which the participant became partially separated from communal mortality and closer to the existential status of ancestors. Becoming *helaga* enabled people to embrace their ancestors' power to a degree. This last achievement is reflected in the English glosses of *siahu* in translation, which include 'power' and 'authority' as well as 'heat'.

Siahu, in the sense of authority, was also a legitimating force when telling a *sivarai* (story),[13] insofar as genealogical connections to specific ancestors legitimated narratives of the past, which might include, for example, stories of the movement of ancestors from place to place establishing or abandoning villages or gardens, fighting battles, killing or being killed and buried. It is in this light that we should understand the Motu-Koita relationship to land, for example. For *siahu* is the word used when talking about what English speakers call land-rights. Through narratives about their ancestors, speakers would iterate their *siahu*, or that of their *iduhu*, to inhabit, or use, or pursue various activities at, the places to which they referred. In other words, their *siahu* derived from their ancestors' presence and actions at a given place. As mythopoeia, these narratives were not articulated as truth claims, nor were they subject to proof in any European legal or philosophical sense. They 'belonged' to the people who told them by virtue of their genealogy, and thereby their content was not challenged by other individuals or groups. *Sivarai* of the past, particularly those asserting 'land-rights' exemplify the way the Motu-Koita phenomenologically viewed the environment as constituted by places which were given meaning for the living by the activities of ancestors.

These briefly-sketched aspects of the traditional worldview of the Motu-Koita indicate the significance of relatedness as an aspect of people's being. Not only was genealogical connectedness a source of authority, but a temporary increase in the intensity of a person's relationship with ancestors (the attainment of degrees of *helaga*) was at the same time a lessening of his or her relationship with the community. The importance of relatedness can also be seen in, for example, Motu use of teknonymy and other encompassing terms of address. Familiar people were not normally addressed by name, but in terms of a relationship to someone else—'mother/father of *x*', 'husband/wife of *y*', 'my sibling', 'my father's sister' and so on. Their social being was in fact acknowledged through explicitly relating them to others. This is demonstrated mythopoeically in the partial social negation, during his youth, of the culture hero Kevau Dagora, who was mentioned earlier. Kevau Dagora was yet unborn when his father was killed in the massacre of Taurama village. His pregnant mother Konio was the only survivor of that massacre, fleeing to her brother's village, where Kevau Dagora grew up not knowing who his father was. He was mocked by other children for not belonging to a place, or having a father. When he went hunting, other children took the game he killed (a further negation of Kevau). Kevau Dagora eventually overcame this negation, after learning the story of the Taurama massacre, in an episode during which he killed one of his tormentors and declared himself. His utterance varies according to versions of the story—in some he uses the name of his father, in others his father's *iduhu* name or an invocation of Taurama, his ancestral home.[14] The variation discloses a commonality; in each account Kevau consolidates his social being through the elaboration of his relatedness beyond his own mother.

A further point of note in this narrative is the very name Kevau is given, in relation to his slaughtered father. Children were commonly named in the first instance by prefixing a name to the 'first' name of their father—thus the son or daughter of a man called 'Kevau *x*—' would be named '*y*— Kevau'. In the case of Kevau Dagora, however, genealogies ascribe to him the whole name of his father (that is, there is a 'Kevau Dagora No. 1' and a 'Kevau Dagora No. 2'). In this narrative, then, Kevau's natal relationship to his already deceased father is articulated through the shared relationship with the woman Konio ('Kevau *adavana*' = 'married of Kevau' and 'Kevau *sinana*' = 'mother of Kevau'), and his emergence as a new *iduhu* head and war leader replacing, rather than simply succeeding, his father through the avenging of the Taurama massacre.

In combination, the foregoing insights into the lack of historical separation of the past and present, and the primacy of relatedness, indicate that the autonomous self, as commonly understood in Western society, was not possible in Motu-Koita society. To elaborate this I draw on the terminology of Maurice Leenhardt, who attempted to represent Melanesian understandings of what Westerners consider to be the person, based on his study of New Caledonia in the early 1900s.[15] Without capitulating to the evolutionist cast of his representation, I find value in Leenhardt's distinctions between three kinds of human beings, which he designated, in French, *personnage, personne* and *individu*. The last of these terms can be translated as 'individual', and denoted for Leenhardt the Western notion of the autonomous, ego-oriented entity, imbued with temporal continuity.[16] In the standard English translation of Leenhardt's *Do Kamo*, Gulati renders *personnage* as 'personage',[17] but I prefer to use the term 'persona'. In contrast to the individual, the persona is constituted by and dependent upon relationships, is intrinsic to the mythopoeic experience of the world, and cannot exist outside of these conditions.[18] Between the two is the *personne*, or 'person', neither mythopoeically structured, nor fully individuated. The relationship between the Leenhardtian 'person' and 'individual', understood by him as a modality of a problematic evolution from archaic persona to rational individual, could be recast in terms of more recent anthropological discussion of the relationship between 'self' and 'person'.[19] My preoccupation here, though, is with the persona, the 'participatory' entity, which, among the Canaques of Leenhardt's ethnology, was known as the *kamo*:

> The *kamo* is a living persona who recognises himself less in his human contour than in his form, one might say in his human likeness.
>
> It is in this form, and not in the exterior contour, that the persona exists. Humanness thus transcends all physical representations of man. It is not perceived objectively, it is felt. It encloses in itself the aesthetic and affective elements which belong to man and which the Canaque experiences as such. It is this living, human, ensemble which he means by *kamo*.[20]

The *kamo*, the Canaque persona, is not defined by his or her body, but is sustained by a set of relationships with similar entities. To a predominant degree, the persona's being is experienced as participation, not as an independent existence. Leenhardt gives a handy example of this in the negative instance, a Canaque cursed and driven out of his society, who feels himself in 'perdition'. Deprived of any relationship through which to find himself, he cannot even assert his being through speech, because he no longer corresponds to any persona. Without a participatory relationship and a corresponding name he has no existence.[21] 'Persona' is, then, a particularly apt term for the mode of being Leenhardt is attempting to portray, being derived from the Latin terms *per* ('through'), and *sonare* ('to sound'), giving the compound *personare*, 'to sound through'.

To return to the Motu-Koita, the culture hero Kevau Dagora is in every sense a persona. In the narratives he is initially in 'perdition', as his social being is denied by others, until he finds himself by establishing the relationship to his father, to his *iduhu*, and to Taurama and declares himself. Consequently in the remainder of the narrative he is, as Leenhardt might put it, a living Motu-Koita ensemble in the qualities he displays and in his achievements. But importantly, the *narrator* of such stories is also a persona, using his or her relationship to Kevau Dagora to establish authority, both to tell the story, and to maintain a practical engagement with the places which the narrative traverses. The narrator declares himself or herself in this mythopoeic fashion. The obverse of this dependence on relationships is a lack of acknowledgement of a self which can exist autonomously outside the mythopoeic context. That is, traditional Motu-Koita did not acknowledge themselves as the autonomous, ego-oriented entities, imbued with temporal continuity, which we might call individuals. Consequently, they could not have an autobiographical consciousness.

An indication of this traditional lack of autobiographical consciousness among the Motu-Koita is found, paradoxically, in the 'autobiographical' reminiscences of Ahuia Ova, written in collaboration with the anthropologist F.E. Williams and published in 1939. Ahuia Ova was prominent in his day, the early colonial period. He was a major informant of C.G. Seligman, who published an ethnology of the Koita,[22] an informant of Malinowski during the latter's short time in Port Moresby,[23] and enjoyed some patronage from the Governor, Sir Hubert Murray. Williams was partly motivated to record Ahuia's biography by Radin's apparent success with a native American.[24] Certainly the finished product contained a significant amount of biographical material and, as Williams observed, was evidence of considerable hubris,[25] but its form was the result of guidance, 'some encouragement', a syllabus and pre-arranged table of contents provided by Williams, significant editing of the manuscript dictated by Ahuia, and substantive rearrangement to achieve the conventional autobiographical structure desired by Williams.[26] The anthropologist expressed 'some disappointment' at the quality and quantity of the finished product, compared to Radin's achievements, and clearly had expectations of what an autobiography should contain which were unfulfilled by Ahuia, whom Williams said was 'more at home in relating legends than in writing personal history'.[27] Indeed, Williams tells us that 'A few quite irrelevant passages have been dropped, and some long-winded ones summarised in square brackets'.[28]

Less interference was involved in another celebrated document, 'Kori Taboro's story' dictated to a literate Papuan in the 1940s and published both in English and in Motu.[29] Kori Taboro was a prominent Koita woman in Port Moresby, a diviner, mistakenly represented by some as a sorcerer,[30] and witness to early government and missionary activity in the area. Some phraseological liberties were taken in the translation, but the substance of Kori's story was preserved, and she appears to have told her story in her own way. Moreover, G.A.V. Stanley, the European at whose house the story was narrated, forbade any questioning of her during the telling. This document is a marked contrast to Ahuia Ova's reminiscences, in that Kori Taboro gives very little autobiographical information. She gives her birthplace and genealogy[31] and testifies to being a child when the missionary W.G. Lawes began translating the Bible into Motu.[32] This information, though, is used only to legitimate and orient her narrative, about migrations, warfare, missionary and other colonially related activities (which are themselves mythologised in the account). Kori Taboro, in other words, refers to herself only to indicate her relationship to the persons whose actions she describes and thereby her *siahu*, her authority to tell the *sivarai*.

The Motu title of Kori Taboro's story, *Kori Taboro Ena Sivarai*, also indicates its lack of autobiographical consciousness. Two types of possession, alienable and inalienable, are marked in the Motu language. *Kori Taboro Ena Sivarai*, unlike its English translation 'Kori Taboro's Story', is unequivocal in meaning. It is specifically 'the story told by Kori Taboro'. To indicate a story *about* Kori Taboro, a different phrase, *Kori Taboro Sivaraina*, would be required, and the speaker would be someone other than Kori Taboro. *Sivaraina* (*sivarai* with a possessive suffix) is the inalienable case, the story and its subject are inseparable, as with the story above about Kevau Dagora. Such a construction cannot sensibly occur with the speaker as the object, such as *lau sivaraigu*, 'the story of me'. In order to use the inalienable construction in a reflexive manner, Kori Taboro would have to tell a story about her *participation in* an event (e.g., *lau Mosbi nala sivaraina*, 'story about my trip to Moresby'). In conformity with the mythopoeic conception of the persona, Kori Taboro cannot represent herself as an entity with its own life history.

Representing Tatana

An autobiographical account, in the conventional sense, by a Motu-Koita person, would represent a significant transition from the mythopeoic worldview and the non-historical self-perception of the narrator as persona, which I have described here. It is worth noting that when Williams elicited the reminiscences of Ahuia Ova more than 50 years after the arrival of Christianity, the latter had long since converted to the introduced religion, and had explicitly denounced the kinds of activities which the administration labelled 'sorcery' and associated with a pre-Christian worldview.[33] Kori Taboro, who continued her traditional divinations and midwifery until her death in 1950, was schooled in her youth by the London Missionary Society.[34] Long experience of Christianity did not foster the degree of individualism necessary for an autobiographical consciousness in either of these articulate narrators. However, in the 1970s, a series of writings, culminating in an account which could rightly be described as autobiographical, was produced by a Motu-Koita man who had internalised the message of legal documents at least as much as the word of God. His name was Bobby Gaigo, and he was from Tatana, a village which had barely been mentioned in academic literature on the Motu-Koita until he began writing history.

Tatana is on a small island, essentially a hill, in the inner harbour beside the town of Port Moresby. At first contact by Europeans in 1873, a village of up to 200 people occupied the northern edge of the island and had only a little gardening land at the base of the hill. Archaeological research suggests that as a result of a fission when the forerunners of the Motu were in a state of migration centuries earlier, Tatana villagers, and the people of another village on the mainland coast, Vabukori, moved into their present sites via a different route from the rest of the Motu.[35] A few oral traditions reinforce this possibility, giving Tatana people different migration routes than the majority of Motuans, mostly from beyond Galley Reach to the west.[36] Early European observers noted that Tatana villagers appeared not to make pots, which distinguished them from most other Motu villages in the area, but specialised in the manufacture of shell beads (*ageva*), and shell headbands (*gema*).[37] They were of less interest to early anthropologists than the much larger village complex nearby known as Hanuabada, and little was written about them. Turner, a missionary anthropologist, wrote in 1878 that they 'have no plantations and so they live by plunder'.[38]

Missionaries and the administration 'bought' land from the Motu-Koita, especially those of the Hanuabada village complex, initially paying with items of clothing and axes. Whether the Motu-Koita recognised this process as a land sale in the European sense is debatable: traditionally land had either been taken by conquest in warfare, or land-use by outsiders was negotiated in terms of ongoing tokens of reciprocation and goodwill. The administration's land acquisition procedure later included rental agreements and more substantial payments, but by the mid-20th century local landholders had become alarmed by the growth of permanent infrastructure and buildings. By the end of the colonial era (the 1970s) the *de facto* loss of their land to what had become a city of migrants was developing into a major issue for the Motu-Koita.[39]

In the 1960s Motu-Koita discontent manifested in a number of claims for compensation in respect of land which they regarded as inadequately paid for, or even illegally acquired, during the early colonial period. The land claims created legal conflict among the Motu-Koita, as various groups occasionally claimed to have been the original owners of the same piece of land, alleging that the colonial authorities had paid the wrong people when acquiring the land, or had made inadequate enquiries as to whether land was owned in the first place. An example of the latter was a tortuous case lasting two decades in which a large number of groups claimed ownership of Daugo Island, near Port Moresby, which the administration had acquired as 'waste and vacant' land in 1889. Tatana villagers became involved in several claims to land in and around Port Moresby, including the Daugo Island claim, in the 1960s.

It is conventionally legally held in Papua New Guinea that the process of establishing genealogical linkages to the actions of apical ancestors is customary and therefore legitimate, and indeed warranted, in land claims. But in relation to Motu-Koita claims, the traditional sense of *siahu* was made irrelevant *a priori*, by virtue of the cases being a contestation of 'ownership' demonstrated according to principles of probability, requiring claimants to reasonably prove their habitation of an area of land and use of its resources during a particular period of historical time. This necessarily obliged commissioners and judges to consider the credibility of claimants' testimony, which could only be done by reference to a measure of historical 'fact', provided by documentary evidence and European testimony. *Siahu*, in its original sense of affirming the mythopoeic simultaneity of the past and present, the incontestable expression of the potentiality of occupation or use of a place by virtue of an ancestor's presence, had no legitimacy in these sorts of procedings.

Of all the claimants to Daugo Island, the Tatana villagers recognised the importance of demonstrating to the court a detailed knowledge of historical facts and articulating themselves with those facts. In contrast to the other claimants, who relied on assertions that they had *traditionally* fished and camped at Daugo, the Tatana villagers claimed that they had *actually* lived and gardened on Daugo. They also claimed to have planted coconut trees on the island (against the documentary evidence that the trees were planted by prisoners working on the government plantation in the late 19th century). As the hearings progressed visits were made to Daugo Island, where Tatana witnesses pointed out pottery sherds, and what they claimed were the sites of their village, and gardens and a waterhole. Tatana witnesses also claimed variously that their grandparents had been active on the island or had lived there in the days of prominent early colonial figures such as Captain Moresby, Governor William MacGregor and the entrepreneur Robert Hunter and had interacted with these people.[40]

Much of what they said contradicts not only the documentary evidence before the court, but the body of knowledge available from a spectrum of academic research (not used in the Daugo claim hearings) touching on Daugo Island.[41] Nevertheless, as the claim continued, their ability to position themselves as actors in the conventional history of the island became focal in convincing the courts of their ownership of the island. A National Court appeal hearing in 1979 was a turning point in the fortunes of the Tatana claimants to Daugo. The Court, reviewing the evidence, was impressed by the extensive historical knowledge of Daugo Island apparent in the witnesses' testimony and in subsequent hearings Tatana village had the ascendancy over other claimants.[42] They were eventually judged to be the traditional owners of Daugo Island, in 1985.

Bobby Gaigo's Story

The Tatana villagers' most prominent representative in the Daugo and other claims was Bobby Gaigo, himself from Tatana village, who died in 1987, shortly after victory in the Daugo claim. Bobby Gaigo had no legal training, but he had developed the ability to read and interpret legal texts, and commonly represented fellow villagers in court cases.[43] During the 1970s while the land claims were in process, Bobby Gaigo started to produce written accounts of the history of Tatana Island and the social practices of its villagers.[44] In all of them, beginning with a short paper on fishing practices, his introductory section included a claim of extensive land holdings. The first of these was as follows:

> According to our traditions the ancestors of the people now living at Tatana Village formed the first community in the Port Moresby area. Their population was large, as were their landholdings. We occupied land around Fairfax Harbour and the offshore islands of Daugo and Gemo. Old village sites may be seen in several places, including a fair sized one on Daugo Island.[45]

In subsequent papers he elaborated by listing specific mainland sites comprising the northern and western sides of the harbour and beyond to Malara. He also listed various islands scattered through fishing grounds around Port Moresby and along the coast to the east and west: for example, 'Tatana owned large traditional fishing areas, including Daugo island, Nadera reef, Gavera islands, Walter Bay, Gemo Island, Hesede reef, Nonorua Island, Konebada and Port Moresby harbour'.

In marked contrast to the oral traditions of migration and movement commonly offered by Motu-Koita, including Tatana islanders in the past, Bobby Gaigo's writings represented Tatana people as the original people of the area. Indeed he stated that other Motu negotiated with Tatana people to be allowed to settle at sites such as Hanuabada. The significant difference between the conventional wisdom informed by the collective oral traditions of other Motu-Koita groups and Gaigo's own claims of territorial priority and extensive landholding by Tatana people was attributed by him to the selectivity of European researchers, whom he claimed never consulted Tatana people. In elaborating this claim he revealed the extent of his own reading, for he listed individuals he considered complicit in the misrepresentation of local prehistory. These included Governor MacGregor, prominent early missionaries, later churchmen and writers, anthropologists, their local informants (specifically, Ahuia Ovia), linguists and colonial officers. He even included publication dates.

While Gaigo's writings contradicted much of the historical evidence about the Port Moresby area, as well as being self-contradictory, and contained a number of anomalies such as attributing some of Owen Stanley's exploratory activities in 1850 to John Moresby in 1873, they are evidence of considerable documentary research on his part. For example, the claim that his forefathers saw ships which may have been Spanish or Portuguese relates to a debate among historians about whether the Spanish expedition of Torres and de Prado sailed close to the area in 1606. Gaigo even includes a reference list in one document, an indication of his acquaintance with academic literary convention.[46] In addition to discursively shifting Tatana islanders from a marginal position in local history to a foundational and central position by claiming that Tatana islanders, and his own genealogical ancestors, were the original inhabitants of the territory, Gaigo provided autobiographical information, particularly in a document entitled 'The Young Bobby Gaigo of Tatana Island', which was clearly produced without editorial assistance.[47]

By his own account, Bobby Gaigo was born at Malara, which is where Tatana villagers were evacuated to during the Second World War, inviting the inference that he was born between 1942 and 1945.[48] His parents were both from Tatana and his father was a village councillor. He attended a London Missionary Society school and then a primary school, but left before completing primary education, due to 'family problems',[49] and obtained work as a tea boy and messenger in the Department of Native Affairs. He worked intermittently in a number of administrative departments as a clerical assistant, and for some private firms as a storeman, frequently leaving his employment—or being sacked for non-attendance—to attend the land-claim hearings in which he was involved for two decades.[50] After dropping out of school he continued to try to educate himself by reading local and overseas newspapers when he could obtain them and, significantly, by spending time in the public library and (from the late 1960s) the library at the University.[51] He also learned the rudiments of typing.

In the 1970s, he attended the University of Papua New Guinea's academic conferences known as the Waigani Seminar, where he gave short seminar papers.[52] Bobby Gaigo was a supporter of the Pangu Party (the party of Papua New Guinea's first Chief Minister, Michael Somare) and later of Papua Besena, the party led by Josephine Abaijah, switching allegiance, he wrote, because Pangu failed to support Tatana's local land claims.[53] He served as a 'village court' magistrate on Tatana in the 1970s and campaigned unsuccessfully as an independent political candidate in the 1977 elections.[54] He spent two periods in gaol during the time he was active as a representative in court cases—one for 'contempt of court' and the other for 'fraud'—implying in his account that he was a political prisoner.[55] He went on to claim that in his youth he lived at Daugo, made gardens and planted coconut trees. The document re-visited the testimony of Tatana witnesses in the land claim, some of whom Gaigo represented as being centenarians, and included a reference list of documents tendered during the hearings of the Daugo Island claim.[56]

Law, History and Autobiography

Bobby Gaigo's collective writings demonstrate a sophisticated understanding of the exigencies of civil legal processes and the value Europeans place on documentary sources and the establishment of historical 'facts'. He was putting a version of history on the record for future scholars in the manner of others he had consulted during his own research for land claims. In pursuing those claims he had come to recognise the importance of demonstrating a detailed knowledge of historical facts and articulating himself with those facts. His accounts, placing Tatana geographically and politically at the centre of the prehistory of the Port Moresby area, were far removed from the mythopoeic narratives which his forebears had told oral historians, but which the Tatana land claimants never told in court, about man-eating giants and migration from somewhere north-west of Galley Reach. Those narratives, he realised, would not satisfy the real criteria by which 'customary' ownership was proved in courts of law, and he probably doubted they would be credited as acceptable history by a western reader.

It was through this praxis, then, that Bobby Gaigo developed a historical consciousness, and thereby the conditions for representing himself as an autobiographical subject.[57] For success in the court cases required stories to be testimony, subject to interrogation requiring proof, or at least probability, whereby the speakers had to represent themselves as witnesses, at first hand or second hand (the latter through recalling what a grandfather or other relative had witnessed). Called upon to describe themselves, their actions, their whereabouts at particular times, their qualifications and authority to make statements of fact, their memories of specific events at specific times, Bobby Gaigo and his fellow witnesses learned to position themselves in historical time, witnessing events from the point of view of an individual, an autonomous, ego-oriented entity, capable of discursively detaching themselves from what they described.

When Bobby Gaigo finally wrote his autobiography it is notable that although he referred to his father and grandfather, he did not narrate a detailed genealogy, in the way Kori Taboro had at several points in her story. His story was the story of himself, his achievements and occasional failures, as an individual historically shaped through his own praxis, not as a persona constituted by and dependent upon relationships, intrinsic to the mythopoeic experience of the world, and unable to exist outside of these conditions. As I said at the beginning of this paper, critical considerations of nascent Melanesian individual-ism contextualise its development particularly in the encounter with Christianity and capitalism, which are commonly seen as the major historical determinants of individualism in the West. But there is not a great deal of evidence of such determination in the stories of Ahuia Ovia or Kori Taboro. Bobby Gaigo's story, though, indicates a link between the encounter with European criteria of proof and legitimacy, for example in legal contestations, and the development of the historical consciousness which shapes the concept of the individual, and thereby, autobiography.

ENDNOTES

[1] For example, Josephine Abaijah, *A Thousand Coloured Dreams* (Mt Waverley 1991); R.M. Keesing, *'Elota's Story: the life and times of a Solomon Islands big man* (St Lucia, Qld 1978); A.M. Kiki, *Kiki: ten thousand years in a lifetime* (Melbourne 1968); Michael Somare, *Sana: an autobiography of Michael Somare* (Port Moresby 1975); Andrew Strathern, *Ongka: a self-account of a New Guinea big man* (New York 1979); Andrew Strathern, *Ru: biography of a Western Highlander* (Port Moresby 1993); V.D. Watson, *Anyan's Story: a New Guinea woman in two worlds* (Seattle 1997).

[2] There is certainly no consensus on the nature of traditional Melanesian 'individuals' beyond the observation that individual-ism was not a part of their worldview. For a comparative range of perspectives see for example A.L. Epstein, *Gunantuna: aspects of the person, the self and the individual among the Tolai* (Bathurst 1999); C.A. Gregory, *Gifts and Commodities* (London 1982); Maurice Leenhardt, *Do Kamo: person and myth in the Melanesian world*, trans. B.M. Gulati (Chicago 1979); K.E. Read, 'Morality and the concept of the person', *Oceania*, 55 (1955), 233-82. Michele Stephen, *A'aisa's Gifts: a study of magic and the self* (Berkeley 1995) and Marilyn Strathern, *The Gender of the Gift* (Berkeley 1990).

[3] Louis Dumont, *Essays on Individualism: modern ideology in anthropological perspective* (Chicago 1992) on the historical shaping of individualism in the West are a handy guide, and Tawney's discussion, in 1922, of the relationship between Christianity and capitalism remains relevant, R.H. Tawney, *Religion and the Rise of Capitalism: a historical study* (London 1990). Examples of the contextualisation of individualistic attitudes in the encounter with Christianity and/or capitalism in Melanesia can be found in T.S. Epstein, *Capitalism, Primitive and Modern: some aspects of Tolai economic growth* (Canberra 1968); Ben R. Finney, *Big-Men and Business: entrepreneurship and economic growth in the New Guinea Highlands* (Canberra 1973); Gregory, *Gifts and Commodities*; Edward LiPuma, *Encompassing Others: the magic of modernity in Melanesia* (Ann Arbor 2000); and Joel Robbins, *Becoming Sinners: Christianity and moral torment in a Papua New Guinea Society* (Berkeley 2004).

[4] T.E. Dutton, *The Peopling of Central Papua* (Canberra 1969), 32.

[5] Dutton, *The Peopling of Central Papua*; N.D. Oram, 'The history of the Motu-speaking and Koitabu-speaking peoples according to their own traditions', in Donald Denoon and Roderic Lacey (eds),

Oral Tradition in Melanesia (Port Moresby 1981); Pamela Swadling, 'The settlement history of the Motu and Koita apeaking people of the Central Province, Papua New Guinea', in Denoon and Lacey, *Oral Tradition in Melanesia*, 240-251.

[6] Oram, 'Introduction', *Oral History*, 7:3 (1979), 2-7; Oram, 'The history of the Motu-speaking and Koitabu-speaking peoples'.

[7] Oram, 'The history of the Motu-speaking and Koitabu-speaking peoples'.

[8] For example, Cyril Belshaw, *The Great Village* (London 1957), 13; Michael Goddard, 'Rethinking Motu descent groups', *Oceania*, 71:1 (2001), 313-3; Murray Groves, 'Western Motu descent groups', *Ethnology*, 2:1 (1963), 15ff.

[9] Lawrence J. Hatab, *Myth and philosophy: a contest of truths* (La Salle 1990), 20, italics in original.

[10] Jadran Mimica, *Intimations of infinity: the cultural meanings of the Iqwaye counting and number systems* (Providence 1988), 5.

[11] Oram, 'Taurama—oral sources for a study of recent Motuan prehistory', *The Journal of the Papua and New Guinea Society*, 2:2 (1968), 79-91; 'The history of the Motu-speaking and Koitabu-speaking peoples'; R.L. Pulsford and V, Heni, 'The story or Taurama village as told by Aire Aire Rahobada of Pari village', *The Journal of the Papua and New Guinea Society*, 2:2 (1968), 97-100; Susan Bulmer, 'Prehistoric settlement patterns and pottery in the Port Moresby area', *Journal of the Papua and New Guinea Society*, 5:2 (1971), 29-91; Jack Golson, 'Introduction to Taurama archaeological site Kirra Beach', *Journal of the Papua and New Guinea Society*, 2:2 (1968), 67-71.

[12] Partial accounts of the Buasi story are given by N.D. Oram, (used by permission of the Australian National Library), 'The History of the Motu-speaking and Koitabu-speaking peoples', 211; Oram Papers, Nigel Oram Collection, Canberra, Australian National Library, MS9436; and R. L. Pulsford, 'Changing attitudes of the Motu-Koita to illness and misfortune', MA Thesis, University of Sydney (Sydney 1974), 18. I was given a version in Pari village in 1994 in conversation with a group including Lohia Daure (head of Idibana Taulamiri Iduhu), Morea Hekoi and Puka Vagi.

[13] *Sivarai* is a general term for 'story'. Another term, *gori*, is translated in the standard dictionary of Motu (Lister-Turner), as 'legend', but would be better interpreted to mean stories told for amusement, for example to children, or to 'pass the time'. *Gori* are the Motuan equivalent of 'tall tales' and 'fairy tales'. Stories of cosmogony, culture heroes, which might be viewed as 'legends' or 'myths' (i.e. exaggerated or untrue) by Europeans, are not regarded as *gori* by the Motu-Koita.

[14] Cf. I.O. Nou, *Pari Hanua Edia Sense Sivaraidia* (Port Moresby 1975), 4-5; Oram, 'Introduction', 2-7; Pulsford and Heni, 'The story of Taurama village', 98-99. In the latter version, his cry is given as '*Gwadagwada Taurama Biri*' which the authors erroneously say is the name of his *iduhu*. An approximate translation is 'Speared by Taurama!' Kevau Dagora's father's *iduhu* is generally understood to have been *Tubumaga*, which Kevau Dagora subsequently re-established at *Tauata*, a site now known as Pari village. The account given here is condensed from a number of versions, as cited and also orally given to me at Pari village.

[15] Leenhardt, *Do Kamo: La Personne et le Mythe dans le Monde Mélanésien* (Paris 1998 [1947]).

[16] Leenhardt, *Do Kamo: La Personne et le Mythe*, 264, 270-71.

[17] Leenhardt, *Do Kamo: Person and Myth*, trans. Gulati, xxxii and *passim*.

[18] Leenhardt, *Do Kamo: La Personne et le Mythe*, 248-251.

[19] Leenhardt, *Do Kamo: La Personne et le Mythe*, 1998, 261-271; cf. Leenhardt, *Do Kamo: Person and Myth*, 162-169. In respect of Melanesia in particular, see for example Kenelm Burridge, *Someone, No One: an essay on individuality* (Princeton 1979); A.L. Epstein, *Gunantuna*; Deborah Gewertz, 'The Tchambuli view of persons: a critique of individualism in the works of Mead and Chodorow', *American Anthropologist*, 3 (1984), 615-29; LiPuma, *Encompassing Others*, 128-152; and Stephen, *A'aisa's Gifts*.

[20] Leenhardt, *Do Kamo: La Personne et le Mythe*, 73-4, my translation of 'Le kamo et un personnage vivant qui se reconnaît moins à son contour d'homme qu'à sa forme, on pourrait dire à son air d'humanité. C'est dans cette forme, et non dans la ligne extérieure, que le personnage existe. L'humain dépasse ainsi toutes les représentations physique de l'homme. Il n'est pas perçu objectivement, il est senti. Il enferme en lui les données esthétiques et affectives qui sont de sont de l'homme et que le Canaque éprouve comme telles. C'est cet ensemble vivant et humain qui'il signifie par *kamo*'. Cf. Leenhardt, *Do Kamo: Person and Myth*, 26.

[21] Leenhardt, *Do Kamo: La Personne et le Mythe*, 251.

[22] C.G. Seligman, *The Melanesians of British New Guinea* (Cambridge 1910).

[23] B. Malinowski, *A Diary in the Strict Sense of the Term* (California 1989), 9-22.

²⁴ Radin cited in F.E. Williams, 'The reminiscences of Ahuia Ova', *The Journal of the Royal Anthropological Institute of Great Britain and Ireland*, 69:1 (1939), 12.

²⁵ Williams, 'The reminiscences of Ahuia Ova', 13 and *passim*.

²⁶ Williams, 'The reminiscences of Ahuia Ova'.

²⁷ Williams, 'The reminiscences of Ahuia Ova', 12-13.

²⁸ Williams, 'The reminiscences of Ahuia Ova', 13.

²⁹ Sinaka Goava, 'Kori Taboro's Story', *Oral History*, 7:3 (1979); and Goava, 'Kori Taboro Ena Sivarai', *Oral History*, 7:3 (1979), 95-123.

³⁰ For example, Caroline Mytinger, *New Guinea Headhunt* (New York 1946) 202ff.

³¹ Goava, 'Kori Taboro's Story', 65, 67, 79; Goava, 'Kori Taboro Ena Sivarai', 95, 96, 107.

³² Goava, 'Kori Taboro's Story', 79-80; Goava, 'Kori Taboro Ena Sivarai', 108.

³³ Williams, 'The reminiscences of Ahuia Ova'.

³⁴ Oram, 'Introduction'.

³⁵ Bulmer, 'Prehistoric settlement patterns and pottery in the Port Moresby area'; Swadling, 'The settlement history of the Motu and Koita speaking people', 245-247.

³⁶ For example, Bulmer, 'Prehistoric settlement patterns and pottery in the Port Moresby area'; Swadling, 'The settlement history of the Motu and Koita speaking people', 45; Oram, 'The Hula in Port Moresby', *Oceania*, 39:1 (1968), 1-35; Oram 'The history of the Motu-speaking and Koitabu-speaking peoples', 215.

³⁷ Bulmer, 'Prehistoric settlement patterns and pottery in the Port Moresby area', 44; Seligman, *The Melanesians of British New Guinea*, 93, 114; W. Y. Turner, 'The ethnology of the Motu', *Journal of the Anthropological Institute of Great Britain and Ireland* 7 (1878), 470-499.

³⁸ Turner, 'The ethnology of the Motu', 492.

³⁹ Nigel Oram, *Colonial Town to Melanesian City: Port Moresby 1884-1974* (Canberra 1976), 175ff.

⁴⁰ Papua New Guinea Law Reports (hereinafter PNGLR) 1979, National Court of Justice (hereinafter NCJ): Re Fisherman's Island, 225-229.

⁴¹ For example, Bulmer, 'Prehistoric settlement patterns and pottery in the Port Moresby area'; T.E. Dutton, *Police Motu: Iena Sivarai* (Port Moresby 1985); R. J. Lambert, 'Some archaeological sites of the Motu and Koiaria areas', in *The History of Melanesia: proceedings of the 2nd Waigani Seminar* (Port Moresby 1969), 411-9; Oram, 'Taurama'; Swadling, 'The settlement history of the Motu and Koita speaking people'. Briefly, Daugo was uninhabited when first visited by Capt. Moresby in 1873 and archaeological evidence suggests that it had not been inhabited for at least 1000 years. The colonial administration acquired it as 'waste and vacant' in 1889 and attempted to establish a coconut plantation which was abandoned after a few years. Various local groups fished around the island, but it remained uninhabited until people from Hula, 100 kms east of Port Moresby, began a settlement on it in the 1950s.

⁴² PNGLR 1979, NCJ: re Fisherman's Island, 225-229; see PNGLR 1986, NCJ: Arthur Ageva v. Bobby Gaigo and Mahada Resena, 160-166; PNGLR 1987, Supreme Court of Justice: Arthur Ageva v. Boby Gaigo, Naime Daure and Madana Resena, 12-15.

⁴³ PNGLR 1971-72, Supreme Court of the Territory of Papua and New Guinea: Rahonamo v. Enai, 58-67; PNGLR 1977, NCJ: Arthur Ageva, Gadiki Sanai, Madaha Resena, Jack Mase, and Bobby Gaigo v. the State, 99-106; PNGLR 1979, NCJ: re Fisherman's Island, 202-46; PNGLR 1979, Gaigo, Representing Mrs Henao Batari and Mrs Dai Bais v. The Employers Federation of PNG, Representing W. R. Carpenters, 92-98; PNGLR 1986, NCJ: Arthur Ageva v. Bobby Gaigo and Madaha Resena, 160-66; PNGLR 1987, SCJ: Arthur Ageva v. Bobby Gaigo, Naime Daure and Madana Resena, 12-15; also Ralph R. Premdas and Jeffrey S. Steeves, *Electoral Politics in a Third World City: Port Moresby 1977* (Port Moresby 1978), 38.

⁴⁴ Bobby Gaigo, 'Present-day fishing practices among the people of Tatana village in Fairfax Harbour, Papua New Guinea', in B.A.C. Enyi and T. Vaghese (eds), *Agriculture in the Tropics: papers delivered at the tenth Waigani Seminar, PNG University of Technology, Lae 28 May 1976* (Port Moresby 1977), 143-9; Gaigo, 'Present day fishing practices in Tatana village', in John H. Winslow (ed.), *The Melanesian Environment* (Canberra 1977), 176-81; Gaigo, 'The history of Tatana village, National Capital District Central Province', *Oral History*, 7:5 (1979), 88-102; Gaigo, 'Social disorder', in Richard Jackson (ed.), *Urbanisation and its problems in Papua New Guinea* (Port Moresby 1980), 209; Gaigo, 'Past and present fishing practices among the people of Tatana village, Port Moresby', in Louise Marauta, John Pernetta and William Heaney (eds), *Traditional Conservation in Papua New Guinea: implications for today* (Boroko

1982), 301-2; Gaigo, 'The young Bobby Gaigo of Tatana Island', mimeo, Attorney General's Department Library, Waigani, no date; Gaigo, 'The history of Tatana', mimeo, Michael Somare Library, University of Papua New Guinea, Port Moresby, no date.

[45] Gaigo, 'Present-day fishing practices among the people of Tatana village', 143.

[46] Gaigo, 'The history of Tatana'.

[47] Gaigo, 'The young Bobby Gaigo of Tatana Island'.

[48] Gaigo, 'The young Bobby Gaigo of Tatana Island', 1. In contrast, Premdas and Steeves, in a biographical note on 1977 election candidates, suggest he was aged 30 in 1977; *Electoral Politics in a Third World City*, 38.

[49] Gaigo, 'The young Bobby Gaigo of Tatana Island', 2.

[50] Gaigo, 'The young Bobby Gaigo of Tatana Island', 3-4.

[51] Gaigo, 'The young Bobby Gaigo of Tatana Island', 4.

[52] For example, Gaigo, 'Present-day fishing practices among the people of Tatana village'; Gaigo, 'Past and present fishing practices among the people of Tatana village, Port Moresby'.

[53] Gaigo, 'The young Bobby Gaigo of Tatana Island', 9.

[54] Gaigo, 'The young Bobby Gaigo of Tatana Island', 10-11.

[55] Gaigo, 'The young Bobby Gaigo of Tatana Island', 12. I have been told by a witness (whom I will not identify here) to the 'fraud' gaoling that Bobby Gaigo was charged with obtaining money from people ostensibly to arrange for their representation in court by lawyers—arrangements which were not actually pursued.

[56] Gaigo, 'The history of Tatana', 12-23.

[57] I am not suggesting that this was simultaneously the demise of a mythopoeic consciousness.

Chapter 4

Mobility, Modernisation and Agency: The Life Story of John Kikang from Papua New Guinea

Wolfgang Kempf

In this chapter I focus on the autobiographical notes and oral accounts by John Kikang, and how I have used these sources in writing a version of his life. My interlocutor came from a village in the heartland of the Ngaing, a people who inhabit the Rai Coast hinterland in Papua New Guinea's province of Madang. Kikang was over 70 years old when, in February 1997, he died in the village of his birth. Throughout his life Kikang had valued the ideals of progress and development. His narratives and writings tell of identifications and initiatives aligned to Western discourses and practices, particularly those of Australian government officers and Christian missionaries. He portrayed himself as someone who played a leading role in modernising his home region and was proud that his personal efforts as a pioneer of modernity were recognised and remembered in his village. I argue that Kikang's desire to record his individual history cannot be detached from this process of modernisation. I see my task as narrating Kikang's life story in a way answering to his notions of modernity.

I owe the term 'life story' to Peacock and Holland,[1] who used it to bring together two different dimensions in the study of biographies. 'Life' represents an approach that seeks via narratives to access historical, cultural and/or psychic facts. The spotlight here is on a reality standing outside the narrative; the narrative as such receives little attention. 'Story', on the other hand, foregrounds the narrative itself and its power to create reality in the act of narrating. Peacock and Holland see life stories as participating in a variety of processes:

> [life stories] do indeed offer a window—though not a perfectly transparent one—on historical periods, cultural practices, and psychic events. And their content and telling no doubt do vary by audience. The communicative purposes, the effort to promote understanding yet sometimes to defend and hide, played out in the production of a life story, do result in narration tuned to, but not totally dominated by, immediate social conditions and communicative intent.[2]

I talk of Kikang's 'life story' with both approaches in mind. In order to illuminate the construction of my account of Kikang's life, I have drawn on the idea of 'mimesis'.

Following Gebauer and Wulf, I conceive 'mimesis' as embracing equally imitation and change, acquisition and articulation. Mimesis thus designates the interplay of internalisation, interpretation and re-enactment. Gebauer and Wulf talk of the subject's capacity to incorporate the outer world into the inner world, thereby creating references and identifications for subsequent use in social performances.[3] Through such mimetic processes of referencing and performing, certainties are created, attachments are generated, and realities are construed. 'Mimesis construes anew already construed worlds.'[4]

My account of Kikang's life is based on his journal entries and oral narratives, themselves the product of diverse mimetic processes. Kikang's representations refer to prior processes of internalisation, interpretation and re-enactment of discourses and practices from the world of the whites, such as allowed him to identify as a pioneer of modernity. His long years away from home working with Europeans changed how he saw his home region; compared with the world of the whites, his home region came to represent one thing: backwardness. Therefore, a leitmotiv in Kikang's self-representations was first the vision, then a concrete commitment, to re-structuring his home region, with a view to implanting the economic, political and religious modernity he had come to know in the capitalist and Christian colonial system. Kikang saw himself as a go-between, adept at organising exchanges between the rural countryside and the world of white modernity—yet also, on a spiritual level, as enabling exchanges between the real world of the Here and Now and the realms of the dead, or the Beyond.[5]

Mobility was crucial for Kikang's mimetic practice. Two forms of mobility need to be distinguished. One is the physical movement of a living person in the Here and Now. Thus the young Kikang left his homeland on the Rai Coast and spent many years in the white colonial world. After returning, he mainly worked for Australian administrative officers, who commissioned him to oversee agricultural projects. His other form of mobility was based on the indigenous belief that a portion of the self, namely a person's spirit-being (*asabeiyang* or *ananuang*), is able to detach itself from the body.[6] When its owner is asleep and dreaming, the spirit-being can have out-of-body experiences. Kikang spoke of dream-journeys that he took to the world of the dead, who, according to his representations, now lived as whites in a Western and largely urban landscape, in material prosperity free from care. In these spaces inhabited by the dead he saw the very modernity that, he believed, still awaited creation in the local world of the living.[7] Through his journeys into these different zones of whiteness, and his interactions with the whites, Kikang acquired cultural experiences, habitual imprints and new forms of power-knowledge, all central to his self-perception and masculine identity, his agency and authority.[8]

When I attempt to fashion from Kikang's notes and oral accounts a life story that tallies with his identifications and initiatives, 'mimesis' describes my practice too. For what else do I explore but a mimetic process when I describe how I tell Kikang's life and change it in the telling? In this chapter, I begin by sketching how our collaboration came about and introduce the two chief sources for Kikang's life story: a) transcripts from tape recordings of our conversations, and b) Kikang's own autobiographical notes. Then I reflect on my decision to tell Kikang's story in chronological order and, finally, discuss my reasons for including in the text excerpts from our conversations.

Methods and Materials

Early in my fieldwork among the Ngaing, several of my interlocutors pointed out John Kikang's achievements. They portrayed him as politically influential and instrumental in introducing both coffee cultivation and Catholic Christianity to the region following World War II. In the national archives in Port Moresby, Papua New Guinea's capital, I came across several reports by Australian administrative officers who depicted a restless, disciplined Kikang, a man with an entrepreneurial spirit, energetically promoting vegetable marketing, coffee cultivation and other economic projects, and outstanding as village headman: 'Kikang is regarded as the most progressive Luluai in the Saidor Sub-District. His village looks a picture, and they have running water … [He] is a tireless worker and a deeply religious man'.[9] His economic initiatives and his loyal cooperation with the local authorities won him standing with the Australian administration. The head of the Department of Native Affairs advised officials in Saidor: 'You should use Kikang as much as possible to spread progressive ideas in the area'.[10]

Upon returning to the village, I told Kikang what I had learnt in the archives; I asked him about this or that historical detail and expressed an interest in his career generally. Then I broached the idea of recording his entire life story. He was communicative—indeed he seemed honoured by my interest—and he agreed to let me tape his reflections on the past. His long years of working together and identifying with white people in Papua New Guinea certainly helps to explain his cooperativeness. He could see in our conversations, perhaps, a renewal of the recognition he had once received for his convictions, ideas, and initiatives.

We agreed on a series of interviews, usually meeting at my house in the evening. Often Kikang would arrive wearing a jacket, long trousers and, on occasion, dark shoes. Our conversations—conducted exclusively in Tok Pisin, the *lingua franca* of Papua New Guinea—were recorded on tape and eventually ran to more than 30 hours. The verbatim transcripts of the interviews form the primary source for my account of Kikang's life story. I see my chief tasks as translating the interviews, selecting salient passages, undertaking any necessary editing (for clarity or to reduce repetition), ordering the material chronologically and breaking it up into chapters. I take my bearings from the structure Kikang himself provided in his remarks and writings. In ordering the interviews, I wanted to keep as closely as possible to Kikang's own narratives. I organised them into a continuous body of text running to 12 chapters. References to historical sources—such as missionary documents or patrol reports by Australian administrative officers—are found in the introduction, but have chiefly been relegated to footnotes in the actual narrative. The timeline of events forms the background against which this life story plays out. As I will discuss in more detail, this chronological ordering, oriented to Western conventions of linearity, accords with Kikang's own express wish.

Kikang's written notes comprise the second narrative format of importance for my construction of his story. When I began interviewing him, I had no idea that for years he had kept a written record of episodes and events that mattered to him. He began bringing photographs, medals, documents and sketches to our sessions. Then one day he came along with two journals he had once kept.

The first of these was an 'Australian Diary' from the year 1958 with various entries for the period between 1960 and 1983. Some entries take the form of registers giving the place, year and number of coffee bushes planted in the region; others are tables listing his personal income and expenditures; others again list the amounts of church collections, as well as donations and membership fees for local associations; there was a clan and family register for his own village setting out dates of birth; reports from board members on local self-administration bodies; also notes that Kikang had made on his political, economic and religious activities; and finally, notes on his personal achievements.

The second journal, written in a school exercise-book, contains entries from the 1980s. Here too are tables listing personal income and expenditures, but most of the space is devoted to writings of a spiritual nature. Kikang writes of events on the local Christian scene, his dreams and visions, his religious insights and initiatives, Jesus and Maria, his encounters with the spirits of the dead, the nature of the Beyond. On the journal's back cover Kikang had inscribed the telling words: 'SANTU BOK 1983' ('Holy Book 1983').

In his 'Holy Book', Kikang set down his thoughts in Tok Pisin, adding the date of entry; and was careful to adopt a business-like, official tone, always referring to himself in the third person. Many entries were rounded off with: 'Kikang wrote this' or 'John has written'. The model for Kikang's entries may have been the notes Australian patrol officers entered in the 'village register'. In his years of service as village headman, Kikang had to keep just such a register;

during my fieldwork, he still had it in his possession, the entries dating from 1956 to 1978. Here is an example of an entry made by an Australian officer:

9/6/61

Tax/Census Patrol. Stayed here for 3 nights. 1 ¼ hours walk from Waibol. Had a meeting with nearby village officials on general progress and economic development. Complaints re pigs spoiling gardens. Owners warned and Luluai told to take action. A good village.

{Signature A.D.O.}

For comparison's sake, here is a brief entry taken from Kikang's 'Holy Book 1983':

March 28/3/88

Bishop Noser came by helicopter and spoke with J. Kikang on what was the best way. And after the two had decided which way was best, he went back.

J. Kikang wrote this.

Interestingly, though Kikang imitates the report-writing style of administrative officers, Kikang's subject is (often) his dreams and visions. Thus the passage above tells of Kikang's encounter with the former Archbishop of Madang, Adolph Alexander Noser, who had died some time beforehand. Noser communicated by dream to Kikang how the souls of the dead were in future to be transported away from the locality. The dream was founded on Kikang's insight that the Catholic Church had modernised transportation for dead souls, having switched from ships to helicopters.

Kikang's two journals are heavy-going in a variety of ways. For a start, they are in a bad state of preservation: many pages are either loose or fragmentary; several have been torn out, and others have probably simply gone missing. Then both journals contain passages that are barely decipherable. Further, Kikang used a Tok Pisin orthography of his own devising, which I had to 'translate' into the standard version of Melanesian Pidgin after Francis Mihalic.[11] Although Kikang dated all his entries, they were rarely arranged in any systematic chronological order. Kikang placed his entries anywhere in the journal as yet unwritten upon. To this mosaic of entries, Kikang added narratives of past events and experiences, these being assigned a year presumably from memory.

It is, therefore, only right to ask how these autobiographical records should be handled. To me, Kikang's writings are valuable historical documents bearing on a specific time of transition. Kikang's primary socialisation was in an oral culture. After leaving his village, he received a rudimentary formal schooling. His journals show how he related to reading and writing. They bear witness to a mimetic practice. Kikang appropriated this 'technology' because he saw he could fashion from it an autobiographical tool. Reading and writing let him actualise in himself his idea of a modern self.

So I have opted for two forms of representation. First, I shall combine a selection of journal entries with Kikang's own oral accounts. I have decided to place the latter at points in the text where journal entry and oral narrative directly bear on each other. Translated entries from the journal have been placed in grey-shaded boxes to set them off from the rest of the text. Thus the reader will be able to see that these entries are not part of the interview transcripts. Journal entries and oral representations thus run on parallel tracks, yet interrelate. This *modus operandi* however requires a number of passages from the journals to be relocated within the chronological framework of Kikang's narratives. Second, so as to compensate for the dislocation of the original journal material, I have decided to give readers access to the two journals in an appendix. There the edited Tok Pisin versions of Kikang's notes may be inspected in the original arrangement—albeit without the tables listing personal income and expenditures and without personal data from the village register about the inhabitants of Sibog.

In my account of Kikang's story, I want his life to be told as far as possible in his own words, therfore my account most resembles books such as *Ongka* by Andrew Strathern[12] or *Elota's Story* by Roger Keesing.[13] If I insert journal entries into the narrative flow, it is not only because I deem this necessary, but also because nothing less will bring out the fragmentary and protean nature of his story.[14]

Chronology

When I first tried to conceptualise a framework to accommodate Kikang's life story, several questions were foremost in my mind: Where should I begin my account? Which of Kikang's episodes should go first? And how would that shape the rest of the story's structure?

I have already pointed out that Kikang wanted his life story to be told chronologically. We agreed that I would re-arrange his testimonies in chronological order. Several entries in the first journal show that, long before our encounter, Kikang had himself attempted to work out an accurate timeline for his life and career:

The Life Story of John Kikang from Papua New Guinea

> STORY BOOK   SIBOG YEAR 1946
> COMMUNICATION FROM MR. J. KIKANG. HE CAME TO THE VILLAGE OF SIBOG. HE BECAME LULUAI IN 1947 AND HE RESIGNED IN 1964 HE LAID DOWN HIS WORK AS LULUAI. AND IN 1970 HE BECAME COUNCILLOR.

'Sibog Year 1946'—this entry exhibits the typical features of a retrospective. Kikang has his life story commence in the post-war era. In 1946 after a long absence he had finally returned to his village of birth. But this note apparently did not satisfy him. Immediately below it, Kikang wrote a new version. There he was at pains to extend the timeline, and dated the beginning of his story from the time of his departure from home.

> STORY OF J. KIKANG WHEN HE LEFT HIS VILLAGE AND IN 1917 WENT TO THE WHITES. HE WORKED WITH THE WHITES AND HE CAME BACK TO SIBOG IN 1946. IN 1947 HE BECAME LULUAI. HE WAS RESPONSIBLE FOR THE VILLAGE AND IN 1964 HE CEASED HIS WORK. IN 1970 HE BECAME COUNCILLOR, COUNCILLOR OF THE LOCAL GOVERNMENT FOR SIBOG IN 1970.
>
> THE PARENTS OF KIKANG SAY HE WAS BORN IN THE YEAR

At this point the entry breaks off. His exact date of birth was something that clearly weighed with Kikang. In some sense, to be a full person required the year of birth. One of the pre-printed headings in Sibog's village register was 'Estimated or known year of birth'. Under this heading, an Australian administrative officer had placed after Kikang's name his (estimated) year of birth: 1917. Yet, in the above entry, Kikang dates his departure for work with the whites to that year. As related to me, this act of leaving home marked the beginning of his life story:

> I was no more than a child when I left my village and set off. In what year that was I can no longer say. Apart from the mission and a few government officers, by the time of my departure not very many whites had ever been to see us. My mother had died and father was now looking after us. A friend of my father's had come up from the coast. Accompanying him was a firm that was hiring workers. They were looking for a couple of young men to work in some plantations. I took

a liking to this man. After all, he was a friend of my father's. I took a good look at him and liked what I saw. Why? He was wearing pants—and the loincloths, you know what I mean? I took a look at them, and then I wanted one for myself. That's why I went away. Father said: 'No way! You're not going.' I said: 'But I want to go!' And so the man took me with him, together with a friend of mine. They paid for us. They gave my father an axe and a knife. That was the price. At the time I was still quite young. I didn't even have a real bark loin-covering. So I went to the coast. That was where the firm was located. Here they gave me a loincloth. I was very glad when I could put it on.

Kikang then narrated how he had arrived with other recruited workers in Madang, the nearest colonial centre. There he met a doctor from England whose job was to examine the new arrivals. Kikang was, the doctor decided, far too young for plantation labour. That was why the Englishman finally took the boy home with him. There Kikang fell in with the indigenous housekeeper, who ran the European-style household, and she became his foster mother.

This episode about the young Kikang leaving his village shows how I take my bearings from Kikang's autobiographical testimonies. His written notes supply me with important indications as to how best to construct Kikang's life story. Hence his life story does not commence with his birth or early childhood. Instead, he chooses to begin it with his departure from home—a phase of transition. In his narrative, he actively brings about this transition against his father's will. In so doing, he positions himself in an interstice, evoking a liminal zone between his home region and the world of the whites. Kikang sees himself as mediating between different worlds—and this image of the mediator will run through his whole life story.

Turning over a few more pages in Kikang's first journal, we arrive at a third entry that further attempts to order his life temporally.[15] Again Kikang chooses to begin with his departure for the colonial settlements of the whites. But then the entry takes new turns. One novelty is that he now numbers (in the left-hand margin) the different phases of his journey through life. Another is that the text is broken into two blocks. In the first, Kikang describes his secular career. The second (and new) block is devoted to Kikang's spiritual experiences and messages.

Rai Coast No 1   MOT AREA SIBOG

No 1 John Kikang left his village in 1917, he went to the white station. And in 1919 he began school at Kavieng. He was the first person from Sibog to go to school. And in 1946 he went back to his village. Sibog was given a Luluai in 1946 and he became Luluai in the YEAR 1947.

No 2 John Kikang became Luluai in 1947. And in 1964 he stopped

No 3 In July 10/7/70 he became councillor.

No 6 On 10/11/77 John Kikang went and was given a message by Christ.

No 1 ON THE DAY OF JUDGEMENT A GREAT FIRE WILL COME DOWN AND ALL PLACES ON EARTH WILL BURN ALONG WITH THE ONES WHO ARE BURDENED WITH GREAT SINS.

No 2 TO KILL PEOPLE and TO STEAL MONEY and GREAT OFFENCES, TO DISOBEY THE WORD OF GOD.

No 3 and he taught a new prayer with a song from Sibog itself he named ATAT.

No 4 And all songs from Sibog itself and also the praying, you shall not only address to the Almighty.

No 5 if you want something, you must let Him know and HOLY MARY too. You want something.

No 6 You must turn to me, so I can send you something. I died on the CROSS.

No 7 Through my blood I have taken all sins on myself. And J. Kikang asked about the Day of Judgement and he

No 8 said, when ALL YOUR TEETH have fallen out, then he will come; take this message DOWN to your people.

No 9 You shall not be afraid of dying. It is a good thing. The body knows many pains. The SOUL knows no pain, everyone is well, without disease and wounds. Then he STUNG each of the eyes of J. Kikang. And he sent him back to EARTH. On SATURDAY IN THE NIGHT. Day 10. Nov. 1977.

Kikang wrote this

Here we see Kikang tightening his story's chronology by means of enumeration. This entry indicates, in my view, that Kikang associated a modern life story with linking together in linear sequence the various stations of his life.

Of special note is that the spiritual part of the entry is given a greater share of space than the secular. This weighting reflects a significant shift in Kikang's own life. After returning home in 1946 he became active above all in the economic and political sector, a role he continued to play up to the 1970s. At the end of the 1970s, however, he began increasingly to identify with the office and functions of a Christian missionary/priest. With his usual application, he took to studying Christian discourses and practices, the End of Days, death and dying, time and space in the Beyond. Kikang's second journal, the 'Holy Book 1983' is not the only evidence for this; in the second half of our interviews he spoke at length on Christian projects as well as on messages and visions. He was now intently anticipating the life that follows death. The closing sequence of the entry above demonstrates this new preoccupation, though the statement that Christ sent Kikang back to earth with a message on death and the Beyond shows how even in this late phase of his life, Kikang continued to present himself as a mediator. Whereas in the early postwar decades he mediated with colonial officers and mission representatives to promote modernisation in his home region, in later years, he increasingly mediated between the worlds of the living and the dead.

Dialogue

In addition to articulating Kikang's written entries with his oral accounts and ordering these chronologically, I have found dialogue indispensable in constructing Kikang's life story. Although I foreground Kikang's self-representations as continuous text, I have inserted selected excerpts from our conversations. These dialogues serve to remind readers that they are dealing with a co-construction—one that has emerged from the interaction of two variously aged men of different cultural backgrounds.[16]

By including passages of dialogue, I can better analyse two core aspects of our cooperation. First, Kikang would often appeal to me explicitly, include me in the flow of his narrative, ask me questions or refer back to previous interviews and statements. To illustrate, let me take Kikang's account of how he came to learn his date of birth. I was most surprised when he raised this matter at our very first interview:

> Kikang: By the way, I know too when my mother gave birth to me. That I can tell you right now. See for yourself. I have written it down [showing me his small notebook]. That's when I was born [pointing to the note 'Mar 3/31/1902']. Wrote it down myself, I did. Just like that.
>
> Wolfgang: *Good. And how did you come across this date?*

Kikang: Well, we're able to dream. You know what I mean, dream?

Wolfgang: *Yes. And so you found that out in a dream?*

Kikang: Yes. I fell asleep. I used to think a lot about my [deceased] mother. And one day she appeared to me [in a dream]. By then I was already a young man. Mother came and said to me: 'The day on which I gave birth to you is this one' [Kikang pointed to the date in his notebook]. So what do you think? Do you think I'm right about this?

Wolfgang: *Well, it's your story. If you look at it like that, it could well be true.*

Kikang: So I immediately got up and wrote it down. Later on I thought: 'That's my day now.' Ever since then I take that day off and rest up a little.

Wolfgang: *Yes, that's what we do too—on a birthday.*

Kikang: At first I wasn't sure if my mother wasn't playing tricks with me. But later, on another occasion, she came to me again in the night. That was during the war.

Kikang then described how he first journeyed to the Beyond in a dream and talked of his experiences during World War II. But the exchange above shows, in my view, just how much having a date of birth to call his own mattered to Kikang. He saw this as a prerequisite for having a modern life story. What he hoped to get from me was more than just recognition of his chosen path, along which he had found his birthday. He was also signalling his equal status with whites generally and with their European notions of personhood. He wanted my confirmation, too, that by possessing his own birthday he qualified as having a modern life story.

My second reason for retaining various dialogues within Kikang's otherwise continuous narrative is because long sequences of it are only there, at least in that form, because of questions I had put. These were due, first, to my interest in local history, prompting me to seek insights into events that had shaped the region. But I also questioned Kikang about entries that I could make no sense of. To illustrate, I reproduce below a page from the second journal. Its entries date from between May and July 1984. The topmost (and the first for May) tells of a fight between Christians and non-Christians in a neighbouring village. The next refers to the Pope's visit to Papua New Guinea in May 1984. Then follows a note on holy men in the same neighbouring village, whom Kikang had seen while he was dreaming. Next, he notes a (dream-)encounter with dead persons from the Chimbu region of Papua New Guinea. The last entry names the places where the souls of the dead may abide; Kikang has also included a small explanatory sketch.

> May 4/84 Message from the catechist at Sisagel. The heathen are fighting, says the Church. The people. The villages of Umboldi, Guyarak, Namga, Amun, Sor, Sibog and Silaling met up. Then there was a fight with the Catholics. And the heathens struck one of the Christians and one remained unharmed, but another was hurt. He later got better though.
>
> May 8/5/84 The Holy Father Pope John Paul is coming to Papua New Guinea.
>
> May 17/5/84 Holy Church message. In Sisagel, there are two groups of holy men, one wearing blue clothing and the other black. These two groups are the holy men in Sisagel.
>
> Jun 13/6/84 J. Kikang saw men from Chimbu, dead men who greeted him.
>
> Jul 2.7.84 John K. saw (1) klinpaia and (2) limbo and (3) pullkatori and (4) heaven. Four places where the souls go to. It is the story of the dead and where their souls abide.
>
> The commandments
> 1 2 3 4 5 6 7 8 9 10
> T N S P K S S G M K
>
> O 4
> O 3
> O 2
> O 1
>
> The four places of God the Father
>
> Church meeting on the 1st of May 84
>
> 10 commandments, taught to the people as the 10 Commandments of Moses.

I asked Kikang about the last of these entries, dated 2 July 1984:

Wolfgang: *You have already spoken a couple of times now about journeying to Paradise or Heaven or Purgatory. Now in these notes of yours you write at one point: 'John K. saw (1) klinpaia and (2) limbo and (3) pullkatori and (4) heaven. Four places where the souls go to. It is the story of the dead and where their souls abide.' And you've made a little sketch as well. And underneath you've written: 'The four places of God the Father.' Can you say a little bit more about what these places are like?'*

Kikang: ... Look at it this way, hell is where we are now—here on our land ... So you have someone here on the land. Then he dies. And he has saddled himself down with guilt. So then he can't just get up and go. First he has to stay here a while. He can't just leave. First he's going to have to stay here on this land. And then the people that's us [the living] we have to pray. Yes, pray! It goes something like this: 'O God our Father, help, help, help.' And you just keep doing that, let's say, for 10 years or even more than that. Good, so the exact number of years is laid down in advance. Now, when he's got the last year behind him, now he'll be able to leave the place. So now he leaves the place and on he goes to the next one. Now if he's not a good person—[that means for him] first of all [a stint in] Klinpaia [i.e. station 1] … That's a bit like Madang. A small town. So [he] stays in Klinpaia for, let's say, 12 to 20 years. And once again it's pray, pray, pray. Well then, so eventually he's done with Klinpaia. He gets the day behind him that was laid down for him. It's time now for him to go on to limbo [i.e. station 2]. So limbo is a good place. It's a good place. It is beautiful. Everything is laid on … So there he stays. Then [what happens is that] he sets off from limbo. From there he now goes on to Pullkatori [i.e. station 3]. This is a perfectly holy place. As for paradise [i.e. station 4], that is the place of the tiny children. We adults never go there. That is for the tiny children—[who are] without sin. They do not know guilt. They were still too little when they died … So I was in contact with the dead people, and I asked them: 'Where are you now?' And they said: 'We are in Klinpaia.' Well, I knew that is just a place like Madang. Nothing special about it … Later—it was in another year—I prayed and then I asked them: 'And where are you now?' I was told: 'I am in Moresby [i.e. Limbo].' So I said to myself: 'Ah, I see, so it's Moresby now you've got to.' Still later I repeated my question—and all the while the praying was going on and on—'When are you going to leave Moresby?' And then I was told: 'I've already left Moresby. Now I'm in Australia.' Then I said: 'So he's finally arrived in the city. Now he's in Australia. That is Pullkatori. That is where Pullkatori is. Very close to heaven. There it's just like being in Australia. The places are like cities.' … Madang is a small town and that's how you have to imagine Klinpaia. Lovely houses. People filled with joy. Now if you leave Madang behind you and go on to Port Moresby, then it's like you're in a big town. Lots of wonderful houses. Good roads. And after that comes Australia. Well you know how it is there, a real city. All of the time you just see machines working. Houses with lots of levels. Well, that's how you've got to imagine this place Pullkatori. All the people living there are happy. They are well-off. No hard work anymore … Those are the messages the dead pass on to me. Well, that's what I ask all of them. All those who have died, I ask them [the same question], and they give me the answer … But if one of them tells me 'I've gone to

Australia', then I don't pray for him anymore. Then I'm through [with praying]. He has already arrived. He's come home ... Well, that's how things stand with us humans after we die.

Kikang's cosmological imaginations of the Beyond depicted a moral trajectory from country to city, blackness to whiteness, sinfulness to redemption. The route to be travelled by the dead was clearly prefigured, leading out of the world of rural villages on the Rai Coast, passing through Papua New Guinea's urban centers, and ending in a land inhabited by white people. Thus the first station on the route was the so-called Klinpaia, a place marked by minor tribulations, which for Kikang was very like the provincial capital of Madang. Limbo, the next station, was something of an improvement, being a major town with many tall buildings; Kikang likened it to Port Moresby—Papua New Guinea's capital and largest city. The third station, which Kikang described as Pullkatori, was a 'holy place' (*ples santu*)—a city located in Australia.[17] The fourth and last place—'Heaven' in this hierarchy of levels—Kikang referred to, finally, as 'Paradise'. To this Garden of Eden, a landscape where all was pure and pristine, only small children, who had died young and so were free from all sin, could have access, according to Kikang. His primary focus, however, was on the sequence of urban landscapes in the Beyond that finally leads into the land of the whites and the heavenly city. This he conceived as a European-style city, at once holy place and epitome of modernity.[18]

Kikang once showed me a revealing photograph from his personal documents. Probably taken by a Catholic missionary at the beginning of the 1950s, it pictures one of the earliest Catholic churches in Kikang's home village. In front stands the man who designed and built it, John Kikang himself. The building, resembling a pagoda, is in a style not usual for this region of Papua New Guinea. But to eyes informed by Kikang's imaginings of the respective abodes of the dead, its stack of four storeys is clearly an architectonic parallel of his four-tiered model of the Beyond.

Final Remarks

A central feature of Kikang's autobiographical writings and oral narratives is the linkage between the two worlds of the living and the dead. Dream-journeys are, therefore, no less significantly implicated in how he constitutes his modern self than are his real-world journeys to, and identifications with, the world of the whites in a colonial and post-colonial Papua New Guinea. Kikang would cite both kinds of mobility when claiming for himself authority and agency as a pioneer of modernity. Travelling provided him with the opportunity to tap into novel power-knowledge from the other world, whether it came from the whites or from the dead. In his writings and narratives, Kikang made the other world of the whites and the dead the central reference-point of his mimetic practice. By taking his bearings from discourses and practices from the other world, he was able to constitute whiteness, power-knowledge and modernity as core components of the local world and the indigenous self.[19] Rural home region and urban centres of modernity, blackness and whiteness, the world of the living and the world of the dead—instead of treating these as mutually exclusive domains, Kikang chose to 'infold' them, by which I mean that he construed each as containing traces of the other. What Kikang's writings and oral narratives make clear is that he constituted his personal identity as a process in which difference and sameness constrain, even as they pervade, each other.

So when we focus on (auto-)biographies in the Pacific region, what value, then, should we ascribe to constructions and experiences of sameness and difference? In terms of the role played by otherness in articulating identity, are idiosyncratic features discernible in Oceania? Might it not be that alterity—in its historically and culturally specific modes of articulation—is a distinctive characteristic of biographies in the Pacific region?

I construe Kikang's representations of his life as products of mimetic processes of transculturation embodied in his person. The account given here of his life is an attempt to comprehend these. His writings and what he told me himself have been my primary sources. Three principles have guided me in constructing Kikang's life story. First, I articulate his written notes with his oral narratives so as to set up reciprocal points of reference, all the while preserving each format's autonomy. In other words, they should be recognisable in their difference, despite being referenced to each other. Second, Kikang's efforts to create for himself a chronologically ordered, individual life story struck me as noteworthy. If I dwell on his initiatives in this direction, it is because they correspond, in my opinion, to his mimetic practice and his notions of modernity. At the same time, Kikang invariably links this chronological order to parallel time-spaces. In Kikang's imaginative world, the borders between spaces and times are rather more porous than is the case in the dominant Western discourse. It is interesting to note how he evades, at least in part, the modern idea of time with its radical separation of past, present and future[20] —as when he receives messages from Christ, or commutes between the worlds of the living and the dead, or reconstructs his date of birth via his dream-journeys. In particular, it was Kikang's explanations of the exchanges between the time-spaces of the living and the dead that persuaded me to incorporate dialogue as a third principle in attempting to construe his life story. His representations concerning these matters were largely prompted by the questions I put to him. It therefore occurred to me that reproducing our dialogues was an excellent way to recall our co-construction of his life story; further, that I could render it comprehensible with the help of selected passages. At the start of this chapter, I stated my conviction that reflection on how we tell Pacific lives and change these in the telling should be seen as reflection on mimetic processes. The literary critic Arne Melberg has pointed out that *'Mimesis* is *never* a homogeneous term, and if its basic movement is towards similarity it is *always* open to the opposite'.[21] Thus mimesis designates a way of articulating similarity and difference.

ENDNOTES

[1] J.L. Peacock and D.C. Holland, 'The narrated self: life stories in process', review article, *Ethos*, 21: 3 (1993), 367-383.

[2] Ibid., 373.

[3] G. Gebauer and Ch. Wulf, *Mimesis: culture – art – society* (Berkeley 1995), 2-4; *Spiel - Ritual – Geste. Mimetisches Handeln in der sozialen Welt* (Hamburg 1998); *Mimetische Weltzugänge. Soziales Handeln – Rituale und Spiele – ästhetische Produktion* (Stuttgart 2003), 102-26.

[4] Gebauer and Wulf, *Mimesis*, 317.

[5] W. Kempf, 'Mobilität und der Traum vom besseren Leben: Routen und Visionen eines Wegbereiters der Modernität in Papua-Neuguinea', in E. Hermann und B. Röttger-Rössler (eds), *Lebenswege im Spannungsfeld lokaler und globaler Prozesse: Person, Selbst und Emotion in der ethnologischen Biografieforschung* (Münster 2003), 43-63.

[6] W. Kempf and E. Hermann, 'Dreamscapes: transcending the local in initiation rites among the Ngaing of Papua New Guinea', in R.I. Lohmann (ed.), *Dream Travelers: sleep experiences and culture in the western Pacific* (New York 2003), 60-85; E. Hermann, *Emotionen und Historizität. Der emotionale Diskurs über die Yali-Bewegung in einer Dorfgemeinschaft der Ngaing, Papua New Guinea* (Berlin 1995), 56-59.

[7] M. Taussig, *Mimesis and Alterity: a particular history of the senses* (London and New York 1993), 131-133.

[8] D. Holland, 'Selves as cultured: as told by an anthropologist who lacks a soul', in R.D. Ashmore and L. Jussim (eds), *Self and Identity: fundamental issues* (Oxford 1997), 171-179; B.M. Knauft, *From Primitive to Postcolonial in Melanesia and Anthropology* (Ann Arbor 1999), 169-180: G.M. White, 'Afterword: lives and histories', in P.J. Stewart and A. Strathern (eds), *Identity Work: constructing Pacific lives* (Pittsburgh 2000), 172-187.

[9] E.V. Smith, Portion Mot C.S.D. Patrol Report No. 8 (A) 60/61. National Archives of Papua New Guinea (Waigani 1960/61).

[10] J.K. McCarthy, Saidor, Department of Native Affairs, Konedobu, Papua, 20th February, 1963, Patrol Report No. 6-62/63, 1. National Archives of Papua New Guinea (Waigani,1963).

[11] F. Mihalic, *The Jacaranda Dictionary and Grammar of Melanesian Pidgin* (Milton 1986 [1971]).

[12] A. Strathern (trans. and ed.), *Ongka: a self-account by a New Guinea big-man* (London 1979).

[13] R.M. Keesing, *Elota's Story: the life and times of a Solomon Islands big man* (Fort Worth 1983 [1978]); J. Fifi'i, *From Pig-Theft to Parliament: my life between two worlds*, trans. and ed. R.M. Keesing (Honiara 1989); A. Strathern and P.J. Stewart, *Collaborations and Conflicts: a leader through time* (Fort Worth 2000); M. Kwa'ioloa, *Living Traditions: a changing life in Solomon Islands as told by Michael Kwa'ioloa to Ben Burt* (Honolulu 1997).

[14] P. Hempenstall, 'Sniffing the person: writing lives in Pacific history', in B.V. Lal and P. Hempenstall (eds), *Pacific Lives, Pacific Places: bursting boundaries in Pacific history* (Canberra 2001), 34-46; M. Goldsmith and D. Munro, *The Accidental Missionary: tales of Elekana* (Christchurch 2002), xiii-xv, 2.

[15] Kikang sometimes writes in lower case and sometimes in upper case, the latter presumably to highlight points of importance. I have reproduced his practice.

[16] V. Crapanzano, 'Life-histories', *American Anthropologist*, 86:4 (1984), 953-960; Peacock and Holland, 'The Narrated Self'.

[17] W. Kempf, 'Cosmologies, cities and cultural constructions of space: Oceanic enlargements of the world', *Pacific Studies*, 22:2 (1999), 107.

[18] A similar conception was documented some time back by the anthropologist Peter Lawrence, who at the end of the 1940s and again in the 1950s did fieldwork in the Madang region with, among others, the Ngaing in the vicinity of the Rai coast. The Heaven to which the dead went, according to Lawrence, was in a part of Sydney or, in another version, it was in the clouds over Sydney. Peter Lawrence, *Road Belong Cargo* (Melbourne 1964), 77-78.

[19] W. Kempf, 'The politics of incorporation: masculinity, spatiality and modernity among the Ngaing of Papua New Guinea', *Oceania*, 73: 1 (2002), 56-77.

[20] M.R. Trouillot, 'The otherwise modern: Caribbean lessons from the savage slot', in B.M. Knauft (ed.), *Critically Modern: alternatives, alterities, anthropologies* (Bloomington and Indianapolis 2002), 220-37.

[21] A. Melberg, *Theories of Mimesis* (Cambridge 1995), 3.

Chapter 5

Surrogacy and the Simulacra of Desire in Heian Japanese Women's Life Writing

Christina Houen

My contribution enquires into how a woman who is born and raised in a patriarchal society where desire is defined by men can become a desiring person in her own right. My argument is based on two propositions. First, that I am a palimpsest, a text that has been erased and re-inscribed by others; I read their inscriptions and try to discern the traces of what is lost. Secondly, that I can rewrite myself through reading texts of other women's lives; in doing so, I make a looking-glass journey into another world, where desire and the self are different, yet strangely familiar. Through the looking glass, I see myself differently and return to rewrite my self.

My working definition of desire is that it is a universal force that produces life in all its different forms. Desire is immanent, productive, impersonal and asocial. Human culture and sexuality are codifications or stratifications of desire.[1] Society seeks to regulate desire, to control its force; part of this regulation has been the attempt to extinguish woman as a desiring subject. Gilles Deleuze and Félix Guattari have criticised the Oedipal family structure, analysed and endorsed by psychoanalysis, as 'one of the primary modes of restricting desire in capitalist societies'.[2] The Oedipus complex has corralled desire within the nuclear family structure, thus individualising it and removing all but residual and commodified traces from the wider social domain, where capitalism regulates relations between groups of people.[3] Jacques Lacan has re-read Sigmund Freud's writings in the light of Ferdinand de Saussure's and Claude Lévi-Strauss's interpretations of semiotics. Lacan sees the subject as defined in terms of lack and loss, through the stages of sexual reproduction, birth, separation from the mother, sexualisation as male or female, and the final and radical alienation from the real with the infant's entry into the symbolic order of language.[4]

Within the male symbolic order, the subject is cut off from the real through language, which mediates all other sources of signifiers.[5] The subject is both opposed to, and constituted by, the other. As an alternative to this oppositional structure for subjectivity and relations, in which desire is a secondary function of language and culture, Deleuze and Guattari propose the connective flow of desire as a primary, free-floating, unconscious and productive force which is immanent to the 'plane of consistency', that is, of 'unformed matter and anonymous forces from which the various strata of expression and content are formed'.[6] Instead of the world of Platonic reality, with its dualism of essence and appearance, idea and image, original and copy, model and simulacrum, Deleuze posits a world where there is no original, only simulacra; no hierarchy of production, only simultaneity and multiplicity.[7] A simulacrum is 'not a degraded copy. It harbours a positive power which denies *the original and the copy, the model and the reproduction*'.[8] Simulation is an effect, in the sense of 'a "costume," or rather a mask, expressing a process of disguising, where, behind each mask, there is yet another ...'[9]

Lacan, Freud and others tell only part of the story about desire and subjectivity, but have made it the whole story, for all cultures and times. I have critiqued their interpretation of the dominant Western discourse of desire and subjectivity elsewhere.[10] In this paper, I will use the ideas of desire and simulation that emerge from the writing of Deleuze and Guattari to interpret some texts written by court women in the mid-Heian period of Japan (late 10th through the 11th centuries AD). I am interested in comparing the writing of court women in a polygamous medieval Asian society with my own story of living as a bourgeois wife, mother and divorcee in a monogamous 20th-century Western society. I find it fascinating that such a different culture, apparently opposite to my own in many respects, could generate writings that speak to me with such power of myself, of my own life. The women whose lives are described in these texts are objects of desire that are dressed to conceal and suppress their individuality and embodied selves, and manipulated to remain hidden from men's eyes except in strictly defined circumstances. Yet, beneath the mask, there is an inner life that can be, variously, passionate, playful, jealous, vengeful, power-seeking, resistant, nostalgic, lamenting, world-weary, desirous of enlightenment. Although the Lacanian construction of desire as the search for the ideal lost object does explain the surrogacy of subjectivity in the Heian world, it does not explain the powerful richness and intensity of life behind the mask, for both men and women, and the remarkable achievement of Heian women's literature, which has stood the test of one thousand years and still speaks vividly to readers today. Such a phenomenon needs a more open-ended, multifaceted and complex interpretation than the binary and totalising view that Lacanian and other poststructuralist and postmodernist theories offer.

As the much-awarded English novelist, A.S. Byatt says: 'It isn't nice not to be writing a book. It isn't nice not to have a more real world than the real world we inhabit'.[11] Speaking of her desire to create more fictional worlds, Byatt claims that the imaginary world created by the author is more real than the world she or he inhabits; by implication, this is also true for the reader who 'inhabits' the imaginary world of the book. The claim can be extended to any literary or artistic work, since all representation involves not only imitation, but invention, in varying degrees. As I read Byatt's statement, fiction is not merely an escape into an imaginary world. There are many reasons why a fictional world can be more satisfying than the world we inhabit, and escapism is only one of them. The permeable borders and points of exchange between fiction and reality are some of the lines of enquiry into the desiring self that this paper will pursue.

Is the mask more real than the inner life it hides? Certainly it does not hide absence, as Jean Baudrillard has told us contemporary culture does.[12] Must we have only two ways of seeing, realistic and disillusioned, or fictional and escapist? Or is there, as Brian Massumi argues, a third way—a way of seeing to which Deleuze and Guattari, in a theory of simulation that emerges from the corpus of their writing, open the door?[13] Like Michel de Certeau, they see mimicry as strategic: '[t]here is a power inherent in the false; the positive power of ruse, the power to gain a strategic advantage by masking one's life force'.[14] Deleuze and Guattari do not, according to Massumi, address the question of

> whether simulation replaces a real that did indeed exist, or if simulation is all there has ever been. Deleuze and Guattari say yes to both. The alternative is a false one because simulation is a process that produces the real, or more precisely, more real (a more-than-real) on the basis of the real.[15]

In a regular world of apparently stable identities or territories, simulation finds points of departure to create new forms that are more real than the real. 'Reality is nothing but a well-tempered harmony of simulation.'[16] There are two modes of simulation, the regular, normal world of surface resemblances, and the world of art, that multiplies potentials. Reproving Baudrillard for whining—'The work of Baudrillard is one long lament'—for his nostalgia for the old reality that was, in fact, made up of simulacra, Massumi offers us Deleuze and Guattari's liberating vision that celebrates the simulacrum as 'a proliferating play of differences and galactic distances' and that opens the possibility of 'becoming realer than real'.[17]

The Heian period in Japan takes its name from the capital, Heian-kyo, now the city of Kyoto. My first acquaintance with women's writing in this period was through *The Tale of Genji*, a gift from my daughter, who was living in Japan with the Japanese man who became her husband. It sat on my shelves unread for some years, while I was doing my Master of Creative Arts degree, but when I picked it up, not expecting to be very interested, I was surprised and delighted by what I found. It became the inspiration for an anthology of contemporary Australian women's writing that I have collected and edited, titled *Hidden*

Desires. In the invitation that I sent out in 2003 to writers' associations and creative writing students, I said:

> Do you have a story to tell? Murasaki Shikibu, a Japanese noblewoman of the eleventh century, escaped from the stifling conditions of a high-born woman's life by writing stories of desire and circulating them amongst her friends and acquaintances. Across the centuries, and across cultures, her tales speak of repressed desire, of the superior power of men, of the wayward nature of passion, and of the beauties of nature, poetry and music. Let us, Murasakis of the twenty-first century in the western world, tell our own tales of desire.

I received about 250 submissions, from which a selection was made; the anthology, co-edited by Jena Woodhouse, was published by Ginninderra Press in 2006. The attraction that I felt then to the remarkable work, *The Tale of Genji*, has become an obsession. I am reading it for the fourth time, and each time I read it, I find more subtle expressions of desire. In this paper, I will draw examples from it, as well as from the poetic diaries of Murasaki Shikibu and other Heian court women. I am aware that the *Tale*, a psychological romance that is recognised as having a strong claim to the status of the world's first novel, is not strictly life writing. However, I am using it as a mirror to my own life and writing; my practice and research focus on the desiring female self as represented in life writing across a spectrum from non-fiction to fiction. There is an element of fiction in all life writing, whether this is declared by the author or not, for the past is accessible only through memory, which is idiosyncratic and selective.

The *Tale of Genji* became widely known to the Western world through Arthur Waley's translation, 1925–1933. I first read this book of two volumes and 54 chapters in the 1976 translation by Edward G. Seidensticker. There has been another translation since his, by Royall Tyler; the latter is the text I will refer to here, as it is recognised as being, in many ways, closer to the spirit of the original text than its predecessors. *The Tale of Genji* is regarded in Japan as a masterpiece, as great as the works of Homer and Shakespeare in the Western world. It has spawned an immense body of scholarly and popular publications in Japan. As Tyler says: 'Scholars build careers on it. It has been turned into movies, plays, dance, modern novels, Kabuki, comic books (*manga*), musical theatre, and opera. A scene from it appears on a current banknote'.[18]

Murasaki Shikibu was born in the mid-seventies of the 10th century, the daughter of a provincial governor, and a member of the Fujiwara family who held power for over a century, from the mid-10th century on. This was a period in Japan of political stability, which allowed culture to flower at a time when, as Ivan Morris says in *The World of the Shining Prince*, much of Western Europe was in one of 'the bleaker periods of cultural history'.[19] It was the period of transition in China from the T'ang to the Sung dynasty. Though Heian culture and political structure derived many forms from China, official embassies to China had ceased in 894, and were not resumed till over four centuries later, and so the Heian was a period of adaptation and cultural emancipation.[20]

Murasaki Shikibu is an interesting example of how women were involved in this emancipation. In her diary, she reflects ruefully on her reputation for learning, which was not an attractive attribute for an aristocratic woman:

> When my brother ... was a young boy learning the Chinese classics, I was in the habit of listening with him and I became unusually proficient at understanding those passages that he found too difficult to grasp and memorize. Father, a most learned man, was always regretting the fact: 'Just my luck!' he would say. 'What a pity she was not born a man!' But then I gradually realized that people were saying 'It's bad enough when a man flaunts his Chinese learning: she will come to no good,' and since then I have avoided writing the simplest character.[21]

She goes on to confess that she gave the Empress secret lessons in reading the collected works of Po Chü-I, a T'ang dynasty poet.[22] Chinese language and culture was the province of the ruling male class in Japan. A learned woman was a contradiction in terms, and women who surreptitiously acquired learning took care to conceal their knowledge. Yet women in the Heian period developed their own form of writing in the vernacular. *The Tale of Genji* is written in Heian Japanese (which is to modern Japanese as the language of Beowulf is to modern English) in *kana* or phonetic script, derived from Chinese characters, as distinct from *kanbun*, the official script of men, government and scholarship. Richard Okada tells us that this mode of writing was gendered feminine and referred to as *onna-de*, 'woman's hand', although men also used it.[23] Okada speculated that this feminine art allowed women 'a degree of freedom and confidence of representation in contrast to the *kanbun* mode'.[24] He goes on to point out that the word *kana* derives from *kari-na*, 'which means 'temporary, provisional or nonregular name', and thus denotes the surrogate nature of this script, and indeed, of writing itself.[25] Women who write in Heian Japan, then, are using a surrogate script to describe and express areas of experience that are themselves surrogate for the real, regular world of Sino-Japanese (male) culture and politics.

It is conjectured that Murasaki wrote *The Tale of Genji* before and during her period of court service, when she served the Empress; the book seems to be unfinished, and there is some scholarly dispute as to whether she is the author of all the chapters, or whether they were written in their present order. We know that the tale existed in something like its present form in 1024, when a young girl, returning to the capital from a distant province, received a complete copy of over 50 bound chapters from her aunt. This same young girl wrote a memoir, known as *The Sarashina Diary*. In it, she describes how obsessed she was with the romance:

> Although I was still ugly and undeveloped [I thought to myself] the time would come when I should be beautiful beyond compare, with long, long hair. I should be like the Lady Yugao [in the romance] loved by the Shining Prince Genji, or like the Lady Ukifuné, the wife of the General of Uji ... Could such a man as the Shining Prince be living in this world? How could General Kaoru ... find such a beauty as Lady Ukifuné to conceal in his secret villa at Uji? Oh! I was like a crazy girl.[26]

The diarist remembers herself as a young girl obsessed by the romance, imagining herself as one of the heroines, loved and pursued by the hero Genji, or by his lesser type, Kaoru. Compare this with the sad picture Murasaki paints of her self in her diary, a disillusioned introvert in the court circle where appearance is everything and gossip is rife; where learning is unwomanly, and even the feminine art of writing in the vernacular is frowned on if it is practised to excess. She describes a scene where the Empress and her handmaids are busy binding the stories (presumably Murasaki's) to send to people, when the Empress's father finds them and scolds his daughter for not resting; yet later he brings her paper, brushes and ink, some of which she passes on to Murasaki. Then, when Murasaki is attending the Empress, he sneaks into the author's room and steals her only fair copy of the *Tale*.[27] His show of disapproval is a front for secret collusion and appropriation of the artist's work, suggesting the envy and disguised admiration felt by a powerful male for the beauty and richness of the woman's writing, which he can only possess in a surrogate and illicit manner. Murasaki follows this vignette, which shows us how influential and yet how vulnerable both her position in court life and her status as a writer were, with a sad passage of reflection:

> As I watched the rather drab scene at home, I felt both depressed and confused. For some years now I had existed from day to day in listless fashion ... doing little more than registering the passage of time. How would it all turn out? The thought of my continuing loneliness was unbearable, and yet I had managed to exchange sympathetic letters with those of like mind—some contacted via fairly tenuous connections—who would discuss my trifling tales and other matters with me; but I was merely amusing myself with fictions, finding solace for my idleness in foolish words. Aware of my own insignificance, I had at least managed for the time being to avoid anything that might have been considered shameful or unbecoming; yet here I was, tasting the bitterness of life to the very full.[28]

Her complaint reflects a bad day, or few days, perhaps, in the life of an author; one any of us who write for an audience beyond our intimate circle can relate to! The loneliness, the introversion, the sensitivity to criticism, the comfort of a few like minds, the anxiety that what one is doing is trivial, insignificant, of little worth in the real world. She expresses the sense that her writing, indeed her very existence—lonely and idle—are surrogate, of inferior worth in comparison with the 'real' world of courtly society. Yet she could not have felt like this all the time, or she would not have managed to write a book that is twice as long as *Don Quixote*, *War and Peace*, or *The Brothers Karamazov*,[29] and well over 1,000 years later, is still being read, enjoyed, and analysed by ordinary people and scholars in Japanese and in translation. Perhaps Murasaki's depression is an effect of her genius; she was pushing the boundaries of identity for a court woman by creating a work of fiction that was read by men and women in aristocratic circles, in a time when, so far, only men had created works of fiction, and other women were writing poetic diaries, but nothing as complex or ambitious as the *Tale*.

'Fictions and foolish words' are all she has to give her life a deeper meaning; the forms and rituals of the court occupy her daily life and give her a place in the real world, but she feels like an outsider at court. She questions the value of her writing: 'I tried reading the Tale again, but it did not seem to be the same as before and I was disappointed'.[30] She loses confidence even in the support of those with whom she has shared mutual interests: 'Those in whose eyes I had wished to be of some consequence undoubtedly thought of me now as no more than a common lady-in-waiting who would treat their letters with scant respect'.[31] In her depressive state of mind, she feels 'as if I had entered a different world'.[32] The world of court, in which she had found a kind of reality, seems empty, and her private life at home is no better. Retirement from the court does not relieve her depression and self-doubt. She misses her constant companions, and receives letters from them, including the Empress, and so she returns.

Murasaki Shikibu is an outsider, an observer of the world she inhabits, one of middle rank who, having lost her husband, has no official status other than through her service to the Empress. She cannot live independently, as a modern woman would have the opportunity to do; she is without a powerful man's favour, and her status as a writer is problematic. So she returns to court life, the pettiness of which continues to annoy her.[33] Later, in a long reflective passage, she reveals more of her situation at court. Even at home, she feels unable to be herself, aware of her servants' prying eyes, and finds that it is worse at court: 'where I have so many things I would like to say but always think the better of it, because there would be no point in explaining to people who would never understand'.[34] 'They' would never understand because of the standards they apply to other's behaviour—standards Murasaki sees as narrow and petty—'So all they see of me is a façade'.[35]

It is that façade that interests me as the frontier or interface between the 'real' world of court and the aristocratic woman's hidden life that is not revealed because if it were, it would be dismissed as being of inferior worth, even inauthentic. The façade allows Murasaki to move and be accepted in the Heian court world. From Murasaki's perspective, it is a frontier between the public fiction that the outside world sees, and the inner reality of her private world. A frontier is an articulation of the difference between the two things or states it divides; though it does not unite them, it allows exchanges to take place. Another way of putting it, perhaps a more culturally correct one, is to use the Japanese terms, *omote* and *ura*. Takeo Doi, in his study of the relationship of the Japanese individual to society, *The Anatomy of Self*, explains the pervasive concept that underlies Japanese culture: the opposite yet complementary ideas of *omote* and *ura*, 'the two sides of everything', which, in classical Japanese, were synonymous with *kao* (face) and *kokoro* (mind, heart).[36] He points out that though the face usually expresses the mind, it can also hide it; so *omote* or face both expresses and conceals *ura* or mind.[37] The relationship is not binary and divisive, but symbiotic and mutually constitutive.[38]

In Heian court life, the construction of appearance and reality is not a mechanistic one where the surface is simply an abstract representation of the qualities that are valorised in that society, hiding emptiness or an inferior level of being. Rather, outer reality is both an outward and visible expression of, and a mask for, inner heart/mind. It is what allows the individual to relate to others while having an inner life that is at least partly hidden. Murasaki's façade is a simulacrum that is seen as authentic by others, but is a strategic device that masks her inner life, which, to her, is more real than her persona and the outer world she inhabits. The outer both discloses and protects the inner. Ambivalence is a way of life. Murasaki moves uneasily between her outward persona, constructed and constrained by her relationship to the powerful figures of the Empress and her Fujiwara relatives, and her inner self, which both performs and resists the life of a court lady, so highly regulated in behaviour and appearance. It is this tension that makes Murasaki fascinating to a modern reader, and allows us to enter and identify with the autobiographical consciousness of a subjugated being; one who manages to escape, in her imaginative life, from the limits imposed on her. The remarkable aspect of Murasaki's diary and fictional writing is that, in recording her sensitive and penetrating awareness of the ambiguity of living as a woman in this society, she achieved so much. The living, aching reality of leading a double life is revealed in her confessions, and in the introspection of the fictional characters she creates. Murasaki's court persona has an extra layer, a mask that self-consciously performs the multi-layered reality she inhabits. This is the mask of the writer, the teller of tales, who traverses between the outer and the inner world, and brings both to life in a form that outlives the author and her society.

De Certeau describes the individual in social life as determined by relations with others and with the surrounding culture; he qualifies this by saying that the individual is neither passive nor docile in his or her culture, but rather, practises everyday life by '*poaching* in countless ways on the property of others'.³⁹ Though he is describing contemporary culture, he sees such practices as an evolution of 'the age-old ruses of fishes and insects that disguise or transform themselves in order to survive'.⁴⁰ Individuals use the products of a dominant economic order in subversive ways that are not intended; for instance, the culture imposed by the Spanish colonisers on the indigenous Indians was used ambiguously. The apparently submissive natives did not reject or alter the rituals, representations and laws of the conquerors, but they used them 'with respect to ends and references foreign to the system they had no choice but to accept'.⁴¹ The colonised people, unable to challenge the power of their conquerors, 'escaped it without leaving it'.⁴² In similar ways, the narratives, both fictional and confessional, of Heian court women show the ambiguity of the female desiring self as *other* within the culture of men, outwardly conforming to rituals, representations and rules, yet inwardly resisting and escaping in subtle ways. One of these ways, their reading and writing of *monogatari* and poetic diaries, became, paradoxically, a flowering of cultural life that has outshone and outlived the works and lives of the powerful men who ruled their lives.

Rather than being artefacts masking an absence of reality, or bearing no relation to any reality whatever, as Baudrillard describes the simulacra of the contemporary world, the texts of Heian Japan dramatise a culture where the images and surfaces of court life conceal and protect, as well as express, a rich inner life that both complies with and resists the dominant codes of behaviour.

Murasaki is an artist who observes and mirrors the society she inhabits in a fictional world that is, to the reader, 'more real' than the historical world of the Heian court, which we can never know except through indirect and fragmented reports. *The Tale of Genji* is a complex and many-layered world of the imagination that we can enter as we turn the pages that number 1,120 in the Penguin edition of Tyler's translation. Though the court women's diaries of the period give fascinating glimpses of this world, they remain glimpses, written from one point of view, discursive and sometimes fragmented.

One such diarist, who lived and wrote a generation before Murasaki, describes the fictional romances that were popular in her time in disparaging terms. This predecessor is known to us only as 'The mother of Michitsuna', and her diary, *Kagero Nikki* (translated by Seidensticker as *The Gossamer Years*) is the record of her unhappy marriage to a Fujiwara who became regent. In the prelude, she describes herself in the third person as:

> one who drifted uncertainly through [these past times], scarcely knowing where she was ... [A]s the days went by in monotonous succession, she had occasion to look at the old romances, and found them masses of the rankest fabrication. Perhaps, she said to herself, even the story of her

own dreary life, set down in a journal, might be of interest; and it might also answer a question: had that life been one befitting a well-born lady? But they must all be recounted, events of long ago, events of but yesterday. She was by no means certain that she could bring them to order.[43]

Of course, the diarist had not read *The Tale of Genji*, and perhaps if she had, she would have revised her opinion as to the value of fiction as a surrogate world. Nevertheless, she is making an interesting comparison here between the artistic and therapeutic value of fiction and that of life writing proper. The claims she stakes for life writing are that it may be interesting, even if it tells a life that has been dreary and uneventful, and that it might question the way in which she was born—indeed constrained—to live her life. The diary starts in 954, at the beginning of Fujiwara Kaneie's courtship of her. What develops is an intense and bitter account of a woman who waits with unsatisfied longing for visits that become less and less frequent.

This dilemma is a common one for Heian women, in a society where women's status is determined by the social rank of their parents, by their relationship to the men who favour them, and, in the case of women in service at court, by their position in relation to the emperor and his consorts. The most desirable position for a woman is to be the official wife of the emperor. Imperial consorts are chosen from daughters of the powerful Fujiwara family, thus insuring that the head of their family will be the father-in-law or grandfather, or sometimes both, of the reigning sovereign.[44] Women are precious wombs, cultivated by their parents to be objects of desire. For a woman to be desired in Heian Japan, she must clothe her body in many layers of voluminous silken robes of blending patterns and colours, have long uncut hair that sweeps the ground, plucked eyebrows and blackened teeth; she must remain cloistered behind screens, curtains and fans, and not be seen uncovered, certainly never seen naked; she must be accomplished in the arts of poetry, poetic conversation, calligraphy, music and preparation of incense. Taste, good birth and artistic sensibility are the primary values by which women and men are judged.[45] It is a polygamous society, which means that even the most favoured women are insecure, since men constantly seek new conquests, and an official wife may be supplanted in her husband's attentions by an 'unofficial' wife, concubine or mistress. There are many degrees of favour, and the only formal way in which a marriage is recognised is for a man to visit a woman for three nights running, sending a poetic letter each morning, and celebrating the union on the third morning with a gift of special rice cakes.

Just as secrecy and concealment are essential strategies for the arousal and expression of desire in the Heian world, so is surrogacy. A surrogate or substitute is sought when the original object of desire is inaccessible. The machinery of desire in Heian Japan is driven by surrogacy. By cloistering their women and rendering them virtually inaccessible, Heian men fuel the desire to penetrate the covers, to unveil the hidden, and if the object is persistently elusive or out of reach, to seek substitutes. In *The Tale of Genji*, desire is imagined through a bewildering range of surrogates, most of them women, whose disguises, substitutions and evasions drive the erotic pursuits of the hero.[46] Lady Murasaki, the central female protagonist in *The Tale of Genji*, is Genji's favourite wife and his 'live-in lover', yet she has lesser status than his principal wife, and is subject to the ambiguity of her status and the errant nature of his passions, just as his other less favoured women are. Murasaki has to suffer the torture of watching Genji, now middle-aged, marry the young Third Princess, not because he wants to, but because his brother, the retired Emperor, pleads with him to take her under his protection (which is, in Heian Japan, usually synonymous with marriage). The Third Princess has higher status than Murasaki, for though the latter is the granddaughter of an emperor, the unceremonious manner of her entry into Genji's life, as a 10-year-old child whom he abducts, marks her status as secondary or unofficial for the rest of her life.[47] She is, in fact, a surrogate for Fujitsubo, her aunt and consort to Genji's father, the Kiritsubo Emperor. Genji had an illicit passion for Fujitsubo, his stepmother, (who was only five years older than him), and fathered a child by her; Murasaki bears a striking resemblance to Fujitsubo, who was herself chosen by the emperor because she resembled the Kiritsubo Lady, Genji's dead mother. So there is a series of substitutions: Fujitsubo substitutes for the Kiritsubo Lady both as favourite consort of the emperor and as mother/mistress to Genji, and Murasaki substitutes for Fujitsubo as Genji's child/lover/secondary wife.

Though Genji has no intention of leaving Murasaki, she is the domestic spouse who has to perfume his robes for his obligatory visit three nights running to the Princess, and urge him to overcome his reluctance to go and do the honourable thing. Genji is caught between his desire for a succession of lovers and his great love and devotion to Murasaki. This tension becomes stronger as he ages, and apart from the Third Princess, who does not meet his expectations, and with whom he is a reluctant lover, he does not follow through with his erotic fantasies as he did when he was younger. On a plot level, the author creates narrative suspense through the dramatisation of Genji's inner conflicts when he courts other women, and of Murasaki's private suffering over his errant fancy. There is tension between the two plot lines, that of the romantic hero pursuing a string of women, some more desirable than others, and that of the shining prince who meets his match in the surrogate wife, whose beauty and grace outshine the attractions of all her rivals. This tension is played out in a minor key, that of the surrogate wife or mistress who wants to be 'the one', who wants to escape from the straitjacket of surrogacy. This theme and variations on it in the *Tale* are echoed in the diaries of other Heian women, such as the mother of

Michitsuna, who recorded that she wanted her lover 30 days and 30 nights a month, not just on the irregular and infrequent occasions that he visited her.[48] The tension of the major theme of the *Tale*—the Genji-Murasaki romance—sustains the narrative for more than half the novel, and is only resolved by Murasaki's death, and that of Genji not long after. It is, for this reader, this tension, and its reflections in the sub-plots of secondary heroes and heroines, which lifts *The Tale of Genji* out of the genre of medieval romance into that of the modern psychological novel, with its chiaroscuro of light and dark, comic and tragic, hope and despair, love and loss.

Though their domestic life continues when Genji takes the Third Princess into his entourage, it is complicated by Genji's obligations to the young wife who is of higher status in the eyes of the world than is Murasaki, and by other wanderings of his fancy. Murasaki believes her only release from the suffering of watching what she sees as the inevitable decline of Genji's affection for her lies in withdrawal from her worldly state into a religious life. Genji, however, refuses to allow her to renounce her sexual being and to cease social intercourse, which is what the religious life demands.[49] For Murasaki and other heroines in the story, 'becoming a nun is an act of self-expression that can only take the form of denial'.[50] She lives on another three years in her secular state, much diminished, and dies 'with the coming of the day' despite Genji's efforts throughout the night to restore her with scripture readings by monks.[51] As Field comments, 'in Murasaki we see that to be a surrogate is to be not only homeless but imprisoned in this world'.[52] The magnificent home that Genji has created for her and bound her to with his love is insecure and becomes a comfortless prison because it houses, in separate wings, not only the Third Princess, but other women who are under his protection. Her worldly state as a surrogate or secondary wife is, by its nature, temporary and subject to loss and rejection. The tragic irony of the *Tale* is that Genji himself suffers deeply because of the fragile and surrogate nature of his bond with Murasaki, and the transient nature of worldly pleasure, and does not survive long after her death, because he has no wish to live:

> Very little in this life has really satisfied me, and despite my high birth I always think how much less fortunate my destiny has been than other people's. The Buddha must have wanted me to know that the world slips away from us and plays us false. I, who long set myself to ignore this truth, have suffered in the twilight of my life so awful and so final a blow that I have at last seen the extent of my failings ...[53]

His death is a hiatus in the text; he dies between chapters. This may be an accident of the fragmented and corrupted state of the text that survived into the 13th century, when two scholars set out to restore it.[54] However, the fact that the reader is denied the tale of Genji's last days has a strangely poetic and haunting effect; his absence casts a shadow over the other characters: 'His light was gone, and none among his many descendants could compare to what he had been', and over the rest of the narrative.[55]

What is the relevance of this story and the poetic diaries of Heian court ladies to my quest for a desiring female self? The third way of seeing finds abundant and fertile play of differences within a rigid social system, such as that represented in the literature of cloistered women like those of the Heian court. The searcher expects to find similar patterns in the literature of other women who have lived and written within patriarchal cultures. And having seen with their eyes, freed from bondage to patriarchal patterns, from the belief that she is determined by them, she will be encouraged, like the replicant in *Blade Runner*, to return to the culture that has created her, and to seek to change the terms of her subjectivity that were her birth legacy, to live a desiring life on her own terms, to unmask the hidden and assume her full difference, and to create a 'more real than real' world of her own through art.

I commented at the beginning of this paper that my journey into the world of Heian women is a looking-glass experience. The differences between their lives and mine are many and obvious. Yet their voices speak to me of emotions that are familiar. They speak of loss, longing, exclusion, separation, loneliness and, above all, of repressed desire for emotional and material security and artistic freedom. If I merely read these texts, I am, as de Certeau says, a nomadic traveller poaching on other's territory, unable to keep for my own what I enjoy.[56] I want a place of my own as a desiring woman writer. My desire as a modern woman is for the freedom to live and love where I choose, to express myself emotionally and artistically.

Born into an Australian rural family, I was brought up in isolation in outback New South Wales by a mother whose values were Victorian bourgeois. My father left the family when I was eight years old, and I spent much of my childhood mourning his loss and trying to support my mother in running the farm. I married young to an older man, and found that security was not enough. My search for love destroyed my marriage and resulted in the loss of my three children, who were taken to America by my ex-husband without my consent. The process of understanding this story of my life began in earnest in 1999 when I enrolled for a Master of Creative Arts degree, and wrote an autobiographical novel and an exegesis on the construction of female desire in the bourgeois family. Since then I have continued to write and study desire, and have reached a point where I feel able to move beyond the syntax of loss and surrogacy.

Part of this freedom comes from visiting a world where women writers have created, in their diaries, poetry and fiction, a world that is more real than the real world they inhabit, to repeat Byatt's memorable phrase. To do this, Heian women developed genres that already existed—the poetic diary and the *monogatari* or prose romance—to a level of complexity and richness unsurpassed before or since. They also developed a script, 'woman's hand', that, though it was a surrogate for the official male script, became the vehicle for a literature that dramatises Heian vernacular culture so powerfully that it has, as Okada says, 'come to be regarded as a great (if not the greatest) flowering of Japanese culture'.[57] It seems, to return to Byatt's phrase again, that we have a circular relationship between fiction and reality, for fiction is a surrogate for a reality that is itself illusory or fictionally constructed, and the fiction becomes more real than the reality within which it is created.

I am grateful to Heian women writers for showing me a world where, though women's embodied selves were concealed and their individuality suppressed, they still managed to have hidden desires and to express them in surrogate and indirect ways. I pass back through the looking glass, a contemporary woman who can desire in her own right and can live and love without surrogacy or subterfuge.

ENDNOTES

[1] Gilles Deleuze and Félix Guattari, *Anti-Oedipus: capitalism and schizophrenia*, trans. R. Hurley, M. Seem, and H.R. Lane (New York 1977).

[2] Ronald Bogue, *Deleuze and Guattari* (London 1989), 88.

[3] Ibid.

[4] Kaja Silverman, *The Subject of Semiotics* (New York 1983), 149-64.

[5] Ibid., 164-5.

[6] Bogue, *Deleuze and Guatari*, 89, 148-9.

[7] Deleuze, *The Logic of Sense*, ed. C.V. Boundas, trans. M. Lester with C. Stivale (London 1990), 226-63.

[8] Ibid., 262.

[9] Ibid., 263.

[10] Anne Christina Houen, 'A deserting wife: the construction of female desire in the bourgeois family', MA, Curtin University of Technology (Perth 2001).

[11] A.S. Byatt, television program, 'Scribbling', ABC TV, Sydney, 10 August 2005.

[12] Jean Baudrillard, 'Simulacra and Simulations' in *Jean Baudrillard: selected writings*, ed. Mark Poster (Stanford 1988).

[13] Brian Massumi, 1987, 'Realer than real: the simulacrum according to Deleuze and Guattari', *Copyright*, viewed 26 May 2005, <http://www.anu.edu.au/HRC/ first_and_last/works.realer.htm>.

[14] Ibid.

[15] Ibid.

[16] Ibid.

[17] Ibid.

[18] Royall Tyler (trans.), *The Tale of Genji*, 2 vols (New York 2001), xii.

[19] Ivan Morris, *The World of the Shining Prince: court life in ancient Japan* (Harmondsworth, UK 1979), 12.

[20] Ibid., 25.

[21] Murasaki Shikibu, *The Diary of Lady Murasaki*, trans. Richard Bowring (London 1996), 57-58.

[22] Ibid., 58.

[23] R.H. Okada, 'Speaking for: surrogates and *The Tale of Genji*' in B. Stevenson and C. Ho (eds), *Crossing the Bridge: comparative essays on medieval European and Heian Japanese women writers* (New York 2000), 11.

24 Ibid., 12.
25 Ibid.
26 A.S. Omori and K. Doi, 'The Sarashina diary', *Diaries of Court Ladies of Old Japan* (New York 1970), 20.
27 Murasaki, *The Diary*, 33.
28 Ibid., 33-34.
29 Morris, *The World*, 275.
30 Murasaki, *The Diary*, 34.
31 Ibid.
32 Ibid.
33 Ibid., 35.
34 Ibid., 56.
35 Ibid.
36 Takeo Doi, *The Anatomy of Self: the individual against society*, trans. M.A. Harbison (New York 1986), 23-24.
37 Ibid., 26.
38 Ibid., 152.
39 Michel de Certeau, *The Practice of Everyday Life*, trans. S. Rendall (Berkeley 1984), xii.
40 Ibid., xi.
41 Ibid., xiii.
42 Ibid.
43 E.G. Seidensticker (trans.), *The Gossamer Years (Kagero Nikki): the diary of a noblewoman of Japan* (Tokyo 1973), 33.
44 Ivan Morris, *The World*, 63.
45 Ibid., 206-07.
46 Professor Royall Tyler, in a conversation on Wednesday, 7 December 2005, indicated that he thought the device of surrogacy in *The Tale of Genji* can be explained in terms of the author's desire to keep her readers entertained. I agree that on the plot level, this is sufficient cause. However, though this accounts for conscious authorial intention, it does not address the unconscious dynamic of surrogacy, which operates on so many levels in the Heian world, not just in *The Tale of Genji*, but in all the literature that I have read from that period.
47 Norma Field, *The Splendor of Longing in The Tale of Genji* (Princeton 1987), 168.
48 Seidensticker, *The Gossamer Years*, 95.
49 Field, *The Splendor*, 189.
50 Ibid., 190.
51 Tyler, *The Tale of Genji*, 760.
52 Field, *The Splendor*, 198.
53 Tyler, *The Tale of Genji*, 768.
54 Ibid., xviii-xix.
55 Ibid., 785.
56 De Certeau, *The Practice*, 174.
57 Okada, 'Speaking for', 23.

Chapter 6

'The Story that Came to Me': Gender, Power and Life History Narratives—Reflections on the Ethics of Ethnography in Fiji

Pauline McKenzie Aucoin

I was well into my fieldwork in Fiji when Vasi, a young Fijian woman, came to visit me. My research into the social construction of gender in Fijian society had been going well. I had travelled to several of Fiji's larger islands, including Koro, Vanua Levu, and Viti Levu, and established a wide network of contacts with men and women in many of their villages. I had conducted interviews with a number of women involved in *Na Soqosoqo Vakamarama,* the National Fijian Women's Organisation, and helped with the organisation of a village women's co-operative store. I had acquired a sound understanding of the routines of daily village life, and attended weddings in several coastal villages and the interior. My trips to the capital, Suva, to conduct archival work had been successful. I was nearing completion of a kinship survey and had identified a preferential marriage rule: when a woman of one generation from Clan A marries into Clan B, then one of her daughters or classificatory daughters in the descending generation from Clan B would then marry, in turn, into her natal Clan A. A marriage rule. Exchange relations. My notebooks were filling up.

Vasi first approached me in a village store where I had occasion to volunteer, and asked shyly if I would teach her to sew. I had offered to teach sewing to women in the local women's organisation, so it wasn't an unusual request. Vasi (a pseudonym) was a young married woman with a small child in tow. Yes, I knew of her; she had married into the patrilocal clan located nearest the store and came from a village in an adjacent district along the coast. Yes, I could place her. I could see her sitting in the doorway of her mother-in-law's kitchen, peeling cassava. She smiled warmly and waved whenever I passed by. I knew who her mother-in-law was—an energetic woman who walked briskly past my house on the way to her gardens in the morning, machete over her shoulder. I could place Vasi socially. Well, yes, I could teach her to sew, I told her, but not this week. I was off to the coast on Friday, the busiest day for the markets. I could buy some cloth for her there. Maybe later next week, we agreed. Impatient I was, still so much research to do. This paper is about this woman's visit; about the story that came to me.

We busied ourselves when Vasi arrived at my house, this time without her children. I threaded the sewing machine I had borrowed from a neighbour; she smoothed the crinkled tissue paper pattern with her hands and spread it out on the floor. I had sent my husband off earlier that morning to the men's house, through the pouring rain. The clan's ceremonial field was deserted and houses around its perimeter were closed up against the rain. Water splashed over my door sill onto the floor and onto our fabric. I shut the door, a normally unacceptable thing to do in a Fijian village. Unsociable, draws suspicions. Passers-by couldn't call in their greetings, glancing in and about as they passed. People performed witchcraft behind closed doors, mixed and drank *yagona*, or kava, alone—directing invocations to their ancestral spirits, *na nitu*, against their enemies. I spread out Vasi's fabric, carefully smoothing the edges. 'I came to talk to you', she said, in a quiet tone. 'Yes', I thought to myself without looking up. 'I know who Vasi is, married in from a nearby village, small child, robust mother-in-law', I recalled. 'I came to talk to you', Vasi repeated, and this time I stopped, something in her voice, mentally noting her clearly spoken English for the first time. I looked over at Vasi. She began to talk.

Rain pounding on the corrugated tin roof of my small house set up a sound barrier, a deafening protective frame within which a story of forced marriage was told. Noise silenced this narrative to all but one. But one who by trade was compelled to tell. And one who, in listening, was able to see—see both the invisible self and the invisible force applied upon this self. To retell a story delivered in silence is to cast a voice outside its protective frame … possibly to invite the visibility of force. This paper explores ethical issues underlying the ethnography of narrative, self, voice, gender and power.

Vasi told me that when she was younger, she had worked in a town on the coast in a restaurant catering to tourists. She had talked to many visitors to Fiji and had learned to speak English quite well. And she had a few years of secondary education. She had had a boyfriend, and they intended to marry. On one occasion she had gone to visit him, and was staying with him overnight at his garden house. And that is when they came to get her. Her uncles, as she described them, using the English kin term to describe their relationship to her. These men were, in genealogical terms, her father's older and younger brothers and his parallel same sex cousins, all same generation members of his patrilineal clan. According to the Fijian kinship system, these men—her father, father's brothers, and classificatory father's brothers—were all classed together and referred to using the same kin term, *momo*, meaning father. Her father's brothers, she explained, were men she had grown up with, close kin who had raised her. They came to the garden house and called out for her. She was to marry her mother's brother's son, or cross cousin: when a woman of one generation from Clan A marries into Clan B, then one of her daughters or classificatory daughters from Clan B would then marry, in turn, into her natal Clan A. A marriage rule. It had been decided by her fathers and ritually confirmed by the presentation of *tabua*, or whale's teeth, which had passed from the groom's family to the bride's kin. *Tabua* are highly prized as traditional Fijian exchange objects: they allow men to do what Micaela di Leonardo has described for women as 'social work'—connect kin groups, make alliances, and confirm political pledges.[1] They are coveted, and someone who receives a whale's tooth will not readily give it back, I have been told.

Vasi had not wanted this marriage. She had not thought they would really force her, she explained. She was going to marry her boyfriend. From outside, they called out to her. 'We were afraid', she said. 'What were you afraid of?' I asked. 'We were afraid of the men outside', she said. After some time, her boyfriend left—she used the word *tuba* to describe his actions, meaning to flee or run away, to escape. 'They stayed outside the house a long time', she explained. 'I was alone, and I was very afraid. I was afraid of them. It became dark and I was alone in the house. They yelled out; they called out to me. They waited. Finally, I left the house. I was afraid. I went with them.' There was a pause. 'Why?' she asked plaintively in a soft voice, tears falling. 'Why did my uncles do this to me?' I heard in her voice fear, and I saw on her face sadness. This is the story that came to me.

Did anyone know she had come to talk with me? She had asked if I would teach her to sew. No suspicions. We were sewing. We cut and pieced as we talked. The sound of the rains enclosed Vasi's narrative in secrecy. We were only sewing.

Her story was one through which Vasi related her traumatic experiences as a narrative and revealed to me as only she could her understanding of self and her social position, her narrative serving as what Riessman terms a 'text of identity'.[2] And yet, as Vasi had asked for a sewing lesson, it appeared to me that she had set up a ruse. This spoke to me, the academic, of agency. This was not so much a story to be told as a story to be heard. The story of a life, a sequence of events, to be heard by someone who was, in this village, understood to be inquiring into and interested in learning about the lives of women. This struck me, even at the time, as ironic, for I was the ethnographer after all; the one who actively sought out women to interview and work with. Yet this story had been brought to me. And this woman, who prior to her visit had represented to me only one of many possible informants, this woman had interjected her voice in my ethnographic enterprise; hers was an experience she wanted included. There was a certain strategy in her telling. By bringing her story to me, her tale would help to construct what it was that I was to understand as her culture and what it was I knew about the lives of women in Fiji. I hadn't anticipated this collaboration.

Vasi's story had moved me. Her narrative conferred upon the events of her life and the male kin involved in the forcing of this marriage a meaning: conveying unequivocally that relationship of power within which she was caught. Her story revealed the trust she had had for those close kin whom she assumed would provide for her as a woman as they had when she was a child. This was a meaning she asserted; it was critical to my understanding of who she was, how she was socially and politically situated as a woman and emotionally constituted as an individual. Through this narrative, I had been drawn into her social world and her point of view,[3] sharing through the course of her narrative in the lived experience of her fear, betrayal, despair, and sadness. Vasi related what Riessman has described as a truly 'moral drama',[4] or in this case a countering drama, one in which she set her male kin and their expectations for her obedience—her acquiescence and emotional denial—as the immoral cast. This re-orientation of value was immediately apparent, but her motives were not so clear. What did she hope to accomplish in bringing me this story? 'Why had she come?' I wondered. How was I to understand this visit and her goals? Why did she want *me* to know about her life? How did she understand my project? Why did she trust me? What was her intent: did she offer this as a representation of self, a voicing of the life she has been forced to live? Or as a representation of collectivity: as a single example of the multifarious exertions of power that women are subjected to, through which men control and dominate their lives? What motive underlay her narrative strategy? Was it revenge? Yet her voice relayed only sadness and resignation, and spoke of anger defused. Was it therapeutic? To lift and throw off the weight of silence? Was it to find solace? To seek out a community of comfort, even if only a community of one?

And if, as it certainly appeared to me, we had to speak in private, that she still lived her life in fear, what was I to do with this story and what would the consequences be for her if I wrote about her life—if I *represented* her as it seemed she intended me to do? To represent her would be to expose her. Or should I even be bothered by the consequences? Who in the village would ever know that I had written up her story? And should I even care? Publish or perish.

The story Vasi offered had moved me and it also disturbed me intellectually for I had already inquired about this. The women themselves had told me that they were free to marry whomsoever they pleased. Young women had told me this. Perhaps they spoke only of themselves and I had assumed they spoke for others, though I had asked the question directly. And my kinship charts had certainly not spoken to me of forced marriage, of fathers' betrayals, of fear. Although, on reflection, I did wonder at the perfect alignment of all those circles—what had it taken to put each in its place, to put each woman in her place? Rather than providing a story which simply set out 'one's life within its social context', as narrative has been described as doing,[5] this story actively challenged that context and engaged me in its reexamination, interfacing not only 'self and society',[6] but also self and social analysis.[7]

Vasi's narrative has expanded substantially my understanding of what I had taken to be, in the anthropological sense, the nature of marriage and the lives of women. I would no longer read with detachment about sister exchange, preferential marriage, generational marriage exchange, marriage rules or compensatory exchange. Not only did this story 'reconstitute' the person I thought I knew as Vasi; the meaning of kinship had also been remade for me by its telling. I could now envision the people who put into practice these inter-generational alliances: I could hear them calling out in the night. This narrative became for me not only a story about self, but also a story about power, about how it is that those in power insert young people into the relationally appropriate places of their kinship systems.

In the course of further research, I learned of two other cases of forced, 'preferential' marriage for young women, though I was unable to record, in these individual cases, how these marriages were realised or what pressures were applied; which is to say, the social contexts within which force, or the immediate threat of force, had become visible. And I heard the story of Sura (a pseudonym), a woman from an inland village who, some years ago, had married a man from another island. She had been killed by her husband in a domestic dispute. To resolve her murder, one of the murderer's sisters had been required to marry into the dead woman's clan in return, as compensation, and her young daughter had been returned to her now deceased mother's clan. There appeared to be a cultural patterning in all this: women exchanged, lives and stories within a matrix of power. The story of Sura's death was related to me by her then 11-year-old daughter.

Vasi's story stands as one of a number of narratives I recorded which have contributed to the ongoing record of truth that I, as an ethnographer, have been engaged in collecting in my pursuit of an understanding of the culture of Fiji, recognising that any recorded truth emerges from the compilation of numerous truth claims. Other forms of narrative I have collected reflect a range of genres: life stories, mythology, and performance. In their various forms, they constitute attempts to make sense of experience—making sense or creating meaning being a transformative process by which meaning is given to, that is asserted and attached to, experience. Life stories such as Vasi's may seemingly be individually cast, reflecting more on a narrator's personal and unique circumstances than on cultural practice. But given the broader range of narrative I met with in this Fijian context, I came to comprehend that collectively they present a discourse, a running collective commentary on gender and power which speaks to the nature of gender ideologies in this hierarchical context.[8] Narratives such as Vasi's life story, along with women's mythology and dance performances, which I have analysed in other contexts, constitute forms of stories that are counter-posed in relation to dominant culture, a variety of what have come to be called countering narratives. In dominant representations of gender in this culture, authoritative images of male power and superiority are presented, a spatial order that symbolically—and in real terms physically—elevates men above women is instituted, and a dominant system of ritual knowledge that excludes women through the institution of the men's house is practised. Women's representations stand as narratives that people 'tell and live which offer resistance, either implicitly or explicitly, to dominant cultural narratives by going against the grain'[9] and resisting prevailing hegemonic understandings. In this sense, narrative represents a site of discourse for both the circulation and contestation of ideas regarding the nature of society, about lives lived, about subjectivity as the experience of positioning within a stratified society, and about power practised. I consider the various narratives of Fijian women I have collected to be forms of counter discourse: some of these simply describe the conditions under which women's obedience is extracted, while others record the subjective experience, the feelings and tensions engaged in the construction of self in the context of political domination. Some of these form part of what has come to be known in anthropology as a subordinate discourse,[10] while others of these constitute forms of what I have called 'insubordinate discourse'—a term which captures the subversive quality that certain women's narratives and performances carry. All express disaffect; all find their place along what Ari Sitas has called the 'continuum' of resistance.[11]

As ethnographers, we must ask where and how dominant meanings are formulated within culture. We must show how they are inscribed, validated and upheld, and alternatively, how they are contested and debated. This brings us to consider the role women play in cultural production, either as consumers of certain versions of reality or as 'generators of signs',[12] asking in precisely what arenas do women contest, contradict or resist dominant ideologies of gender? And we must also ask how and why certain versions are silenced.

How can we understand the significance of a contemporary life story such as Vasi's to history, and Pacific history in particular? How do they intersect? Vasi's story seems removed from the course of historical events we know from our reading of Fiji's colonial past. Or does it? What of the colonial regulations forbidding Fijian women from leaving their villages to visit coastal towns that were being established at the turn of the century? What of petitions that were made by Fijian men to have their kinswomen brought back to the village? Could this seemingly isolated narrative of Vasi's forced marriage relate to a wider and ongoing discourse on the social control of women? On the politics of gender, space and movement?

As an ethnologist, where do I go with a story such as this, recognising as I do the continued vulnerability of this woman and the circumstances that allowed only enough privacy to let her tell her story to me. Do I deny this risk to my informant—I have collected records that tell of women having been killed—how do I gauge this risk, the risk posed to her by her exposure, her potential identification? Villagers would certainly know who she is; they would know who told me this story. The relating of this narrative is an act which at once recognises the structures of power that surrounded us as Vasi told her story in the privacy of my house, while also revealing the fear she had for her kin, and potential consequences of her telling. Yet this story also spoke to me of her initiative in engaging me as an audience. I have come to appreciate that my ethnographic understanding of how lives are lived within this culture would have been incomplete without this woman's tale, I humbly admit, no matter how thorough my kinship charts and surveys might have been. Elinor Ochs and Lisa Capps,[13] in their review article 'Narrating the self', have argued that a narrative, in its telling of the experiences of one life lived, provides 'an opportunity' [for the narrator] to insert and 'impose order on [what might otherwise appear to be] disconnected events'. In the course of hearing and trying to understand the significance of Vasi's story, it has become evident to me that it was her narrative that *inserted reality* into the events surrounding this case of preferential marriage, into what came to be my understanding of this society's 'imposed' kinship order.

In trying to understand Vasi's story as a narrative of self, constituted within relations of power, I have reflected on this woman's initiative in bringing me her story, as well as my responsibility in both recording it and relating it, which, as a feminist anthropologist, is problematic any way I look at it. Would it be unethical, or ethical, to leave her story in her village? This is a question which must be posed as we collect our narratives: what are the consequences of telling Pacific lives?

ENDNOTES

[1] Micaela di Leonardo, 'The female world of cards and holidays: women, families, and the work of kinship', *Signs*, 12: 3 (1987), 440-453.

[2] Catherine Kohler Riessman, 'Strategic uses of narrative in the presentation of self and illness: a research note', *Social Science and Medicine*, 30:11 (1990), 1195-200.

[3] Ibid.

[4] Ibid., 1197.

[5] Deborah Reed-Danahay, 'Introduction', *Auto/Ethnography: rewriting the self and the social*, ed. idem (Oxford and New York 1997), 10.

[6] Elinor Ochs and Lisa Capps, 'Narrating the self', *Annual Review of Anthropology*, 25 (1996), 19-43.

[7] On the topic of gender, self and society, see Martine Brownley and Allison B. Kimmich (eds), *Women and Autobiography* (Wilmington 2000); Peter L. Callero, 'The sociology of the self', *Annual Review of Sociology*, 29 (2003), 115-33.

[8] Glynis George, 'Contested meanings and controversial memories: narratives of sexual abuse in Western Newfoundland', in Michael Lambek and Paul Antze (eds) *Tense Past: cultural essays in trauma and memory* (Toronto 1998), 45-64. See also Sally Cole, *Ruth Landes: a life in anthropology* (Lincoln 2003).

[9] Molly Andrews, 'Introduction: counter-narratives and the power to oppose', special issue, 'Culture and Counter-Narratives', *Narrative Inquiry*, 12:1 (August 2002), 1-6. See also Liz Stanley, 'On auto/biography in sociology', *Sociology*, 27:1 (1993), 41-52; and Julia Swindells, 'Hanging up on Mum or questions of everyday life in the writing of history', *Gender and History*, 2 (1990), 68-78.

[10] Brinkley Messick, 'Subordinate discourse: women, weaving and gender relations in North Africa', *American Ethnologist*, 14:2 (1987), 210-25; Janice Boddy, *Wombs and Alien Spirits: women, men and the Zar Cult in Northern Sudan* (Madison 1989), 158.

[11] Ari Sitas, 'From resistance to co-operative alterity: South Africa's labour movement and the negotiated revolution', plenary paper presented at the International Sociological Association's (ISA) Research Council Conference, Ottawa, 29 May 2004.

[12] Claude Levi-Strauss, *The Elementary Structures of Kinship* (Boston 1969), 496.

[13] Ochs and Capps, 'Narrating the self', 19.

Chapter 7

A Tartan Clan in Fiji: Narrating the Coloniser 'Within' the Colonised

Lucy de Bruce

People continue to think of contemporary Fiji as belonging to natives who look and behave in anticipated ways. The popular notion of a Fijian thus becomes someone who is a considerably different creature to the rest of the people living in Fiji. In most peoples' minds, a Fijian is someone who is friendly and lives in a village; whose menfolk play superb rugby and participate in kava ceremonies and tribal dances; whose womenfolk sing, dance and weave mats and baskets in their villages. Above all, a Fijian is someone who speaks the Fijian language and is a smiling, God-fearing Christian with big hair and dark skin.

As a light-skinned, English-speaking Fijian who does not fit this profile, it is my view that people inside and outside Fiji find it difficult to accept anyone claiming to be a Fijian who falls outside this strict ethno-biological profile. In Fiji, anyone who lives and looks like me is relegated to the realm of otherness and prompts those familiar questions, 'what are you?' and 'to which side do you belong?' I am certain that changing this mindset is a tall order in a land where colonial racial thinking is an inherited part of life that few have bothered to interrogate or challenge.

The antithesis to the 'Fijian realm' is the 'Indian realm', those folk whose ancestors arrived on our shores more than a century ago to work the sugarcane plantations as indentured labourers, and whose descendants must tolerate a reputation as land/money-hungry dissidents locked in perpetual turmoil with their ennobled landowning hosts, the indigenous Fijians. The landscape is thus dominated by two contrasting cultures that reinforce the image of Fiji as a xenophobic backwater, lacking in human diversity and cultural complexity. Persons born of this landscape who do not belong to the Fijian or Indian realms have a tough time getting a hearing and are doomed to irrelevance and invisibility.

A Culture of Forgetting

Where do I begin to tell the story of an invisible people who simultaneously claim a European and Fijian heritage that gives an alternative history of Fiji? I shall begin by acknowledging invisibility and describing what it means to come from an invisible people. By invisible I do not mean that we are a ghostlike people with transparent skins. No. We are invisible by virtue of how others react to us. They do not accept our reality and act as though they do not see us—because the system we live in has been created this way.

Take for example Fijian *kailoma*—known also as 'Part-Europeans' or still in some circles 'half-castes', many who live in villages and towns across Fiji and whose presence and histories go mostly unnoticed owing to their ambiguous looks, language(s) and lifestyles that defy racial pigeonholing. This paper seeks to overcome a 'culture of forgetting' that many Fijian *kailoma* have learned to internalise in their own homeland.

In the colonial environment, the prevailing thinking was that Fijian mixed-bloods were a fragmented identity and therefore were neither authentic Fijians nor Europeans. Yet as the fine grain in my story reveals, Fijian mixed-bloods by virtue of their racially-mixed heritage have routinely crossed all barriers of their mixed heritage that were designed to determine race, culture and place of belonging. Nevertheless, in such an ecology one of the dilemmas for most Fijian mixed-bloods was that human diversity could not be comprehended by colonial administrators schooled in black/white thinking; so when they were confronted with the human evidence of the fusion of the European 'within' the native child, that truth was not easily grasped nor accepted.

Background to a Colonial 'Problem'

The colonial obsession with herding citizens into separate, tidy, racial boxes meant that the separation and management of Fijian mixed-bloods in relation to their natural families was often a haphazard operation and a bizarre, sometimes harsh experience. It is something that is seldom discussed among those who were 'ethnically' at the receiving end of such treatment.

The management of 'ambiguous' Fijians was conducted in ways that involved the systematic carving-up of Fijian society into elites, commoners, half-castes or Part-Europeans. For example under certain colonial conditions a half-caste child born of a Fijian chiefly mother and a European or half-caste father could be deemed a Fijian chiefly 'elite' with land rights and colonial privileges; another child from the same family could be deemed a commoner with no land rights and a village-bound existence; while yet another could be judged to be a Part-European and allowed to live in town with rights to private property and a Western way of life. At certain points in a mixed-blood's life it was not uncommon to receive different treatment (sometimes different race classification) to another member of the same family since physical appearance played a major role in determining racial belonging, with those most resembling Europeans having the greater privileges.

Some *kailoma* who were reared as Fijian children in their maternal villages later 'progressed' to a half-caste status after being encouraged away from their families by missionaries and given a missionary or Western education. Some 'progressed' even further to the status of quasi-whites (Part-European) who could be employed in the government or private sector and allowed to live in the towns. A select few became 'sponsored' whites and were sent abroad for schooling, sometimes returning home as strangers to a villager mother and an extended clan of full-descent and mixed-descent clan members. The legacy of such social engineering has had far-reaching effects among Fijians divided in this way to determine a child's life chances. The major difference was the way that the system determined place of residence (village or town); participation in the colonial economy; and significantly, eligibility for inclusion in the native land register or V*ola ni Kawa Bula* (VKB)[1] and recognition as a 'real' Fijian.

Much of this activity was conducted in a spirit of goodwill that separated family members along the lines of skin colour, geography, rank, education and cultural competence. This mechanism followed imperial England's patriarchal system that ignored the legitimate status of a Fijian woman in her tribe; her right to inherit and bequeath land; and her right to raise her children as full members of her clan. Thus, at every point in our history the lives of *kailoma* Fijian mixed-bloods were scrutinised and carefully managed in the ordering of colonial society.

European Assimilation

Spearheading the mustering of 'stray' half-castes into central observable locations were the state-approved Christian missions which in the early 19th century established themselves doing God's work among the Fijian chiefs and their people. Of greatest influence were the Wesleyans and Roman Catholics Marist missionaries who, as agents of the state, were given a virtual free rein to evangelise. Missionaries were charged with the elevation and management of half-caste children from plantations and squatter settlements in rural pockets into centralised day and boarding schools.

Europeans widely regarded mixed-bloods as debased, contaminated or immoral. To many whites, half-castes were the products of a regrettable union and the confronting evidence of white men's weakness towards native women. Half-caste children were thus inculcated with Christian values at an early age and taught English in a highly disciplined environment at church-run native mission boarding schools great distances from a child's home. The intensification of this mission increased from 1936 to 1970 following a government report that recommended closer supervision and training of half-castes at the earliest possible age and preferably away from their native mothers and natural families.[2] This drive coincided with colonial alarm at the steady increase of the half-caste population that threatened to swamp European interests in their own colony. A schizophrenic relationship thus developed where half-castes came under the direct control of whites in an authoritarian atmosphere that variously tolerated, ostracised and assimilated half-castes into European schools. Controlled habitation, family monitoring and regular home visits were part of this state/religious campaign to instill white ways in half-castes and assimilate them towards accepting European domination.

Race Mixing and the Blended Child in a Colonial State

In much of Fiji's colonial literature, the perilous lives of the early European settlers and their mixed-blooded/*kailoma* offspring have sadly escaped the history books in the recording of frontier history. Typically, the main players in Fijian history have been European administrators, Fijian elites and Fiji-Indian leaders, a prevalent theme to this day.

As many *kailoma* will attest, our lives have been remarkably altered by the fickle hand of time. We know that both culture and the negotiation of a cultural identity are ongoing processes that can dramatically alter a life at different times and places. We know that as we move back and forth among other cultures and worldviews, we adjust our values and behaviours accordingly. We know that deep inside we are the same person of yesteryear, yet we have been permanently affected by this fluctuation of an identity that makes us quite different people from before. For instance, we see this change occurring in our European forebears who arrived in Fiji in the early 19th century, who took Fijian wives, who gave birth to a different-looking individual from themselves and their husbands, and this child being the inheritor of cultural and linguistic influences from both parents.

Because the fabric of our present is stitched deeply into our past, it is critical to view history as a two-way channel that can explain things about the way people lived and the rules that governed their lives. So it is worth reflecting on the neglected history of those who hail from Fiji's *kailoma* community in order to assess the powerful legacy bequeathed by our Fijian and European forebears during early white settlement and into the colonial era.

Narrating the Coloniser 'Within' the Colonised

At this point, I wish to provide a brief outline of my family history as a way of explaining human interaction and diversity in the Fijian landscape. In this short story of my father, William Henry de Bruce and his European and Fijian forebears, I seek to illustrate how the mechanism of racial thinking operated in a colonial state and how certain individuals challenged, and continue to challenge, the very rules upon which the concept of 'race' depended. This 'sociography' depicts the quality of life of a Fijian *kailoma*/mixed-blood born in 1917 during British colonialism.

Little is known about this period between 1881 and 1911 when miscegenation between whites and non-whites was at its peak, and subsequently when this population began to interbreed and steadily outnumber Europeans between 1921-1946 to the present day. The story of this racially-mixed Part-European/Fijian born in 1917 tells us about 'life on the border' for someone who recounts what it was *like* to live ambiguously under a system that could not account for a person's racial hybridity nor their routine interactions with members of their natural families.

It shows how the mechanism of race functioned across colonial Fiji and how the lives of half-castes were closely monitored and manipulated in the ordering of Fiji society. The outstanding feature of this narrative is the creativity and fluidity of racially mixed/*kailoma* Fijians as border-crossers between all aspects of their racially mixed heritage and between other ethnic groups. This chapter shows the great difficulty in creating single races and maintaining them within tightly controlled ethnic borders when the very large presence of racially mixed people like William Henry de Bruce continue to defy racial thinking in Fiji. This begs an important constitutional question: are such persons at risk of having 'no race' in a land obsessed with 'race'?

The following narrative highlights the quality of relationships between two distinct cultures, Fijians and Europeans who, for whatever reason (food, sex, guns, concubines) found mutual benefit and intimacy at a certain place and time. Inspirationally, it shows that the life of an ordinary Fijian citizen can be as compelling as that of a prominent citizen. I especially seek to fill a wide gap in Fijian-European interactions and to provide a fresh look at the peopling of the South Pacific.

An American Tartan Clan in Fiji

The original William Henry Bruce, my great grandfather, came to Fiji from Portland, Maine. My father said he had fought in the American Civil War as a private and was in the 16th Maine Infantry Volunteer Regiment, Company B, mustered in 1862-1865. His regiment fought in many of the major Civil War battles including Antietam, Fredericksburg, Gettysburg and Petersburg. No one knows exactly how Bruce came to Fiji, but his occupation as a shipwright was a needed skill in 19th century Fiji. Bruce settled in Levuka, the old capital of Fiji, and is listed in the Fiji Planters and Commercial Directory of 1879. Another person listed in the same directory was a Miss Sarah Watts. On 18 May, 1881 at the Church of England in Levuka, Bruce married Sarah, an Australian spinster 15 years his junior, who came from the Melbourne suburb of Collingwood. Some say she was a schoolteacher, others say she arrived with the 'Fiji rush' of Australian women looking for husbands in the 1870s. Like many of Fiji's first white settlers, Bruce was a shipbuilder, island trader, and landowner who served as the American Commercial Agent in Fiji during the 1880s.

Still, he became dispossessed of 2,000 acres of his land in 1892. Bruce's land-claim battle against the British in 1892 along with several other American citizens in Fiji proved fruitless. Nonetheless, he retained possession of 705 acres of freehold land. Following his wife's death in 1892, Bruce had transferred his estate to the Roman Catholic Marist Missionary Fathers of Levuka, Fiji, whom he appointed as trustees and potential guardians of his estate and his three children upon his death. In 1909, the Mission transferred the land to Bruce's two eldest children when his son Donald attained the age of 21. Bruce had four children in Fiji but not all of them survived him. They were Essie Atalanta Callerhoe, Cora-Mona, Douglas William Washington and Donald William Henry Bruce (my grandfather). Bruce was considered independent, hardworking, respectable and comparatively prosperous considering he belonged to the unstable planter class of his day.

Despite being an American, W.H. Bruce and my Fiji-born grandfather still identified with Scotland, the land of their forefathers. Following in his American father's footsteps, my Fiji-born Grandpa Donald Henry Bruce took up a similar line of work in planting and boat-building, receiving his early education in Fiji at Levuka Public School, then at Marist Brothers Fiji, and later at St Patrick's College in Wellington, New Zealand. Upon the death of their pioneering American father in 1897, Grandfather Bruce and his older sister Essie jointly inherited 705 acres of sugar cane plantations in the Ba province of northwestern Viti Levu, that were held in trust for them by the Marist Fathers of Fiji which they received in 1909. The untimely death of their Australian-born mother Sarah, in 1892, at the relatively young age of 40, had brought the Bruce children and their American father under the pastoral care of the Marist Catholic Missionary fathers of Levuka, Fiji, who saw to their spiritual and educational needs.

It is thought that the children were given to the Mission when their widowed American father could not cope following his Australian wife's death (a pattern that was to follow in his son's generation). Bruce nevertheless remained in touch with his children through the mission and in close friendship and counsel with the Marist fathers. It is clear from family correspondence that his children benefited from their American father's wisdom and foresight. Bruce's second child, Donald, my Grandpa, had an older brother, Douglas, who died as a baby and in whose grave Grandpa's Australian mother was also buried.

Family correspondence reveals that Grandfather was most unhappy during his schooling years at St. Patrick's College in Wellington, New Zealand. He seemed like an oddball to the New Zealand Marists and he did not get along with the school's superintendent, Father 'K'. Letters between him and the Marist Fathers in Fiji reveal that Grandpa was anxious to return to Fiji to work the land he had inherited. New Zealand during 1905-1907 was experiencing a downturn in the economy with an oversupply of immigrants from England and Europe. New Zealand was a dismal place to live and find work. Consequently, Grandpa followed his dream back to Fiji in the footsteps of his American planter/shipwright father. In Fiji, Grandpa was a loner who shunned the company of other white men, preferring to live alone among the natives, being his own man, and always with his guns close at hand.

My father remembers my gun-toting Grandpa roaming the beach spraying the air with bullets to remind the natives he was armed. (More than a few discovered he was serious as they abandoned Grandpa's boats and fled for their life.) Paybacks were frequent, but Grandpa didn't seem to care since he was brought up among Fijians and knew their ways well. In some ways he was a Fijian in a white man's skin, coming and going between both races. He seemed happy with his lot living at the edge of both societies, operating as a shipwright, copra planter and trader. Unlike his Fijian neighbours, Grandpa was a reserved and fiercely independent man, some say mean and unfriendly. Despite this he was tolerated by the Fijians and to some extent befriended by a nearby village chief, whose daughter he later married—my grandmother, Marica Kenona.

Like many white men of his day, Grandpa Bruce spoke Fijian as well as a native and kept company with native women. He had grown up among them and felt comfortable in their presence. The piano-playing white girls of his old Levuka Public School were not for him. After a previous de-facto marriage and three children to a Fijian woman from another island who had died young, Grandpa took up with Adi Marica Kenona, my chiefly grandmother, from the Navitabua tribe on the neighbouring island of Nacula. Her father was Ratu Taitusi Bebe, the chief of Nacula Island; her mother was Adi Senimili, also a chiefly daughter from the neighbouring island of Malakati. (This de facto union, discussed below, took place before my father's birth in 1917 who was registered and raised by his white father, Grandpa Bruce.) Grandpa Bruce and Marica, my Fijian Grandma, made their home on the idyllic island of Nanuya Lailai which Grandpa had purchased by leasehold from the Burns Philps South Seas Trading Company. Six half-caste children followed this union, my father William Henry Bruce being the eldest (Bill, the central character of this narrative). Bill's siblings were Sarah, David, Henry, Sophie, Joseph. The island was a copra plantation, a shipbuilding works and a happy home where Grandfather traded in *bêche-de-mer*, trocus shells and copra. The following story is based on my father Bill's life.

Bill grew up in a warm and close-knit family in modest but comfortable surroundings. Nevertheless his natural environment was pleasant and abundantly luxurious. The ocean was his playground where he learned from his Fijian uncles how to spearfish and dive for octopus at a young age. He was named after his chiefly grandfather, Ratu Viliame Taitusi Bebe, but was known by his tribal name, Bebe—pronounced 'Bembeh', meaning butterfly in Fijian. Both Fijian and English were spoken in the home. The family homestead was a large grass hut (*bure*) built by the menfolk of his mother's clan. There was no electricity and water was brought in from a nearby stream that trickled down from the lush tropical hills. At night kerosene lamps lit up the *bure* that gave a hushed and cosy atmosphere under the stars. With his guns and Bible at his bedside, Grandpa slept with his family amid the breakers of the vast South Pacific Ocean. The *bure* had Fijian and European furnishings and native mats covered the floor. There was a high wooden bed for his parents with its firm coconut mattress and soft Fijian mats for covers. The embroidered pillowcases were the work of Grandma and her sisters. The children slept huddled together on the floor on a pile of soft-hand woven mats with China blankets. A curtain divided them from their parents. Bill remembered the Blue Willow crockery on the top shelf of their cosy outdoor kitchen that also had a food cupboard made of timber and wire gauze. In the far end was a fireplace housing Grandma's big clay pots and a collection of Indian tin pots. In the corner of the living room stood a colossal His Master's Voice gramophone, Grandpa's prized possession that blared out his favourite tunes, 'Swannee', 'Mammy' and 'Yes sir, that's my baby'. On the wall of the homestead hung Grandpa's faithful barometer, the most precious symbol of the planter class that told him it was light showers, a passing blow or a gigantic hurricane and to bring the boats in and batten down.

The family's daily diet was fish, crab and *kuita* (octopus), eaten with cassava, taro, yams, *bele* (island spinach), *rou rou* (taro leaves cooked in coconut milk). Cooking was done on an open fire in clay pots, and on Sundays in a ground oven (*lovo*). When trading times were good, stewed beef made it onto the menu, and maybe a cake or pudding (*purini*). Grandma's colourful dresses and shiny adornments were also subject to the whims of the copra trade. The family's breakfast was the same each day: cabin crackers from a shiny tin box, or giant dumplings (doughboys or *topoi*) spread with CSR golden syrup and washed down with 'Bushells Tea' or *draunimoli* (lemon leaf tea). Sometimes there was jam, but butter was scarce. Bill's upbringing was almost totally bi-cultural with a slight leaning towards his mother's people owing to their proximity and her own strong influence as the daughter of a chief.

Within our Fijian *mataqali* (clan) my grandmother was from a line of kingmakers and communicators whose role to this day is to relay community news, preside at clan meetings and formally appoint tribal chiefs. At a young age Bill was initiated into his mother's clan and became familiar with tribal songs, storytelling, dance and rituals. Fishing, planting, and learning the ways of his mother's people were his normal childhood pursuits. My grandmother took her tribal duties seriously and despite living with a *kai valagi* (European), remained active in her clan attending frequent ceremonies and rites of passage. Bill inherited from his father (my grandfather) an appreciation of his Scottish heritage and was fed regular reminders as to the family's links to the Scottish Crown. 'Never forget you are a blue blooded Scot and a descendant of the great Robert the Bruce, King of Scots!', Grandfather Bruce would exhort. These narratives were absorbed by the half-caste boy and interwoven with the elaborate tales of his Fijian people who had once chased the beleaguered Captain Bligh from the cannibal-infested waters of his own islands.

Bill's timeless island life in his South Pacific cocoon did not prepare him for the events that would follow. Things turned bad when his mother began a love affair with a Fijian chief from a neighbouring island and ran away to live with him, abandoning her husband and their five children. The runaway chief's daughter was pregnant with Grandpa's sixth child when she ran away. She later confirmed that the light-skinned boy with soft wavy hair was in fact Grandfather's son, not the chief's, however the boy now belonged to the chief. When a desperate and grief-stricken Bill swam out in pursuit of his deserting mother, the angry chief struck the boy's fingers with his oars as the crying, screaming boy struggled in vain to climb aboard the chief's wildly rocking boat. A decisive jerk of the chief's oar finally sent Bill flying backwards, submerged into the depths of the Pacific Ocean, to the startled stare from a worried octopus swaying there among the seaweed. Grandpa Bruce, it seems, had paid the ultimate price for his contempt towards Fijians.

Life quickly deteriorated for the shattered white planter whose self-reliance and wealth had dwindled accordingly. After a month or two alone, he struck up a deal with an unmarried half-caste girl half his age to come and live with him and look after his family. She turned out to be a 'wicked witch' who was cruel to his children and soon became pregnant with her own brood for Grandpa to feed. One morning while Bill and his two younger sisters were playing at the back of the house, they were called to come inside by their solemn-faced father who was in the company of two strange men, one of them in a long black robe. Before the children could ask questions, they were bundled aboard the stranger's boat and transported across rough, dangerous green waters on a terrifying journey to an unknown destination on the other side of Fiji. Their captor was a tiny-framed Catholic priest, an Indian I was told. His silent oarsman was a large Fijian battling a dodgy engine in gigantic waves that sprayed the boat incessantly as the terrified children clung to each other. Bill and his sisters' journey took them five days.

Their first landing was at Lautoka wharf where they were taken to a small convent during its school holidays. There the white nuns gave them a bath and a meal and they slept in an empty dormitory before heading off with the priest in a public bus through the dusty canefields of Ba and Raki Raki and to the wharf at Londoni where they boarded another boat for Levuka the old capital on the faraway island of Ovalau. Their final destination was a remote Catholic mission on Ovalau where Bill, then 14, was handed over to the brothers of St John's College, Cawaci, while his two sisters, Sarah and Sophie, aged nine and four, became wards of the European sisters at the nearby Loreto Convent where they were housed behind the main school building in a barrack called 'Sola'.[3]

The mission was a native residential school that trained Fijian boys and girls for agricultural work and domestic duties. A handful of half-castes were among them and European nuns and brothers gave instruction in Fijian and English. Some were not competent Fijian speakers and often made comical errors, much to the childrens' amusement. The syllabus was rudimentary reading, writing and arithmetic with most of the time spent in the fields planting staple food crops such as *dalo* (taro), *tavioka* (cassava) and *bele*. Standard English was taught only as a foreign language, otherwise Fijian was the main language of instruction. Life on the mission was physically demanding and the discipline harsh. The nuns and brothers at the mission station were understood to be French, English, Irish and Australian who often used the cane as a teaching tool, yet mischievous Fijians children retained their humour, never fully cowering to white authority.

My father told me a light story about a cane-wielding nun who once whipped a 'class clown' (a Fijian chief's son). Feigning pain, he fell to the floor, gripping his stomach and writhing in agony, but who suddenly leapt up and sought refuge under the nun's long black robe in his mischievous clowning way. The jumping, shrieking nun had to dismiss her class because the children were collapsing with laughter. Nevertheless, the children learned to pray morning, noon and night and the school bell was a constant reminder of calling them to prayer. Although supervised in the dorms and in the fields by Fijian lay teachers (*vukevuke*), the children learned to plant their own crops, cook their own meals and look after one another.

The older children took care of the young ones, showing them how to bath, dress and comb their hair. Aunt Sarah has poignant memories of Bill, her older brother, turning up at the convent gates on Christmas Day clutching a tin of corned beef that he had brought for his two sisters' Christmas lunch. This he got from the money he had earned selling his coconuts and vegetables in the town markets. No food was provided by the mission and the children's garden-grown meals were the same each day—boiled *tavioka* and *bele*. Whenever he could, Bill would go spear fishing, returning with his catch to throw on the fire and share with his friends. Apart from that, life's luxuries were paw-paws, bananas and mangos grown in the school gardens. 'We were vegetarian', Bill said.

Yet Bill often spied sumptuous meals on the tables of the missionaries who kept cows and chickens and made their own milk, butter and cheese. 'You could smell those bacon and eggs coming from the refectory', he would say. They even had cornflakes, porridge,[4] and roast meat on Sundays. Since no letters or money came from their father, some of the European nuns took pity on the three Bruce orphans and sewed them clothing made from scraps of material. Bill remembered his round-necked tapestry 'blouse' and his blue baggy shorts made from old convent curtains. When the homesick Bruce children inquired after their parents and the possibility of going home, they were told by the nuns that their parents were dead and that the mission was now their home. The hardest times were during school holidays when the mission would close and the other children would go home for their holidays. Only the Bruce orphans remained behind at the mission.

Bill did not consider himself a promising pupil. He was unable to understand the lessons in the classroom and he found school life confusing and irrelevant. It is now a family legend that one night he prayed to God to make him understand what was going on. God heard his prayer. Suddenly he began to read, write, and add up numbers. His mind opened up to his studies and he began to shine in the classroom and on the track field. Every night he prayed and began to find great comfort in God the Father, the Son, and the Holy Ghost. This man called Jesus, the apostles, and all the saints that the brothers and nuns had been teaching him about became his new family. As an orphan with now a keen interest in his school work, Bill gained access to the brothers who gave him the special attention he needed to succeed. The brothers responded to his missionary values and it also helped that he had a religious air about him and a maturity beyond his years. Bill's prowess as an athlete and track star in the 880-yard run led him to become a national champion who ran from the mid-1930s and in the war years. He retired unbeaten after the war. Unfortunately we will never know how fast he ran because in his day races were not timed in Fiji. Bill's identity had now shifted from a 'native-half-caste' to a 'de-tribalised' 'Part-European'. He became somewhat like the 'marginal man' of social theory straddling two cultures but alienated from both. His journey into a shifting and changing colonial identity had begun.

Bill became Fiji's youngest qualified school teacher at the age of 17. The Marists encouraged him to join the brotherhood and train in New Zealand, but a teaching career in Fiji appealed more. He taught at a number of Catholic missions across Fiji, learning all the regional dialects in the course of his work.[5] At the outbreak of World War II, and like many of his Fijian compatriots, he enlisted in the Fijian army to fight the Japanese in the Pacific War. He joined the 1st Battalion attached to the New Zealand contingent that fought with the Americans in Guadalcanal and Bougainville during 1943-1945. Enlisting in the army proved an interesting exercise with regard to Bill's identity.

At first, recruiters processed him as a Fijian, issuing him with his uniform and allocating him to his barracks where he was delighted to join many of his old schoolmates and former pupils, some of them the sons of Fijian chiefs. But after a couple of days he was moved to the European barracks after a recruiter who knew his father pointed out that Bill was in fact 'Part-European', not Fijian. Such was the colonial attitude that rendered the mixed-race identity fluid while the war also enabled Part-Europeans to become token whites, regardless of skin colour. On 13 April, 1943, the 1st Battalion and the 1st Commando marched through the streets of Suva among sobbing crowds of relatives and friends. Among them was Don Bruce, the old planter, who had journeyed all the way from the islands to be there. That was the first time Bill had laid eyes on his teary-eyed father since he was taken away from his island paradise as boy. The two men managed a brief embrace before Bill boarded the *USS President Hayes* to join in one of the bloodiest battles of the Pacific conflict, Guadalcanal.

On his first rest and recuperation leave in 1945 Bill met Andie, my mother, in Lautoka, Fiji, where they were introduced by mutual friends. It was the proverbial love at first sight for the two mulattos who lost no time in getting married. In his choice of bride it seems Bill was staring at himself in the mirror as their ethnic and social backgrounds were remarkably similar. Permission to marry Andie first had to be obtained from the European Marist sisters who were intimately involved in her upbringing—their 'little Rose', as she was often called. Bill's wife (my mother), was the daughter of a British district commissioner, Jack Charles Barley, and a Fijian woman, Nakesa Luisa Naite, from the west coast of the main island. The wedding-ring Bill bought my mother was earned from the prize money he had won at a showdown 880-yard race in Lautoka in 1945. Being already familiar with Andie's English father and Bill's reputation as a good missionary boy and an outstanding local athlete, the Marist nuns gave them their eternal blessings and sang at their wedding in Lautoka on April 7, 1945.

And so ends this narrative of a changing identity of a colonial Fijian child as played out in the hybridised life of William Henry de Bruce and his European and Fijian forebears. The outstanding features of such a narrative are the creative identities that mixed-bloods were compelled to construct in order to justify their existence in a race-conscious and artificial milieu. Contemporarily, it provides food for thought on how an evolving Fiji might manage its multi-ethnic, interracial population in its coming years when the issue of 'race', racial categorisation and place of belonging will be a far more complex determinant in the distribution of wealth and resources in Fiji.

ENDNOTES

[1] 'The VKB is a register of names of the members of each *mataqali*, or land-owning unit, maintained by the Native Lands Commission (NLC) since 1914. The registry is the product of evidence-taking by the NLC staff since the early days of colonisation. A person is usually registered in the VKB as a member of a particular *mataqali* at birth, by the filing of an application with the NLC. The VKB is highly confidential, and the names of the members of any *mataqali* are available only to other members of that *mataqali*. The NLC is a government body under the authority of the Great Council of Chiefs'. Annelise

Riles, 'Part-Europeans and Fijian', in Brij V. Lal and Tomasi R. Vakatora (eds), *Fiji in Transition: research papers of the Fiji Constitution Review Commission*, vol. 1 (Suva 1997), 128, note 15.

[2] CO83/215 and CO83/214; Arthur Mayhew *Report on Education in Fiji* (Suva 1937), prepared after a visit to Fiji in September, 1936. On Christian indoctrination in Fiji, Narayan noted that Fiji was not a conquered country in the sense of invasion by physical force but that Fijians were a people conquered at the level of beliefs and values. Jay Narayan, *The Political Economy of Fiji* (Suva 1986), 81-2.

[3] 'Sola'—Latin, *solo*, only, alone, possibly orphan…of the 'Five Solas' or the 'Five Onlys' of Christian doctrine that teaches (1) Scripture/the Bible 'alone' teaches the authoritative word of God, not traditions; (2) Christ 'alone'; (3) Grace 'alone'; (4) Faith 'alone'; (5) Glory to God 'only'. http://www.monerg-ism.com/thethreshold/articles/topic/fivesolas.html

[4] This probably explains why porridge and cornflakes were Bill's cherished foods in his later, more prosperous years.

[5] Bill even spoke the Nadroga lingo that was much like his own Yasawa language, and are two of the most difficult dialects to master.

Chapter 8

Telling Lives in Tuvalu

Michael Goldsmith

Tuvalu is an independent low-island microstate of 9,500 people in the central Pacific. It used to be the Ellice Islands component of the Gilbert and Ellice Islands Colony (GEIC) before separation in 1975 from the Micronesian Gilbertese, or i-Kiribati. Its inhabitants, who are mainly Polynesian and mainly Protestant, do not have a long tradition of 'life writing' and one could argue that such practices are inconsistent with Tuvaluan culture. My response to this suggestion is that the relationship between Tuvaluans and other Polynesians to their life histories is more complex; but there is a school of thought concerning Pacific conceptions of personhood that supposedly lends weight to the argument. I will return to this problem briefly later.

Whether or not the practice of life writing 'fits' their culture, a small number of Pacific Islanders who were either Tuvaluan or had a profound influence on Tuvaluan history have been the subjects of published biographies or autobiographies. The following three persons almost certainly comprise the sum total so far.[1] One is the subject of a biography that I co-authored, one wrote his own autobiography, and the last appeared in that hybrid kind of auto/biography, a life history dictated by him but written up by his interlocutor.

First in order of appearance was Elekana, the Cook Island London Missionary Society deacon credited with having introduced Christianity to the archipelago in 1861. As the survivor of a so-called miraculous drift voyage to Nukulaelae, Elekana cropped up in many missionary narratives illustrating the workings of divine providence but also appeared in scientific accounts of voyaging and tales of seafaring. I became interested in Elekana during the course of my doctoral research, as his story (or rather stories) seemed to shed light on how Christianity took root in Tuvalu as the first great institutional transfer of the mid-19th century central Pacific. After some preliminary published interpretations,[2] the magnum opus of this research so far has been a book by Doug Munro and me entitled *The Accidental Missionary: tales of Elekana.*[3] Because so much has been written already on this historical figure, in this paper I will refer to him less than I do to the other two.

The second subject is Frank Pasefika, a former civil servant in the Gilbert and Ellice Islands Colony administration, who published a short autobiography under the aegis of the University of the South Pacific in 1990.[4]

The last subject is Neli Lifuka, the self-proclaimed leader of Kioa, a Tuvaluan colony island in Fiji purchased through the good offices of the GEIC administration after World War II for the use of people from Vaitupu. His story was compiled by an anthropologist, Klaus-Friedrich Koch, and published as *Logs in the Current of the Sea* in 1978.[5] This was the result of Koch deciding to switch from an ethnography of the displaced community of Tuvaluans on Kioa to 'an ethnohistorical biography' of its most charismatic leader. The biographer first came into contact with his subject on Kioa in July 1968 and returned to record the story in June 1969. They secluded themselves for a week in a crude shelter on the other side of the island from the main village and talked, interrupted only by sleeping, eating and the daily visits of Neli's son or daughters to bring more provisions. By the end of that time, Koch had recorded 48 hours worth of reminiscences (some eight reels of taped conversation). Not all of that material, by the way, figures in the published version.

The first very obvious pattern of note is that these three subjects are all men (as are all the subjects of the briefer pieces or passages referred to in footnote 1). Call it a wild hunch, but I don't think that this particular inclusion/exclusion is a coincidence. The dominant pattern of personhood in the Pacific reflects the domination of male persons in the vast majority of societies.

The common gender of their central figures aside, however, the stories do vary in other respects. The biography of Elekana, *The Accidental Missionary*,[6] was written well after the life it attempted to portray was over. It was also based exclusively on documentary sources, both primary and secondary (though these did include the transcript of a face-to-face interview with a knowledgeable elder conducted by another ethnographer, Niko Besnier, on Nukulaelae). Although he has been the most recent of the three men to receive extended biographical treatment, Elekana's life of course was much the earliest in a chronological sense, preceding the other two by several decades. Neli Lifuka (b. 1909) and Frank Pasefika (b. 1914) were more recent historical actors and their lives overlapped not only with each other's but also with many people still alive.

They also both participated actively in the recounting of their lives—Frank by writing it down and Neli by telling it into a tape-recorder. On this score, nevertheless, any apparent difference from Elekana is somewhat illusory. True, he never authorised a biography but it's my guess that he wouldn't have resisted one being written and he was happy enough to be turned into a legendary character in missionary folklore (though less happy to be made an example of in other respects). He also wrote an extended account of the drift voyage that established his status as one of God's chosen.

An important part of the framework for understanding all three is that their biographies have appeared only in English, not in Tuvaluan. That has a great deal to do with the exclusions and disciplines of missionisation and colonialism (and of present-day publishing) but in a complex kind of way.

Elekana almost certainly did not speak, read or write English fluently though he may have acquired some of the language through contact with the LMS's British missionaries. In fact he didn't even know the language of Tuvalu until he drifted there and the language he was probably most comfortable with was Cook Island Maori (both the Manihiki dialect of his home island and the southern dialect, which had become the official church language of the Cooks group through the spread of the Church). Residence in Tuvalu—on Nukulaelae after the drift voyage and later on Nukufetaeu after being stationed there as a native teacher—probably forced him to acquire oral fluency in the vernacular but at that time it was not a written language. Rather, Samoan became the LMS central Pacific language of instruction, of the written scriptures and of preaching. Consequently, it was Samoan that Elekana would have had to learn when he went for missionary training at Malua.

After his first sojourn in Tuvalu, Elekana did write a couple of brief accounts of his exploits but Doug Munro and I were only able to find translated versions that the LMS had commissioned for the edification of its members, especially the juvenile ones. The language of the originals was probably Cook Islands Maori but we just don't know for sure. Virtually all the material we consulted to write his story was available only in English. It is also the language that Doug Munro and I have done most of our publishing in, though he is one of the few Pacific historians to have had some of his works translated into the vernacular.[7]

Neli Lifuka and Frank Pasefika both knew English pretty well, partly through their involvement in the elitist male secondary education system of the British-run GEIC. Neli, however, left school early after he rebelled against the regime of the dictatorial headmaster of Elisefou, D.G. Kennedy,[8] and seems to have been mostly self-taught. From internal evidence, I suspect English was the main language of Neli's life history interviews but Koch left that point implicit, perhaps because he thought it was obvious. (He died not long after the book came out so I've never been able to get an absolute confirmation.) Neli himself attributed his command of English to the help of the fourth engineer of the second ship he worked on: 'He gave me newspapers to read and gave me paper and pencil to practice my writing. When I didn't know a word, I asked him, and he explained it to me'.[9]

Frank lasted longer in the formal education system and states that the choice of language for his account was deliberate: 'I have written this story in simple English because I thought that by the time this story was published everybody in Tuvalu may be able to read and write in English'.[10] He's probably right because, at least since independence in 1978, Tuvaluan children have learned English from an early age. This contrasts with their 19th century counterparts, for whom written language consisted mostly of scriptures and religious tracts in Samoan, which was the first language of most of the native teachers and missionaries posted to the Ellice Islands until well into the 20th century. There were, of course, a few important exceptions like Elekana, whose singularity confirms the rule because of having to learn Samoan as an adult.

Elekana was different in other respects as well. Like his biographers, his biography is unreliable at the best of times. That was actually one of our main interpretive points. But *The Accidental Missionary* is also radically 'incomplete' for a biography. We don't know exactly when Elekana was born or when he died; in fact we don't know much about his early life or his later career at all. We focused on the years when he was most famous to missionary audiences and most useful to missionary bodies. This, and the fact that our approach was deliberately Tuvalu-centric, was not just because of our research blinkers but also because that was virtually all we could find in the records. As a result, Elekana's written life is much more fragmentary and partial than Neli's and Frank's. In our defence, it may be that all such lives are partial from this distance.

The shape of the other two life stories is more conventionally rounded. Neli begins with his childhood and rather turbulent schooldays at Elisefou on Vaitupu, his early employment on freighters and on phosphate boats at Ocean Island/Banaba, and his promotion up the ranks to engineer. At other times he worked on a government boat and a missionary vessel but argued with his commanding officers over pay and conditions and resigned in each case. Interestingly, he then found employment blasting reef passages with his old headmasterly nemesis, Kennedy (who had morphed into a resident District Officer (DO)). Later he even went back to Vaitupu to work as a caretaker at Kennedy's former school. Eventually he returned to Ocean Island to work on the phosphate boats but gained a foothold in the Colony administration by being appointed as a hospital dresser and Ellice community liaison person. True to form, he also led a strike of Ellice Island workers against the British Phosphate Commission.

Kennedy turned up again and, resistant to the idea of a posting to the Solomons, suggested to Neli that they sail a canoe back to Tuvalu. (Given Elekana's prior example, it's probably fortunate that they didn't.) The two old antagonists were now firm friends, according to Neli, and he waxed lyrical over Kennedy's contribution to development in Tuvalu.

Frank, meanwhile, endured the school regime more successfully than Neli but seems to have enjoyed it even less. When Elisefou was shut down on Kennedy's appointment as DO in 1931, Frank was one of five boys selected to go to King George V School at Tarawa in the Gilberts, the headquarters of the GEIC. There he found life 'a bit easier and more independent'.[11] He joined the civil service on Funafuti (the headquarters of the Ellice district) as a clerk and interpreter in 1933. This appointment entailed a wide variety of tasks (which he recounts in great detail) and also required him to work alongside Kennedy a lot of the time, which was not to his taste. Though a student and colleague of Kennedy for 16 years, he always found him 'difficult to like'.[12]

For both Neli and Frank, the Pacific War was a pivotal experience. From 1941, Neli was involved on Vaitupu in coast-watching and, later, in choosing labourers whom he accompanied to work at Funafuti helping to build the American base there. This became the headquarters for the assault on the Japanese bastion of Tarawa in November 1943. Neli was astonished by the number and size of the warships at Funafuti and, in a trope familiar from other parts of the Pacific, marvelled at the Americans' material wealth and enjoyed their egalitarianism.[13] 'We always ate together, we had the same food.' Unloading ships 'was hard work but the Americans looked after us very well. The only trouble was with the British. They didn't want the Americans to give us the wages they wanted to pay. ... The Americans were very kind to us. They used their dive bombers to drop our mail and parcels at Vaitupu and the other Ellice Islands. ... The Americans were really very good to us'. And so on.

In one revealing deviation from the nativist ideologies that the Americans and their largesse inspired in places like Vanuatu, however, Neli was not impressed by the presence of black troops: 'After the Americans had taken Tarawa, other marines came from the United States. They were all Negroes, only the captain was a European. ... They always said bad things about the [white] Americans, and that they would get back at them sometime in the future. They reckoned that they were not treated like the European Americans. I think they were wrong because they were educated by the Europeans; they didn't know anything by themselves. How can I go against a person who teaches me things? That's bad. The Negroes were natives just like us, but they always talked smart'.[14] I have had students who, in assuming a retrospective ideological alliance among all non-white Pacific Islanders, attribute Neli's views to having internalised the self-hate of the colonised subject. In my opinion, he was much more likely to have been reflecting the standard racial hierarchies of the time, which placed blacks (including Melanesians) lower on the great chain of being than Polynesians.

For Frank, the war meant that his duties increased and for extended periods he was often left to operate without the direct supervision of a *palagi* (white) official. But, like Neli, what he remembered most vividly was the American 'invasion' in September 1942. In fact, he was on board a ship in the massive convoy from Suva when it anchored in Funafuti lagoon.

After the battle for Tarawa, Frank was put in charge of travelling around the Colony to repay government officers their salary arrears. This temporary transfer to the Treasury became permanent and he spent the rest of his career in that branch of government, mainly at Tarawa, retiring once at the age of 50, then operating the government hotel on Funafuti for a few years until required for short-term redeployments back in Treasury and as part of the team for the 1973 Colony census. When those duties came to an end, he settled on Funafuti as head of a large extended family and worked voluntarily for the Ellice Islands/Tuvalu Church until he finally retired for health reasons in 1984 at the age of 70.[15] Of the three subjects of this essay, he is the only one I have met personally. That was in the late 1970s when he was working, as I recall, on the church newsletter—but I have to confess he didn't leave a strong impression on me.

Neli was appointed magistrate on his home island of Vaitupu soon after the war came to an end. Almost inevitably, he alienated many of the elders (for being too young), the pastor (for questioning his authority and privileges), and some *palagi* members of the administration (for not enforcing laws where he felt no wrong had been committed). But he had enough allies to remain in power for a while and claims that he restored Vaitupu to its favoured position with the government.[16] His lively period of rule survived numerous complaints and inquiries until 1951. The final straw was being caught *in flagrante delicto* with the pastor's young wife—in church, no less. There followed successful stints working for the Colony Cooperative Society and as an officer on one of the inter-island boats. After five years he even received an invitation to return to the magistrate's position on Vaitupu, an offer that he clearly relished being able to turn down.[17] In the end, having been instrumental in the purchase of Kioa in 1946, he joined the community and quickly became chairman of its council (thereby annoying yet more people).

Lack of time precludes my continuing a detailed narrative of the lives of Neli and Frank and I have provided hardly any information on the life of Elekana. In the rest of this chapter, I wish to use the historical and ethnographic snippets of information provided so far to address some more general points concerning the issue I mentioned at the beginning of this paper—the question of whether or not (auto)biography, in a Western sense, conflicts with Pacific cultural frameworks.

The question arises because of a theory, popular in some circles, that Pacific conceptions of personhood are at odds with the standard 'Western' model of atomistic individualism. One variant of this approach postulates an image of *heroic* personhood, especially in relation to political leaders such as Polynesian chiefs; another variant prefers the more egalitarian image of *consocial* personhood. On this latter view, Pacific Islanders are generally less interested in 'inner' motivations than their 'Western' counterparts, their sense of individual agency is inseparable from wider social or group relationships, and their sense of selfhood is changeable across different contexts (perhaps even 'partible', which I understand to mean as distributed fractionally across those different contexts).

Consocial personhood has its clearest expression in a collection of anthropological essays edited by Jocelyn Linnekin and Lin Poyer, *Cultural Identity and Ethnicity in the Pacific*.[18] But its advocacy is by no means restricted to anthropologists. Tongan educator Konai Helu Thaman supports the idea of consocial personhood and has found it persuasive for explaining the importance of cultural rights—which are collective, she claims, unlike the individual human rights of Western modernity.[19]

The concepts of heroic and consocial personhood at first glance seem rather opposed to each other but they can be seen as mutually reinforcing. Thus the theory of heroic personhood proposes a view of leaders as emerging integrally from the group. Canonically, the group is named after its founding individual whose repeated incarnation through succession means an unbroken sense of the leader's self. This endlessly reconstituted chief may be said to represent the whole group in an almost physical sense. Just as there is no individual without a group, there can be no chief without a people. Ruminating on Hawai'ian mythology, Marshall Sahlins puts it thus: 'The king assumes, and in his own person lives, the life of the collectivity';[20] and, the 'king encompasses the people in his own person, as projection of his own being'.[21]

However, if one applies the overall frame of heroic/consocial personhood to the few contemporary published examples of political biography or memoir in the Pacific, including those addressed in this paper, the picture becomes murky. The men I have discussed arguably saw themselves as heroes but in an individualistic manner quite recognisable to *palagi*; and their views of personhood do not strike me as particularly 'consocial'. I can cite many instances where each of them (but especially Neli) prided himself on going against the grain, claimed to be right when everyone else was wrong, and took great satisfaction in being able to say 'I told you so'. Consocial? More like anti-social.

In any event, I hope I have presented enough pertinent material on these three men in this brief account to suggest that they are not obedient and unthinking bearers of group identity. They strike me all as clear-cut individuals. Frank Pasefika's passive-aggressive style contrasts with both the self-belief and self-righteousness of Elekana and the gleeful nonconformity of Neli Lifuka.

At the same time, not only were they rarely in control of their own destinies, they could never have been the unalloyed creators of their own subjectivities. As an aging survivor of the Foucauldian revolution in social thought, I am continually struck by the relevance of Michel Foucault's work to the historiography of the Pacific. The most influential of these ideas stem from his histories of the rise of modernity in Europe, an era that established new boundaries between reason and madness[22] and concomitant procedures of exclusion and confinement.[23] While Foucault never turned his attention directly to this region of the world, his writings shed light on the subjugated knowledges and forms of personhood produced, for example, by the forces of religion and colonialism—partly, of course, because Europe exported them. I also remain convinced of the theoretical grasp offered by his analysis of the productivity of subjectification in relation to how lives may be constructed. While people are subjects of a kind, the very notion of the bounded autonomous subject is an effect of power. Narratives that emphasise the free agency of individual lives are themselves examples of technologies of the self.[24]

Studies of the Pacific and elsewhere demonstrate the major role played by literacy in relation to such technologies. For Tuvalu, this topic has been most intensively studied by Niko Besnier by means of some insightful analyses of connections between religion, personhood and literacy on Nukulaelae, one of the more isolated Tuvaluan atolls.[25] Besnier's work represents a major contribution not only to Tuvaluan ethnography but also to studies of the cultural shaping of literacy in general. In some ways, however, it seems tangential to the processes that led to the more individualised life stories that concern me here. For example, the only kind of literacy practice in his work that has a sense of 'authority' similar to the *authorship* of the accounts I address is the Nukulaelae tradition of writing down sermons for delivery in church. Such occasions, underpinned by the putative authority of the scriptures and the word of God, turn the sermonisers (who are not just pastors but a substantial body of lay preachers as well) into much more forceful and even authoritarian figures than the usual codes of interpersonal conduct on the island allow. Besnier convincingly argues that this culturally sanctioned 'deviation', rather than evidence for transgressive individuality, is actually *support* for the view that on Nukulaelae, as elsewhere in the Pacific, notions of personhood are highly context-dependent.[26] I am not persuaded, however, that such an explanation is pertinent to the idiosyncratic case-studies I have outlined, with their intricate connections between individual personality and the technology of literacy that helps to create that sense of individuality in the first place.

There is no time to pursue these points in any detail here but my brief sketch does suggest that disciplinary regimes, exclusions, prohibitions, displacements and colonial subjectifications played a major role in shaping these Tuvaluan life stories and the very possibility of their publication.

Ian Burkitt recently bemoaned the fragmentation of everyday life and its deleterious effects on the ability of people to shape meaningful life narratives.[27] I take a different view. A decade ago, in one of my first attempts at understanding Elekana, I argued that 'ethnographic life histories and cross-cultural biographies actually emanate most richly from marginality'. I went on to say:

> Biography as a genre is marked by the traces of people crossing cultural and physical boundaries, transitions from one state to another (often literally). ... In part this pattern occurs because the crossing of geopolitical boundaries throws up administrative and bureaucratic information... by springing the subtle and not-so-subtle tripwires of governmentality. ... Lastly, it may come about because crossing cultural boundaries makes received assumptions about what constitutes a life more problematic as well as easier to structure as a sequence.[28]

Elekana's famous drift voyage, his involvement in converting a whole culture, his rise and fall in the missionary pantheon, and his appearances in the margins of many of the documents recording his restless career; Neli's constant troubles, disputes and nomadic escapades; the upheaval of his and Frank's world by a war between huge powers that saw Pacific islands serve merely as stepping-stones, their fears of Japanese bombardment and occupation (albeit a less terrifying ordeal than life under Kennedy at Elisefou); and their episodic registration in the bureaucratic affairs of the GEIC—all of these lend support to a view of biography that, whatever the vernacular cultural plausibility of the genre, sees dispersal, interruption and exclusion as central to the exercise involved in telling lives in Tuvalu.

ENDNOTES

[1] Others have featured in memoirs (Michael Goldsmith, 'Alovaka Maui: defender of the faith', in Doug Munro and Andrew Thornley (eds), *The Covenant Makers: Islander missionaries in the Pacific* (Suva 1996)), in briefer pieces on various pastors and traders (Doug Munro, 'Kirisome and Tema: Samoan pastors in the Ellice Islands', in Deryck Scarr (ed.), *More Pacific Islands Portraits* (Canberra 1978); 'The Lagoon Islands: a history of Tuvalu 1820-1908', PhD thesis, Macquarie University (Sydney 1982); 'The lives and times of resident traders in Tuvalu: an exercise in history from below', *Pacific Studies*, 10:2 (1987), 73-106; 'Samoan pastors in Tuvalu, 1865-1899', in Munro and Thornley, *The Covenant Makers*; 'The humble Ieremia: a Samoman [sc. Samoan] pastor in Tuvalu, 1880-1890 [sc. 1895]', *Pacific Journal of Theology*, Series II, 23: 40-48 (2000) and as bit players in longer works (Munro, 'The Lagoon Islands', Michael Goldsmith, 'Church and society in Tuvalu', PhD thesis, University of Illinois (Urbana, IL 1989); see too Nicholas Thomas and Richard Eves, *Bad Colonists: the South Seas letters of Vernon Lee Walker and Louis Becke* (Durham, NC 1999) on Louis Becke's sojourn in Tuvalu.

[2] Michael Goldsmith and Doug Munro, 'Encountering Elekana encountering Tuvalu', in Donald H. Rubinstein (ed.), *Pacific History: papers from the 8th Pacific History Association Conference* (Mangilao 1992); Michael Goldsmith, 'Decentering Pacific Biographies', in Alaima Talu and Max Quanchi (eds), *Messy Entanglements: the papers of the 10th Pacific History Association Conference, Tarawa, Kiribati* (Brisbane 1995).

[3] Michael Goldsmith and Doug Munro, *The Accidental Missionary* (Christchurch 2002).

[4] Frank Pasefika, *The Autobiography of Frank Pasefika* (Suva 1990).

[5] Klaus-Friedrich Koch, *Logs in the Current of the Sea: Neli Lifuka's story of Kioa and the Vaitupu Colonists* (Canberra 1978), xi; Michael Goldsmith, Review of Klaus-Friedrich Koch, *Logs in the Current of the Sea*, *Journal of the Polynesian Society*, 87:4 (1978), 361-62.

[6] Goldsmith and Munro, *The Accidental Missionary*.

Tito Isala and Doug Munro, *Te Aso Fiafia: Te Tala o te Kamupane Vaitupu, 1877-1887* (Suva 1987).

[8] Klaus-Friedrich Koch, *Logs in the Current of the Sea*, 9.

[9] Ibid., 12; see too 32.

[10] Pasefika, *The Autobiography of Frank Pasefika*, 7; see also 54.

[11] Ibid., 22.
[12] Ibid., 21.
[13] Klaus-Friedrich Koch, *Logs in the Current of the Sea*, 28-29.
[14] Ibid., 29-30.
[15] Pasefika, *The Autobiography of Frank Pasefika*, 42.
[16] Klaus-Friedrich Koch, *Logs in the Current of the Sea*, 33-44.
[17] Ibid.
[18] Jocelyn Linnekin, and Lin Poyer (eds), *Cultural Identity and Ethnicity in the Pacific* (Honolulu 1990).
[19] Konai Helu Thaman, 'Cultural Rights: a personal perspective', in Margaret Wilson and Paul Hunt (eds), *Culture, Rights, and Cultural Rights: perspectives from the South Pacific* (Wellington 2000).
[20] Marshall Sahlins, 'Hierarchy and humanity in Polynesia', in Antony Hooper and Judith Huntsman (eds), *Transformations of Polynesian Culture* (Auckland 1985), 207.
[21] Ibid., 214-15.
[22] Michel Foucault, *Madness and Civilization: a history of insanity in the age of reason* (New York 1965).
[23] Michel Foucault, 'Orders of discourse: inaugural lecture delivered at the Collège de France', *Social Science Information*, 10:2 (1971), 7-30.
[24] Michel Foucault, *The History of Sexuality*, vol. 3: *The Care of Self* (New York 1986).
[25] Niko Besnier, 'Literacy and the notion of person on Nukulaelae Atoll', *American Anthropologist*, 93: 2 (1991), 570-87; 'Christianity, authority, and personhood: sermonic discourse on Nukulaelae Atoll', *Journal of the Polynesian Society*, 103:4 (1994), 339-78; *Literacy, Emotion, and Authority: reading and writing on a Polynesian Atoll* (Cambridge 1995).
[26] Besnier, 'Christianity, authority, and personhood', 368-69; *Literacy, Emotion, and Authority*, 162-63.
[27] Ian Burkitt, 'Situating auto/biography: biography and narrative in the times and places of everyday life', *Auto/Biography*, 13:2 (2005), 93-110.
[28] Goldsmith, 'Decentering Pacific biographies', 7-8.

Chapter 9

My History: My Calling

Alaima Talu

I was born a Protestant on my home island, Nanumea, in Tuvalu, on 7 August 1948. I attended school in Tarawa, Kiribati, from January 1963-1968. On 12 January 1980, I made my final vows as a Catholic Nun in the Congregation of the Daughters of Our Lady of the Sacred Heart, in the Cathedral, Tarawa, Kiribati. In taking this step, I had chosen to serve as a Catholic missionary and Kiribati to be my home.

Mission History

Kiribati and Tuvalu were evangelised by the American Board of Commissioners for Foreign Missions (ABCFM) and the London Missionary Society (LMS) in the mid- and late-19th century. Reverend Hiram Bingham and a handful of Hawaiian missionaries arrived on Abaiang on 17 November 1857 and from there evangelised the northern islands as far south as central Kiribati.[1] In the 1870s Protestantism was brought to Tuvalu and the southern islands of Kiribati by the London Missionary Society through Samoan pastors. Catholicism was brought to Nonouti, in Kiribati, first by Betero Terawati and Tiroi in 1881. They had gone to work on the coconut plantations in Tahiti during the labour trade era and had embraced Catholicism. On returning to their home island of Nonouti in 1881, they sent a request to Rome for priests. In response, the Missionaries of the Sacred Heart, priests and brothers arrived in May 1888 and the Daughters of Our Lady of the Sacred Heart in August 1895.[2]

Tuvalu and Kiribati became a British Protectorate in 1893. From 1916 until 1975, they formed the Gilbert and Ellice Islands Colony, when they separated to prepare for independence.[3] The Ellice Islands became independent on 1 October 1978 and took the name Tuvalu which literally means 'a line of eight' and the Gilberts changed to Kiribati, the local version of Gilberts, on 12 July 1979.

Tarawa with its good anchorage was the main island in the colony and the centre of colonial administration and commerce. On each island there was a Magistrate who presided over both the island and lands courts. He was assisted by four other men, three *Kaubure* (Councillors) and a Secretary. All were elected by the people and had to be approved by the Resident Commissioner, with the help of the District Officers for each section.

Nanumea is the northernmost island in the Tuvalu group and, therefore, the closest to the southern islands of Kiribati. In the 1960s, the LMS had one secondary school for boys in the Ellice Islands on the island of Vaitupu. It had two secondary schools—Rongorongo on Beru in the Southern Kiribati, Morikao on Abaiang to the north of Tarawa—and a Theological College at Tangintebu on South Tarawa. The Catholic Church had two secondary schools, St Joseph's College, Tabwiroa, Abaiang for boys and Immaculate Heart College, North Tarawa, for girls. Both churches had been engaged in primary education since the arrival of their early missionaries. By the 1960s, the LMS in Kiribati handed over its primary schools to the colonial government. The Catholics continued with primary education until just prior to independence in 1976. The Seventh Day Adventist also ran one secondary school, established in 1949, and one primary school on Kauma, Abemama, in central Kiribati. The colonial government secondary schools for both boys and girls were located in Bikenibeu in South Tarawa.

Family Background

The LMS school in Nanumea which I attended was run by a Samoan pastor, Enoka Alesana and his wife, Usoali'i. The other teachers were Taulu Teuo, who had been a leper on Makogai in Fiji, and Tafaoata Pulusi, one of the few who were educated in Papauta, Samoa, as well as a few young women and men who had completed their studies under the pastor himself. Classes were from Standards 1-6 and the subjects were: Bible Study, English, Arithmetic, Social Studies and Hygiene.

My father was the eldest in a family of eight: four boys and four girls. Of the boys, one died in his teens and the other in an accident in Suva. My mother was the youngest in a family of four. There were three girls and their only brother was killed on Banaba during the Japanese occupation. My father was the local government warden at the time when he sent me to school. He looked after the government station, prisoners if there were any, and attended the Nanumea council meetings. He also looked after colonial government guests on the island. Before this, he had been a policeman and chief of police on Nanumea, after he and my mother had spent 1949-1956 working on the phosphate mine for the British Phosphate Company on Banaba.

It is amazing how memory stores so much history. As part of keeping Nanumea clean, all the pig-sties were located in one area outside the village. It was here that my father met Viane Tabuanaba, the Kiribati Catholic catechist on Nanumea. Viane must have spent around 12 years as a catechist on Nanumea where he learnt the Nanumean dialect. My father also spoke Kiribati from having grown up on Nui (one of the islands in Tuvalu where the people speak a mixture of Tuvaluan and Kiribati dialect) and from his years in Banaba. From Viane my father learnt that the Australian and Irish Sisters in Kiribati ran schools and took care of girls in schools. Viane's eldest daughter was in school in Tarawa.

One day in 1962, after evening prayer and meal, I was preparing for bed. My father called, 'Alaima, come here for a minute'. As I sat in front of him, he asked me, 'Do you like school?'

I said, 'Yes, I like school'.

He continued, 'Would you like to go to school in Tarawa?'

I said, 'No, I do not want to go to school there'.

My father went on as if he had not heard me, 'In Catholic schools on Tarawa, the Sisters look after the girls well. Think about it'.

I repeated, 'No, I do not want to go to Tarawa'. I thought that was the end of that and returned to my bed.

I was just settling down to sleep when my mother called me. She was surprised I could go to sleep without giving my father a positive answer. She told me to apologise to him. I told her I had nothing to apologise for as I had not done anything wrong. She said I was disobedient. I got up and went to tell my father that I was sorry. In my mind I was apologising for disagreeing with him, not for what I said. I continued to attend the pastor's school as usual. But to my surprise he took my apology as a 'yes, I would go to school in Tarawa', for one evening my father took me to have classes with Viane in preparation for the school on Tarawa. That was a very dark period in my life. I was sad at the idea of leaving home. Tarawa seemed so far away!

I am the eldest in a family of 11: two girls and nine boys. The boy immediately after me was born deaf and dumb. He spoke a language of his own, and the third child died in infancy. He had been adopted by one of my aunts. She took him from Banaba to Betio where she lived with her Kiribati husband and the fourth one was too small at the time to go to school. Nine years separated my sister and me. She was also adopted by another aunt. Today it is still a mystery to me why my parents sent me to school in Kiribati. At that time, I could not bring myself to ask them, nor did it occur to me to ask. Perhaps, this is due to the fact that I was given to my grandparents when I was about 14 months old and returned to my parents when I was eight. I learned this story in 1994 from my father. They left me with my grandparents when my parents were employed in the phosphate mine in Banaba. My mother said, 'Your grandparents wanted us to leave you behind with them'. That was why I could relate to my grandparents better. For this reason I could ask my grandparents anything since I grew up with them. However, it did not stop my feeling of being unloved. I always felt I was being passed around like a parcel—as if I was an object. This created a kind of resentment within me. It is a burden I have carried during my religious life. I generally react strongly to anyone who tries to make decisions for me. It is also one of the reasons why I have not been open to share the 'real me'. When I first wrote my story, I gave it to one of the Sisters to read. At the end of the first draft she commented: 'There is no soul in your story'. I was avoiding having to deal with the hurts I have buried for many years.

My father probably envisaged I might be an asset to the family by earning an income. Since I was the eldest, I could help with the education of my young siblings. I can only speculate. I never plucked up enough courage to discuss this issue with my parents. Thus the insatiable quest for the unknown has remained in my heart. This has caused me much pain over the years. In retrospect, it shows how important it is to have good communication skills. This has perhaps been the most regrettable part of my life since the event has left a deep void within me. It has worsened over the years because, with my parents' passing, I cannot know for certain what was in their hearts for me.

However, those were difficult days for me and only the close members of my family knew I was being prepared to go to school. I was not even sure if the pastor knew about it. The pastor knew my grandfather very well. My paternal grandparents lived on the islet of Lakena. For years my grandfather was the caretaker for the pastor when he visited the islet for the Sunday services. My grandfather also beat the *lali* for Sunday services, as well as for the daily evening prayers.

My father knew how I loved my grandparents and it seems he exploited this too. He went to fetch them to live with us. When I appealed to my grandmother to help me get my father to change his mind about sending me to school in Tarawa, my grandmother said: 'It would be alright if we could live together and die together; but since we're getting old, we will die soon. We would have to leave you behind anyway, so it is better for you to go to school'. I knew then that I was going and there would be no turning back. While these were indeed visionary words, I did not appreciate it then. For I was only a child and I thought like a child. Again, communication failed. Nothing was said to comfort me or to make my journey more bearable and meaningful.

For the purpose of finding meaning in my life, I have chosen to look at this topic. I read somewhere that life is encyclical and not linear. In order to become complete or whole, one has to take into account one's past or learn from one's history and experiences. Some have even gone as far as stating that 'history is therapeutic'. And it is this that I hope to gain from writing my story. It would be impossible to do justice to all that could be remembered, so what I have written is but a slice of that short period of time.

Looking through the list of autobiographies in the library for directions in writing my own story, I was hesitant. I felt insignificant and feared that my story might not be interesting enough. In fact, it was the titles of the books that determined my choice. I like Sidney Poitier from his films and Mahatma Gandhi from history. Now having read their stories I found that threads of their experiences resonate with my own.

In his *Memoir* (2000), Poitier's preoccupation was to write about 'life itself'.[4] He had dealt with his Hollywood life in his first book. Now at 70 he had the compelling desire to put into writing how he had lived all those years. He explored his childhood memories on Cat Island and the values he had acquired at that formative period from his family and environment. For instance, failure in tomato farming caused his family to move from Cat Island in the Bahamas to the capital city of Nassau. At the age of 15, Poitier again left for Miami, Florida and then New York to follow his dream. His dream was to get into the film industry. Again in the evening of life, he wished to take stock by closely examining how he had fared in living up to the values he had set for himself especially in the areas of 'integrity' and 'commitment', 'faith' and 'forgiveness', 'simplicity' and 'joy'. I can identify with Poitier's growing up in an island environment. He left home to follow his dream. I had to leave home to follow the dream of my parents and in doing so I had unexpectedly found my own. As he grew he took stock of how he had lived up to his values. Now at this time in my life I am looking back to assess where I have been and what I have done in order to deepen my understanding of the call I have received and readily embraced.

The second autobiography that caught my attention was Gandhi's.[5] He wanted it to be called *The Story of My Experiments with Truth* (1927). Since India was still under the British at the time, Gandhi did his law studies in England and then worked in South Africa before returning to India. He was encouraged by his friends to write his story but Gandhi's primary aim was to tell the story of his many experiments with truth. From his spiritual path he gained the strength to carry out his work in the political arena. Like great men and women in the history of humankind who had lived life to the full through service of others, Gandhi did not credit these experiments to himself only. For this reason he hoped that all who read his story would find something useful for their own life's journeys.

He echoed St Paul, that great apostle to the Gentiles, in his striving to capture Christ. All aspects of his life—speech, writing, 'non-violence', 'celibacy' and other forms of conduct—were aimed at 'self-realisation' or winning salvation. Gandhi's deep reverence of God made him realise his own unworthiness. To Gandhi the chief principle is truth which involves truthfulness in words and thought. Like Poitier, Gandhi was aware of the vulnerability of the human condition. Just as Gandhi left India to complete his studies in London, so I went to study in Kiribati when the Gilbert and Ellice Islands were a British colony and stayed to work there. Like Gandhi who experimented with truth, so I am carrying out research, to search for truth, my truth. As Gandhi strove to win salvation through the practice of non-violence, celibacy and other forms of good conduct, so I value celibacy and other forms of good conduct because I have faith in God and I believe there is an after-life.

Beloved Infidel (1959), is the autobiography of Sheila Graham (Lily Sheil),[6] who came from the slums of East London. Raised in an orphanage, at 14 she had to go home to care for her mother who was suffering from cancer. Lily had an ambition to be wealthy and well connected. To every man who showed interest in her she told a made-up story about her family background. She could not retract the family she had made up for herself, even the phony photos on the wall. She married a man 20 years older than herself and enlisted as a show girl. Young and beautiful, she was pursued by many men from high society. The couple's financial difficulties led to Lily's departure for Hollywood to try her luck as a newspaper writer. There she met F. Scott Fitzgerald whom she grew to love deeply. He became the only one who knew about her and her pretences. They were not able to marry since Fitzgerald's 'wife was in an institution and [he had] a daughter who still needed him'. Among the many things Lily learnt from Fitzgerald was 'an appreciation of literature'. It was he who encouraged her to write her own story and after his death she did.

Lily was so grief-stricken after Fitzgerald's sudden death that she returned to England. At the time she co-authored her own autobiography with George Frank, she was married with two grown-up children. Her fear of public opinion had prevented her from writing her story earlier; and then there had been her children to consider. Gradually as her children grew up, she found the courage to tell them the truth about her background. Fitzgerald's struggle with his dark side, his drinking, which he conquered towards the end of his life, gave Lily the courage to write her story. I can say I share Lily's fear of public opinion. In this seemingly promiscuous character, Lily, with her outrageous lies about her background, feared being found out. I feared sharing my desire to become a Catholic and further a nun because of my Protestant background. I feared my parents and public opinion because in those days there was much bigotry among the members of these two churches.

The Autobiography of Mother Jones (1980) is the story of a brave and courageous woman of action, fired with zeal to champion the cause of miners.[7] Mary Harris Jones was of Irish origin and a teacher and dressmaker by trade. She lost her husband and son in the yellow fever plague of 1867 in New York. Her memoires tell of her trade union activities. She lived in Chicago but her work took her all round the United States and West Indies. She supported various efforts to build labour solidarity among railroad workers and miners. She worked for the abolition of child labour, especially for miners' daughters who were employed in the mill for 10 hours every day. She gave talks and supported miners' strikes for better wages and to cut down daily working hours to eight. She wrote her story at the request of friends when she was a very old woman. These same friends who knew her from her work helped put the events in chronological order. But her personal story was very much bound up with the national history of trade unions in the United States from 1868-1924. She made history and her story is an inspiration. I admire this brave woman. I found in her story a woman who was totally selfless. I share in the element of being for others through a particular and unique way of life, the religious life. Through my vow of chastity I have given up the power of having a family of my own so that I may be totally available for the mission of the Congregation within the Catholic Church; through Obedience the power to direct my own life, and through Poverty I own nothing and have to ask for what I need.

Kanaka Boy (1985) is an autobiography by Sir Frederick Osefilo, published by the Institute of Pacific Studies, Suva, and the University of the South Pacific Centre, Honiara, the Solomon Islands.[8] Beginning with the author's childhood, the story moved from school, to World War II in the Solomons, his work in the colonial service and Independence, ending with his discovery of faith. I enjoyed reading about Osefilo's culture, which was very different from my own.

I found it fascinating to see how these five people in their autobiographies were so engrossed with life. Their stories made me question myself. Did I make conscious choices in my life or did I just float with the tide? I like the way Sidney Poitier reflected on his life as a little boy on Cat Island; he had all the time in the world to explore, to think his own thoughts and to observe his family, the people around him and his environment. To him this was the very 'first part of his education'. Here on Cat Island and Nassau where he learned his values, the very values that steadied his course in the excitement and storms of life and against the adverse racial winds of the United States. Even in religious life, one cannot escape racial discrimination. Living very closely together sometimes the very diversity of backgrounds can become a huge cross. I share these authors' search for truth. I admire their humility and courage in facing their truth.

While Poitier, Gandhi and Osefilo were decisive from the outset, Lily was fearful at first. Being able to share her truth with Fitzgerald liberated her from her fears of being found out. On the other hand Fitzgerald, though he was well known and had no reason to hide his family background, had a dark side that not everyone knew. This was his drinking—his 'demon'. From this Lily learnt that her pretences, her made-up family background and false family photos were her 'demons'. Just as Fitzgerald conquered his drinking for her friendship, so did she write her story for him. By contrast we have in Mother Jones, who reached 100, someone who always lived her truth in fighting the cause of the downtrodden. She was the picture of total availability and selflessness in the service of others.

In writing my story, I speculated a great deal on why my parents and grandparents sent me to school. For me this question is basic. I can remember thinking that my grandparents could get me out of it, but that did not happen. It seemed to me I was being 'ganged-up' against. Today, in retrospect, I can say that they must have wanted me to make a 'better life', one that would be different from their own. Having come from a Protestant island where church services and prayer times were regulated and very much part of the fabric of daily existence, I chose another religious life when the time came for me to decide.

1963-1968 Te Po o Tefolaha — Departure Day!

I left Nanumea on 8 January 1963, *Te Po o Tefolaha* (the day of Tefolaha). Tefolaha was the ancestor the Nanumeans regarded as the founder of the island. This great Tongan warrior drove out two women, Pai and Vau, who were the first settlers on Nanumea. Tefolaha is believed to have left behind three sons to whom all the inhabitants of Nanumea trace their descent. The church term for *Te Po oTefolaha* is Asopati. This day is commemorated every year because it was the day Nanumea embraced Christianity brought by the London Missionary Society through the Samoan pastors. It is celebrated on 7-8 January. In significance it equals Christmas Day and New Year. The people assemble in the *ahiga* (public hall), feasting and having games and, in the evening, dancing and contributing money throughout the night. The church welcomes those who wish to receive the Body and Blood of Jesus Christ in a special service held every month after the usual Sunday service. Looking back I cannot remember what happened on these big days of that last year of 1962. I remember deciding to dance (local dancing) the night out; it is the decision that I can remember, but whether I actually did dance or not, I cannot. Towards the morning, I remember going home to sleep hoping to miss the *Santa Teresa*, the Catholic Mission ship, from the Gilberts. Our house was full, there were people coming and going all the time. I was woken to get ready for the ship. Departure time had come and I was too sad even to think. How I wished I did not have to leave behind those I loved. Since it was my first time to leave home, I was heartbroken; and going to Kiribati was like going to the end of the earth! I was crying, my mother was crying and my grandmother was crying. Though there were others there, I do not remember the faces even of those who kissed me goodbye. My father took me to the ship on his canoe with three other men. I did not shed a tear when I said goodbye to my father. I held him responsible for my going away so I had no tear for him. He had explained that no one would accompany me to Tarawa because Viane had arranged that his two brothers on the ship, one the captain, the other a crew member, would look after his three children—his eldest daughter Taeaniti, Ioane, Teresa—and myself.

The Trip to Tarawa

The trip to Tarawa took a whole week. We arrived on Beru on our third day at sea. I was as sick as a dog. I vomited all the way there. We went ashore and were welcomed by a number of families. I took for granted that they were Viane's relatives because Beru was his home island. We were back on the boat before dark and arrived at Tabiteuea where the ship stayed for two days. We were taken to Buota village by a woman whose husband was away in Nauru. On Tabiteuea, I noticed that young girls of my age were going round with grass skirts only. Our caretaker wore the same grass skirt and *tibuta* every day. Because there were four of us the woman came with us to sleep in the *maneaba*. It seemed other people sleeping there all the time. We used mosquito nets because the mosquitoes were bad. The woman was very kind: she made us new clothes. I realised then that people were wearing grass skirts not because of lack of clothing or money, but because that was the ordinary daily wear.

Before boarding the ship Ioane, Viane's son, and I were standing outside the church in Tanaeang, the Catholic centre on Tabiteuea North. He was trying to show me the church. It was made of thick cement walls with its white paint wearing off. While looking at the sanctuary, a Sister entered and she seemed to be fixing something around the altar and then disappeared to the back. Ioane said, 'See that's what the Sisters do. They pray every day and look after the church'. I did not have anything to say.

Nonouti was our next stop. Here the Sisters were on the beach to meet the new arrivals. Taeaniti could not make me approach the Sisters to say hello. I walked in the other direction. They were dressed in white long dresses that reached to their ankles, with long sleeves, and veils which seemed like hats showing only their eyes to their chins. Their ears were well hidden away. Here, too, in Nonouti I attended my first Mass. The Sisters ran a primary school in the Catholic station and had girl boarders with them. These girls took good care of us. We only spent a day here. By evening we were back on the ship and left for Abemama. We went ashore at Manoku only for the day. It was a relief to be able to go ashore because I was so sick on the ship. Though the ship spent the night in Abemama, the four of us had to return to the ship for the night by order of the Captain. The last stop was Kuria. Viane had another brother living there with his family. They were very kind to us. We finally reached Tarawa on 16 January. We stayed in the Captain's home in Teaoraereke, the headquarters of the Catholic Mission.

First School

When school started, I went in as a boarder and was put in Standard 4. There were quite a number of Sisters in Teaoraereke, but Sister Ursula Begley, Irish, and Sister Callistus Flynn, an Australian, were the only two involved with the school. Boarders came from other villages on Tarawa and from the outer islands. The day students were from Teaoraereke village. Classes were Standards 1-4 and three classes in the Infants' Section. In Standard 4 the girls sat the entrance exams at the end of the year to Immaculate Heart College, Taborio, and the boys to St Joseph's College, Tabwiroa, Abaiang and the government secondary schools: Elaine Bernacchi School for girls and King George V for boys, both in Bikenibeu. I found the girls very kind, and we communicated in English as I could not speak a word of Kiribati. The radio had just arrived and every Sunday afternoon Sister Callistus sent for me to listen to the news in the Ellice language. I would be the only one in the parlour because the other three Ellice Island girls could speak Kiribati and they joined the others for the news in the Gilbertese language. One day we were called to see the first bus on Tarawa. The causeway between Nanikai and Teaoraereke had just been completed and the bus was on its first trip up to Bikenibeu. It was a big truck that had been furnished with long seats painted white, and had support posts along the sides to hold up the top as shelter from the sun and rain. I was still in Teaoraereke when I received my first letter from my parents. I took my letter and went off on my own to sit under the trees. To this day I do not remember what I read in that letter, but I was crying my eyes out. The Sisters came to hear of it and sent for me.

'Did you receive any bad news?' Sister asked.

I replied, 'No Sister'.

Sitting down with me she said, 'If there is no bad news, why so much tears?'

I said, 'I am just sad and very homesick, Sister. This is my first letter from my parents'. She spent some time talking to me and then called one of the big girls and sent me off with her.

The Nuns and *Te Buaka*

Because Teaoraereke was the headquarters of the Catholic Mission, there were many comings and goings during that first term. Sisters and priests from the outer islands came in on business and then disappeared back to their stations. Sister Ursula had to leave to take up responsibilities of the school in Marakei because Sister Dennis O'Shea was going on leave and Sister Ursula was replaced by Sister John Bosco Donnelly from Immaculate Heart, Taborio. One day Sister Oliva Glynn visited from Taborio. The girls were all calling her 'Mother'. To me she looked ancient and forbidding. When I finally got close enough to hear her talk she talked in a quiet way and did not waste words but she had the most beautiful smile. What I remember most about my term in Teaoraereke was the salt fish I had to eat, the long singing practice and the kind Sisters and girls. Every Saturday we went to the movie in the school field.

'What is the movie tonight?' I asked my friends.

They answered in the Kiribati language, *te buaka*.

I was thrilled because *te puaka* in my language is a pig. I went off to the movie eager to see a pig or pigs. Sitting there with my eyes glued on the screen I saw people being shot dead or people shooting at each other and killing going on non-stop. I closed my eyes because I could not stomach watching people being killed in the film. Crossly, I asked my friends, 'Where is *te puaka*?

They said, 'Open your eyes and see—what is going on'.

So it dawned on me then that *te buaka* meant war. During Holy Week Sister Christine Clark took me shopping with her since I was a non-Catholic and Holy Thursday and Good Friday did not mean much to me. We travelled on the Mission launch from Teaoraereke to Betio. I found Betio hot and we had to walk from place to place as there were hardly any cars. After Easter I was told to get my things ready to leave for Taborio. The Sisters said to me, 'Taborio is better for you. There are more Ellice girls there and the girls speak English in school. You do not need to learn Kiribati'.

I travelled with Sister John Bosco who was going back to Taborio for a week's holiday.

Immaculate Heart College, Taborio

That was where I was going when I left home. Taborio is situated on three and a half hectares of land surrounded by sea on all sides or reef-mud at low tide except where it is joined onto Nootoue village on its southern end. It was a girls' school of just over a hundred boarders, and conducted by the Sisters of the Congregation of the Daughters of Our Lady of the Sacred Heart. There was nothing spectacular about the place except for its timetable. Girls spoke English at all times except for one hour after afternoon work. When I arrived in Taborio there were Forms 1-4 but in the following year Form 4 was phased out and the Colonial Form 3 examination was introduced. This examination was taken by Form 3 in the five secondary schools in the Gilbert and Ellice Islands Colony. The subjects included: English, Arithmetic, History, Geography and Health Science. The girls also learnt needlework, typing, singing, music (musical instruments, recorders, mouth organ and others). A primary section was attached to the school with just three Classes 2, 3 and 4 for limited numbers only. The primary section was phased out in 1965, the year I left. Drama and figure-marching were very much part of Taborio in those days: drama for the College's prize-giving at the end of the year and figure-marching for its annual sports day in early August. Extracurricular activities in a school depended on the talents and generosity of staff. There were only four Sisters, and didn't they work hard!

The girls in Taborio came from all over the Colony, the majority from the Catholic islands of Butaritari, Abaiang, Tabiteuea and Tarawa. The Ellice girls were mostly daughters of government workers from South Tarawa or those whose parents were working on the phosphate mines on Ocean Island and Nauru.

The day began with a 'call', a prayer and then Mass. Charges were followed by breakfast and then school. After lunch, there was a break of an hour and then study and the afternoon lesson. There was work followed by drama and music. After charges were the evening meal, prayer, study and bed. The lights went out at 9.30. The weekend programme was slightly different. Saturday morning was general cleaning, and the midday meal was held outside in the open as the dining room was still wet after the scrub. There was personal washing and sports. The school's four teams competed against each other: Fatima, Lourdes, Carmel and Issoudun. The games were basketball, volleyball, tennis, other ball games, and races. The afternoon charges were usually weeding and watering the gardens, serving the meals, and getting firewood from the bush. After the evening meal were prayers and the movie. The movie was the highlight of the week. For this reason the girls tried to speak English because one would get bad marks for speaking Kiribati. With more than three bad marks one would stay in the classroom to do homework while the rest enjoyed the movie. The Sunday programme was more relaxed. After Mass at nine in the morning was singing with Father Hirsch, a French MSC, the parish priest for North Tarawa and the College, who taught us hymns. After lunch there were sports for those interested, reading for the bookworms and letter-writing to parents and penfriends.

Conversion — First Signs

In the school there was what we called an 'Honour Roll'. Each girl received ten points every week. Marks were deducted for not speaking English, arriving late for or disturbing study. Good marks were awarded for extra efforts at speaking English, being helpful and generous around the place. This was done every Friday evening at a meeting with the principal. The girl with the highest points on the Honour Roll was crowned Our Lady at her feast on 31 May. She received the prize for conduct at the end of the year. Also every year, a visiting priest gave us a weekend retreat.

The Sisters usually put out many religious books for us to read during the retreat. For the first time I encountered the riches of the Catholic Church in the lives of these young girl martyrs. I enjoyed reading their lives, especially that of St Barbara, whose father secluded her in a tower. Barbara studied and prayed and was rewarded with the gift of faith. Secretly she received baptism from a Catholic priest. When her father learnt of it he was indignant and had her handed over to the magistrate for torture and execution.[9] St Cecilia had consecrated her life to God before she was given to Valerian in marriage. Through prayers she won her husband over to God; and because of this she was thrown into a fire that did not burn her and in the end her head was cut off.[10] St Agnes refused an offer of marriage and was subjected to ill-treatment until she was put to the sword.[11] St Philomena, because of a vow she had made to belong to God alone refused the marriage proposal of a prince from another area in Italy. Her father disowned her and she was tortured to death.[12] These are but a few of the many martyrs whose lives I read. I admired their courage, their love of God and the manifestation of their faith. It was from these courageous young women that I received the inspiration to go against my parents in my 'fight' to become a Catholic. It was at this time, too, that I began to think about religious life. I was not yet a Catholic and I also knew the problems I would have to face. In one of his talks during the retreat, Father Rinn, MSC, was trying to explain the parable of the wedding feast where the bridegroom found one of his guests not dressed in a wedding garment.[13] Father kept repeating, 'No one can do it for you; you have to do it yourself'. The message for me then was the way to heaven is not automatic. I had to respond to God's grace in working out my own salvation.

The life of the 'Little Flower', St Therese of Lisieux truly inspired me to give my life to God.[14] That was when I heard the call to religious life, but because I was not a Catholic I felt silly in sharing this with anybody. Also I feared my parents. St Therese's little way of doing everything, small things for love of God, touched me deeply. This was something I could do, so I thought to myself. My mother's words rang in my ears: 'You are going to school and not to become a Catholic'. During religion class, Sister was reading to us a passage from the Gospel: '… what would profit a man if he gains the whole world and suffers the loss of his soul?'[15] This further confirmed for me that I had to follow my call. In trying to help me decide about a career, this Sister advised me that I would go further and obtain a higher salary if I worked for the government. After hearing that passage from the Gospel, I could not. I had already decided in my heart to stay in the Catholic Church. I had good friends in school who taught me to say certain prayers besides praying with me. I found the principal very approachable, firm but caring and interested in every student. She was an excellent teacher.

Changes in the Church

The 1960s saw a number of changes in the Catholic Church in Kiribati. When I first arrived, the Mass was still said in Latin. With the death of Pope John XXIII and his successor, Paul VI, there followed a number of visible changes. The Mass was translated into English and the Kiribati languages and the priests started to say it in the vernacular. The Sisters' habits also became simplified. We began to learn the hymns normally sung in Latin in the vernacular. This was Father Hirsch's domain. He was very musical and fluent in the Kiribati language. He was a kindly person who was patient with us during choir practice.

I settled down in Taborio and began to enjoy school life. In August 1963 my father signed up for indenture on the phosphate mine on Nauru. In the few talks we had before I left, my father had said, 'Alaima, when you have gone to school in Tarawa, I shall leave this job in the same year for Nauru. What I earn here is just enough for us here; but not enough for you in school and us here as well'. My father kept his word and I was not in any kind of need in school. I did very well in school and chose not to continue to do Forms 4 and 5 at the government secondary school in Bikenibeu. Instead, I went to the Tarawa Teachers' College (TTC). When I was accepted, I had to make up my mind whether I would teach for the Catholic Mission or for the government. I decided to teach for the Catholic Mission.

Tarawa Teachers' College

I found the Teachers' College challenging in many ways. Our group was made up of students from Taborio, Tabwiroa, King George V and Elaine Bernacchi and Hiram Bingham, Rongorongo, Beru. Since we were admitted from Form 3, ours was a three-year course. Those students who were admitted from Form 5 and those who had been abroad on scholarships in New Zealand or Australia followed a two year course and therefore joined whatever group was in their second year at the time of their entrance. We entered in 1966, the year after the main building was completed and opened. Members of staff were mostly English and two locals for the vernacular, the Kiribati and Tuvalu languages. In all, there were 60 students: 30 boys and 30 girls. In TTC I kept company with the Taborio girls and continued to attend Mass and religious instruction for Catholic students. Gradually I began to enjoy life and made new friends. I still wanted to become a religious.

In the Christmas holidays of 1966, the *Santa Teresa* went to Nauru, and Takenrerei Taukoriri, Bwebwenteiti Tebwebwe, Ioanna Ben Kum Kee and I took the trip to visit our parents who worked there. The trip to Banaba took three days and we stopped there for several days before setting off for Nauru. Banaba and Nauru are raised coral islands, and from the ship it appeared we were looking up at them. On Banaba we met some ex-Taborio students who were working as typists for the British Phosphate Company, and as nurses in the hospital. We were also able to catch up with our relations from our home islands. We stayed for Christmas and the New Year in Nauru.

In my second year in TTC, Sister Berness Claxton joined the staff. Her fields were maths and education. We met over a boyfriend I had whom she thought was too old for me and too much of a playboy. She even told him to leave me alone. She became someone I could trust. She was the very first person with whom I shared my desire to be a religious. She listened attentively and offered encouragement every now and then but did not push me. From then on, we began a friendship that lasted till her death in 1990. In my last year at TTC, Air Nauru began flights to Tarawa. My parents invited me over for the Christmas holidays. I was apprehensive about going because I was finishing from TTC and my parents could keep me in Nauru. Sister Berness advised me to go and see my parents and I must trust God to get me out of Nauru. Consoled by such words, I had my first trip by plane at the end of 1968 after graduation from the Tarawa Teachers' College.

Just as I had feared, my parents wished me to stay and work in Nauru. They had already approached the principal of the location school for a teaching position for me, but my father's boss had advised him not to keep me in Nauru but to let me return to work in Kiribati. My father wanted me to go and see his boss, an Australian, to ask him to let me stay. I told my father that I could not do it. One day my father asked me who was writing to me from Australia and Hong Kong. My little brothers just loved going through my things, my bag and my suitcase and they had shown him my letters. Because the letters were in English he could not really understand the content. I told my father who my correspondent was. He was from Nanumea but at that time was studying abroad. My father expressed his displeasure at the thought of having him as my future husband. He had nothing against him as a person but he preferred I did not marry into that family. To me he was a good friend but there was nothing serious. Then he said, 'You do not have to get married if you do not want to'. I was surprised to hear that from him.

On New Year's celebration some cousins of my father were at our house. In front of my parents one of them said to me: 'You can stay in Kiribati to work for as long as you wish. When you have had enough you come home to Nanumea. We shall choose a husband for you. We will make sure that you settle down well into your new home. If not, we shall take you back'. This I found disturbing for I was not ready to have anyone choose a husband for me but I also knew they could. This confirmed for me that it would be better to become a nun. When they had gone and my parents said no more about the matter, I assumed they agreed with them. One evening the Kiribati catechist on Nauru saw my name in the Catholic *Itoi ni Kiribati* (Catholic quarterly newsletter) among the Catholic teachers for the New Year 1969. In joy he poured out his heart to my father saying how happy he was that I was going to teach for the Catholic Mission even though I was not yet a Catholic. My father listened but was shocked as he was not aware of this. At home he quietly told me to change from the Catholic Mission to the government school. On this note I returned to Tarawa. It was not a pretty scene. In their displeasure my father cried and my mother was furious.

Back in Kiribati, I went to see the Chief Education Officer, Mr Urqhart. I thought he could make the change for me so I would not have to bother the Catholic Education Office. He was the principal of TTC in my first year and he used to give us oral English lessons. In fact he was not pleased with my visit nor the subject I discussed with him. He told me so. I sought the Catholic Director of Education, Sister Mary John Bosco Donnelly and Sister Berness. After much discussion Sister John Bosco and I went to see Bishop Peter Guichet, MSC. Sister tried to explain my problem with my parents to the Bishop. After listening to Sister, the Bishop simply asked me, 'Do you want to teach for the Mission or for the government?' I replied from my heart, 'For the Mission'. That was the end of our interview. He turned to Sister and stated: 'She stays in the Mission'.

1969-1972 — First Teaching Experience

My first teaching post was Immaculate Heart, Taborio! I was thrilled even though my training was for the primary level. Among the Sisters, four were for the College and the fifth one was for St Dominic's primary school in the village. The principal, Sister Veronica Hollis, taught me in my last year as well as the principal when I was in school. Among the other three Sisters was Sister Mary Gormley who had also taught me. I really enjoyed my three years in Taborio. I enjoyed working with the Sisters as well as the students. In mid 1971 we said goodbye to Sister Veronica and Sister Nora Hanrahan who had won scholarships to study in Nova Scotia. Also at this time we had the sad tragic loss at sea of Sister John Bosco Donnelly and Sister Rita Mary Skinner and the boatmen who were travelling with them.

Conversion to the Catholic Church

In 1970 I asked to be admitted into the Catholic Church. The present Bishop, Paul Mea, MSC, was the parish priest of North Tarawa. He gave me catechism lessons to prepare me for admission into the Catholic Church. That memorable day fell on 22 October 1970 and I was confirmed on the Sunday of that same week. I did not ask my parents but informed them when they again invited me to go over to Nauru for the Christmas holidays. I must have shocked them tremendously because they stopped writing. The following year brought me a letter from my mother. She just wanted me to know she was very disappointed and displeased with what I had done. I wrote back apologising and then told them that what I was doing was not a bad thing and would they please trust me.

Why I Became a Catholic

As a young girl far from home, far from parental guidance, I found the Sisters' teaching substantial, genuine and meaningful. They did not only teach in the classroom but they were personally involved with us outside class. I felt they were interested in my life and nurtured me as best they could. For instance, they made me listen to the radio in my language. When they discovered I felt isolated they sent me to Taborio where there were other Ellice Island girls. All these efforts gave me a sense of belonging and identity. There was a strong tendency within me to identify with what I was learning since the desire for identity and a sense of belonging is strong at that age. I found this identity in the Sisters and in the lives of those early martyrs I read about during my school days. They say that 'God can write on crooked lines'. It certainly was true in my case. Amidst all my adversities, loneliness and emptiness and the longing to be loved by my parents, somehow I sensed that God was watching over me and drawing me to a call I wanted to embrace. The call had a dual dimension. It was primarily the call to embrace the Catholic faith, and secondly the call to the religious life. These two calls were no small challenge particularly for one with a Protestant background like myself. It meant going against my parents. This brought a lot of unhappiness to me because I knew that my parents strongly disapproved of my 'conversion'. However, like the simple girl that I was with a simple faith, I plucked up courage and took the necessary steps for my own inner peace of mind and heart. I felt my call was a very personal response to God's personal love for me and my desire to follow a way of life that would enable me to serve others, fulfill my aspirations, and enrich my purpose in this life.

The following year I asked to become a nun, a Carmelite. Sister Oliva Glynn kindly informed me that if I wanted to become a Carmelite I should go to Samoa instead of Papua New Guinea. One of the Kiribati Sisters of the local Order, the Sisters of St Teresa, had gone to Papua and New Guinea to join the Carmelites there. She had returned and rejoined the Sisters of St Teresa. Samoa would be better for me. To me at that time Samoa was too far away and I could not imagine it. Then she said, 'Why don't you join us?' I said, 'Oh, no. You work too hard'. She laughed and said, 'But you are doing it'. I did not take long to think about it because in that same year I wrote to Sister Marie Timbs, who was in charge of aspirants in Sydney, to be admitted into the Novitiate. There were two of us, Witake Tawita and myself. We left for Sydney on Easter Monday of 1972.

The Novitiate: 1972-1975

Five of us entered on that same date. Anne Ihlein, Anne Searson and Catherine Howard were Australians, Witake Tawita and myself from Kiribati and Tuvalu. After the feast of the Sacred Heart in June 1972, we were joined by an American girl, Dale Maxwell. All of us had been teaching with the exception of Cathy Howard who had come straight from Year 12. Five Sisters made up the Novitiate staff—the Novice mistress, her assistant, the Music and Sewing mistress, the Sister in the kitchen and the Sister who gave us Theology. There are two parts in the Novitiate, the first one is the postulancy where we were gradually introduced into religious life. We learnt about the Order, its spirit, charism, prayer and lectio-divina and mission. Work consisted of cleaning, laundry, gardening and cooking. Once a week we went to Mater Dei in North Sydney to attend talks on Scriptures, Prayer and the Vows with Postulants and Novices from other Congregations. The Novitiate also invited speakers from other Congregations to give talks especially on Scripture, Theology and Church history.

Since we were to make our vows to live religious life according to the Constitutions of the Order, we had to learn the Constitutions by heart. That was a time of learning about the Congregation and discerning if religious life was for me. On the other hand, the Congregation tested and discerned if I was suitable for religious life.

After six months in the postulancy we were accepted into the Novitiate programme. The first year in the Novitiate is also called the canonical year when the Novice starts on the religious path, as it were. As an external sign we wore a simple religious dress with a veil which we received on our reception day. We studied in some depth the constitutions of the Daughters of Our Lady of the Sacred Heart and tried to apply it in our daily lives. It is during the canonical year that a novice is confined to the Novitiate and is not allowed to leave the Novitiate for any length of time. In the Novitiate I used to think that we were always praying and working. Silence was to be observed at all times except at recreation after the evening meal and sometimes in the afternoon when we were out in the garden. Also on big feast days we would be given extra recreation time. This silence does not mean that we could not talk if we had to. There was the monthly retreat on the first Friday of every month as well as the annual eight-day retreat before and after Christmas. Usually when we came off retreat we would go to visit the old people at Harbison Home in Bowral. It did not take long to walk there.

In the three years I was in the Novitiate we used to prepare the place for the Sisters coming in from the missions—from PNG, Kiribati, the Philippines, Port Keats, Thursday Island, and Darwin where they worked as teachers, nurses or social workers. They usually came to Hartzer Park Novitiate to make the eight-day retreat. I used to look forward to seeing those great missionaries at the end of the year. When Hartzer had calmed down and all the retreatants had left we all went to Austinmer in early February on the coast of Woollongong for 10 days' holiday. There we slept, swam, ate, wrote letters and went for long walks. That was our holiday for the year before plunging into the new year's programme. Sometimes the Novice mistress gave us some quiet days to catch up with unfinished homework and to write home. I wrote to my parents every month, trying to share with them as best as I could what I was doing in the Novitiate. I tried to tell them about the application of the vows in my life after the Novitiate. My father wrote to me but not my mother. He did not say much beyond keeping me posted with family news.

The second year of the Novitiate is spent preparing for first profession, when the Novice makes a public profession of the simple vows of chastity, poverty and obedience. So I was in the Novitiate from 9 April 1972 to 12 January 1975, when I made my first profession. Dale left the Novitiate for good at the end of 1973 and Anne Searson in March 1974 due to illness. After she recuperated she re-entered the Novitiate when it moved to Manila in 1982. Again her sickness returned and she was able to make her vows just before she died in 1984. Sister Anne Ihlein's and Sister Catherine Howard's families came for their profession. For Sister Rotia Tawita and me, some Sisters from Kiribati came. A few days after that memorable day, Sister Rotia and I left for Melbourne by train to catch Air Nauru back to Kiribati.

One setback in the joy of 'coming home' was that the Gilberts and Ellice Islands were separating. I had heard talk of separation before leaving for Australia, but I did not realise it would be so soon. I was glad I was able to see some of my relatives before they left, but the impact of the separation stayed with me. It was something that I thought long and hard about in deciding whether to make final vows. In the Novitiate, the novelty of learning about religious life and the knowledge that I was there only for a short time did not make missing home too bad. I knew if I made final vows I would be going home for holidays only. And then how could I practise my faith in Tuvalu? Around September the *M.V. Nivanga* left the Betio wharf for the Ellice Islands, never to return.

Once in Kiribati the two of us were stationed in Teaoraereke, our headquarters. Though we had been professed we were 'the babies' of the Kiribati region and had to be around headquarters at least for our first year in the field. It was my very first year too to teach in primary school and I was given the senior classes—7, 8 and a handful of supposedly Class 9. Our Lady of the Sacred Heart Primary School at the time was a selected school and the teachers were paid by government. Since I had not taught for the government before, my salary was that of a new graduate teacher from the Tarawa Teachers' College. I enjoyed teaching these students as well as my extracurricular duties. I collected the 20c that all the students paid every month for the building of the teachers' houses. Some of the teachers were Mission-trained and had not yet been to the TTC so they were paid by the Church. Their salaries did not amount to much. Whatever funds we raised through extracurricular activities went to the teachers and the construction of houses for them. The school bought a deep-freezer and one of these teachers' wives helped me make ice blocks and sandwiches to sell to students and teachers. Once a year the school raised funds in their teams by selling food they had made. For the Open Day at the end of the school year, the students learnt dancing for the entertainment of their guests and parents. The year went very quickly and after Christmas, New Year and the annual retreat I was assigned to Catholic Junior College, Tabwiroa, Abaiang.

Abaiang is the outer island to the north of Tarawa where I had spent time before. In Tabwiroa there were five Sisters—three Australians, an I-Kiribati and myself. The principal was Sister Veronica Hollis. She had returned from Nova Scotia where she had studied Theology for three years. The other two I also had worked with in Taborio. I was new to Tabwiroa which is far bigger than Taborio. There were four other I-Kiribati teachers and three VSOs. Tabwiroa at that time was a co-ed and catered for Forms 1-3 with two classes for each form. Those who passed the Form 3 examinations would continue either to Catholic Senior College, Taborio or Elaine Bernacchi and King George V, Bikenibeu, to do Forms 4 and 5. In the Christmas holiday of 1977 Sister Rotia and I went back to the Novitiate in Bowral to prepare for renewal of vows early in the following year. We met up with Sister Catherine Howard and Sister Anne Ihlein. The latter made her final vows while the three of us made renewal.

In the Provincial visitation of 1979, Sister Berness, who was then on the Provincial Council in Australia, was part of the team that came to Kiribati. Since I had not been home at all she advised me to go home to see my parents. I was due for final vows the following year. I had come to a point where I could no longer postpone seeing my parents. I went, but in my heart I was scared. I was afraid of my parents. I did not know how they would receive me. My grandparents had passed away. Were I going home to see them, I would have had no fear. Even if I had committed the worst crime on God's earth, I still would fear nothing from my grandparents. Such was my certainty of their love and acceptance of me. But I had always seen my parents as forbidding and formidable. I was never sure of myself when with them. Had I grown up with them or had they not given me away to my grandparents when I was small, perhaps I would have felt differently. Perhaps I would have been assured of their love.

When I got to Funafuti, the main island in Tuvalu, I waited for the country's only ship to go on its trip to the northern islands. I had a month's holiday and it was almost two weeks before *Nivanga* left. Because it had to call on two other islands to drop passengers and cargo, as well as pick up those bound for Funafuti, the whole trip to Nanumea would take almost a week. To wait on Nanumea for the next trip was another two weeks. Perhaps I could have taken the time to give myself one month at home, but I did not think of it. I meticulously counted the month from the day I left Tarawa to the day when I should get back. For the life of me I do not know why I thought like that. I did not give myself time nor did I give my parents time. I did this on each of my trips home every four years. Yet the first time I went home after they had both left this world, I took three months. Looking back now I do not know who I was punishing, my parents or myself.

I did not let them know I was coming for a holiday. Members of the extended family on Funafuti sent many messages from the time I arrived on Funafuti to let my parents know I was on my way. Tuvalu is a Protestant country and on achieving independence in 1978 had called its church, the Church of Tuvalu. In a small place like that, a nun, even if she is a Tuvaluan, became something of a curiosity to the people. I regarded the stares rude and I preferred to stay in the house all the time. When I finally reached Nanumea, my parents had prepared for my arrival and this is why looking back I am sad I did not stay, even if it had meant going over the normal holiday time. The ship arrived during the night and the captain let me go ashore with the Minister in the Tuvalu House of Parliament, Maheu Naniseni, my mother's cousin. With the familiar smell of food I knew then all was well. My parents had been preparing for my arrival. They had just turned down the lantern to go to sleep thinking passengers would be coming ashore in the morning. It was a happy reunion and after telling stories for awhile, we slept. Little did I know, that was my only time with my parents.

The next morning I wanted to go everywhere. I wanted to see everything—even Lakena, the islet where I had lived with my grandparents. When I returned to the house it was noon and the extended family had gathered. I wanted very much to see my parents alone but I realised there was no time. Then from among the people sitting there, a lady cousin of my father spoke up. From the many things she said I could remember only one. 'You go back to Tarawa and when your vows are expired in January, we shall meet here when you return.' I knew then I could not tell my parents my news. When I left in my heart I said goodbye because I was not sure if my parents would want to see my face again. I had meant to tell my parents that I wanted to make final profession.

Final profession in Kiribati is a big event because it involves the Sisters' families. I wrote to my parents explaining that I was making my final vows and I did not invite them. Because I did not invite my parents I could not bring myself to invite anyone of my relations either. Sister Rotia's family came from Abaiang and because they had known me from there they included me in their preparations. They were very kind. Somehow my relatives on South Tarawa must have heard because they got together and prepared food for the feast after Mass. Some of them even came to the Mass, participated in the liturgy and the feast in the *maneaba*. I was very grateful for what they did. Their presence made me feel good. I was not alone after all. I was home!

ENDNOTES

[1] Barrie Macdonald, *Cindarellas of the Empire: towards a history of Kiribati and Tuvalu* (Canberra 1982), 31.

[2] Ibid., 50; U.F. Neemia, 'Tuvaluans in Kiribati', Research Paper (mimeo).

[3] Gilbert and Ellice Islands Colony, *Memorandum on Post-War Reorganisation Administrative Policy*.

[4] Sidney Poitier, *The Measure of a Man: a memoir* (London 2000).

[5] M. K. Gandhi, *An Autobiography or the Story of My Experiments with Truth* (Ahmedabad 1927).

[6] Sheila Graham and Gerald Frank, *Beloved Infidel: the education of a woman* (London 1959).

[7] Mary Field Parton (ed.) *The Autobiography of Mother Jones* (Chicago 1980).

[8] Sir Frederick Osifelo, *Kanaka Boy: an autobiography of Sir Frederick Osefilo* (Suva 1985).

[9] Henry Sebastian Bowden of the Oratory (comp.), *Miniature Lives of the Saints (with Reflections for Every Day in the Year)*, ed. and rev. by Donald Attwater (London 1960), 559.

[10] Ibid., 529.

[11] Ibid., 31.
[12] Ibid.
[13] Mtt 22.12.
[14] Bowden, *Miniature Lives of the Saints*, 447.
[15] Mtt.16.26.

Chapter 10

Researching, (W)riting, Releasing, and Responses to a Biography of Queen Salote of Tonga

Elizabeth Wood-Ellem

Researching Queen Salote was *not* my first foray into biography. I was employed as a book editor for five years in Sydney and then nine years in London. In 1969 Macmillan London decided to move the editorial department from Little Essex Street—just about equidistant between the Thames, the Law Courts, Fleet Street, and the Middle Temple (and only 20 minutes walk from the National Gallery and other delights)—to Basingstoke. Not the Basingstoke of Gilbert and Sullivan (a 'word that teems with hidden meaning'), but a factory town. After the brass handshake from Macmillan, my friend Nick Furbank asked me if I would be his research assistant, as he was writing the biography of the novelist E.M. Forster.

The research was fruitful. After I had spent some time in the British Museum Library (now the British Library), the London Library, and the Colindale Newspaper Library, Forster obligingly died in June 1970. I was then asked to go to King's College in Cambridge and catalogue all Forster's papers, which were to be found in his set of four rooms at King's.

After that initial catalogue for the Forster estate, King's College, the main beneficiary of Forster's will, asked me to do a more detailed catalogue and arrange for the binding of many of the papers. Thus I became the first Archivist of the Modern Manuscripts at King's. I returned to Australia after 15 years abroad just in time to take advantage of Prime Minister Gough Whitlam's abolition of university fees. I was tempted to do something to make up for my lacklustre undergraduate degree, and the idea of doing a postgraduate degree on the late Queen Salote of Tonga came to me in a flash while I was having my hair cut. Well, not quite. My father had written the chapter on Queen Salote for Noel Rutherford's book *Friendly Islands: a history of Tonga*, and asked me if I would do some checking of the dates. So it was a kind of pre-destined flash.

That was the only part of the whole experience that happened with any speed. After a year, my candidature for an MA being converted to a PhD, I felt liberated—able to undertake something I hoped would be significant and fulfilling. I had by then realised that my research was something of a 'roots' exercise, as I had been born in Tonga to missionary parents.

When I submitted my topic to the History Department at the University of Melbourne, I broke many of the rules I now endeavour to impress on students (if any ask my advice): to know your archives before you begin, or at least their locations; whether they have been catalogued of not; whether permission is required; and last but not least what languages the papers are written in. I had an unfounded conviction that my first language (Tongan) would just come back to me once I encountered it again. It didn't.

It came as somewhat of a shock (a) to find very little in any library or archive in Australia about Queen Salote, who had been a mythical figure of my childhood; (b) neither Tongans nor Australians who had lived in Tonga for many years seemed to know very much about anything connected with Tonga.

I had already discovered in a game that some people have astoundingly poor memories of anything that happened more than a week earlier. Others, particularly former missionaries, had acquired a loyalty to the kingdom of Tonga that prevented analysis or criticism. So the myth of the Friendly Islands lives on.

Once in 1974 and twice in 1976, I visited the Western Pacific High Commission Archives in Suva to read their papers. The British High Commissioner (also Governor of Fiji) had oversight over Tonga, the British Solomon Islands Protectorate, the New Hebrides, Pitcairn Island, and the Gilbert and Ellice Islands. The Archives were located in the Suva Botanical Gardens, and as I sat waiting for files to be delivered, I could watch the prison inmates labouring in the Botanical Gardens and listen to the intermittent drumming of tropical rain on the roof—a sound reminiscent of my childhood.

The procedure at the Archives was to look in large registers that listed the inward and outward correspondence of the Western Pacific High Commission (WPHC). There were also the British Consul Tonga (BCT) files, relating specifically to Tonga. And registers for the correspondence between the High Commissioner of the Western Pacific and the Secretary of State for the Colonies in London.

Each item of correspondence in the main WPHC registers, which could be to or from any one of the WPHC territories, had a brief (about four words) description of the contents. Using these registers I requested those files that looked as though they might be relevant and interesting. I ignored files about exports and imports (these were summarised in the *Tonga Government Gazette*, another useful source) and ordered any to do with religion, as I knew these would really be about politics. A few files had nothing, or referred to attachments that had been removed. I assumed that the missing attachments had been forwarded to the Colonial Office in London.

In the late 1970s, the Western Pacific Archives papers went to Milton Keynes in the United Kingdom. Since 2002, they have been in the care of the Library of the University of Auckland. In January 2005, in Auckland, I requested some files from the 1950s and found they had been removed in the UK because they were considered too 'sensitive' for us colonials to read.

Alas, nothing like the Western Pacific Archives existed in Tonga, and still does not. When the late King became Minister for Education in 1943 *or* when he became Premier in 1949, he decided to make a big bonfire of most of the papers lying around in the 'Stone Building'—which then housed several government departments—in order to make space for his own records.

The papers of the Free Wesleyan Church are now being well looked after (although requiring more detailed cataloguing). In the 1970s the large registers of baptisms, marriages and deaths, and the minutes of District and Quarterly meetings were stored in cupboards and odds and ends in the old stables. Some of the letters and other loose papers I read and copied in the Mission House in 1974 and 1976 I never saw again, although a sighting of some letter books was reported to me in 2005.

The Catholic Bishop Finau was most helpful, but the ancient French priest who looked after the Catholic Archives assured me that the only relevant papers in the Catholic Archives were some surviving diaries of 1912-1934 of Bishop Blanc, which were in French. I borrowed a French-English dictionary from the nuns and spent a number of weeks at the Catholic office (Toutaimana) translating Bishop Blanc's diaries and sharing morning tea with the nuns and young priests.

The real goldmine in Tonga was the collection of papers then stored in the Palace Office. When I first arrived to make inquiries, the Acting Private Secretary to the King was the noble and musician Fielakepa, who had been a student of my father's many years before. Each morning I borrowed his keys and went into a back room, climbing over bicycles, boxes full of bottles of champagne, and rolls of wire to reach the top shelf of the book-case on which there were boxes labelled by decades. Someone had started this sorting venture some time before, but after an inch or so of the designated decade, other papers had just been dumped in on top. I took one box at a time and retired to the Privy Council room to read them.

As there was nothing much to do in the evenings, I studied Churchward's *Grammar*, and learned lists of Tongan words off by heart. The latter was not a particularly useful exercise, as there are many homonyms in Tongan, and the meaning is determined by the pronoun and context. The outcome of these evenings and keeping Churchward's *Tongan-English Dictionary* always at hand was that I was able to do quite a lot of translation on my own—especially when the *Tonga Government Gazette* also included a summary in English, a practice abolished by the late King.

For my purposes, the most valuable of the documents then in the Palace Office and now in the Tongan Traditions Committee Archives were the diaries kept by Queen Salote's Private Secretary (Sione Filipe Tongilava), which gave me some idea of the daily comings and goings at the Palace. Presentations of food were listed in great detail, also lists of *koloa* (mats, barkcloth, etc.) presented to Queen Salote, but alas no details of dances beyond a bare number, such as 37 *lakalaka*. He noted when the Queen presided over a kava circle or *mavae kava*—a kava root was presented, but was not immediately used. Tongilava was also Clerk to the Privy Council Minutes and kept the Privy Council Minutes, but I did not have the time to read all of these, nor the Hansard of the Parliament of Tonga. The last would have been beyond me, as Tongan speeches are allusive, using metaphors abundantly.

An unknown person had already translated the diary Queen Salote had kept of her visit to England in 1953. When Tongan friends offered to help with the translation of letters, I found *they* could not understand the documents, partly because of the allusive language and partly because the would-be translators did not have the context. Tongan history as taught in schools was bland, respectful of the royal family, and tended to ignore the 20th century. I had to explain why the documents were interesting to me before they could attempt translation. Another difficulty is that the Tongan language is not gender specific. In a letter to Rev. J.B. Watkin did Queen Salote reproach him for trampling on 'me'—i.e. the Queen—or on 'it' (her plan)? No one will ever know.

My father had read papers in 1972 that were no longer there, and on later visits I could not find papers I had read earlier. But it was worth asking on the next visit whether the papers had reappeared. I cannot remember the number of times I asked about photographs, and was told there were none. After my book was published I was shown a photograph album bursting with pictures of Queen Salote and her family. The denial of the album's existence was not malicious, it was just easier to say no than to actually go and look!

After my three visits to the Western Pacific Archives in Suva and two visits to Tonga (one for three months and one for a year) I put the papers I had copied in those countries and in Australian libraries and private papers into date order. The 5 x 3 cards on which I had made notes I put into alphabetical order, indicating the date and source of each of the notes. It was only then that I got any sense of sequence, and hence of cause and effect. I would phone a friend and say, 'Guess what! If A and C happened then B must have been the link!'

By this time, having written and thrown away a number of chapters, I realised that the focus of my thesis was the partnership between Queen Salote and her consort, the great chief Tungi Mailefihi and their dual leadership, which was derived from the traditional relationship between 'eldest sister' and 'eldest brother' as leaders of their clan; and in the case of the highest titles, as sacred and secular ruler.

Traditionally the 'eldest sister' was the keeper of genealogies and provider of *koloa* (wealth) in the form on barkcloth, mats, and other durable goods, and the 'eldest brother' was the keeper of the land and distributor of the food that grew on it. Salote and Tungi were fourth cousins. Thus, in political terms, they took on the traditional roles of 'eldest sister' and 'eldest brother' and made their goal the unification of the whole kingdom. Salote had married Tungi (the choice of her father, Tupou II, and much loved by her) when she was 17 years of age and he was 29. Seven months after the wedding she was proclaimed Queen, and was pregnant with the first of three sons.

Salote alone was installed in the pre-eminent title of Tu'i Kanokupolu. Salote alone was addressed in the sacred language, although both she and Tungi were descended from the ancient line of sacred rulers. Tungi was addressed in the language appropriate for chiefs. Salote appointed him as her Prime Minister; but his real influence was exercised through his role as a very high-ranking chief, especially in matters relating to land. 'He was a farmer', people told me. He initiated the annual agricultural show and won many prizes there. He made lists of local fish. He planted as many species of yam as he could find and kept cattle. He encouraged people to grow for export, not only copra, but good quality bananas and other fruits: a frustrating enterprise since the inspectors employed to ensure the fruits were of good quality were often relatives of the farmers. There was always a line of people outside his office waiting to ask for money: to pay for taxes, a wedding or funeral or special birthday.

Oral history in the 1970s was quite a problem. 'If we knew we would tell you, Besi', was the cry of my Tongan friends, friends bequeathed to me by my parents and my sister and brother-in-law, who had also been missionaries in Tonga. Reflecting on this later, I realised they thought I was seeking really 'important' information, rather than the humdrum insights that mean so much to a biographer. These insights came to me in casual conversation, *not* by my sitting with a tape recorder or notebook—both of which caused Tongans to clam up. The cup of tea was, in my case, mightier than the pencil.

Part of the reason for the almost universal silence was that, even in the 1970s and 1980s (Salote died in 1965), Salote's *mana* was so great that she might reach out from the grave and punish someone for being *fie'eiki* (presuming to know matters reserved for chiefs).

What surprised me even more was that Queen Salote's sons did not have much to say. Both had been students of my father, and so there was no difficulty in getting audiences. The youngest son held back, I think, also because of the great *mana* of his mother.

This was not the case with the late King. It took some years for me to realise that although he had kindly provided me with a letter giving me permission to do research, he was simply *not* interested in what I was doing, or in anything about the past. He was sure he was more intelligent, better educated, higher-ranking, more interesting, and altogether had more of everything than the late Queen, and he could not understand why people were interested in her when *he* was there to be admired. Was he jealous of the love and respect people had for her?

I was fortunate that when I suffered 'culture shock' in 1976, Epeli Hau'ofa, who had just returned to Tonga from Canberra and was being very bolshie (wearing a black beard and a kaftan made of mattress ticking), was writing his best short stories, and would read them to his wife, Barbara, and me and other friends in the evenings. Another guide along the way was a Danish man known as Tavi, who had lived in Tonga since 1953 and had privileged access to the Palace. His cynical view of Tonga, which had been the paradise of my childhood, was a great corrective.

Best of all was being introduced by Tonga's best-known *fakaleiti* to his grandmother, a woman of high rank, who loved talking about the old days. Twice a week I visited her and (without my taking notes) we had wide-ranging conversations. As soon as I returned to my place, I would type out everything I could remember her saying. I could check some omissions on my next visit. Alas, as a postgraduate student, I did not have the money to have her wonderful collection of photographs copied.

After the PhD thesis was submitted and approved, I was really burnt out, and wanted to do something else for a while. That was possibly a mistake, but at the time I was happy to become a freelance book editor and indexer and write occasional papers on Tonga for conferences and publication.

At last, in 1994 and 1995, I was awarded two fellowships in New Zealand, which enabled me to do further research and writing. My thesis had covered only the years 1918-41. Although I had incidentally researched much of the remainder of her life and times, I had many gaps to fill, which was possible through papers, books, and theses in the University of Auckland Library, and the archives in Auckland and Christchurch of the New Zealand Methodist Church. Queen Salote was, and her grandson now is, the only Methodist monarch in the world.

In an early draft of the book, the first two chapters had described the hierarchical structure of Tongan society in much detail. Then I thought: 'The *papalangi*s won't be interested in all this detail, and the Tongans know it already'. Then I remembered the question people in Australia always asked me: 'Where is Tonga?' So I started the book by answering that question. Salote was born in a palace beside the sea, within a town about a mile square. Beyond the town were the villages and allotments and the chiefs and people who lived there. Then there were all the other islands of Tonga, then Samoa and Fiji, and the rest of the Pacific, until I reached the ends of the earth.

I believe in following a chronological line as far as is reasonable, so once the scene was set, past history summarised, and a brief account of the social ranking systems given, I was able to structure the book so that chronologically the narrative moved on while each chapter dealt with a different theme. Fixing the structure of the book was the most satisfying experience.

At the end of 1995, I returned home to Melbourne with a complete book: long and somewhat doughy. In the next 18 months I rewrote the whole book, keeping the structure, but with a lighter tone, bearing in mind my audience: the Tongans themselves and anyone who knew enough about Tonga to be interested. I deliberately avoided academic jargon (a decision made also, but independently, by two of my colleagues: Helen Morton Lee and Cathy Small) in favour of simple language.

Many times people told me how they had been in the crowd in London when this wonderful Queen Salote rode by in a carriage with the hood down in spite of the rain so she could share the excitement of the people who had waited all night and all day to see the procession. A man in Rotorua, New Zealand, gave me a cutting about Queen Salote at the coronation that he had kept for 40 years. As the Queen had attracted attention before Queen Elizabeth II's coronation by her obvious enjoyment of everything she witnessed and her friendliness to all she met, it was not surprising that the coronation edition of the *Daily Express* included a diagram of Westminster Abbey, showing the seat allocated to Queen Salote (only a few of the invited guests were so distinguished). Salote had been 18 years old when she had been crowned in the royal chapel in Tonga, so it is not surprising that she empathised with the young Queen of England then making her coronation vows.

My major 'conclusions' were (1) that Salote was a very intelligent person, very shrewd, and very good with people; (2) that Salote had not always been beloved and secure in her position as Queen; (3) that her allies (both Tongan and *papalangi*), especially her consort, were totally committed in their loyalty to her.

I was concerned about some things that were common knowledge, but I could not decide how to handle. I consulted a high-ranking chiefly woman who encouraged me by saying, 'It is time to tell the truth'.

One example of a truth that needed to be told related to the Queen's half-sister, Princess Fusipala, daughter of Tupou II's second marriage (Salote's mother having died when Salote was only two years old). Princess Fusipala's mother's family set up a rival court in Tonga, and did everything they could to enhance the status of Fusipala and diminish that of Salote. Eventually the half-sister died, in

Sydney, in 1933. I was told by Tongans (a) that Fusipala had died from a broken heart because the Queen would not allow her to marry the commoner she loved; (b) that Fusipala had committed suicide because she had been engaged to four high chiefs and angered all four and their families by breaking the engagements; (c) that Tungi (who was in Sydney at the time) had poisoned Fusipala. The truth was that she had died of tubercular peritonitis. Did my account stop the romantic stories being told? Probably not.

Although Fusipala was related to Tungi in a way that required his loyalty (her mother's mother's mother was sister of his father's father), Salote's consort was totally loyal to the Queen. When Tungi and his most trusted ministers were impeached by his enemies in 1939-40, the Queen was solid in her loyalty to him, while (to *papalangi* eyes) appearing to be calm and impartial. The attempted impeachment failed. In the following year, 1941, the Queen was devastated by the death of Tungi when she was only 41 and he was 53.

When the late King Tupou IV (then Crown Prince) returned from Sydney University with both a BA and an LLB (the first Tongan to take a university degree) in December 1942, he assumed he would take over from the Queen. As Prime Minister, he relieved Salote of many onerous duties, particularly the bureaucracy and tedious government matters, so that she could get on with the *real* governing, with influencing the people. Her *mana* increased each year, and she was much loved and admired for what were her genuine qualities.

The time eventually comes when one must stop writing a book (even when one has not finished) and start looking for a publisher. New Zealand had given me the space to write the book, and it was Auckland University Press (AUP) that accepted it for publication. Fortunately, AUP did not ask me to cut the text, as another publisher might have done, since the book is around 110,000 words. And they accepted almost all of the 130 photographs I offered, and chose someone who designed a most wonderful cover. ('Is yours the book with the blue cover?' I am sometimes asked.)

One very good thing that AUP did was to offer a 40 per cent discount for any direct order of at least 10 books. Many Tongans in Melbourne and Auckland—and perhaps other places—were able to order boxes of books, and sell them to their fellow church members or friends at considerably less than retail price.

I visited Tonga after the first printing in 1999. The first 500 copies ordered by the Friendly Islands Bookshop had sold out and another 700 copies had arrived. One Tongan lady bought six copies, one for each of her granddaughters. There was a signing session. I paid the late King a courtesy call.

Tongans and non-Tongans alike have thanked me for writing the book, as it covers a period in Tongan history that no one else has written about. Reviews were many. I had omitted the story about Noel Coward at the coronation for my own reasons, and the index to my book has the entry 'Coward, Noel, not mentioned' with no page references. Nevertheless some reviewers insisted upon telling the story. Chagrin.

One criticism (repeated to me 'anonymously') was that I had written about the illnesses and causes of death of members of the royal family and of other high-ranking people. No one in the royal family commented on or reproached me for this. However, in a subsequent book, *Songs and Poems of Queen Salote*, our translator insisted that all reference to such matters were taken out of the notes that headed each section of poetry. As editor, I complied with her request, but put the information into my essay that introduced the book.

An Australian lady, Rosary, had lived for many years in Tonga, and in the year 2000 she was living in Fairfield, Victoria, the suburb next to mine. She read *Queen Salote* and phoned the History Department of the University of Melbourne to ask how she could get in touch with me, as she would like to meet me. She was told I was *dead*. Rosary showed the book to her next-door neighbour, Pat, and told her how sorry she was that I was dead. 'She is not dead', said Pat. 'I see her every Sunday. She is a member of our Uniting Church congregation here in Fairfield.'

The most recent response was unexpected. A contract has been signed for *Queen Salote of Tonga: the story of an era 1900-1965* to become part of the History E-Book Project, so it is in cyberspace courtesy of the American Council of Learned Societies.

Financially, of course, the PhD and the writing of *Queen Salote* were a total disaster, costing me immeasurably more than I shall ever recover from minuscule royalties. I am glad I did not realise that relative poverty would be the outcome, or I might not have proceeded. I learned not only about the paradise of my childhood (which is no paradise, but I cannot help being loving and wanting the best for Tonga), but my mind was stretched, and I made many friends, both Tongan and *papalangi*, in the course of researching, writing, releasing, and listening to responses about *Queen Salote of Tonga: the story of an era 1900-1965* (first published in 1999) and, subsequently, to the *Songs and Poems of Queen Salote* (first published in 2004).

Chapter 11

On Being a Participant Biographer: The Search for J.W. Davidson

Doug Munro

Books do not write themselves, unfortunately. There is always a behind-the-scenes story of research, writing and getting published that is sometimes more interesting than the story related in the book itself. This is especially the case with biography. What might seem the straightforward task of writing the life of an individual is often fraught with difficulty; and the biographical enterprise has engendered some particularly bitter disputes. For every encourager, there can be an ill-wisher. Friends and family can be obstructive. Unwilling prospective subjects of a biography have been known to take pre-emptive legal action; John Le Carré, for example, has deterred two would-be biographers by such means.[1] Literary estates can nip a project in the bud by refusing access to personal papers and denial of quotation rights.[2] Such obstruction is serious, precisely because biographies have to be 'produced' and a precondition of that production is more often than not access to archival sources. My own work towards a biography of J.W. Davidson has not landed me in court. But it has taken me to archival repositories in the search for anything and everything on Davidson as well as in locating documents in private possession and in securing access to personal papers that were decreed off limits to me (but not to others). It is all part and parcel of the business of 'producing' biography and a tale worth telling.

Jim Davidson (1915-1973) was the New Zealand expatriate and Cambridge don who became Professor of Pacific History at The Australian National University. He emerged as the founding father of modern Pacific Islands historiography as well as constitutional adviser to a succession of Island territories in the throes of decolonisation. Far from being a run-of-the mill academic in his ivory tower, Davidson prided himself on being unconventional, notably for his promotion of 'participant history' and his advocacy of the advantages of personal experience.[3] As well as writing history, he helped to make it, and he combined the two in his major book, *Samoa mo Samoa*, large parts of which detail his role in the making of the independent state of Western Samoa.[4] All things considered, Davidson is an attractive biographical subject. He was significant and influential within his profession. He was a man of affairs as well as a scholar. He was controversial and there are certain mysteries about his life. He had a singular and complex personality in which the elements were strangely mixed—patrician yet egalitarian; gentle yet abrasive; the soul of discretion when confidences were involved yet outrageously indiscrete when it suited him; respectful of authority figures in other cultures yet disparaging of those in his own; and apt to be an outright pain to strait-laced colleagues to the extent that they were apt to doubt his seriousness of purpose.[5]

I knew Jim Davidson in the last years of his life and now find myself writing his biography. If someone said that biographers choose their subject by selecting and idealising a hero figure, I could respond with mock-dismissiveness that this is a very Freudian interpretation. But Freud did hold that view,[6] and in my case it happens to be true because Jim Davidson meant a great deal to me personally and he had an influence on the course of my life. Also, I feel a sense of connection with the person about whom I am writing, and not simply because I once knew him as a person. We were both brought up in Wellington, where I have returned to live. As well as archival research, I was then able to engage in 'optical research' the term coined by a biographer of Mary Queen of Scots who 'visited every conceivable castle, quagmire, byre or whatever associated with the Queen in three countries'.[7] There was a time when I daily walked past the house where Davidson was born and the church in which he was baptised (both in Upland Road). There was the occasion, in the manner of Richard Holmes' *Footsteps*, when I traced his daily trek from the family home in Tinakore Road, via the Botanical Gardens, to the (then) Victoria University College. There was the occasion when I went to see that same house to discover that it had been demolished for freeway development. The feelings of loss and emptiness on that afternoon are part and parcel of the biographer's journey, where the thrills and spills intermesh.

I did not initially intend to commit myself to a book-length biography but, rather, an 'intellectual biography' in article form: an assessment of Davidson the Pacific historian—the type of Pacific history he promoted and practised, notably his advocacy of 'participant history'; the formative influences; his academic legacy. Davidson's published corpus provided the basis for the investigation, but was not sufficient in itself.[8] It is impossible to deconstruct adequately a historian's writings on the basis of the writings alone. Detailed biographical material is also required; and I needed to consult personal papers. It seemed simple and straightforward enough. But I was to find, as most biographers do, that there were surprises in store, not all of them agreeable.

I cannot recall the moment I decided upon this course of research. A distant influence was the impact of a couple of superb books on the American historical profession, which showed what could be achieved through the use of historians' personal papers.[9] The immediate impetus was probably writing a couple of journal articles on Pacific Islands historiography in the early 1990s in which the Davidson legacy was mentioned.[10] In July 1994, at the Pacific History Association Conference at Tarawa, I spoke about planned research on Davidson with David Hanlon of the University of Hawai'i; and David remarked that I was well qualified, having known Davidson personally and been his student. But any such intentions were relegated to the backburner because I was midway through other research. Also, I was then working at the University of the South Pacific in Fiji, remote from both archival sources and people whom I could interview about Davidson.

The project began in September 1996 on a fortnight visit to Canberra during a mid-semester break from teaching to consult the Davidson Papers. There are two sets of Davidson Papers, the main body at the National Library of Australia and a smaller miscellaneous collection at the ANU Archives. I understood that both collections were on open access but the smaller collection was restricted, and continued to be so for a further three years.[11] The fact that Davidson died without issue, and had no literary executor, contributed to the difficulties concerning access and the reproduction of archives. Finally, I gained access. I discovered there was nothing untoward or of a sensitive nature in those papers, and they proved valuable in answering a number of questions about Davidson's academic life, including the completion of *Samoa mo Samoa*.[12]

Most of my time during that fortnight in Canberra was spent consulting the National Library of Australia's collection of Davidson Papers. That larger collection is disorganised. Davidson himself was never particularly careful in keeping his papers in much order, and when he died suddenly in 1973 his muddled papers were transferred to the National Library and have never been properly sorted. There were 63 archival boxes of papers, according to the finder aid, and the single largest category comprised a miscellany of official printed papers relating to Davidson's constitutional advising. The first three boxes contained scattered correspondence from the 1950s and I concentrated on these, making handwritten notes because there was seemingly no one able to grant permission to photocopy. The note-taking was time consuming and the information fragmentary and inconclusive. There were plenty of leads but few 'answers' to my questions. But I did manage to purchase a recent official history of The Australian National University by Stephen Foster and Margaret Varghese, who were accused by an admiring reviewer of being 'in serious danger of giving commissioned history a good name'.[13] Although the authors made a couple of factual errors about Davidson, they provide a remarkably frank and engaging account of the ANU's first 50 years. Both in terms of specific information and background material, Foster and Varghese saved me an enormous amount of legwork.

My next archival foray was the visit, in December 1996, to St John's College, Cambridge, where Davidson was a PhD student (1938-1942) and Fellow (1944-1951) and for which he maintained a lifelong affection. Through the good offices of Malcolm Underwood, the College Archivist, I consulted what he could find. The bulk of these records were in the Tutorial File, containing the records kept on Davidson by his tutors. There was also a smaller bundle of papers, on the cover of which was written 'Found while cleaning up'—a chilling reminder that archives can be at risk even in well-appointed institutions. There was not as much material as I had expected—nothing, for example, on Davidson relinquishing his fellowship upon being appointed to a professorship at ANU or the arrangements regarding affiliation during his 1956 study leave. But the records I saw were in more concentrated form that I had hitherto encountered; and I was fascinated to see resonances of the Davidson I knew as an older man jumping out at me from the pages: a love of travel; leaving things to the last minute; always having a plausible excuse for a seemingly habitual pattern of not having done something quite on time; and an equal facility at knowing how to work the system. Again, I came across a secondary source that was important to my work, although in a different way to the ANU official history. The book in question was Bryan Palmer's memoir of the English historian E.P. Thompson (1924-1993), famous for *The Making of the English Working Class* and notable for his wholehearted involvement in the Campaign for Nuclear Disarmament.[14] In its attempts to connect Thompson's personality to his writing, and sympathetically written by someone who knew Thompson, whose activism informed his scholarship, Palmer's book suggested how I might approach my work on Davidson.

But I still did not have enough material for an intellectual biography, even in article form, and I was still immersed in other projects. As part of a long-delayed study leave, in 1997, I consulted some of the papers of H.E. Maude (1906-2006), who had been Davidson's loyal lieutenant at ANU. I had toyed with the idea of doing a full-scale biography of Harry Maude, but Susan Woodburn, the librarian in charge of the Special Collection at the Barr Smith Library, University of Adelaide, where the Maude Papers were housed, had beaten me to it.[15] I told Susan that I had abandoned any intention of a biography but would still like to write a historiographic paper about Harry Maude, whom I had known since 1972. Also, I was working on Davidson and would it be possible to see relevant material among the Maude Papers? Susan was completely unfazed at the prospect of a potential rival and facilitated my research. It is difficult to suggest anyone else to be as obliging in the circumstances. And Harry Maude, despite initial unease, gave permission to consult his papers, with the exception of the general correspondence. It was a win-win situation. Over the next few years, Susan and I enjoyed a rewarding professional relationship as we shared our findings and gave each other every assistance.[16]

Still, my work on Davidson was proceeding slowly. From Fiji, I could make only occasional visits to archival sources in Australia and New Zealand. There was also the distraction of my other research commitments. But I did begin what has become a large correspondence with former friends and associates of Davidson. I got away to Canberra again in September 1997 during a week-long mid-semester break from teaching. It wasn't nearly enough time to make an impact on National Library's collection of Davidson Papers, but I did on this occasion locate material among the papers of the Australian historian Brian Fitzpatrick, on whose behalf Davidson unsuccessfully attempted to secure an academic position.[17] Events then started to take another trajectory. Shortly after returning to Fiji I wrote to the social anthropologist Sir Raymond Firth (1901-2002), who had worked with Davidson during the Second World War in the Naval Intelligence Division[18] and who, as one of the ANU's Academic Advisers in the late-1940s, had recommended Davidson for the position of Professor of Pacific History. He responded enthusiastically, but voiced concern when I later mentioned that the scope of my work was limited to an intellectual biography. He wrote back:

> You say you are only 'incidentally' concerned with Jim's constitutional advising. Indeed to deal fully with it would need a big book. But I do hope you can give it fair space, since it was an integral part of his intellectual life. It was a fusion of the scholar and the man of affairs, concerned directly with people, which I think he loved and which let him express himself most fully. I should stress that it also allowed him a sense of power, of the kind which [the social anthropologist] Audrey Richards once described in quite another context as 'Let me just plan your life for you!'

The 'sense of power' to which Firth refers is apposite—not power for its own sake but the opportunity to be centrally involved in the process of decolonisation and not simply to comment from the sidelines.

At that point I started to consider writing a full-scale biography. Not only did Davidson lead a varied and eventful life but it was evident that his reputation was on the wane, as a shadowy and not very relevant ancestral figure. A comparable example is that of W.K. Hancock who is making a comeback on the basis of publications on his life and work.[19] Yet in his time, Davidson had clout and was well known: he pioneered the study of Pacific history as a specialisation in its own right; his department trained nearly all the practitioners; and he founded *The Journal of Pacific History*, which influenced the research agenda. These in themselves would probably not justify Davidson being the subject of a full-scale biography; and it is noticeable that historians usually only rate chapter-length biographical treatment. While there is no firm pattern, usually historians who combine public affairs with academic work, or at least have a multi-faceted career, are more likely to attract a biographer[20] —and Davidson's constitutional advising, not to mention his advocacy of participant history, put him in this category.

I was mulling over this possible change of plan in December 1998 during a two-month tenure as a Visiting Scholar within the newly created Centre for the Contemporary Pacific, to work both on Davidson and on a book on the collapse of the National Bank of Fiji.[21] My time was spent interviewing former associates of Davidson, and to my astonishment I discovered that his younger sister Ruth was alive and still living in the house that Jim had built for her in the Canberra suburb of Garran. I had not seen her in over 25 years. A feeble and immobile old lady in her early-80s, we instantly recognised each other. Although eager to help, she tired easily in interviews. She then brought out some memorabilia (photo albums, offprints of early publications), including a marvellous photograph of Davidson in his early 20s walking along a city street in Wellington. Taken in the days when street photographers were plying their trade, the photograph was quintessential Davidson—the tall, gangly, uncoordinated figure accentuated by an ill-fitting suit, and the sunny smile. She also agreed that I could photocopy archival material authored by her brother, which would save hours of transcribing at a later stage. I went away heartened by Ruth's endorsement of my work and kept in touch until her death in 2000.[22] I interviewed numerous other people in Canberra. On the archival front I started consulting material from the ANU Archives, notably Davidson's personal file. The major story to emerge from this was the sheer difficulty that Davidson had in persuading the ANU for extended leaves-of-absence to engage as the Samoans' constitutional adviser between 1959 and 1961. This was new and subsequent enquiries revealed that Davidson was largely successful in keeping this facet of his constitutional advising under wraps. Fortunately, Davidson was sufficiently senior for his ANU personal file to have been retained. Those of many junior and middle-ranking academics have been culled.

At the end of my Visiting Fellowship, in late-January 1999, I encountered a rather unexpected difficulty when I presented a seminar on Davidson. Members of the audience included people who were opposed to my work on Davidson and I am under no illusions that I was not considered a fit and proper person for the task, despite Ruth Davidson's support. I am uncertain what went on behind the scenes directly afterwards but about an hour later I was more or less warned off. This reaction was at odds with my notion of cooperative collegiality; and fellow biographers will attest that I routinely pass on relevant material from my own researches. It was an unpleasant experience, and in such contrast to the support I was receiving from complete strangers, who were enthusiastic about my project. I readily recall the unaffected delight of Ian Fairbairn over the telephone, whose PhD thesis was supervised by Davidson.[23] I was later to learn that bumpy rides are the biographer's frequent lot, something I wish I had known earlier because it might have given a measure of grim comfort.[24] Matters have since been smoothed over, but I felt aggrieved for months afterwards.

Back in Fiji, and again remote from archival sources, I continued tracking down and corresponding with Davidson's former associates. Locating informants has certain similarities to locating archival sources: systematic searching is a necessary but not sufficient condition. Luck and serendipity are just as crucial, although good researchers often make their own luck. My single most important stroke of good fortune was mentioning my biography-in-progress in a footnote to an article published in the journal *History in Africa*.[25] My footnote caught the eye of a student of Davidson's at Cambridge during the late 1940s, Paul Hair (1926-2001), who went on to become a history professor at the University of Liverpool. He in turn put me on to another of Davidson's Cambridge undergraduate students, George Shepperson, who had likewise gone on to a full professorship. Their written reminiscences, which attested to Davidson's pivotal role in channelling them into academic life, were so compelling that I cobbled them together, with my own commentary, and published the resulting manuscript—again in *History in Africa*.[26] As well as having high regard for Davidson's intellect, both Hair and Shepperson had a profound affection for their old teacher. Although Davidson was an indifferent lecturer, he had the ability to inspire and enthuse on a one-to-one basis, and above all to instil the self-confidence in a student to realise his potential. I was aware of these qualities, including the poor lecturing style, but had no idea that they had resulted in the 'making' of two distinguished Africanists.

Even when things go wrong, luck and lady fortune still find time to smile on you. I put a notice in the 1999 issue of *The Eagle* (the magazine of St John's College, Cambridge), asking former students and associates of Davidson to contact me. Disastrously, I gave an incorrect e-mail address. Even then, another former Cambridge student of Davidson, Michael Wolff (Emeritus Professor of English at the University of Massachusetts, Amherst) managed to track me down. He too owed a great deal to Davidson, who had helped him through severe personal difficulties. Wolff had even written a poem for Davidson ('I Have Sat at the Feet of Gamaliel'), composed directly after their first meeting, but had lost the copy. From these former students, I obtained much helpful information. But I was nevertheless uncomfortably aware that my overall knowledge of Davidson's years at Cambridge was thin.

During 1999, my last year in Fiji, I made further short visits to Wellington and Canberra. On the former occasion, I obtained material in private hands—from Colin Aikman (1919-2002), who had served as a Constitutional Adviser with Davidson in both Western Samoa and the Cook Islands, and from Mary Boyd, herself a historian of Western Samoa. This information helped in the writing of a paper on Davidson's covered-up difficulties getting leave from ANU to be involved in Western Samoa's final stages of decolonisation.[27] On the visit to Canberra, I learned that I had been awarded Harold White Fellowship at the National Library of Australia, tenable during 2000, to continue working on Davidson. I took up my Fellowship in November and experienced over the next three months the nearest thing to heaven on earth. I had many privileges, and I enjoyed enormous support from Graeme Powell and his staff in the Manuscripts Section. In return I was asked to present a staff seminar at an early stage of my fellowship, a formal lecture towards the end, and to make the most of my opportunities.

I consulted the papers of several of Davidson's former colleagues, and at last I had the time and leisure to thoroughly go through those 63 archival boxes of Davidson Papers. Because they were, organisationally, such a dog's breakfast, I never knew what I would find next, and I found things I never expected to be there. The original copy of Michael Wolff's poem 'I Have Sat at the Feet of Gamaliel' materialised after all these years (and is reproduced at the end of this chapter). George Shepperson had told me that Davidson supported his application for a lectureship at Edinburgh, and Davidson's referee's report also turned up. Such was the clutter that it was generally pointless to go looking for something among the Davidson Papers. During those heady days of discovery, I was tripping over one unexpected find after another, not daring to wonder what serendipitous delights the next archival box might have in store.

The real treasure of the collection is a story in itself. Back in early 1999, I asked Ruth Davidson if she had any correspondence from her brother. Ruth said that Davidson was a dutiful son who wrote long, regular letters from Cambridge to his family in New Zealand, and that these had been deposited in the National Library. I couldn't tell Ruth that she had to be mistaken, for neither the National Library's on-line catalogue nor its finder aid to the Davidson Papers indicated the presence of any such letters. Before taking up my fellowship, I raised the matter with Graeme Powell. Back came the astonishing reply that there were indeed such letters, some 250 between 1938 and 1942. The reason I had not known about these additions to the Davidson Papers was because the original finder's aid had not been updated. Another surprise was in store. I had only asked Graeme whether letters existed between 1938 and 1942 (the years of Davidson's PhD candidature), and he had replied in the affirmative. Upon arrival, I discovered that the letters went up to 1956 on a regular basis, with a few more until the early 1960s. They occupied three archival boxes. Davidson's mother had kept all his letters. Upon her death they had passed into Ruth's keeping and from there, unheralded, to the National Library of Australia. Because I had Ruth's written permission to have copies made of archival material created by Jim, I was able to photocopy the whole lot, free of charge. Unhappily, the other side of the correspondence is almost entirely lacking because Davidson seldom kept personal letters.

Davidson's long letters home provide a running commentary of his life and cover a wide range of subjects. He assumed that his mother shared and understood his academic interests. This regular supply of information over 18 years, from his departure as a postgraduate student through to first seven years at ANU, has been invaluable, especially for the 1940s. That decade had been something of a blank. Now there was an abundance of the very material I so badly needed. Also, it finally made possible my initial, more limited, objective of an 'intellectual biography'. With these letters as my main source, I have been able to trace the various strands of Davidson's academic outlook to their origins. This was the subject of my Harold White Fellow Lecture in late January 2001, on 'The Prehistory of J.W. Davidson', where I argued that the real Jim Davidson and the elements that made up his thinking were intact before his arrival at ANU.[28]

Davidson's letters contain no major surprises; they reveal nothing that would fundamentally alter my view of a person whom I got to know reasonably well in the last years of his life. Rather, the letters provide detailed basic information. At several points they confirm exactly what I remember Davidson telling me—for example, his distress that his father died before the two had patched up their differences and his intense disappointment at the failure of his first attempt at election to a Fellowship at St John's College. Other things that Davidson told me in the early 1970s have also been confirmed from the written record, notably his negative views on the office of Director for ANU's Research Schools and the reasons for Oskar Spate joining the (then) Department of Pacific History after relinquishing the role of Director of the Research School of Pacific Studies.[29] That confirms that Davidson's honesty and memory are not matters over which to exercise undue skepticism. He was not above representing an event in a false light (the letter to his mother about the termination of his residency at 'Gungahlin' in 1951 being a case in point[30]) but he avoided telling deliberate and outright untruths and his account of events is remarkably precise both in expression and in accuracy.

One aspect of Davidson's life that is absent from the letters home concerns his broader artistic interests (music, painting, literature, theatre). These were mentioned but summarily. The actual mainsprings of Davidson's artistic tastes go unrevealed in his letters to his mother. I was not much interested in such higher matters when I knew Davidson, so they were seldom topics for discussion—although he once berated my willful ignorance of contemporary fiction. My indifference was unfortunate for the future biographer because Davidson's broader artistic interests and aesthetic senses were integral to his personality, and I much regretted that my eventual biography was likely to be lacking a whole dimension. The salvation was one of those events that every biographer can only dream come true.

In 2004 I was trying to locate members of the Natusch family, a name that crops up in Davidson's correspondence, who might be able to help me to find out more about Davidson's earlier life. It was suggested that I contact Sheila Natusch in Wellington, who referred me to Guy Natusch in Napier. It turned out that he had gone to Hereworth School in Havelock North (Hawkes Bay) with Davidson in the 1920s and had fond memories of the slightly older boy. Guy mentioned my name to Caroline Greenwood of Kahuranaki Station, some half hour's drive from Havelock North, and shortly afterwards I received a voice mail message from Caroline. She had located 41 letters from Jim Davidson to her uncle Miles Greenwood as well as his diary of a bicycle tour of Ireland with Davidson in 1939. That not only cleared up the identity of the mysterious 'Miles' who regularly crops up in Davidson's letters home. It also transpired that Miles, and his English wife Cecilia ('Pipps' to family and close friends), shared Davidson's artistic interests and these were a recurring subject in his letters to them. During the late-1930s to mid-1940s, Miles Greenwood was a drama student at the Old Vic in London. Realizing that he was never going to get lead parts on English stages, Miles returned to farming in Hawkes Bay and painting water colours in his spare time. Caroline told me that the only way he could face weeding a row of lettuces was to imagine that they were heads in a theatre audience. The letters themselves were survivors of several boxes of papers that Miles destroyed shortly before his death in the early 1990s. I easily persuaded Caroline to deposit the letters in the National Library of Australia. Sadly, Pipps, who was very fond of Davidson and who could have told me much about him, passed away only in 2002.[31]

Soon after reading the letters to Greenwood, I consulted Davidson's letters to the composer Douglas Lilburn (1915-2001). They were students together at Waitaki Boys' High School and their studies in England overlapped. Again, Davidson reveals much about his broader artistic interests; and he unexpectedly dropped a concrete clue about his sexuality. The general feeling at ANU was that Davidson, who never married, was a closet homosexual in inclination if not in practice; but I had been unable to establish—and not through lack of trying—whether or not this was the case. The topic frequently arose during interviews and conversations, but I had no concrete evidence. Davidson loved youth and he was definitely homoerotic. I also suspect that he was bisexual. But I got fed up with people insisting, with no evidence, that he 'had to be gay'. In Davidson's time, homosexuality was a criminal offence and one that incurred tremendous social disapproval. So it is highly unlikely, if Davidson indeed had homosexual tendencies, that he would have advertised them or left a paper trail.[32] Yet the matter is important to establish, if possible, because it could have been an influence on his creativity.

There is a clue in a letter to Lilburn, who himself was gay. Lilburn's and Davidson's fathers died in successive years (1940 and 1941, respectively). Four months after George Davidson's death, Jim Davidson wrote to Lilburn: 'You will know how I felt on getting the news of Dad's death. You have know[n] more than I have of such sorrows. It was bad—I got over things by going to bed with you: it reduced the tension. Thank you for your sympathy'.[33] When I read this letter, I had a strange feeling of anti-climax that I cannot explain. I should have been shouting 'Eureka!', but was seized by no such impulse. What did amaze me was the letter being sent in the same envelope along with another letter to Davidson's sister Ruth. The letter for Lilburn was duly forwarded and in a fresh envelope and addressed in Mrs Davidson's handwriting to 'Mr. D. Lilburn'. It seems an extraordinarily careless slip on Davidson's part to send a letter of that nature which might be read by third parties, no less his mother and sister. Did Mabel Davidson read the letter before passing it on? If so, did she choose to ignore it? Or did she miss the incriminating part? That is a possibility: the part just quoted begins on the bottom of the last page of the letter and continues around the margins of the first page. There is no way of knowing what Mabel Davidson might or might not have read. But that letter does provide something concrete on Davidson's sexuality, although how much to read into a single statement is problematic. What makes this letter even more problematic is that events could not have unfolded the way they are recounted—because Lilburn was already back in New Zealand at the time of George Davidson's death in February 1941 and Davidson was still in England.[34] I simply do not know what to make of such a mistake on Davidson's part, because it is so out of character.

A biography of a recently deceased individual does not rely on archival evidence alone. There is also the question of how to obtain and use interviews from living witnesses, and in this particular case how far I should rely on my own memory of events.[35] Discussion of these matters will have to await another occasion, but I will say now that people who disliked Davidson are generally reluctant to talk. In the meanwhile, I trust that I have conveyed a sense of what it can be like for a biographer to conduct archival research. In some respects, it is a very different type of research to 'straight' history—especially in the need to develop a different mind set, one that is not easy to define but palpable none the less. But there are eternals, one of them being following up every clue. I am horrified at the prospect of incomplete research resulting in 'some unforgivably elementary error to be picked up and waved around by the reviewer in triumph'.[36] At the same time, I am not prepared to accept responsibility for mistakes or omissions resulting from being denied access to archival material. There have been some dispiriting moments to be sure, but the highs far outweigh the lows. All the same, a biographer's archival adventures can be bizarre. In order to find out how Daniel Defoe got out of gaol, Paula Backscheider consulted the hitherto unexamined records of the King's Bench Courts, which were rolled tightly and in a filthy condition; she emerged from the archives each day looking like a coalminer.[37] I have had no experiences of that nature, and neither have I completed my biography of Jim Davidson. In my various papers on Davidson, I have fulfilled the original objective of an intellectual biography;[38] and it is fortunate that I started when I did because in excess of 20 of the people with whom I corresponded or interviewed have since died.[39] So bear with me and one day my biography of the late, great Jim Davidson will appear.

[Untitled]

I have sat at the feet of Gamaliel,
I have learned in one brief hour
What one soul means to another,
What water means to the flower.

I have marked, with a panting of wonder,
How purely a man can see
Through form and shape and deception
What a friend is meant to be.

And then, lost in the depths of my thinking
And crossed without power of thought,
I have felt in my heart that now never
My fight shall alone be fought.

I have seen with unwanted perception
The morrow is weak and small;
That now and what now is passing
Is ever and always all.

With gratitude,
Michael Wolff
(republished with the author's permission)

ENDNOTES

[1] This is a modified version of a paper originally published in the October 2004 issue of *Archifacts* (Journal of the Archives and Records Association of New Zealand). I am grateful to Dr Kevin Molloy, the editor of *Archifacts*, for permission to republish. The revisions benefited from comments by Graeme Whimp.

Carl Rollyson, *A Higher Form of Cannibalism? Adventures in the Art and Politics of Biography* (Chicago 2005), 27-28, 72.

[2] Ian Hamilton, *Keepers of the Flame: literary estates and the rise of biography* (London 1992); Michael Millgate, *Testamentary Acts: Browning, Tennyson, James, Hardy* (Oxford 1992).

[3] J.W. Davidson, 'Understanding Pacific history: the participant as historian', in Peter Munz (ed.), *The Feel of Truth* (Wellington 1969), 25-40; Niel Gunson, 'An introduction to Pacific history', in Brij V. Lal (ed.), *Pacific Islands History: journeys and transformations* (Canberra 1992), 4-6.

[4] J.W. Davidson, *Samoa mo Samoa: the emergence of the independent state of Western Samoa* (Melbourne 1967).

[5] O.H.K. Spate, 'And now there will be a void: an appreciation of J.W. Davidson, 1915-1973', *Journal of Pacific Studies*, 20 (1996), 21-22.

[6] See Peter Hempenstall, *The Meddlesome Priest: a life of Ernest Burgmann* (Sydney 1993), xii.

[7] Antonia Fraser, 'Optical research', in Mark Bostridge (ed.), *Lives for Sale: biographers' tales* (London 2004), 113.

[8] Honore Forster, 'Bibliography—James Wightman Davidson', *Journal of Pacific History*, 28:2 (1993), 278-81 is reasonably comprehensive.

[9] August Meier and Elliott Rudwick, *Black History and the Historical Profession, 1915-1980* (Urbana/Chicago 1986); Peter Novick, *That Noble Dream: the 'objectivity' question and the American historical profession* (Chicago/London 1988).

[10] Doug Munro, 'Who "owns" Pacific history? Reflections on the insider/outside dichotomy', *Journal of Pacific History*, 29:2 (1994), 232-37; 'Pacific Islands history in the vernacular: practical and ethical considerations', *New Zealand Journal of History*, 29:1 (1995), 83-96. Both articles were submitted for publication in 1993.

[11] Sir Isaiah Berlin's biographer eloquently rebuked All Souls College, Oxford, for denying him access to their records relating to his subject: 'It is regrettable that a community of scholars who depend for their work on accepted conventions of access to archival material should deny a biographer access to papers on a fellow who was a credit to their institution for over 60 years'. Michael Ignatieff, *Isaiah Berlin: a life* (London 2000), 304.

[12] Without the latter material I would have been severely hampered in writing 'Disentangling Samoan history: the contributions of Gilson and Davidson', in Doug Munro and Brij V. Lal (eds), *Texts and Contexts: reflections in Pacific Islands historiography* (Honolulu 2006), 225-37.

[13] S.G. Foster and Margaret M. Varghese, *The Making of the Australian National University, 1946-1996* (Sydney 1996). The reviewer is Eric Richards (Professor of History at Flinders University), *The Australian*, 2 Oct. 1996, 31.

[14] Bryan D. Palmer, *E.P. Thompson: objections and oppositions* (London/New York, 1994).

[15] Susan Woodburn, *Journeys through Pacific History: a guide to the Pacific Islands library and papers of H.E. and H.C. Maude* (Adelaide 1995).

[16] Susan Woodburn, *Where Our Hearts Still Lie: a life of Harry and Honor Maude in the Pacific Islands* (Adelaide 2003). See my review in the *Journal of Pacific History*, 40:1 (2005), 124-5.

[17] Fitzpatrick's biographer does not bring out that Davidson was Fitzpatrick's strongest supporter in his quest for an academic position. Don Watson, *Brian Fitzpatrick: a radical life* (Sydney 1979), 273. This has been rectified by Stuart Macintyre, 'The radical and the mystic: Brian Fitzpatrick, Manning Clark and Australian history', in Stuart Macintyre and Sheila Fitzpatrick (eds), *Against the Grain: Brian Fitzpatrick and Manning Clark in Australian history and politics* (Melbourne 2007), 12-36. Fitzpatrick's children went on to become distinguished professors of history—Sheila at the University of Chicago and David at Trinity College, Dublin.

[18] R. Gerard Ward, 'Davidson's contribution to the "Admiralty Handbooks"', *Journal of Pacific History*, 29: 2 (1996), 238-40; Hugh Clout and Cyril Gosme, 'The naval intelligence handbooks: a monument to geographical writing', *Progress in Human Geography*, 27:2 (2003), 153-73.

[19] D.A. Low (ed.), *Keith Hancock: the legacies of an historian* (Melbourne 2001).

[20] E.g., Carole Fink, *Marc Bloch: a life in history* (Cambridge 1989); David Cannadine, *G.M. Trevelyan: a life in history* (London 1992); Fay Anderson, *An Historian's Life: Max Crawford and the politics of academic freedom* (Melbourne 2005); David S. Brown, *Richard Hofstadter: an intellectual biography* (Chicago 2006); Tim Beaglehole, *A Life of J.C. Beaglehole: New Zealand scholar* (Wellington 2006).

[21] Roman Grynberg, Doug Munro and Michael White, *Crisis: the collapse of the National Bank of Fiji* (Adelaide 2002).

[22] But there was an unhappy sequel. In July 2000, I received an email from the caregiver who tended Ruth during her last months when, unbeknown to me, she had been moved to a nursing home. Ruth had passed away in early March and the caregiver, who found my letters and Christmas card to Ruth, had been trying to locate me ever since. I enquired about the memorabilia, and especially the photograph. It transpired that Ruth was unable to take many of her belongings to the smaller quarters of the nursing home and the memorabilia had been 'disposed of'. See the obituary in *Reflections* [Quarterly Journal of the NSW Branch of the National Trust], October-January (2001), 37.

[23] Published as *The National Income of Western Samoa* (Melbourne 1973).

[24] My experiences pale by comparison with the treatment dished out by Sonia Orwell to her late husband's prospective biographers. Gordon Bowker, 'Nuts about St Cyps: lessons and quarrels in the lives of George Orwell', *Times Literary Supplement*, 15 Sept. 2006, 13-15.

[25] Doug Munro, 'The Vaitupu Company revisited: reflections and second thoughts on methodology and mindset', *History in Africa*, 24 (1997), 235 note 10.

[26] George Shepperson, P.E.H. Hair and Doug Munro, 'J.W. Davidson at Cambridge University: some student evaluations', *History in Africa* (2000), 215-27. Davidson's work at Cambridge, especially his key role in mounting the famous Expansion of Europe course, is recounted in Ronald Hyam, 'The study of Imperial and Commonwealth History at Cambridge, 1881-1981: founding fathers and pioneer research students', *Journal of Imperial and Commonwealth History*, 29:3 (2001), 81-84, 98-99.

[27] Doug Munro, 'J.W. Davidson and Western Samoa: university politics and the travails of a constitutional adviser', *Journal of Pacific History*, 35: 2 (2000), 195-211.

[28] The revised version of the lecture is intended as the opening chapter to a book of biographical essays on Pacific historians which I am working on.

[29] O.H.K. Spate, 'The history of a history: reflections on the ending of a Pacific voyage', *Journal of Pacific History*, 13: 1 (1988), 5-6.

[30] Davidson to his mother, 14 Sept. 1951, Davidson Papers, National Library of Australia, MS 5105, Box 66; Foster and Varghese, *The Making of the Australian National University*, 149-50.

[31] It also turned out that my father, a professional singer, has fond memories of the vibrant Pipps. As Secretary of the British Music Society (Hastings Branch), she was able to give my father much-needed recital work in the 1950s. She was also the regional representative for the New Zealand Opera Company, which my father founded, and facilitated the Company's touring throughout the Hawkes Bay area. Doug Munro, 'The early years of the New Zealand Opera Company, 1954-1957', *History Now*, 11:1-2 (2005), 19-23.

[32] The evidential difficulties are illustrated in other ways by Davidson's friend, Eric McCormick (the biographer of Omai, among other books), who hid his sexual preferences in the face of societal prejudice and legal repression and 'came out' in a more tolerant climate. McCormick's later insistence that his homosexuality must no longer be concealed created problems for the editor of his autobiography. First, McCormick's scattered autobiographical writings, which were written in the age of intolerance, contain few explicit references to his sexuality. Second, while McCormick was eventually frank about his own sexuality, 'he felt he had no licence to be so about his partners, many of whom later married and had children'. E.H. McCormick, *An Absurd Ambition: autobiographical writings*, ed. Dennis McEldowney (Auckland 1996), x-xi.

[33] Davidson to Lilburn, 5 Jun. 1941, Papers of Douglas Lilburn, Wellington, Alexander Turnbull Library, MS-Papers-2483-052.

[34] The matter is also discussed in Philip Norman, *Douglas Lilburn: his life and work* (Christchurch 2006), 80, 429 note 34.

[35] An illuminating account of a biographer's excursions into oral history is Andrew Roberts, 'La-Di-Da', in Bostridge, *Lives for Sale*, 124-33.

[36] Michael King, *Tread Softly For You Tread On My Life* (Auckland 2001), 43. An exemplary example of the primacy of research over 'style' is Bernard Crick, *George Orwell: a life* (London 1980). Crick once said, 'Damn the ring of truth, give me the footnotes'.

[37] Paula Backscheider, *Reflections on Biography* (Oxford 1999), xvi-xvii.

[38] My publications on Davidson, in addition to those already itemised are: 'Davidson, James Wightman, 1915-1973', in *Dictionary of New Zealand Biography*, vol. 5 (Auckland and Wellington 2000), 135-6; 'J.W. Davidson: the making of a participant historian', in Brij V. Lal and Peter Hempenstall (eds), *Pacific Lives, Pacific Places: bursting boundaries in Pacific history* (Canberra 2001), 98-116; 'Becoming an expatriate: J.W. Davidson and the brain drain', *Journal of New Zealand Studies*, 2-3 (2003-2004), 19-43; 'J.W. Davidson's Contribution to New Zealand Historiography', Treaty of Waitangi Research Unit Occasional Paper, no. 9 (Wellington 2005), 49; 'J.W. Davidson and W.K. Hancock: patronage, preferment, privilege', under consideration for publication.

[39] This bears comparison with the biography of the New Zealand Prime Minister, Peter Fraser, who sent Davidson on his first tour of duty in Western Samoa in 1947. See Michael Bassett with Michael King, *Tomorrow Comes the Song: a life of Peter Fraser* (Auckland 2000), 11-12. Sir Alister McIntosh (the long-serving permanent head of the Prime Minister's Department, who suggested to Fraser in 1947 that Davidson go to Western Samoa) intended to write Fraser's biography as a retirement project, but by then his health was not up to the task. He enlisted Michael King's collaboration in the late 1970s but a few years later King suffered a lengthy illness and the project went into abeyance. In 1996, Michael Bassett was asked to take over and the biography was duly published in 2000. The book took a while to complete but the early start did mean that King was able to interview at length not only McIntosh

(one of the few people in whom Fraser confided), but Fraser's surviving contemporaries and members of the family. Most of these interviews would not have been possible by the time Bassett entered the picture. Moreover, the almost complete absence of personal papers meant that these interviews were crucial to the eventual biography. In like fashion, starting work on Davidson when I did has resulted in oral testimony and written reminiscences that are no longer available.

Chapter 12

'You Did What, Mr President!?!?' Trying to Write a Biography of Tosiwo Nakayama

David Hanlon

At the time of this writing in March, 2006, Tosiwo Nakayama lies gravely ill in Waipahu, a former plantation town on the island of Oʻahu flattened, paved over and built upon with shopping malls and track houses. Japanese and later Filipino immigrants once worked the sugar cane fields of Waipahu. More recently, the town has become home to an increasing number of people from Micronesia; most notably those from Chuuk and the Marshall Islands. Their presence is the result of provisions within the Compact of Free Association between the United States and the governments of the Federated States of Micronesia (FSM) and the Republic of the Marshall Islands that allow for the free movement of Micronesians into the United States and its territories. Tosiwo Nakayama, the first president of the FSM, helped negotiate that compact.

There is considerable unease surrounding his present situation in Hawaiʻi; those who tend to him in that two-story townhouse in Waipahu are his most immediate family members: his daughter Sydiniha, his youngest son Masami, and other female members of his extended family resident on the island. The United States government has extended no recognition to this former head of state lying ill within its borders, and members of the FSM consulate in Honolulu struggle with the lack of established protocol for his presence. Nakayama's current circumstances seem a less than dignified or respectful culmination to a distinguished life. Perhaps the uneasiness surrounding his situation suggests something of the ways in which the nation-state he helped build is regarded by those who reside within its borders and by those who are bound by diplomatic treaty to respect its sovereignty. Or do the restrained responses to his weakened condition remind us of how belittling the prefix 'micro' is? Micro as in 'Micronesian', meaning tiny or small, and not terribly important to those for whom size matters. That is the way Micronesia has been viewed historically and historiographically; that is the way Micronesian immigrants tend to be viewed now in Hawaiʻi. Tosiwo Nakayama, then, dies as a 'micro' man whose contributions to the founding of the Federated States of Micronesia do not allow him to escape the belittling, still colonising gaze cast upon people from small, distant islands to the west of Hawai'i. I am interested in the meanings of Tosiwo Nakayama's life that precede, include and transcend his current condition.

Born to a Japanese father and a local woman in 1931 on Piserach, a part of the atoll complex of Onon in the Namonuito group of islands that lies some 200 miles to the northwest of the main Chuuk Lagoon group, Nakayama grew up during Japan's colonial administration of greater Micronesia. Perhaps, the skills he developed negotiating the different worlds from which his father and mother came help explain his success in later forging a national government from a collection of disparate island groups. Before he reached the age of 15, Nakayama had lived through a world war and a subsequent change in colonial administrations. Nakayama proved adept at adjusting to life in post-war Chuuk, then known as Truk, and under the United States Trust Territory of the Pacific Islands. He learned English and graduated from the Pacific Islands Central School (PICS) on Weno Island, also called Moen and the administrative center for Chuuk during the Trust Territory period. Nakayama later went on to spend time studying at the University of Hawai'i's Mānoa campus.

Returning to Chuuk in 1958, Nakayama advanced quickly through a series of administrative positions to become assistant district director for Public Affairs. Most notable in this time period are his efforts on behalf of autonomy and self-government at both the local and trust territory-wide levels. He served first as a representative from Namonuito and then as president in the Truk District Congress. In 1965, Nakayama won election to the House of Delegates of the Congress of Micronesia. In 1968, he succeeded Amata Kabua of the Marshalls as president of that legislative body. More than any other individual, Tosiwo Nakayama is credited with managing the complex, sensitive political negotiations on Saipan in 1975 that resulted in a draft national constitution for the different Micronesian states or districts seeking political autonomy from the United States.

A proponent of independence for Micronesia since his student days at the University of Hawai'i, Nakayama served as an early member of the Congress of Micronesia's Future Political Status Commission, and was a key player in the long difficult negotiations with the United States government that culminated in the Compact of Free Association. Nakayama worked aggressively on behalf of the compact, arguing for its passage throughout the islands and against strong opposition in the Northern Marianas, the Marshalls, and Palau where sentiment for separate political negotiations with the United States ultimately prevailed. Despite this separation, the Federated States of Micronesia came into being as a result of the constitution's ratification in 1978 by the remaining island states of Chuuk, Kosrae, Pohnpei, and Yap. These same four states later approved the draft Compact of Free Association with the United States in a 1983 plebiscite.

By vote of his congressional colleagues, Tosiwo Nakayama was chosen as the first president of the FSM. His inauguration took place on 15 May 1979. More than seven years would pass before the United States Congress completed its review and approval of the compact. In the interim, Nakayama concerned himself with matters of government. During his first four-year term in office, Nakayama focused on transition issues, nation building, economic development, and the distribution of power and responsibilities between the national and four state governments. He worked in his second term to establish the FSM's regional and international credibility.

A study of the life of Tosiwo Nakayama, however, involves much more than a narrative of political events. From a small atoll complex whose survival depended upon voyaging and navigation, Nakayama's career parallels the current regional reemergence of these nautical abilities as powerful testaments to cultural pride and dignity. Similarly, Nakayama's personal and professional travels foreshadowed the current migration of Micronesian peoples; as previously noted, his efforts on behalf of the Compact of Free Association have enabled Micronesian migration to the United States and its territories. Nakayama's rise to prominence in Chuuk constitutes a remarkable story given the physical, political, and cultural distance that separates the Namonuitos from the main Lagoon group. Put another way, he was an outer islander.

Complex engagements with colonialism, decolonisation, and nation-making were central to Nakayama's career; these encounters place him squarely in the middle of some of the most complex, important issues in 20th-century Pacific Islands history. Nakayama's career also affords the opportunity to examine the gap between political theory and practice. While anthropologists, historians, and social science researchers debate modernisation, development and the appropriateness of the term 'Micronesia', Nakayama had to call upon historical linkages, common experiences, and shared aspirations among varied and diverse groups of island people. Tosiwo Nakayama's life, then, offers a critical focal lens through which to examine a host of key themes that link Micronesia to the larger Pacific region and beyond.

I first met Tosiwo Nakayama on Pohnpei in 1973. My wife and I were Peace Corps volunteers preparing to leave the island after three years of teaching English and social studies at a Catholic mission school in the south of the island. We were in Kolonia at the time, the aptly named capitol of the island. The Congress of Micronesia was holding a session on the island, one in a series of visits designed to better connect this still fledgling representative body with its widely dispersed constituency of atoll and island dwellers spread across an area about the size of the continental United States. Negotiations with the United States over a new political status had already begun, and members of the congress's Future Political Status Commission were also seeking the input of elected and traditional leaders in the different island districts. There was a reception for the congress near the Catholic Mission in Kolonia to which my wife and I were invited. I remember sitting in one of the chairs that lined the walls of the long, rectangular meeting room with tiled floor, thinly panelled walls and a corrugated tin roof. Nakayama, then president of the Congress of Micronesia's Senate, came up to us, extended his hand, and said simply 'Tos Nakayama'. I remember being struck by his modesty and good looks. Twenty-seven years later, I met him again, this time in the restaurant of the Honolulu Airport's Best Western Hotel where I agreed to work with him on the story of his life.

Why? Living for almost eight years on the island of Pohnpei had taught us to look beyond labels such as 'underdeveloped'. I learned something of how rich life could be amidst communities bound together by a strong sense of kin, clan, family, and church relationships. I remember marvelling at how in control people seemed to be of their lives—of how focused they were on their social relationships—despite a succession of colonial regimes in the region. In more academic environments of the early 1980s, the word 'agency' spoke to the realisation of peoples' roles in the making of their own worlds and in their encounters with others. I wrote a general history of the island of Pohnpei that sought above all else to portray a rich and dynamic island world that persevered against an array of external threats, not the least of which was epidemic disease. I authored a later book entitled *Remaking Micronesia* that took a larger regional view of the way people engaged with both the discourses and forces of development. While the balance of power in this engagement was decidedly asymmetrical, I saw agency too in different peoples' efforts to make a better world that was still their world. I saw agency in the person of Tosiwo Nakayama in 1973.

I used to teach a course in World Civilisations at the University of Hawai'i; it was an impossible course that sought to acquaint students with the variety of human experiences over time. I subverted the conventions of that course by including a section on the peopling of the Pacific and by advertising that settlement as being one of humankind's greatest historical accomplishments. I would describe the creation of the Federated States of Micronesia in less effusive terms, perhaps, but nonetheless as a remarkable achievement.

A study of Tosiwo Nakayama's life also offers the opportunity to glimpse local engagements with the American colonial presence, and the creation of a nation state against a formidable array of local and external forces, not the least of which were the divisions among Micronesians themselves. The approval of the constitution of the FSM was but the beginning of a difficult foundational period. There were the complex negotiations with the Trust Territory government over separation and transition; the physical and political difficulties of establishing a capitol for the new government on a reserved, not always appreciative Pohnpei; and the intense debates over states rights, powers, and revenue entitlements. Within the FSM, there was concern over the possible domination of Chuuk at the expense of the smaller states, most notably Kosrae and Yap. Nakayama was at the center of all this, and his mediation skills were sometimes required in the settlement of more immediate, personal and ethnic crises such as the stabbing of a Pohnpeian by Chuukese youth in 1983 on Pohnpei.

Nakayama committed himself early on to independence. He said, in the course of a week-long series of interviews at his home on Weno in early January of 2001, that his early work for the Trust Territory government in Truk had convinced him that Americans could not administer the islands effectively or prepare them for self-government. He thought Micronesians needed to govern their own islands. There is more than a little irony in Nakayama's call for unity and independence. To be sure, it was the Chuukese or Trukese delegation in the Congress of Micronesia that was most critical of the American administration in the late 1960s and early 1970s. Members of the Chuukese delegation in this period were also quite adamant in their insistence on independence for the future Micronesian state. Nonetheless, Chuuk is considered the most divided and contentious of the Micronesian island groups. It's a description with a historical pedigree that goes back almost to first contact between the islands and the larger world. 'Dreaded Hogelau' is the term used by some historians to describe the factionalism and rivalry that seemed to characterise the lagoon group then. It's a characterisation that in the minds of many still fits in the first years of the 21st century.

Chuuk's alleged backwardness was a concern of the Trust Territory government. More recent assessments, such as the United States Government Accounting Office's report on the use of compact monies in the FSM, have stressed the corruption that has impeded Chuuk's development, making it a major drain on the struggling government. The prejudice is not necessarily a colonial construction or artifact. Distrust of Chuukese is acute among other Micronesian peoples and is pointed too as a potential cause for the dissolution of the FSM.

Nakayama, however, dismissed criticisms of the region as too diverse and divided. He believed differences among Micronesians were exaggerated by outsiders whose own interests, prejudices and world views were served by the presumption of divisiveness. He did not share understandings of Micronesia as a colonial construct. He saw links, connections and commonalities that the name 'Micronesia' spoke well enough too. He articulated his belief on numerous occasions during the ratification campaign for the FSM constitution that the resources of the surrounding seas could easily provide the revenues to sustain a unified government. During his trip to various islands during the ratification campaign, he often told the story of a previously dismembered ocean deity made whole again by those who believed in him.

If there are reasons enough to justify a life history of Tosiwo Nakayama, what then are the themes, patterns, or interpretive lens through which Nakayama's life might be understood? Voyaging is an often used (perhaps too often) metaphor in Pacific studies. Voyaging, however, is a metaphor that might serve us well in understanding something of Nakayama's lineage. I'm thinking here of Nakayama not so much as the navigator for the FSM ship of state or of the extensive travel that was a feature of his public life. Rather, I have in mind something more immediate and personal. Nakayama hails from Onon in the Namonuito group of islands. One of Nakayama's uncles was a respected navigator who sailed the seas around the Namonuito group. Nakayama himself once thought about leaving his public career to return to Onon to learn the navigator's craft. He was certainly competent and comfortable on the ocean. Fishing was a passion of his, especially during his days as FSM president on Pohnpei. There are stories of him putting his ear to the boat floor to listen for fish. Another account speaks of an earlier incident when he successfully took over as navigator for a field trip ship whose radar system had broken down on the way to the islands of Yap. We might think of him, then, as a would-have-been navigator had his life been less affected by colonialism and war.

Tosiwo Nakayama is quite literally a child of the Japanese colonial presence in Micronesia. His father was an employee of the Nan'yō Kabushikigaisha (Nambō) trading company that was so commercially prominent in the islands during Japan's tenure. Nakayama and his family accompanied their father on different assignments that included extended stays on Lukunor in the nearby Mortlocks, and on Tol and Tolawas in the Faichuk area of the Chuuk lagoon. Nakayama describes his father as being quite adept in English and with a sense of the importance of that language for the islands' future. Nakayama never mentioned learning any English from his father; he may, however, have had his father's ear for language as he developed over his career a good ability in English despite his limited formal schooling.

The American repatriation of all Japanese nationals from Micronesia following the end of hostilities separated father from family. One of the more intriguing anecdotes from Nakayama's personal history involves the search for his father during a trip to Japan in the late 1960s. The Chuukese son eventually brought his Japanese father back to Weno to live with him in the family home by the shore. Nakayama's father now lies buried just outside of that home in a marked grave surrounded by a modest wooden fence and covered by a small tin roof. Towards the end of his life, Nakayama's father, somewhat senile it seems, tended the family's small retail store. He was a popular sales clerk as he often returned people's money with their purchases.

One of the more remarkable aspects of Tosiwo Nakayama's life is the network of relationships throughout the Chuuk group and further west that would later translate into political support. Prejudice within the Chuuk lagoon group against people from the outer islands remains pronounced. Nakayama's birth on Onon gave him no advantage on Weno or in the surrounding lagoon area, and by itself could have been a very limiting factor for anyone with ambition. The personal relationships established on those islands where his father resided for extended periods of time as a commercial agent of Nambō came strongly into play in his election to the Congress of Micronesia and later to the Congress of the Federated States of Micronesia where popular electoral success was a condition of eligibility for the presidency.

Nakayama claims to have had no ambition, certainly no plan for a political career. But his travels, multiple residences, and close personal ties with the people among whom he lived as a boy and young man go a long way toward explaining his electoral success. His ability to garner support from the many island areas that made up Truk district, later Chuuk state, allowed him to overcome the disadvantages of a candidate not from Weno or the lagoon proper.

There is also Nakayama's paternal ancestry. It linked him to a group of people who became quite prominent in Chuuk during the Trust Territory period. These island men, born of Japanese fathers and Chuukese women, were known for their energy, drive, and entrepreneurial ability. They were often called upon to serve as representatives or go-betweens in matters involving governance or economy with the Trust Territory government. Nakayama's association with this prominent, commercially successful network of individuals proved a decided asset. Perhaps, the most politically strategic of relationships was his marriage to Mihter, a member of the Sopwunipi clan that was dominant on Weno and prominent in the larger lagoon area. The geographical distribution of Nakayama's own clan stretched from Nomonuito west into Yap. This link to Yap would provide him with strong support at critical times during his career in the Congress of Micronesia and as president of the FSM.

Nakayama was a facilitator, a consensus seeker not given to confrontations or public posturing. He showed little emotion and was a quiet man who preferred private conversations and small social gatherings. As president of the Congress of Micronesia's Senate from 1968 to 1979, he rarely spoke for the congressional record on key matters affecting policy or legislation; he confined himself instead to procedural matters, and left the more public speeches for others. Nakayama was also a self-effacing leader; he voted for his opponent, Amata Kabua of the Marshalls, in the 1968 election that brought him the presidency of the Congress of Micronesia's Senate. He was a pragmatic man as well. When I asked him why he settled for free association with the United States rather than the independence he had initially and vigorously championed, he replied simply that free association was the best deal that could be gotten.

Those closest to him note that he grew quieter when angry. Emotions and the threat of violence swirled about him nonetheless. He responded to threats of violence against his person in one election by travelling to Tolowas in the Faichuk area to meet with then congressman Kalisto Refalopei, the source of those threats. At the end of the 1975 Micronesian constitutional convention, he brokered a last minute deal that made possible the approval of a draft constitution despite deep dissatisfaction within the Palau, Marshalls, and Mariana delegations. At that closed door session, Nakayama sat between John Ngiraked of Palau and Leo Falcam of Pohnpei. Tensions ran high between the two men on either side of Nakayama. Words, gestures, glances, and body posture, reported those present, conveyed the two men's deep unease with one another. Falcam, himself a future president of the FSM, spoke for unity and the draft constitution; Ngiraked was committed to a separate government for Palau. Nakayama, personally closer to the Pohnpeian than the Palauan, would sometimes step on Falcam's foot when exchanges became particularly heated. Ultimately, the convention delegates approved the draft constitution but with the tacit understanding that not all of the districts would join the Federated States of Micronesia.

Violence would become associated with the careers of both Falcam and Ngiraked. Falcam in 1986 promised that blood would run through the streets of Pohnpei should the Faichuk area of Chuuk be recognised as a separate and second Chuukese state within the FSM, a development that threatened the very tenuous and fragile balance of power among the four existing states of Chuuk, Kosrae, Pohnpei, and Yap. Ngiraked would be arrested, tried, convicted, and jailed for masterminding the assassination of the Republic of Palau's second president, Haruo Remelik.

The pressures on Nakayama were many and constant throughout his public life. There were threats against his life, and intense surveillance on his movements and activities especially during negotiations with the United States over the Compact of Free Association. His absence from home placed considerable pressure and hardship on his family, most especially his wife and two eldest sons. Nakayama, however, did not use his position for private gain. His own public career is remarkably free of controversy or scandal. The same cannot be said for family members. His brother-in-law was impeached as governor of Chuuk State in the early 1980s for misuse of public funds. More recently, Nakayama's daughter and son-in law were indicted, again for the misuse of public funds and as part of a wider investigation into fraud and corruption in Chuuk state carried out by the attorney general's office of the FSM government.

It would be a mistake to see Nakayama as more than he actually was. He brought people together and through dialogue, reassurance, and persuasion. His most important political asset may well have been his patience. Nakayama did not act alone, but rather in consort with others who shared his belief that Micronesians were best able to govern themselves. A life history of Tosiwo Nakayama will need careful attention to his friend and colleague Andohn Amaraich, now chief justice of the Federated States of Micronesia. Amaraich, like Nakayama, was a largely self-educated man who served in the Congress of Micronesia and later headed the Congress of Micronesia's Future Political Status Commission in its negotiations with representatives of the United States. Amaraich shared Nakayama's vision for independence. There are those who view Amaraich, more than Nakayama, as the visionary and architect for what became the Federated States of Micronesia.

Betwel Henry from the outlying island of Mokil or Mwoakilloa in Pohnpei state served as the speaker of the Congress of Micronesia's House of Representatives for many years. Henry is credited with being the tactician who actually brokered many of the compromises that made possible the emergence of the FSM. The three—Amaraich, Henry, and Nakayama—are often spoken of as a triumvirate. Other prominent names from this period of state formation include Petrus Tun and John Mangafel of Yap, Lazarus Sali and Roman Tmetuchl of Palau, and Ambilos Iieshi and Bailey Olter of Pohnpei. One of the reasons behind Nakayama's cooperation in this biography project is the belief that the story of these early formative years of the FSM is being forgotten and that current leaders have lost a sense of vision and commitment to the nation in favour of more immediate parochial and personal interests.

The issues surrounding and even confounding a biography of Tosiwo Nakayama are many and considerable. This is a project that I was asked to do by those close to Nakayama personally and professionally. They perhaps seek a life history that celebrates a man and his many accomplishments. It would be easy enough to make this biography a hagiography. Among the more than 35 formal interviews I have recorded with Nakayama's colleagues and associates, only one individual ventured comments that were substantively critical of Nakayama and on grounds that he was far more a politician than a leader. The vast majority of individuals I have interviewed across Micronesia over the last few years have spoken glowingly of Nakayama, including those in the Marshalls and Palau who opposed him in his efforts to promote Micronesian unity. It would be naive, perhaps, to expect that I as a stranger to most of these men could elicit within a single meeting comments that were other than positive.

The artificiality of formal interviews is but a part of the larger problem of doing a life history of a Micronesian. Biography can certainly be an alien, intrusive venture into lives whose parameters are defined, even subsumed, by a complex, interlocking network of kin, clan and family. There is the fact too that we are dealing with multiple identities and inter-subjectivities. Nakayma was a man whose life involved numerous relationships and accompanying responsibilities; he was a son, brother, nephew, husband, father, uncle, friend, clan mate, student, church member, government worker, elected official, national leader, and president of his country. Depending upon circumstances, he would identify himself by home island, clan membership, family affiliation, and as Trukese, Chuukese, or Micronesian. At different times in his life, he dealt with people who called themselves Chamorros, Guamanians, Kosraeans, Marshallese, Palauans, Pohnpeians, Yapese, Americans, Australians, Fijians, Israelis, Japanese, and Samoans to list a few. And there is the very fundamental question as to what kind of man Tosiwo Nakayama was. The anthropological literature suggests that modernisation has had a highly disruptive effect on Chuukese masculinity. This does not seem to be a prominent issue in Nakayama's life. If so, then the question is why. What is it that allowed Nakayama to be secure, assured and confident in his identity?

It would be a mistake to speak or write of Tosiwo Nakayama only in his more political and leadership roles. He was much more than the public descriptions and accounts provided by Trust Territory officials, diplomats, compact negotiators, American negotiators, and academic observers that constitute the written archive on his life. It would be wrong as well to frame his life solely against the discourses of governance and development with which he engaged. But how to do it? How to tell his life story in a way that captures his complexity, his humanity, his significance, and in a way that he and his people would recognise?

I have already indicated in this essay something of the issues around sources. Let me expand. Soon after agreeing to take on this project, I asked Tosiwo Nakayama if I could have access to his personal papers. He replied that had he any, he would most certainly make them available to me. Unfortunately, he continued, he had thrown them all away shortly after leaving the presidency in 1986. I was dismayed. My inner voice cried out: 'You did what, Mr. President!?!?' The public records of the Federated States of Micronesia for the Nakayama presidency pose another kind of problem. I have been told they exist, but have yet to locate them or identify anyone who knows where exactly they are stored. Given the climatic conditions in Micronesia, the often erratic power supply there, and the generally low priority accorded the preservation of government records, my fear of what I might find sometimes approaches my fear of finding nothing.

Nakayama's life is certainly not without documentation. There are the microfilmed records of the Trust Territory administration housed at the University of Hawai'i, Mānoa, and other selective sites throughout the region.

This rather extensive collection includes over 2,500 reels of microfilmed reports, correspondence, minutes of meetings, and government publications, much of it concerned with matters of governance and future political status. This will help. The secondary and periodical literature is also considerable; Nakayama's name figures prominently in studies of politics, governance, constitutionalism, and the Compact of Free Association. Official American records from Nakayama's time are more difficult to access; many are still classified. Those that are available can be accessed only though a time consuming and costly application process as specified in the United States Congress's Freedom of Information Act. There are too the highly sensitive psychological profiles of Chuukese leaders commissioned by Trust Territory government officials and done by the American anthropologist Jack Fischer in the early 1950s. The Pacific Collection on the fifth floor of the University of Hawai'i's Hamilton Library holds the university's international student records on Micronesians from the 1950s and 1960s; these include quite detailed, even intimate reports on the many future political leaders of Micronesia who studied in Hawai'i during this period. Finally, I did spend considerable time with Nakayama himself in late December of 2000 and early January of 2001. I visited his home on Weno where I conducted 13 hours of recorded and since transcribed interviews with him. These, of course, are invaluable but nonetheless are affected by Nakayama's self-admitted memory loss and poor health.

To be honest, I think Nakayama was also careful, selective and even evasive at times in these interviews. His stated reason for cooperating in this biography project is the belief that the story of the FSM's formative years has been forgotten by those local leaders desperately in need of remembering it. It is, then, a political biography he would have me write and for contemporary political purposes. While I understand Nakayama's life as being about much more than politics, this biography project may well end up concentrating on his public life. If so, I still have many questions to ask. I want to know more about his Japanese ancestry, about his father's forced repatriation to Japan, and about how growing up during Japanese colonial times may have influenced his later political views. I have questions too about what strikes me as Nakayama's denial of the very real divisions within the FSM. Tosiwo Nakayama is unable to answer these questions, however. He is desperately ill in Waipahu, conscious and alert but no longer able to speak.

I return to the circumstances surrounding Nakayama's current presence in Hawai'i. It may be that they reflect his noble but flawed vision of an autonomous government not much believed in by some of its citizens and not much respected by the United States with which it is associated. Still, I contend that a biography of this individual is important for what he tried to do, for the historical and contemporary issues with which his life engages, and for the ways in which he sought to redefine the boundaries of a Micronesia and reconfigure the self-imaging of Micronesians. This is what makes trying to do a biography of Tosiwo Nakayama a worthy and important project.

Postscript:

Tosiwo Nakayama passed away on March 29, 2007 in Hawai'i.

Chapter 13

Telling the Life of A.D. Patel

Brij V. Lal

Ambalal Dahyabhai Patel, or 'AD', as he was universally known, was the greatest leader of the Indo-Fijian community in colonial Fiji and, arguably, one of the country's most brilliant public intellectuals. Steeped in the Gandhian tradition of politics, at whose dawn he came of age, possessing astute political skills, widely read and far-sighted, at home in several languages, the most outstanding criminal lawyer of his day, he strode the public stage like none other. Often at the centre of the most momentous events in Fiji's post-war history, he was nevertheless unable, in his own lifetime, to realise the vision of a non-racial political culture based on the principle of the common roll. Born in Gujarat in 1905, Patel came to Fiji in 1928 and died there in 1969, a year before the colony became independent.

The most ardent advocate of Fiji's independence is now a forgotten figure in Fiji, remembered, if remembered at all, in a few primary and secondary schools which bear his name and among the fading generation of National Federation Party supporters, the party he founded in 1963. On the other hand, Patel's counterpart among Fijians, Ratu Sir Lala Sukuna, is honoured in public memorials and a national holiday named after him, his legacy of chiefly leadership commemorated in an authorised biography.[1] In recent years, Sukuna has become somewhat of a national public icon while the public knowledge of Patel's enormous contribution to the political life of his adopted country, and the inclusive non-racial vision he espoused all his life, has receded, a result, no doubt, of a deliberate policy of manicuring reputations and accentuating things Fijian in the broader scheme of things. However great or worthy a non-Fijian, it is unlikely that he or she will be allowed to compete for national limelight with the stars of the Fijian establishment.[2] Fiji's icons will always remain Fijian.

In 1997, after a decade of interrupted research, I published my biography of A.D. Patel, *A Vision for Change: A.D. Patel and the politics of Fiji*.[3] I reflect here on how I came to write the biography, the sources I used and how these helped or hindered my research effort. Ten years on, new sources of information, principally the Colonial Office records at the Public Record Office (PRO) in Kew Gardens, have became available on the most crucial decade of Fiji's political evolution—the 1960s—in which Patel had a major role to play.[4] Does the new archival material require revision of the conclusions I reached in the book? Does it fundamentally alter the terms of the debate about Fiji's decolonisation? These and related questions form the substance of this chapter.

I do not quite know when I first heard A.D. Patel's name. There was our neighbour, Mr Ram Dayal Singh, an illiterate but wealthy cane farmer and bus-owner, whom we grew up calling Patel. He was nicknamed after A.D., apparently for his ingenious, irrefutable arguments in village meetings to sway decisions in his favour, as A.D. Patel, the canny criminal lawyer, did in the court room. But this connection came to me much later. I must have heard Patel's name during the 1959 strike, prolonged and devastating, causing a shortage of sugar at home and often making us go without it. Patel was the leader of the strike. His name, mentioned in disapproving tones on the radio which had just arrived in our settlement, was at the outer edges of our political consciousness during the 1960s as Fiji hurtled towards independence. Labasa was a rural, isolated backwater then, and politics was never discussed at school except perfunctorily and surreptitiously among teachers and then, too, away from the earshot of students.

It was at university that I first became aware of Patel's role in Fiji's public life. I soon discovered that most official records and recollections, oral and written, either deified or demonised him; frequently the latter among the urban elite who sought to shore up not shake the colonial establishment. The *Fiji Times*, the only local daily then, portrayed Patel always as a dangerous man bent on wreaking havoc on the country to gain political power at any cost. I realised the full range and scope of Patel's contribution after I had finished my postgraduate studies at The Australian National University, published my dissertation, and, getting interested in the more recent history of Fiji, was on the lookout for a new topic. It was then that A.D. Patel's life suggested itself. Existing references to Patel's ambition and his dubious commitment to Fiji simply whetted my appetite.[5] There was, on reflection, another reason for my interest in the man. Soon after returning to Fiji, I began to take scholarly interest in contemporary national politics.[6] The National Federation Party was tearing itself apart over leadership in the 1970s. As I sought to understand why, I got more and more interested in its early history and, as an extension, in the charismatic leadership of its founder. By the 1970s, Patel had become, in the eyes of his supporters, a mythic figure, similar in influence and stature to Ratu Sir Lala Sukuna.

Having resolved to work on Patel, I wrote to his widow, Leela, expressing my wish and seeking her permission to consult Patel's papers (if they existed). The reply never came: people in Fiji do not generally write letters, but permission was generously given when I began the project and approached the family in person. The family cooperated fully, but not once did they ask to see the manuscript when it was completed or seek to know about my lines of enquiry.

I was welcomed with open arms and allowed to consult whatever papers I wanted, including Patel's private letters and his diary, his official correspondence.[7] His children, especially Patel's two daughters, Pratibha and Vasantika, placed at my disposal letters their father wrote, and Leela answered questions about the family scene: the long car rides, the Sunday picnics, the late night games of bridge, the music and singing, the personal quirks of her late husband, his occasional absent-mindedness as he became absorbed in preparing for important court cases, his incessant appetite for reading. In these conversations, Patel came through as a warm, caring father to whom the happiness of his family was paramount. But the timing was wrong. Soon after writing to Leela, I left Suva for Honolulu where I turned my attention to other topics, the coups of 1987 and the modern history of Fiji. For a while Patel faded from my research radar. A heavy teaching load took its own toll on my time and energy. But upon returning to Australia in 1990, and with books on the coup and 20th century history of Fiji written, I returned to Patel, now with purpose and determination to finish a project I had first contemplated a decade ago.[8]

In Canberra, I was fortunate to have two major sources which were to prove highly relevant to my research. One was the Colonial Sugar Refining (CSR) Company archives at the Noel Butlin Archives of Business and Labour. Patel had been at the centre stage of the sugar industry disputes in 1943 and 1960, and the key advocate for the cane growers before the Denning Arbitration in 1969. His role in the disputes was the cause of much controversy, some of it continuing to this day.[9] The CSR papers, I hoped, would enable a deeper probing of a controversial subject, which they did but not to the degree I had expected. They were useful in providing an insight into the CSR view of things and how the company sought to influence people and events to its advantage. But apart from the strike papers, I did not find much of direct value to me. The bulk of the archival material deals with the day-to-day operations of the company, correspondence between various mills in Fiji and the CSR headquarters in Sydney. Like the Patel family, the CSR, too, gave me unconditional access to its papers and placed no restriction on what I might or might not see. Clearly, as far as the company was concerned, its days in Fiji were a part of a receding history. It could be magnanimous because for it, the past was truly past.

The other major source in Canberra was the complete set of the weekly journal *Pacific Review* which Patel started in 1949. In its early years, the *Review* was remarkably liberal and informative, bringing to Fiji news from around the world that was critical of imperial and colonial practices, news which the *Fiji Times* would never publish. The weekly died with Patel. Past employees and correspondents of the *Pacific Review* had told me that in the 1950s, when Patel was out of active politics and to a lesser extent in the 1960s, when he was the centre of it, he wrote most of the editorials. The *Pacific Review* proved indispensable for my research, providing me access to material, sometimes confidential, that I could not find in the archives. *Pacific Review*'s Hindi counterpart, *Jagriti*, was less informative but important in gauging the pulse of the Indo-Fijian farming community. Both these newspapers were effective counterweights to the *Fiji Times* and the *Fiji Broadcasting Commission*. In 1989 and 1990, I wrote to several former colonial officials who knew Patel and worked closely with him, especially when he was Member of Social Services between 1964 and 1967. I also wrote to former governor Sir Kenneth Maddocks and Lord Denning, whose responses are discussed later on.[10]

By the time I went to Fiji in 1992, I had gathered much material of direct relevance to the project. In Fiji, I was keen to pursue three sources. The first was archival. Much of the material before 1947 I had already seen when researching my *Broken Waves*. Unfortunately for the 1960s, the critical period in Fiji's transition to independence, the files were not available under the 30-year rule. They were available now, but were not of much value. The substance of the most important policy papers was already available in the newspapers or in private collections. I was told by a very senior colonial official about five years ago that much of the sensitive, personal material about prominent leaders had actually been destroyed just before independence, apparently a fairly standard practice at the close of colonial rule. Besides unpublished files, I systematically read all the *Hansard* for the years Patel was a member of the Legislative Council (1944-1950 and 1963-1969) to gauge his views on controversial public issues of the day. The second mission I had to accomplish in Fiji was to consult Patel's private papers, and the third was to interview people who knew Patel or were in some way associated with him.

By 1994, I began writing the book, and by 1995 had managed to produce a substantial draft. But I was then called to serve on the Fiji Constitution Commission from 1995-1996. The disruption was prolonged and intense. Nevertheless, I used whatever free time I had to write and revise chapters. In one important sense, the timing was fortuitous. Writing and reflecting on Patel's life, often deep into the night, kept the forgotten struggle for a just and fair constitution for Fiji and all its people at the forefront of my mind. I was acutely aware of the missteps and failures of past efforts and keen to move beyond Fiji's constitutional cul-de-sac. An awareness of the past weighed heavily on my mind during these two critical years when we ourselves were charting a new course for Fiji. I had written in my *Broken Waves* that Fiji's modern history was a history of missed opportunities, and I hoped very much that our work would not take that route.

I will not revisit the central arguments of the biography here. The reception has been warm, both in published reviews as well as in private correspondence. I particularly cherish a private, unsolicited, letter from Peter France, sometime

Secretary for Fijian Affairs and the author of the great *Charter of the Land: custom and colonisation in Fiji*. He wrote on 19 March 1998: '[Y]our book made me feel at the same time a regret that I had not got to know AD better and a satisfaction that I had been able to live, for a time, inside his head. You demonstrate superbly that AD often spoke and acted, from a position not only of intellectual, but of moral superiority. This was emphatically not widely recognised during his lifetime and we are all in your debt for pointing it out'. But privately, some individuals, usually former politicians bitterly opposed to Patel but who had now joined the National Federation Party after leaving the Alliance Party for a variety of reasons, wrote to me to say that I had grossly exaggerated Patel's role, elevated him to the level of statesman when he was nothing more than a common garden variety politician, a grasping Gujarati feeding off the ignorance of cane growers whose case he claimed to champion. But negative responses were few. Some pointed out, gleefully or helpfully, minor errors which will be corrected in any future edition.

This leads me to the value of private correspondence for my research. Most of these were from British colonial officials who had served in Fiji on lengthy tours of duty, most of them in departments directly dealing with the Fijians. They elucidated points, clarified doubts and suggested other contacts or lines of enquiry. Their value is immeasurable, not least because they provided a counterweight to the Patel papers. I shall illustrate this with a small sample of responses I received. The first is from Sir Kenneth Maddocks, governor of Fiji between 1958 and 1964, a critical time for the colony, coinciding with the industrial disturbance in Suva in 1959 and a strike in the sugar industry in 1960 and the first official move, after nearly 30 years, towards constitutional change preparing the way for greater internal self-government. Patel was pilloried in the press and by his critics for his vaulting ambition, his heartless attitude to the suffering of the cane growers he was representing. The *Fiji Times* wrote about Patel and his followers as 'cowards who hide in cane fields to destroy by fire the fruits of other men's labour ... self-seeking, politically ambitious, emotionally twisted grabbers of power by lies and intimidation'.[11]

Maddocks, who had come to Fiji from Tanganyika where he had been governor, saw Patel as a 'very capable, quick-witted and experienced advocate, determined to press his case forcefully and inflexibly'. The strike had antagonised some Fijian cane growers, caused violence and necessitated the declaration of emergency in the sugar belts of Fiji to protect farmers who wanted to harvest or, in effect, break the strike. All that was on the debit side. 'On the other hand', Maddocks continued, 'there is no doubt that he had a case'. But this is *not* what the governor said at the time or in his correspondence with London. Throughout the '60s, everyone denied that Patel had a case. For its part, the CSR viewed cane growers as a lazy, profligate lot whose sorry fate was entirely their own doing.

The strike was broken, and a commission of enquiry under Sir Malcolm Trustram Eve instituted. The Eve report criticised Patel as an intelligent but misguided man who could, if he wanted to, provide leadership of the 'right kind'. Eve accused Patel and his colleagues of causing disruption in the sugar industry 'in the hope of gaining advantages for themselves and of trying to drive the millers out of Fiji'. The sugar industry had become a vehicle for 'ambitious politicians'.[12] Ambitious politicians: these are almost exactly the same words used to describe the strike leaders in 1943. Privately, Eve respected Patel's integrity, according to Robert Sanders, a senior colonial civil servant who served as Secretary to Cabinet for many years after Fiji became independent and who ghosted Ratu Mara's memoirs. Whatever the differences between himself and Patel, Eve said to Sanders, 'one loyalty he was convinced Mr Patel had was his loyalty to his Inn [Middle Temple]' and 'whatever other misgivings he might have he could rely on this'. Patel's opponents seized on Eve's public condemnation in his report to excoriate him. But in truth, as Patel had divined, the contract based on the Eve report broke many farmers and sent them into bankruptcy. Vijay R. Singh, who had led the anti-Patel faction during the strike, later called Patel the greatest leader the growers had ever had, as did N. S. Chalmers of the rival cane growers' group. Interestingly, when Patel went to London for the 1965 conference, Eve, by then Lord Silsoe, invited Patel for tea at his house, the man he had condemned four years back.

After a decade of grief in the sugar cane growing community, when the Eve contract expired, Lord Denning, Master of the Rolls in the United Kingdom and a highly respected judge in the Commonwealth, was appointed to arbitrate a new contract.[13] The atmosphere was charged. In 1969, Fiji was just a year away from independence. The war was on for the vote for the Indo-Fijian community in the cane belts of Viti Levu and Vanua Levu. Ratu Mara, keen to bolster his image as a multiracial leader, and encouraged by the members of the Indian Alliance and the Alliance-oriented Kisan Sangh, courted the Indo-Fijian vote assiduously. At the arbitration, the Alliance was represented by the lead counsel Geoffrey Brennan QC, later the Chief Justice of Australia. The Federation of Cane Growers, affiliated to the NFP, was represented by A.D. Patel (and Karam Ramrakha and Siddiq Koya). In his report, Denning confirmed what Patel and others had been saying throughout the '60s about the Eve contract, that it was heavily biased towards the millers and prejudiced against the growers. '[U]nder the Eve formula', Denning wrote, 'the risk of loss is all on the growers. None at all on the millers: or, at any rate, none to speak of'. Denning regretted Patel's death during the course of the arbitration and praised his advocacy skills: 'He was an accomplished advocate who presented admirably to me the case of the Federation'. But the Alliance went out of its way to claim that Denning's pro-grower report was the result of its own representation before the arbitration.[14] It was a popular claim, effective in the 1972 election campaign when the Alliance managed for the first—and the last—time nearly to win a quarter of the Indo-Fijian votes.

What was the truth? Did Patel's advocacy have any effect at all on the outcome of the arbitration? To find out, I wrote to Lord Denning himself, not really expecting a reply, not knowing whether the good Lord was still alive and active. To my great delight, I received a handwritten letter on House of Lord's stationery on 20 January 1990. 'I remember A.D. Patel well', Denning began. 'Of all the lawyers who appeared before me, A.D. Patel was outstanding. He even out-shone Mr Brennan (now of the High Court of Australia). He was a master of all the facts and particularly of the sugar industry in Fiji. He presented them with skill and understanding. It was his persuasive advocacy that led me to my report which was in favour of the growers and against the millers'. And what about Patel the man himself? 'A.D. Patel was intellectually the most brilliant, as a character the most honourable, and as an advocate, the most persuasive. Quick in mind, fluent in speech, he stood out above all.' But this fact came to light only in 1990, 20 years after Patel's opponents pilloried the man and downplayed his enormous contribution to the sugar industry in Fiji. Denning's priceless letter sets the record straight once and for all on a matter of great political moment in Indo-Fijian history: the beginning of the end of the CSR in Fiji. The value of such private correspondence cannot be overemphasised, nor the importance of luck. Parts of Denning's letter have been quoted in speeches in Fiji, but to no observable effect as far as I can tell.

Between 1964 and 1967, Patel was the Member for Social Services in the colonial government. Ratu Mara was the Member for Natural Resources and John Falvey the Member for Communication. The Membership System was an intermediate step toward full internal self-government later. About this period in Fiji's history, no outsider was a closer observer of events than Leonard Usher, then editor of the *Fiji Times*. Usher was an unapologetically, energetically, pro-establishment journalist whose assumed air of objectivity was insufficient camouflage for an intense dislike of Patel and his brand of politics. Acting Governor P.D. Macdonald wrote to London on 6 August 1965, criticising Usher who 'slyly hints at the unreasonableness of the attitude of the Federation group, and the rightness of the stand taken by the other groups; he stresses the difficulties and deadlocks at the conference, hinting that these are all the fault of the Federation group rather than encouraging the hope that statesmanship and compromise will prevail'.[15] The Fiji Intelligence Report for December 1965 reported of Usher having 'developed an almost pathological dislike of the Federation Party, and A.D. Patel in particular'. Trafford Smith, Assistant Under-Secretary of State for the Colonies, had a different opinion: 'A charming man to meet, not the bogey-man the Fiji Times makes him out to be'.[16] I knew of Usher's political leanings and prejudices. The records in London confirmed them in unambiguous terms. But I do not know if the government, knowing the facts about Usher's mischievous role in fanning the anti-Indian flame, ever cautioned him. Probably not, for the propaganda continued unabated.

The pages of the *Fiji Times* in the 1960s were full of anti-Federation invective. In an interview early in 1990, I asked Usher of his views on A.D. Patel. He praised Patel's intelligence and learning, his mastery of the English language, his rhetorical flourish (as virtually everyone I spoke did), but thought he was stubborn, uncompromising, politically ambitious for himself and his community and dangerous for Fiji. As Member of Social Services, Patel was a disaster, Usher said, because he did not take his responsibilities seriously, coming in late to the office, cursory with his administrative duties. The pattern was predictable. In Usher's mind, Patel was intent on wrecking the Membership System if only to vindicate the view that complete independence was the only answer to Fiji's problems. I asked Gordon Roger about this. Roger, a New Zealander like Usher, was a long-time Director of Education in Fiji, who had served directly under Patel in the mid-1960s. Roger had a completely different story to tell. According to him, Patel was an ideal mentor for senior civil servants. He differed from his successors in two main ways, Roger said. First, 'he had (or at least he gave the impression of having) no axe to grind. This meant he was able to look at educational ideas and problems in terms of *education*, not in terms of votes; and because we (his senior staff in the Edn Dept) had been brought up to do likewise there was in fact very little friction between us'. He goes on: 'I doubt whether we really appreciated at the time just what an easy introduction to the future ministerial system A.D. was in fact giving us'. There were differences between Patel and his staff in setting priorities, but Roger says that 'once we started looking at things through his eyes—he was a very persuasive teacher!—our generally negative attitude became much more positive'.

Roger gives an example of the way in which Patel 'handled' his staff. When he and his deputy Max Bay opposed an idea Patel had put up, he summoned the two to a morning tea-time meeting to explain their opposition to his proposal in person. 'It was the first time he'd used this ploy, and it proved very effective, because a hurriedly-convened staff meeting at 8am had shown me that the idea wasn't in fact nearly as impracticable as it had sounded 20 minutes earlier. When I subsequently told him how near I'd been to saying "no" again, he smiled engagingly and said, in the nicest possible way, "You know, Gordon, it's good for all of us to be made to think sometimes"'. Kenneth Bain, Patel's Permanent Secretary for Social Services, concurs. 'The circumstances of our coming together in this [the Membership System] were unusual and our relationship became one of considerable interest and, I believe, trust.' This, Bain, goes on to say, 'in spite of the fact that my wife stood for election to he Legislative Council as an Alliance-endorsed candidate'. In the circumstances, one must give preference to Roger's and Bain's version, based as it is on direct experience, over Usher's based on hearsay and prejudiced evidence. The extent of harm to race relations and to political negotiations by Usher's jaundiced views is beyond measure.

A constant refrain throughout the 1960s was that Patel was anti-European, which Patel denounced as a 'wicked lie'. How could he be anti-European when his first wife was an English woman? When his young children were attending school in England? 'If A.D. was anti-European', Roger recalled, 'I do not recall his ever showing it in my presence. Personally, I doubt whether he was. But even if he were, why not? There were plenty of Europeans around at the time who made no secret of the fact that they were anti-Indian'. Ray Baker, District Officer in the Fiji in the 1960s, did not think European colonial officials were overtly or deliberately anti-Indian, but it was 'probably true to say that most expatriate administrators were at that time pro-Fijian in the sense that we felt in sympathy with their perception of themselves as the *taukei*—the owners of most of the land but economically backward and overtaken in population by immigrant races'. On this aspect none other than Governor Derek Jakeway was in complete agreement. He said on a visit to Australia in February 1965, just as preparations were under way for the constitutional conference in London in July, that 'it was inconceivable that Britain would ever permit the Fijian people to be placed politically under the heels of an immigrant community'. Jakeway got it wrong. In truth, the Indo-Fijian leaders did not want *any* community to be dominated; they wanted political equality, and equality of representation. Patel was not anti-European: he was certainly anti-colonial. In the minds of colonial officials the two were one and the same thing.

Those who relied solely on the reports and coverage in the *Fiji Times* would, unsurprisingly, form a decidedly unpopular impression of Patel and his followers. But A.C. Reid's private recollection suggests another view. Reid was the trusted Secretary of Fijian Affairs and member of the hugely influential Fijian Affairs Board. In 1949, Patel, then a member of the Executive Council, visited Labasa with Swami Rudrananda. Reid then was Commissioner Northern. The official team was invited to the opening of a new school at Tuatua, on the outskirts of the local township. As Reid was walking up from the main road with Patel and Swamiji, they 'were suddenly confronted by one of the guests—annoyed at the flying of the Sangam flag over the gathering. As I remember, the management was Sangam but the school would be expected, under the rules, to fly the Union Jack on official occasions. There was an embarrassing pause until, bearing in mind A.D.'s senior position in the government, I sought his assistance and he turned to the Swami. While I did not know the precise content of what was said, it was clear that A.D. was determined to adhere to the rules, notwithstanding the Swami's glum reaction. I may add that a very new-looking Union flag was brought out of the school and hoisted up the flagpole'. Patel was, first and foremost, a constitutionalist in the rather old-fashioned way, acutely aware of the need to respect certain protocols and conventions.

Private recollections of the type I have quoted above, mostly from people who, at the time, were on the opposite side to Patel, help to complicate a picture of a man reviled in his time. My conversations with people in Fiji provided further insights into how Patel approached politics. He was a born politician who kept his finger squarely on the pulse of the community, finding time to talk to ordinary people about their problems and concerns. Every Saturday, without exception, he would go to the Nadi market to do the family's vegetable shopping—less to buy things than to mingle with the people. Whenever he returned from Suva to his home in Nadi, he would stop his car and buy fruits and vegetables Fijians sold by the roadside. When his wife protested at his extravagance, he would say, 'When that boy returns to his village, he will tell his family and friends that he sold vegetables to Patela. That is free publicity for us'. Whenever Patel addressed rallies, especially in western Viti Levu, he would ask the local chairman of the party what was being said on the ground so that he could adjust his speech accordingly. In 1963, Siddiq Koya, a Muslim, stood for election in a predominantly Hindu constituency. His opponent was James Shankar Singh, from a large and powerful Arya Samaj clan in Ba. His supporters, so it was reported, were telling people to vote for Singh and not Koya. When Patel was told this, he began his speech by saying 'It is true that Mr Koya is a Musalman, but at least he has remained true to his faith'. He did not need to mention 'James' Shankar Singh's name to drive home the point about Singh's conversion to Christianity. Religion never again surfaced in the campaign. Stories like this abound in the fading memories of a passing older generation.

When I wrote the biography, I had seen all the records, both open and confidential, under the 30-year rule at the National Archives of Fiji. But I had not seen the enormous archives at the Public Record Office. These contain dispatches from the governor in Fiji, records of deliberations in Whitehall about the future directions of policy regarding Fiji's independence, conference proceedings, and petitions and letters from Fiji. Would I have written a different book if I had seen the London records? At first, I was naturally nervous as any researcher would be, writing a book without consulting a major repository! What if I got the story all wrong? We historians pride ourselves on doing as exhaustive research as possible before putting pen to paper. We all aspire to some sort of definitiveness, a longer shelf life even though we know how utterly impossible that goal can be. So I was nervous.

But now, having seen all the London records, I honestly do not believe that I would substantially change anything I have written substantially: revisions at the margins, yes; major amendments, no. To be sure, it would have been good to have seen the records before I wrote the biography, if only because they would have deepened and reinforced many of the conclusions I reached. All important policy discussions found their way into print in one form or another, although not always the thinking which led to a particular policy recommendation. I will give just a few examples to illustrate the point. It was common knowledge, as Jakeway and Baker confirmed, that official sympathy lay with the Fijians, and that the United Kingdom government would pay close attention to Fijian aspirations and concerns when formulating policy. Nor was there much sympathy for Patel's advocacy of common roll. Fijians and Europeans were opposed and so too was London. That was common knowledge; the London records show just how pervasive that sentiment was.

The extent of London's concern was stated by Julian Amery, the parliamentary Under Secretary of State for the Colonies, who visited Fiji in 1960 during the sugar cane strike. Upon returning to London, he penned a memorandum whose central concerns echoed in all the major correspondence and political negotiations between Suva and London throughout the 1960s. Amery was a well connected, supremely self-confident and given to expressing sharp, unequivocal opinion.[17] 'The Fijians and Indians are more distinct as communities than Jews and Arabs in Palestine, Greeks and Turks in Cyprus or even Europeans and Bantu in South and Central Africa.' Fijians deeply feared Indian domination, he said, and their confidence in the government had been shaken by reports (Burns and Spate) calling for fundamental overhauling of Fijian institutions and opening up the traditional society to greater individual freedom. He reminded London that it was the Fijians who had been the loyal community, a reference to enthusiastic Fijian participation in the Second World War and in the Malaya campaign in the 1950s. The Fijians provided 75 per cent of the colony's armed forces. 'The islands could hardly be governed without them, let alone against them.' In the circumstances, Amery advised London, it was 'impracticable to think if terms of a single Fijian nation of a common roll'.

Amery's views were widely discussed in the Colonial Office. Many accepted that his prognosis was probably correct though his rhetoric heated. Nonetheless, everyone agreed to respect the Fijian position. Even when Fijians were contemplating some minor concession to common roll, London was not keen to nudge them along. As Jakeway put it, 'some gentle selling of the attractions of a limited common roll element in the next constitutional stage has been done with all three (Ratu George Cakobau, Ratu Penaia Ganilau and Ratu Mara) and does not appear to have fallen on entirely unreceptive ground'. In the 1965 conference, London actively sought to engineer an outcome that would put Fijians in control, within the overarching ambit of Westminster-style parliamentary democracy. The conference failed to reach consensus, and the Colonial Office was quick to blame Patel and other members of the Federation Party for the debacle. They started the conference on the 'wrong foot' and spectacularly mishandled their case, as Trafford Smith put it in a confidential letter to Jakeway.

A close and careful reading of the Colonial Office records in fact leads to another conclusion, one which becomes all too obvious when London's thinking is borne in mind. London was concerned to appease the Fijians, and Eireen White, the parliamentary under-secretary and chair of the conference, held private talks with both Ratu Mara and John Falvey, but not with the Indian delegation, to impress upon them the need to meet others halfway. This contradicted the Colonial Office advice that White hold private discussions with all the three parties separately to gauge the extent of compromise each was prepared to make. Trafford Smith was especially critical of the Federation group bringing up the matter of common roll late in the conference proceedings. But the Colonial Office itself had recommended the avoidance of the issue at an early stage to prevent the 'striking of attitudes' which could conceivably lead to a deadlock. To argue later that the Federation group should have declared their hand earlier directly contradicts the Colonial Office advice. Patel told his audiences in Fiji that the London conference was merely a 'rubber stamp' for a constitution already decided by Her Majesty's Government.[18] He was condemned for saying this, but as the records show, he had spoken the truth. He was also right that London's mind was focused elsewhere—on Aden—when the conference took place.

The London records show clearly how personal chemistry between the principal participants played a role in the way events unfolded. Sir Derek Jakeway, coming from Sarawak as its chief secretary, had developed empathy for the Fijian people, had seen them in action against Chinese communist insurgents in Malaya, and in Fiji he was active behind the scenes trying to get the Fijians and Europeans to organise politically.[19] The Alliance Party was in fact his brainchild. The Federation Party attacked Jakeway's partisan statements and even petitioned the Colonial Office for his recall. London denied any impropriety in the governor's behaviour, but once again, suspicions about the governor's bias were well founded.

Fijian leaders were chosen to attend specialised courses in London, and many of them formed close friendships with officials in London. Officials from the Colonial Office were assigned to the visitors, sometimes to help them find accommodation and schools for the children, or take them on tours of London. The closeness was reflected in private letters. During the course of an interview with a visiting official from the Colonial Office, an Indian journalist, Krishnamurthy, collapsed and died. In a handwritten letter, Ratu Mara asked Harold Hall, Assistant Secretary and Head of Pacific and Indian Ocean Department at the Colonial Office, to send more such officials. Humour in extremely bad taste, you might say, but this was not uncommon.[20] Richard Kearsley, a member of the Alliance Party, felt socially close enough to the UK officials at the 1965 conference at Marlborough House to call Patel a 'rat'. John Falvey chimed in 'Of course we all hate the Indians'. The English had a patronising, romantic, affinity for Fijians and things Fijian,[21] but coolness and distance, perhaps even suspicion and muted hostility, characterised their attitude to the Indo-Fijians, especially their leaders and especially Patel. Many in London and Suva—from Trafford Smith to Sir Robert Foster—expressed open respect for Patel's intellect and integrity, but personal rapport was absent. No Indo-Fijian politician enjoyed the closeness with European officials that Fijians did.

It did not help matters that in one encounter with Jakeway, Patel humiliated the governor and forced him to back down. Sketchy details are available in the Fiji newspapers, but the full extent of the damage was revealed in the PRO papers. As preparations for the 1965 conference intensified in Fiji, garbled versions of private discussions began to appear in the media and on the Fiji Broadcasting Commission (FBC). The latter came under Patel's portfolio as Member for Social Services. In one meeting, Patel said that, having studied at the London School of Economics, he could call himself an 'economist' and he was an 'optimist' about Fiji's future. The Public Relations Office reported that Patel had called himself a 'communist' and an 'opportunist'! The FBC called Federation leaders 'badmash', hooligans. When Patel attacked the Commission for its anti-Federation bias, Jakeway rebuked him and forthrightly asked for his resignation if he could not observe the rules of collective responsibility governing the Membership System. 'Anything other than a public dissociation from these attacks on the Public Relations Office must bring into question your continued membership of the Executive Council.' Jakeway was determined to get the better of Patel, determined to discipline him once and for all.

Patel replied that he could not be expected to 'defend wrongful acts of civil servants or defend them against public criticism' when he himself, as Member for Social Services, 'had no power to hold officers in his portfolio to account'. He pointedly reminded the governor of the terms and conditions upon which he had accepted his appointment, saying that his present action did not breach them. He had joined the government, he said, 'to serve my people—not to forsake them: and I am not prepared to sell my soul for a mess of pottage'. He offered to resign if that was what the Secretary of State wanted. Jakeway had asked the Colonial Office to take a hard line against Patel. Trafford Smith sympathised with Jakeway, but warned him of the 'serious and far reaching' consequences of not having Patel, the dominant leader of the Indo-Fijian community, in the Executive Council. Expelling Patel would do the government more harm than good. And, after all, Patel did have a case. There was nothing that Jakeway could do but to bite his tongue, accept this advice, retract his ultimatum, and keep Patel in government. London hoped that the 'whole incident has not so seriously undermined the confidence of the other communities in the Indians as to make progress between now and the conference impossible'.[22] It had, and Jakeway had to share a part of the blame for the fiasco. I had an inkling of all this when I was going through the Patel papers and reading the *Pacific Review*: the London records provided the details and clarified the picture.

The 1965 conference was a triumph for the Fijian and European delegation and utter defeat for the Indo-Fijians. Soon after returning from London, some within the Federation Party began questioning whether its constitutionalist stance was appropriate to extract concessions from the British. I was told of a rift between Siddiq Koya and A.D. Patel, indeed a private, potentially party-splitting confrontation in Ba, when Koya threatened to leave the party. Several people confirmed the episode but none knew precisely the cause of the rift between the two men. I mention the episode in the book, but do not, could not, elaborate. The monthly 'Fiji Intelligence Reports' provide one plausible clue. Koya was 'restless with Patel's autocratic control of the party machine and his apparently passive attitude to the outcome of the London conference'.[23] He told his colleagues that Patel's approach had failed and that he wanted to form a 'Subhash Party'. This was after Subhash Chandra Bose, the leader of the Indian National Army, who wanted to eject the British from India by force.

Apisai Tora, whom Koya had defended against the charge of arson in the longest running criminal case in Fiji history (burning down the Korolevu Hotel near Sigatoka) and who had converted to Islam (assuming the name of Mohammed), reportedly told someone that he was twice offered 2,000 pounds by Koya on behalf of the Federation Party if he would pledge his support for 'certain courses of action'.[24] What course of action, the police were unable to ascertain, but 'physical persuasion' was mentioned to embarrass the government and to force a commission of enquiry into the workings of the Native Land Trust Board. I am not convinced that the Federation Party sanctioned the approach. In fact, I doubt it. Patel, Gandhian at heart, the strict constitutionalist, the follower of protocol and procedure, the loyal member of the Middle Temple, would never countenance such a course of action.

The London records, as mentioned before, clarify and amplify, confirm tentative conclusions and deepen understanding of official thinking. But they do not, I think, substantially alter the picture I sought to draw in the book. On many points, they simply confirm my line of enquiry. An important reason for this is that on most matters of importance, Patel published his letters and messages. He recalled conversations with both the governor and officials from the Colonial Office in public, and these found their way into print, especially in the pages of the *Pacific Review*, which Patel founded in 1949 and whose intellectual inspiration he remained throughout. When the 1965 conference broke down, Patel and his colleagues, 'out of respect' for the Secretary of State for the Colonies, accepted the new constitution under protest, but not before writing a lengthy letter to him outlining their reasons for dismay at the final outcome, and promising to 'oppose these proposals by peaceful and constitutional means'. The letter was published in the *Pacific Review*. So, too, was Greenwood's reply.

This exchange would not have been available to me under the 30-year rule even if I had travelled to London to consult the records. The newspaper is full of such disclosures. Patel's case for the common roll, his views on the problems in the sugar industry, his fraught relations with Ratu Mara,[25] his condemnation of colonialism, his speeches in national and international forums (such as at the 1965 conference in London), the substance of letters people wrote to him, all found their way into the pages of the *Pacific Review*. Besides this journal, the *Hansard* was also an important source of information. Patel first entered the Legislative Council in 1944 and remained a member until 1950. He re-entered the Council in 1963 and remained its member until his death in 1969. The words, in cold print now, do not convey the passion and precision with which they were spoken, but they display a mastery of the language and eloquent thoughts on a range of issues of urgent importance to the country.

I was particularly lucky that Patel left behind a rich collection of private papers. Some had been destroyed in the 1972 hurricane, but many survived. Patel was decidedly old-fashioned in preserving his correspondence. He kept personal letters (the oldest being his letter to Swami Avinashananda in 1939), letters others sent him, drafts of speeches,[26] confidential memoranda he received both as the Member of Social Services and as the Leader of the Opposition, newspaper clippings containing his addresses. Patel's large library contained well-thumbed books on many subjects, but there was a predilection towards philosophy and religion.[27] Patel was a Vaishnavite, a follower of Swami Vivekananda and vice president of the Ramakrishna Mission in Fiji. Together with Swami Rudrananda, his life-long spiritual confidante, he held regular discourses on the *Bhagvada Gita* at the Mission *ashram* (lodge) in Nadi. His political speeches were full of references to Indian philosophical texts. Perusing his papers and his library, I came away with the firm impression that two of Patel's greatest attributes were his brilliant intellect and his deep faith which sustained him in the many political failures and obstacles he encountered in his career.

The personal letters to his children were the most useful and revealing about the man. Much to his wife's distress, Patel never phoned his children whom he had sent to England for private education. Not that he could not afford it: he was a wealthy lawyer and owner of large freehold properties. But, like the English gentlemen of leisure in the late-19th and early-20th centuries, he preferred to communicate with his children through letters. In these letters he advised his children about their course of study, about the need to keep the company of good people, meaning those who were determined to make something of themselves. But he also discussed political developments in Fiji. In one letter to his eldest son, Atul, he talked of Mara being the 'blue-eyed boy of the British', and complained about the obtuseness of Indian officials towards political developments in Fiji. In a 1967 letter from the Ocean Island to his tiny daughter Vasantika, he wrote about the iniquity perpetrated by the British Phosphate Commission on the Banaban people whose Chief Legal Counsel he was before the United Nations Committee on Decolonisation. His mastery of the language and fluency of his writing are impressive.

It is almost 10 years ago since I published my biography of A.D. Patel, following a decade of interrupted research. Do I still stand by the words I wrote then? Were there things I simply missed, gaps exposed by evidence and papers which have since become available, such as the records at the Public Record Office at Kew Gardens? Can I say with absolute confidence that the broad picture I painted remains intact? Nothing that I have seen since I wrote the book would cause me to change my mind, except on low level details. What the records, which were not available to me when I wrote my book, do is to deepen the picture and sometimes enter qualifications. I wish I had seen them when I wrote the biography, but, fortunately for me, they confirm rather than derogate from the picture I painted then.

Patel has had his critics, and been subject to carping comments from some scholars. But these often say more about the prejudices and intellectual predilections of these individuals than the man they wrote about. Patel was not perfect, as I showed in my book. He could be—often was—stubborn, uncompromising, and haughty towards opponents he considered unprincipled or opportunistic.[28] The worst that was said of Patel, his harshest criticism by officials, was that he was a practitioner of Gandhian politics, but no one ever spelt out precisely what was wrong with Gandhian politics. People told me that Patel was a hard landlord, demanding full rent on time and requiring the highest levels of husbandry of his tenants. That was probably true, but in this Patel was following the example set by others, including the CSR. Many in Fiji will agree that lack of professionalism in agriculture is one of the serious problems facing the sugar cane growers of Fiji.

When all is said and done, what remains beyond doubt is that, 37 years after his death, his vision for Fiji remains as relevant as it was when he was alive. Racial compartmentalisation was no way to build a cohesive multiracial society, Patel had argued all throughout his life. Long before it became fashionable, Patel talked about the nation as an 'imagined community'. Nationalism, for him, he said in 1964, was 'a question of the mind, it [was] not a question of the colour [of skin]'. Patel received bad press during his life time because he questioned the values and assumptions which underpinned the colonial order, although privately, and much later after he was gone, his critics conceded ground. 'A.D. was a fine man', Q.V.L. Weston wrote privately after Patel's death in 1969, 'stubborn, sometimes too much for comfort'. Weston knew: he was Commissioner Western, colonial officialdom's principal representative, in the heart of the fiery cane belt in western Viti Levu. But, he added, 'it was through his stubbornness that he got his way'. He continued: 'Mixed societies such as Fiji contain a lot of inborn prejudices, which get out of tune with the times and take the leader of the quality and convictions of A.D. to shift. When the tale is told by historians, it will be usually accepted that his way was right'.

ENDNOTES

[1] See Deryck Scarr, *Ratu Sukuna: soldier, statesman, man of two worlds* (London 1980).

[2] An authorised, partly taxpayer-funded biography of Ratu Mara is currently being written and negotiations are under way for a Ratu Mara Chair in Fijian Studies at the University of Fiji.

[3] Published in 1997 in the 'History of Development Studies Series' by the National Centre for Development Studies, The Australian National University.

[4] An extensive collection of documents covering the period 1960 to 1970 has been published in Brij V. Lal (ed.), *Fiji: British documents on the end of empire*, Series B, vol. 10 (London 2006).

[5] Thus Deryck Scarr, the historian of the Fijian establishment, in his Sukuna biography, writes disparagingly about Patel's role in the 1943 strike, commenting on his 'new-found patriotism' (*Ratu Sukuna*, 133). K.L. Gillion, in his *The Fiji Indians: challenge to European dominance, 1920-1946* (Canberra 1977), 172, provides an assessment of the strike that repeats almost verbatim the colonial government's view: 'Once again in the history of the Fiji Indians, communalism, factionalism, pettiness and personal political ambition had triumphed over unity and statesmanship'.

[6] An early result of this interest was my edited collection *Politics in Fiji: studies in contemporary history* (Sydney 1986) and articles on Fiji elections from 1982 onwards.

[7] Patel's papers have been microfilmed by the Pacific Manuscripts Bureau and will be made available to bona fide scholars, with the permission of the family (for a limited period of time).

[8] My book on the 1987 coup was *Power and Prejudice: the making of the Fiji crisis* (Wellington 1988, 1990), and my broader history was *Broken Waves: a history of the Fiji Islands in the twentieth century* (Honolulu 1992).

[9] See, for instance, the National Farmers Union publication *Children of the Indus, 1879-2004: a history of Indians in Fiji portraying the struggles of an immigrant community for justice, equality and acceptance* (Suva 2004).

[10] These letters are in my papers which will be donated to the Pacific Manuscript Bureau in due course.

[11] *Fiji Times*, 22 Aug. 1960. On 26 August, the newspaper wrote about political demagogues 'who would scramble, scuffle and skirmish for power as soon as the Colony came within the sight of substantial measure of self-government'.

[12] See Sir Malcolm Trustram Eve, *Report of the Fiji Sugar Inquiry Commission* (Suva 1961).

[13] See *The Award of the Rt. Hon. Lord Denning in the Fiji Sugar Cane Contract Dispute 1969* (Suva 1970).

[14] See, for instance, 'The Sugar Contract Scorecard', *The Fiji Nation*, October 1969.

[15] Acting Governor to Secretary of State for the Colonies, 6 August 1965 in CO 1036/1216, E83.

[16] CO 1036/1551, no. 1, March 1965. The publisher of the *Fiji Times* was no less anti-Indian. Writing in the *Pacific Islands Monthly* in February 1952, he said 'I have little liking for the Indians. In the main, they are arrogant and disloyal and are dishonest in so far as their evasion of taxation is concerned'.

[17] His father Leopold Amery was Secretary of State for India in the 1940s.

[18] CO 1036/1216/E91, Fiji Intelligence Report, 12 December 1965.

[19] Jakeway told Nigel Fisher on 17 Jan. 1966 that 'Behind the scenes I have encouraged the Alliance leaders to look for professional advice on party organisation and running an election campaign, and it was I who gave Falvey the name of Sir William Urton well as those of his counterparts in the other occupants of South Square, the Labour and Liberal Offices. This was done with the knowledge and agreement of Trafford Smith, and also Mrs White'. CO 1036/1586, Jakeway to Nigel Fisher, 17 Jan. 1966.

[20] Sir Vijay R. Singh told me at a dinner with Praveen Chandra Vijendra Kumar in Brisbane in late 2005 another Mara story. As Patel's funeral pyre was alight and as the plane taking Mara and Singh back to Suva flew over the crematorium, Mara called Singh to his side and said, pointing to the fire, 'Look Vijay, give people what they want and they will flock to you'.

[21] The feeling continued. A. Crosbie Walsh, who taught at the University of the South Pacific in the late 1970s, wrote that 'I had a dislike of Indians (a not uncommon attitude held by Europeans seeking to protect Pacific indigenes from every race except their own) and I did not want to be like this'. See his 'A scatter of islands: reminiscences from Tonga, Rarotonga, Niue, and Fiji,' in Eric Waddell and Patrick Nunn (eds), *The Margin Fades: geographical itineraries in a world of islands* (Suva 1993), 106.

[22] See CO 1036/1263 no. 26 and no. 27.

[23] CO 1036/1216, E1/88, Fiji Intelligence Report for September 1965.

[24] See CO 1036/1216, E/91 Fiji Intelligence Report for November 1965.

[25] Mara recalled Patel as a 'brilliant lawyer, an eloquent speaker, a charismatic leader of his party, and a doughty opponent. But it has to be admitted that political negotiation with him had proved difficult, and on occasion impossible. In particular he was irrevocably committed to the policy of common roll as a first step, not as an aim for the future, which we were prepared to concede. Therefore, sad as his death was, and a great loss to the Indian community, it did seem to open up for our negotiations a spirit of compromise that might have been hard to achieve otherwise'. See his *The Pacific Way: a memoir* (Honolulu 1997), 97.

[26] People often told me how Patel could speak for hours scarcely glancing at his notes. The truth was that he carefully composed his speeches, wrote them down and then committed them to memory. Patel had astounding powers of recall.

[27] Among the many philosophy books in the Patel library are several by Nicolas Berdyaev such as *Slavery and Freedom* and the *Destiny of Man*.

[28] As Sir Vijay R. Singh told me in early 2006.

Chapter 14

On Writing a Biography of William Pritchard

Andrew E. Robson

Biography offers a unique opportunity to resist the generalisations and stereotypes spawned by older, positivist historical schools of thought and more recent theory-based postcolonial approaches. The relatively small scale and specific nature of biographical inquiry avoids the grand themes and pronouncements that lead to the propagation of radical generalisations, whether conservative or liberal, on large-scale topics such as imperialism and colonialism. It offers the opportunity to concentrate on historical specificities, local histories, and individual stories. Such is the case in my study of the mid-19th century British Consul, William Pritchard, who was born in Tahiti in 1829 and served in Samoa and Fiji before being fired, following a Commission of Inquiry that I show to have been little more than a kangaroo court. In *Culture and Imperialism*, Edward Said advocates 'studying the map of interactions, the actual and often productive traffic occurring on a day-by-day, and even minute-by-minute basis among states, groups, identities'.[1] Nineteenth-century archives can produce (surprisingly, perhaps) this kind of excitement, for a careful reading of memos and letters going to and from the Colonial Office, for example, gives one a sense not only of the slowness of communications, but also of the immediacy of discussion once a document arrived or was in preparation. Minutes scrawled on letters, sometimes by more than one person, and dates attached as documents passed from person-to-person, all evoke a sense of immediacy and sometimes of the character of those involved. We don't see the people, but we see their writing and we read their observations and decisions. This is why I included not just portraits of key people involved in Pritchard's career, but also their signatures. It is a gesture not just to them, but to the archives as well.

Many often-heard assumptions about imperialism, missionaries, and relationships between Europeans and Pacific Islanders become more complicated when seen in the context of Pritchard's life. For example, among those with imperial ambitions in the mid-century Pacific Islands was Tonga's King George Tupou; conversely, the British government, at the urging of the Colonial Office, rejected offers of cession from Fiji and deflected requests for protection from Tahiti and Samoa. In the Colonial Office, Permanent Under-Secretary Fredric

Rogers, remembering the lessons of the American Revolution, believed independence, with its attendant loss of investments, to be inevitable, and he was unenthusiastic about new colonial ventures. Pritchard brought samples of high quality cotton from Fiji; this was of great interest to merchants in Manchester, but it left Rogers unmoved. The on-going Maori Wars and his personal resistance to the idea of European settlers moving into Fiji further strengthened Rogers' scepticism, despite vigorous support for the cession of Fiji from high naval officers such as Admiralty Hydrographer Captain John Washington who saw in cession the possibility of better defending the shipping lanes between the goldfields of Australia and Britain.

Pritchard, backed by the authority of Cakobau, spent most of 1859 in London, working in the Foreign Office (FO), and he had extensive written communication with the Colonial Office (CO) over a still longer period. My archival work on Pritchard's interactions with the FO and CO over the proffered cession of Fiji makes clear the paradoxical reality of Rogers as an anti-imperialist (or at least a sceptical imperialist) in the Foreign and Colonial Offices. It also makes plain that these government offices benefited from the large talents of a number of permanent officials, including Rogers and his immediate predecessor, Herman Merivale, who seemed inclined to recommend accepting the offer of cession when a change in government and Merivale's move to the India Office altered the state of play. Both Merivale and Rogers won firsts at Oxford and were impressive on many fronts. Rogers was one of the founders of the *Manchester Guardian* newspaper. These were talented and able men who often worked for ministers who spent little time on the job. On a lower level, some of the 'dispatch-reading draft-writing heads of departments' took their work seriously, but others 'were gay and frolicsome spirits who came late, strutted from room to room, had brandy and cigars, flourished their crested sleeve-links, and left early to dress for my Lady Angelina's "at home", or to dance at the Honorable Miss Emily Evening's ball'.[2]

For missionaries and Pacific Islanders too, the reality that emerges from Pritchard's story is one in which the stereotype of the missionary as a cross-culturally inept imperialist is challenged time and time again. In the post-colonial and secular world of many writers and critics, the motives and impact of the missionaries are often dismissed with something like contempt, but to understand this phase of history we must understand not only the missionaries—who were diverse in background, education, commitment, and effectiveness—but also the people of the Islands, who, with a few violent exceptions, allowed the missionaries to stay and eventually decided to embrace the new religion. The story becomes more interesting, not less, if we take both missionaries and Islanders seriously and look at them with a critical but less cynical eye. Several contemporary historians have made a similar point, including Andrew Porter, Jane Samson, and Greg Dening.

If the Wesleyan missionaries in Fiji were blazing the trail for Empire, they certainly went about it in a diffident and unconvincing way. The Anglican Bishop of New Zealand, George Selwyn, influenced Commissioner Smythe to oppose the Cakobau/Pritchard attempt at cession, and Smythe received the same message from John Binner and other missionaries in Fiji itself. Even before he reached New Zealand and Fiji, Smythe met Sir William Denison, the Governor of New South Wales, who also expressed concern over attempts to attract settlers to Fiji. Why was there such opposition? A desire to avoid disputes over land, such as were wracking New Zealand; a desire to avoid too much government (read 'Anglican') interference in Wesleyan and other nonconformist missionary activities; and concern over the political influence and religious ecumenicalism of Consul Pritchard each played their part, but, whatever the cause, the story certainly complicates any stereotypical vision of the missionaries as stalking horses for builders of Empire. Other questions also arise: we might well ask why the missionaries persisted (of course, many didn't) when in some cases—as in Tahiti—for so long they enjoyed no success. Why did their Polynesian hosts put up with them for all this time? And why did the missionaries ultimately succeed in converting their hosts—or, to use Lamin Sanneh's terms, how and why did individual Polynesians discover Christianity and eventually embrace it? Sanneh writes mostly about Africa, but when he says that he prefers to speak of the '*indigenous discovery of Christianity* rather than the *Christian discovery of indigenous societies*',[3] his words resonate powerfully in the context of Oceania as well. Conversion did not come quickly in most cases, and it did not come without serious deliberation among the local people.

For 40 years, the missionaries worked in a Fiji under the protection of chiefs and their communities, and the eventual colonisation of the islands by Britain in 1874 was certainly not the result of a long campaign by missionaries or London civil servants to achieve this end. Throughout the South Pacific, the power of the missionaries, traders, and other foreigners was limited, and their religious and commercial messages to the people of Oceania were embraced with greater or lesser enthusiasm depending on how useful they seemed to be to the latter. In Tahiti, Pomare II embraced Christianity slowly and this hesitation was returned by the missionaries, most of who continued to be appalled by Pomare's private behaviour and stalled on accepting him for baptism. Pomare was astute, however, choosing his moment and using his alliance with Henry Nott and other missionaries to his political and commercial advantage. For a few years after 1815, when Pomare triumphed in battle over his enemies and was baptised, something akin to a 'missionary kingdom' prevailed in Tahiti, with Nott and others helping to draft laws that were in some respects politically liberal but socially oppressive; this situation persisted after a fashion, but when Pritchard was growing up bilingual in Tahiti (he was born there in 1829) he was subject, like other missionary children to Tahitian influences that were at least as strong as his English ones; in his memoir he remembers thinking of himself as Tahitian as well as English, and sometimes preferring the former.[4] Neither the vulnerability of traditional cultures nor the influence of Europeans should be exaggerated in discussions of the social impact of the Pacific missionaries and later colonial officers. Albert Wendt, the Samoan writer, has rejected the label of Pacific Islanders being 'hapless victims and losers' in their contact with imperial Europeans, instead celebrating the 'marvelous endurance, survival and dynamic adaptation' that he sees around him.[5]

In Samoa and in Pacific histories, Malietoa Vainu'upo[6] is widely acclaimed as the crucial first contact for John Williams in 1830 and thereafter the guarantor of the safety of the Polynesian missionary teachers who stayed after Williams left and the British missionaries who arrived some years later. Malietoa, however, was always cautious and pragmatic about the new religion, and my most recent research finds his role in the conversion of Samoa to be paradoxical and worthy of reassessment. In each of these examples, it is clear that the chiefs, far from being manipulated by the missionaries, were able to use the outsiders and the *lotu* (church) to their own advantage. In Samoa, Malietoa's monopoly on the teachers was short-lived, partly because other *matai* would not tolerate such exclusivity. No cynicism is implied here; as was suggested above, this was largely a Samoan process, and today, it is interesting to note that Samoan theologians, commonly seen as being traditionalist and conservative, are also drawing on traditional *fa'a Samoa* values to put the weight of Samoan religiosity behind a push for ecological integrity, women's rights, and more.[7]

Telling Pritchard's story necessitated a lot of archival work, in part because almost nothing was known about his personal life, even by family descendants, and the only way to find him was through his personal writings and through the archives—the National Archives, the School of Oriental and African Studies, and British Library, all in London; the Turnbull Library and National Archives in Wellington; the Mitchell Library in Sydney; the National Library and more in Canberra; the Fiji Archives in Suva; and more in Samoa, the USA, and elsewhere. Such research, of course, gives great pleasure and calls for appreciation and gratitude for archives and archivists alike. In addition, I was able to draw on the family knowledge of today's Pritchard *aiga*, living in New Zealand, the Samoas, Australia, England, and the USA. This contact was of enormous importance, for I received nothing but encouragement from the family, and the few private documents that exist relating to William Pritchard (including two photographs) were made available to me. I'm grateful for this, as I am also for the support of the Austrian South Pacific Society (and their sponsors in turn), headed by Dr Hermann Mückler. Dr Mückler and his team did a splendid job, and their Novara series, subtitled 'Contributions to Research on the Pacific', is in itself a wonderful and much-needed contribution to Pacific research.

Prior to the publication of my work, Pritchard's personal life was the subject of speculation in histories and even in one play, written for and performed at the Pacific Arts Festival in Suva in 1972.[8] Very little was known about Pritchard at that time, and some widely-reported 'facts' turned out to be wrong, including Pritchard's purported death at the hands of American Indians in 1870, as reported in a letter to an English newspaper from Pritchard's friend, the naturalist Berthold Seemann. My scepticism about Seemann's account was based on nothing more than a gut feeling, and so it was a moment of elation when, after several years of searching, I found at Tulane University in New Orleans a 1907 copy of *The Mexican Herald* that carried on its front page Pritchard's obituary; this image, of course, also appears in *Prelude to Empire*. This kind of basic information was missing when I began this project, and so one vital line of research was aimed at filling these gaps. Another breakthrough occurred in the National Archives in Wellington, where I found certificates identifying Pritchard's first wife, a Samoan named Patisepa, and their two daughters, and giving birth dates, marriage date, and Patisepa's death certificate—a treasure trove! A few years later, friends in Samoa were able to find and show me Patisepa's burial place—an emotional moment of a different kind. What I couldn't do was describe what Patisepa looked like or even why she died so young—the consular death certificate reads 'affection of the brain', but medical experts tell me that this was a generic term used in the 19th century.

Pritchard himself was elusive too, but three images exist, including the two photographs mentioned above and an engraving in Pritchard's *Polynesian Reminiscences* in which he is on board HMS *Pelorus* with Cakobau, Mata'afa, Captain Seymour and others. These figures are not identified in Pritchard's book, and so it gave considerable satisfaction to determine who they were—more detective work! Pritchard writes virtually nothing about Patisepa in his memoir and never even gives her name. What does the biographer do with such blanks, and is speculation legitimate? Is Patisepa's absence from Pritchard's writing evidence of a hard heart? It seems unlikely, as he had delayed taking up his appointment to Fiji during her illness and, when Patisepa died, Pritchard took their daughters with him to Fiji, first securing land for them in their Samoan grandparents' villages. I found the record of this land transaction at the National Archives in Wellington, and it is worthy of note that the agreement states explicitly that Pritchard himself was not a beneficiary; Patisepa's family and Pritchard were aware of the possibility of foreign involvement in Samoa and the possible threat to land ownership, and this land was strictly for the daughters. Perhaps Pritchard found it too painful to write about Patisepa—an opposite but equally speculative suggestion. Curiously, Patisepa is not mentioned in the Mexican obituary either. What we do know from Pritchard's own accounts and those of others is that he was 'a tough guy' (to quote a family source) who knew how to use his fists, who loved to hunt and fish with his Samoan friends, who was linguistically talented and politically adept, who studied and relished the genealogical relationships and political intrigue of the Samoans and Fijians, who tried to establish a reading room in Levuka, and who married three times— to Patisepa, who was Samoan, to Ellen Fanny Glover, who was English, and to Guadalupe Ramirez, who was Mexican. He was massively sociable and energetic, and appears to have had a very wide range of friends and acquaintances from all segments of society in Samoa and Fiji, and was familiar too with the more transient or occasional visitors such as naval officers and their crews, whalers, and traders. He travelled extensively, and we often get a taste of his exuberance, as when he climbs the pyramid of Cheops in Egypt on his first journey to England from Fiji, when he describes a fight in Samoa and in his excursions into the interior of Viti Levu with his friend Seemann.

In writing *Prelude to Empire*, I found that an accumulation of fragments was enough to reveal the person outlined above. Even those who contrived to bring him down, such as James Calvert and Colonel Smythe, acknowledged Pritchard's political skills, and his religious tolerance infuriated the fiercely anti-Catholic Calvert and other Wesleyans. The fact that the Fijian chiefs gave Pritchard 'the full, unreserved, entire, and supreme right, authority, and power to govern Fiji' upon his return from England in 1859 surely reflects a remarkable level of trust and confidence, perhaps even astonishing, given the fact that Pritchard at that time had spent only a few weeks in Fiji. Of course, the acceptance of Cakobau's offer of cession was probably expected, and some have accused Pritchard of bullying, but it is hard to imagine the chiefs acting as they did unless they had decided that Pritchard could deliver things that they wanted, such as the renunciation of Tongan claims in Fiji. In this, they were not disappointed. Pritchard, with no force at his disposal unless the navy happened to be making a visit, and with only the slowest of communications with London, decided to act when he believed action was warranted, as in the Macuata War, when Ma'afu came close to achieving a Tongan-led triumph over Fijian forces allied with Cakobau. His actions got him into trouble with London for 'interfering in native affairs', and his behaviour was certainly unconventional and caused alarm in London, but there can be no dispute over his political and intercultural skills or his personal energy and efficacy. It is also worth stating again that the Fijians, like other Pacific people, were not mere pawns in a game devised by the Colonial Office, Pritchard, or the missionaries. Far from it; they made choices, and these choices were made with their own best interests in mind.

I have not invented any 'conversations' in the biography, and I report only those provided or alluded to by Pritchard or others in the archives and other documents. The story is vivid enough without this, I believe, and it would have introduced an element of fiction running counter to the intention of this particular work. Instead, I have allowed Pritchard's voice to be heard through extensive quotation from his own writings. Sadly, no personal letters appear to be extant, but there is plenty of official correspondence, a few articles written in England and Mexico, and, of course, his book, *Polynesian Reminiscences*, which was completed by Seemann from Pritchard's notes after the latter left England for Mexico. Frustratingly, I have not found these notes, despite my approaches to Pritchard family members and archives in many places, including Seemann's native Germany.

More productively, the various archives provided detailed information about Pritchard's professional life. The National Archives at Kew (London)[9] were, of course, the principal source, and here I found not only the correspondence that passed to-and-fro between the Pacific and London, but also the minutes of Pritchard's trial[10] in Fiji. A close reading of these minutes revealed the flimsy, sometimes farcical, nature of the evidence against him, and this, along with other sources, led me to conclude that Pritchard was badly treated and that he was the victim of a campaign against him. The machinations of the people involved in London and Fiji are apparent in the documents that survive, and they presented me with the evidence that achieves what Pritchard failed to achieve in 1863, the restoration of his reputation; it is a long-delayed piece of justice. The principal villains of the piece, if they can be so-called, were undoubtedly Calvert and Smythe, but others also played their part. Some were traders who had disputes with the consul, but in the complicated finances of the day, when barter and exchange were common, commodities often substituted for money, and money itself could be 'Spanish' dollars (actually Mexican), American dollars, or pounds sterling, disputes were inevitable. More troubling were the decisions by the government auditors, Arbuthnott and Davis, to disregard almost everything that could have exonerated Pritchard, and the even more egregious behaviour of the members of the Commission of Inquiry, who are revealed in their own minutes to be unreliable. Illustrating the truth of Said's remark, quoted earlier, about the rewards of studying 'day-by-day and even minute-by-minute' interactions, is the clear evidence of a conspiracy against Pritchard, including the passing along from Colonel Smythe to T.H. Farrer at the Board of Trade and then to Sir James Murray at the Foreign Office of the idea that no correspondence from the accused should be taken in evidence at the Commission of Inquiry because Pritchard was 'amazingly plausible on paper'.[11] This phrase passes *verbatim* from man to man.

On the other hand, naval officers such as Commodore Seymour; the American Consul, Dr Isaac Brower; many Levuka traders, such as Frederick Hennings; and some missionaries, including the Reverend William Moore, offered favourable comments on the consul's behavior and character, and, as noted above, even his enemies, such as James Calvert, acknowledged Pritchard's skills and impact in the political sphere, especially with regard to Tongan involvement in Fiji. In weighing such a range of commentary, one comes to some conclusions about the man himself and also about the people and institutions around him. While the actions of many were reprehensible, others, such as Sir Frederic Rogers (later Lord Blachford), were intellectually and professionally impressive. The multi-talented naturalist Berthold Seemann was, of course, Pritchard's friend, and he offered, belatedly, a ringing protest at the way the consul was treated. Similarly, the literature on William Pritchard shows divisions between admirers and critics, the strongest admirers including Ronald Derrick, who described Pritchard as 'a sincere friend of the Fijian people at a period when friends were few'.[12]

I chose Pritchard as a subject because I liked his story in *Polynesian Reminiscences,* and because, like him, I had worked in Samoa and Fiji and was thus able to imagine what he and others described. I also found the period endlessly surprising. It is post-contact but pre-colonial, and everything was in a state of flux. The Europeans, through their illnesses, had inadvertently brought demographic calamity in their wake, and trade, money, alcohol, firearms, evangelism, and literacy all introduced, for better or worse, new realities into the Pacific world. Rumours of imperial designs on Samoa and Fiji were not uncommon, but the fact is that Samoa and Fiji were independent political entities at this time, and in all matters of significance, including trade and religion, it tended to be the chiefs, not the foreigners, who called the shots. In this context, the career of William Pritchard in Fiji is perhaps even more interesting because of its exceptionality, but his authority in some ways came from the chiefs more than from London. This is what eventually led to his dismissal.

A close look at Pritchard's life reveals that ending the Tongan threat to Fiji was both Pritchard's most important achievement and the immediate cause of his downfall, for 'interfering in native affairs'. It also reveals the influence of the evangelical revival in England in the late 18th and early 19th centuries that produced a successful anti-slavery movement and also a paternalistic but still important desire to protect the Islanders from aggression, exploitation and, later, 'blackbirding' and other abuses. The evangelical belief in the common origins of humankind complicated the missionary response to even the more egregious realities of life in some of the islands, such as infanticide and cannibalism. Revulsion pulled one way, but a sense of common humanity and their belief in the universal possibility of redemption pulled the other. Naval officers, as Jane Samson describes,[13] while not always averse to shelling villages in retribution for perceived 'crimes', did so rarely; they frequently sided with the local people in disputes with European traders and other residents, and one of their tasks was to deter the colonial ambitions of other powers who threatened the independence of the various groups. The children of the early missionaries, including Pritchard, grew up at home in Tahiti, Samoa, and elsewhere; many of them married locally and their descendants remain there today, as is the case with Prichard's older brother, George, and his wife, Atalina. If Pritchard's daughters had lived, Pritchard might well have had direct descendants in Samoa today, but, as young children, they drowned at sea in a hurricane, and his two sons by his second wife appear to have no living descendants. Pritchard's losses make a mournful list: two daughters drowned as children; one wife dead from 'affection of the brain' and another from post-natal complications; and a career that ended in public and unjust disgrace. But his life was also social, exuberant and well-lived. It makes a good story.

My interest in Pritchard was reinforced, as noted above, by its parallels in geographical terms with my own experience, but I soon discovered that the realities of his life, and those of others in the political and social worlds of the period, offered a stark and enticing challenge to widespread preconceptions connected with race relations, imperial ambitions (and lack thereof), missionary motives and behaviour, and the lives of Victorians. The stereotypical stuffy colonel certainly bears a striking resemblance to William James Smythe, but people such as Seemann and Pritchard are very different, as are the beachcombers and traders. European residents liked to identify a 'King' or 'Queen' from among the local chiefs, but strong parallels with European lineages and monarchs were few and far between. In Samoa, for example, rivalries and a tradition of decentralised authority soon dissipated Malietoa's monopoly over the distribution of missionary teachers (a decentralisation reinforced on his deathbed by Malietoa himself, who forbade the future accumulation of certain titles by a single person). Ironically, the more centralised monarchies, such as existed in Tahiti, proved ultimately less successful than Samoa in resisting foreign occupation and securing again their independence. One sees in stories such as Pritchard's the emergence of the modern world, where lives are lived in places of transition and intermingling—'on the beach', so to speak. What could be more modern and surprising than the three wives of the Victorian tearaway-turned-gentleman, William Pritchard? There is a grand tradition of Victorian adventurers, male and female, but the intercultural skills and openness of people such as Pritchard are seldom heralded. Similarly, the subtlety and adaptability of Polynesian and Melanesian leaders becomes apparent in this story. Ma'afu had great skills, and he and Cakobau both invested in naval power and were shrewd negotiators. Each of these and other leaders in the Pacific were faced with shattering circumstances, with dramatic population decline and social upheaval on a large scale. Individuals, villages, and whole societies made decisions about profound spiritual and material questions, and each created its own blend of change and continuity. The Pritchard story complicates, and sometimes destroys, the conventional wisdom, and it does this through an account that has the weight of hard-won evidence from archival research and the pleasure and enlivening quality of real-life experience.

ENDNOTES

[1] Edward Said, *Culture and Imperialism* (New York 1993), 20.

[2] William Pritchard, *Polynesian Reminiscences* (London 1866), quoted in Andrew Robson, *Prelude to Empire: consuls, missionary kingdoms, and the pre-colonial South Seas seen through the life of William Thomas Pritchard* (Vienna 2004), 89.

[3] Lamin Sanneh, *Whose Religion is Christianity? The Gospel beyond the West* (Michigan 2003), 10.

[4] Pritchard, *Polynesian Reminiscences*, 1.

[5] Albert Wendt (ed.), 'Introduction', *Nuanua: Pacific writing in English since 1980* (Honolulu 1995), 3.

[6] Other spellings are sometimes used, including 'Vai'inupo'.

[7] Charles W. Forman, 'Finding our own voices: the reinterpreting of Christianity by Oceanian theologians,' *International Bulletin of Missionary Research*, 29:3 (July 2005), 118.

[8] Isobel Whippy, *Pritchard*, performed at the South Pacific Festival of Arts, Suva, May, 1972.

[9] Formerly known as The Public Record Office.

[10] Formally, a Commission of Inquiry.

[11] See Robson, *Prelude to Empire*, 137.

[12] R.A. Derrick, *A History of Fiji* (Suva 1968), 155.

[13] Jane Samson, *Imperial Benevolence: making British authority in the Pacific Islands* (Honolulu 1998), 130ff.

Chapter 15

Writing the Colony: Walter Edward Gudgeon in the Cook Islands, 1898 to 1909

Graeme Whimp

In 1903, half way through his 11-year tenure as New Zealand's principal colonial administrator in the Cook Islands, Lieutenant Colonel Walter Edward Gudgeon told an old military comrade:

> I am here the absolute Governor of some 17 Islands, Chief Judge of the High Court, do Land Court, Surveyor General, Treasurer, & Civil Engineer to the Group. Encouraging the natives to plant when they think they ought to be sleeping, slanging the lazy, repressing those with swelled heads (a dangerous disease in the Islands) & flattering the vanity of those who are a little better than their fellows. Such is my life, rather lonely but full of interest for those who like myself love the Maori with all his faults.[1]

Since as early as the 1860s, New Zealand governments' intermittent desire for a sub-empire in the South Pacific had been thwarted by the lack of interest and imperial mistrust of the British Colonial Office. In 1888, however, British protection was declared over the southern islands of the Cook group and, in 1890, Frederick Joseph Moss became the first New Zealand-appointed British resident. Having installed a number of progressive measures for a considerable degree of native self-government, Moss eventually fell foul of a variety of local interests. Failure to implement new legislation setting up a Federal Court and a consequent inquiry finding that his position had become untenable led to his replacement by Gudgeon in September 1898. After annexation by New Zealand in June 1901, Gudgeon became Resident Commissioner and remained in office until August 1909.[2]

The last two decades have witnessed a variety of calls for a closer and more complex reading of colonialism and of its texts by, among others, Frederick Cooper and Ann Laura Stoler, Nicholas B. Dirks, Gyan Prakash, Thomas Richards, and Nicholas Thomas. There is general agreement that colonialism was neither monolithic, nor omnipotent, nor unchanging and Richards has characterised as 'fictive' the illusion of imperial control. Thomas has pointed to a haunting sense of insecurity on the part of colonisers, fear of an inaccessible 'native mentality', and despair at their inability to reconcile an elusive reality with its accepted representations. At the same time, he has questioned the validity of denying complexity and agency to those accused of the same offence and Stoler has appealed for the same degree of differentiation as would be extended, for instance, to ruling elites of the colonised. In this terrain, it is clear that the analysis of colonial autobiography has unrivalled potential to illuminate both realities and representations and this essay will examine that potential in one such autobiographical project.

Thomas has also observed that colonial projects are often and more precisely projected than realised, their intent deflected or vitiated by opposition, competition, or internal inconsistencies, a perspective summarised by Cooper and Stoler as an 'overarching tension between what colonialism *was* and what colonial regimes *did*'. In considering the texts produced by those regimes, Prakash has advocated making their 'silences, contradictions, and ambiguities essential elements in the colonial story'.[3] My purpose in this essay, then, is to outline, in the spirit of those observations and injunctions, a reading of Gudgeon's private Cook Islands journal and to identify some consequent questions for the present.[4] First, however, it will be worthwhile briefly to mesh biography with the present exploration of the imperial project and consider the range of experiences, intellectual and political baggage and equipment, and mandate that Gudgeon took with him to Rarotonga.

Arriving, by his own account, in New Zealand from London in 1849 at the age of seven, he became a farm worker at 11 and later, largely self-educated, a colonial soldier in the Land Wars, a resident magistrate, a controversial landowner, acting under-secretary of defence, commissioner of police, and native land court judge. Long interested in Maori language and history, this position gave him the opportunity for deeper study; he participated in the vanguard ethnography of the Polynesian Society, chaired the inaugural meeting in 1892, and published prolifically in its *Journal*.[5] He was, apparently, fluent in Te Reo Maori and held a strong opinion that 'much as the manners and customs of the Maoris may differ from ours, they may—so far as that people are concerned—be equally right and salutary'.[6] He equally strongly asserted, however, that the missionaries had destroyed 'the even balance of the Maori mind' and 'all that is interesting in a Native race'.[7]

He would certainly have believed Maori a dying or diminishing race (a great impetus to ethnographic inquiry); contradictorily, he would have accepted that the close relationship between Maori and other Polynesians and New Zealand's 'success' in dealing with 'its own Maori people' conveyed some right or responsibility to govern all Polynesians. He expected that only major land confiscation would achieve Maori industriousness.[8] As a progressive, if somewhat sceptical and abrasive, small-'l', liberal then,[9] Gudgeon would have been comfortable with British Liberal J.A. Hobson's endorsement of the validity and virtues of imperialism, an idea with few European enemies, if many perspectives, at this particular time.[10] And he probably would have shared, at least in theory, Hobson's belief 'that the progress of world-civilization is the only valid moral ground for political interference with the "lower races"' and only if evidenced by their 'political, industrial, and moral education'.[11]

His brief from the New Zealand government comprised little more than passage through the Cook Islands parliament of the Federal Court Bill and achievement of annexation to New Zealand.[12] Beyond that there was a vague proposal for a land court on the New Zealand model, a catalogue of largely illusory mutual benefits set out by Premier Richard Seddon in his 1900 visit to the Cooks and in the consequent parliamentary annexation debate,[13] and a general intention to 'leave the Natives, as far as practicable, to manage their own affairs'.[14] Far from serving any major political, strategic, or commercial interests, New Zealand's first sub-imperial acquisition demonstrates Eric Hobsbawm's observation that, by this stage, 'the acquisition of colonies itself became a status symbol, irrespective of their value'.[15]

Gudgeon's 'A Journal of My Residence in the South Seas and of the Causes that Led to that Residence' is a remarkable combination of invective, self-justification, perceptive insight, and passing ethnographic note. Foremost is his predecessor, Moss, haunting both Gudgeon and his Journal, who, together with his associates, is the excoriated object of the bulk of the Journal's 68 pages. In policy, the only criticisms of Moss are of the manner and fact of his introduction of island councils for self-government, his failure to secure passage of the Federal Court Bill, and the lack of increased revenue and the material fabric of colonial government. Administratively, Moss is accused of a variety of fraudulent activities, benefiting to the point of illegality one particular commercial company, employing and favouring one 'Jimmy te Pou', and committing a variety of minor peccadilloes. In character, however, Moss is, from the first page, lacking in 'temper, tact, and common sense', vindictive, swollen-headed, a fool, 'a liberal of the carpet bagger type', unwise and 'an Hysterical old woman', arrogant, inebriated and 'an infabulous liar', insane and idiotic, an absolute despot, absurd, crooked, rabid, a mere crawler behind Sir George Grey', 'God in the Car',[16] secretive, obstinate, and a good deal more.

The Moss administration inquiry report (characterised by Gudgeon as 'ingeniously colourless') found him guilty of error, want of judgement, and overbearing conduct but not of corruption, fraud, or dishonesty,[17] and later assessments of him and his regime generally find both benevolent. Although it is true that Moss maintained an—often justified—critique of the successor regime until his death in 1904, the intensity and duration of Gudgeon's invective is surprising. While he may be defining and establishing himself in opposition to his predecessor, other undercurrents appear in both Autobiography and Journal. In the former, Gudgeon's origins include 'Suffolk people of good social standing' fallen on hard times;[18] in the latter, there are innumerable references to the low status and appearance of his many enemies.

Furthermore, there is a series of progressively intensifying anti-Semitic slurs, beyond even the standards of the day, against Moss 'the half bred jew'. In one episode, stemming from the antipathy between Moss and Gudgeon's later friends, allies and, in one case, son-in-law, the Craig brothers, he asserts:

> there are very few instances on record, of a member of the family of Fagan, Shylock and Co, having told a Highland gentleman that he had no use for him. half [sic] a century ago *we* [my emphasis] should have settled matters by drawing the Resident's teeth until he disgorged all his ill gotten dollars, and annexed the island to Scotland.[19]

The contempt of the once-genteel, military (but not Highland) Gudgeon for the Anglican (not Jewish) but once-commercial and parliamentary Moss calls to mind H. John Field's suggestion of the influence on 'Imperial Man' of the public school values of Character and Duty as 'the two magnetic values of the Victorian that most represent the imperial need' as well as his hypothesis that individual commitment depended upon 'the close association that empire came to have with valued character traits'.[20]

Having conveyed the tone and texture of the Journal, I shall more summarily complete the 360 degree view of Gudgeon's colonial world. The second villain is the *mataiapo* (major lineage chief) and senior public servant Makea Daniela Vakatani, almost invariably referred to contemptuously as Jimmy te Pou, who appears throughout the Journal and occupies more than a quarter of Gudgeon's final address.[21] In eight minutely detailed pages, Gudgeon spells out defalcations, misdemeanours, crimes, and perjuries, for which he succeeded in gaoling Daniela, yet fails to mention an extravagant welcome and three weeks of feasting on his return.[22]

The balance of Moss's former associates, the Law and Order League or the *Piri Moti* (Stick to Moss), fare little better. 'In Appearance [sic] and manner the friends of Mr Moss were of a lower type than his Enemies [sic]. the [sic] former I find to be men of shady antecedents and many of them foreigners.'[23] Among that 'gang of thieves', the collector of customs is imbecile and must be replaced; Sherman is 'Mischievous ... Conceited, Religious, and Vindictive'; Henry Nicholas an unblushing robber 'as crooked in mind as he was in body', a sly-grogger, murderer, and, with Chas W. Banks alias Scard, an embezzler; Gelling a disreputable young hanger-on; Garnier is incapable and faces prosecution; Henry Ellis is loathsome, an embezzler who 'fled to Rarotonga to avoid arrest'; Caldwell 'a fanatic but not a fool', and Richard Exham a forger and thief. Thos Sherman has the appearance 'of a Houndsditch Jew', an impediment to his relationship 'with the better class people'; and the major trading company of Donald and Edenborough is a corrupt and fraudulent manipulator of Moss and the entire administration.

Gudgeon's common attitude to the administration officials is revealed in his exclamation, 'Some of the men with whom I have to work are beneath contempt'. Customs officer Albert Whitty is involved in 'irregularities' and dismissed; the trusted Frederick Goodwin kills himself firing a rocket and is found, along with Gudgeon's nephew, Ralph Gosset (imprisoned for two years—Gudgeon wished he had died too) to have been swindling the accounts and audit; a new customs officer is an 'incompetent fool'; his formerly favoured Mangaia island resident, Large, is increasingly vindictive, excitable, vain, absurd, and quarrelsome, constantly calling on Gudgeon for help; Miller, collector of customs, is Seddon's spy and a lunatic; and Panapa Vairuarangi, the best man in the north, embezzles public money.

The mission and its missionaries, *Papaa* and Maori, are cruel, mischievous, above all intolerant and tyrannical, guilty of supporting the *ariki* (high chiefs) and the old ways, and 'consistently opposed every european [sic]'. As early as 1899, Gudgeon had decided that 'sooner or later [he] must put the Mission down'. It 'is at the bottom of and responsible for all Maori troubles', 'the decadence of the race began with their evangelisation', and 'the L.M.S. Polynesian is a born criminal'. In trying to 'make a Maori into a third class Britisher' and failing, it ground 'the very life of a happy laughter loving people ... out of them'. As to the lives of women, the mission is guilty of physical abuse, degrading women's originally fairly happy lot by putting 'into their heads the modern idea of the woman in the House and the man in the Field', and 'turning out the most lazy, immoral and extravagant lot of drabs known to modern days'.[24]

The *ariki* have been feudal, despotic, greedy, and oppressive, and 'the time has come when the Crown must take up the duties of the Ariki' in order to protect the 'little people': 'it will be good for the place when the present lot of Arikis die out'. Under Gudgeon, an *ariki* has 'no pull over her people' in court and is now subservient to the governor of New Zealand (in practice, the resident commissioner). For the most part, *ariki* play a fleeting role; 'Queen' Makea Takau, head of government who had made herself paramount chief not just of Rarotonga but of the whole group, 'is not a Makea at all, she is a mere mission fake', and her agency and enterprise are obscured in allegations of tyranny and greed.

Unfortunately, the *unga* (common people) are unable to see the need to curtail or destroy 'the irresponsible powers of the Arikis'. In 1902, Gudgeon observed that 'it has long been clear to me that a large majority of the present generation prefer [the old] system with all of its oppressors, to european [sic] rule'. These, however, 'are the people whom I have to protect, and therefore it is advisable that Rarotonga should be surveyed with the least possible delay'; this because 'the Cook islanders are a dying race and the Govt their natural heirs'.[25] As to 'the Cook Islander' in general, he 'is at times described by his friends, as lazy, sensual and thievish', but is 'not a lazy man when he perceives the necessity for exertion'. Perhaps the relationship between Gudgeon and the Cook Islanders, as far as it can be generalised, is best conveyed in 1902:

> It is not easy to decide what policy ought to be pursued in this group, for the Natives are peculiar, and the difficulty is to fing [sic] out what policy they will accept and approve.[26]

Perhaps, however, the impact of the mission has, as in New Zealand, destroyed 'all that is interesting in a Race' as suggested by the infrequent, fragmentary, and abrupt ethnographic observations that, eventually, peter out almost entirely.

Women, Maori and *Papaa*, including Gudgeon's own wife and daughter, are largely absent from the Journal and, except for *ariki* and an occasional and incidental European, nameless. They most often appear in the context of domestic conflict or sexual relationships in which Maori at least are, apart from mission abuse, far from subservient.

The New Zealand governor, government, and parliament are mistrustful, deceitful, got-at, uncomprehending, and pusillanimous, contributing nothing to the Cooks' prosperity, and, above all, very distant, the latter demonstrated in Gudgeon's plausible assertion that he himself formulated his objectives, strategy, and tactics as resident commissioner. Only in this relationship with New Zealand is he an 'absolute Governor'.

Given the personalities and circumstances portrayed in his Journal, Gudgeon must be admired for the restraint of his opinion 'that this was not a pleasant community to be connected with'. It is a matter of some interest, however, that the handful of residents of whom he approves are never as carefully characterised nor so vividly and visually presented as are his reprobates. Yet, alongside the persona of the colonial administrator, his character and duty delineated in contrast to the lack of character and derelictions of his opponents, there appears the person, often vitriolic, but occasionally engaging, more rarely wistful or even regretful. Enough of vitriol; the engaging quality, however vitiated elsewhere, appears in his continuing validation of the Maori point of view, in personally paying off his nephew's misappropriations, in his observation of changed gender roles, and in his refreshing acceptance of the sexual adventures of young men and women; wistfulness in his desire to 'see some regret in the faces of the people when [he leaves] the Islands'; and something close to regret in his observation after an absence 'that the Maoris had persuaded themselves

I was not coming back' and 'the Polynesian is unreliable but afraid of me when I am here'.

Harking back to Gudgeon's boast to his old comrade, the Journal illuminates the contrast between the projection and the project, a contrast captured at another level in Allen Curnow's poem 'The Unhistoric Story':

> Vogel and Seddon howling empire from an empty coast
> A vast ocean laughter
> Echoed unheard, and after
> All it was different, something
> Nobody counted on.[27]

Here is fertile material for a closer analysis of a colonial world. In this case, however, I want to leap over that to consider some questions for the present that arise from the reading. First, does such a marginal example add to our general understanding of the nature of imperialism and colonisation? Although I am not yet clear on that, the understanding of New Zealand's marginal Cook Islands sub-imperialism promises to make some contribution to the appreciation of the complexity of the broader imperial webs.

Second, does this kind of work re-centre rather than decentre the coloniser, or even provide support for new kinds of imperialisms? My provisional answer is that it depends—depends on what is done with the work. And that, in turn, opens up questions about the most productive relationships between insiders and outsiders, however strained those terms—questions of the sort that have been raised in the past by Donald Denoon and Doug Munro.[28] For myself, I see this work as one half of a project the other half of which, the re-centring of other participants, may more sensitively and accurately be taken up by others.

Third, are New Zealand governments, just as much as in Gudgeon's day, more interested in *being* something in relation to the South Pacific than in *doing* something? And that raises in turn the control of diplomats, aid and development officials, and consultants in the region. Anyone who has travelled in the Pacific in the last two decades will have witnessed New Zealand's disciples of economic fundamentalism operating quite as untrammelled as was Gudgeon in his imperial day.

Fourth, might empty or even loaded calls for democracy (limited to the holding of dubiously 'free and fair' elections and devoid of equity and economic and social justice) result in 'democracy'—another idea with few enemies but a number of perspectives in the West—becoming as degraded a concept in the future as was imperialism in the later 20th century? A little less posturing and a little more partnership might be of benefit to New Zealand, the countries of the Pacific, and real democracy itself.

And last, for me personally, a realisation of how much an outsider I am to my colonial predecessor (another interesting aspect of the insider/outsider debate) and yet how much I must resemble him to an outsider of us both—an alarming but salutary insight.

ENDNOTES

[1] Gudgeon to unknown, 2 May 1903, W.E. Gudgeon Papers MS-Papers-3253, Alexander Turnbull Library, Wellington (ATL).

[2] This paragraph draws on Richard Gilson, *The Cook Islands 1820-1950*, ed. Ron Crocombe (Wellington 1980), 57-109; Angus Ross, *New Zealand Aspirations in the Pacific in the Nineteenth Century* (Oxford 1964), 234-44, 252-69.

[3] Frederick Cooper and Ann L. Stoler, 'Introduction—tensions of empire: colonial control and visions of rule', *American Ethnologist*, 16:4 (1989), 609-21 and particularly 609, 616; Nicholas B. Dirks, 'Introduction: colonialism and culture', in idem (ed.) *Colonialism and Culture* (Ann Arbor 1992), 1-25, 7-8; Gyan Prakash, 'A view from afar (South Asia)—an interview with Gyan Prakash', in Robert Borofsky (ed.), *Remembrance of Pacific Pasts: an invitation to remake history* (Honolulu 2000), 296-302, 296; Thomas Richards, *The Imperial Archive: knowledge and the fantasy of empire* (London and New York 1993), 2; Ann Laura Stoler, 'Rethinking Colonial Categories: European communities and the boundaries of rule', in Nicholas B. Dirks (ed.), *Colonialism and Culture* (Ann Arbor 1992), 319-52, 319-21; Ann Laura Stoler and Frederick Cooper, 'Between metropole and colony: rethinking a research agenda', in Frederick Cooper and Ann Laura Stoler (eds), *Tensions of Empire: colonial cultures in a bourgeois world* (Berkeley 1997), 1-54, 5-6, 9, 21-2, 29; Nicholas Thomas, 'Partial texts: representation, colonialism and agency in Pacific History', *Journal of Pacific History*, 25:2 (1990), 139-58, 147-9; Nicholas Thomas, *Colonialism's Culture: anthropology, travel and government* (Cambridge 1994), 1-3, 13-16, 50-1, 105-6.

[4] Brief quotations from the journal are generally not footnoted.

[5] This biographical note draws on Walter Edward Gudgeon, Autobiography [1910], in Walter Gudgeon, Autobiography and Related Materials fMS-079 ATL; E.W.G. (Elsdon) Craig, *Destiny Well Sown: a biography of Lt.-Col. W.E. Gudgeon, C.M.G. etc* (Whakatane, NZ 1985); David Green, 'Gudgeon, Walter Edward 1841-1920' (updated 7 April 2006), *Dictionary of New Zealand Biography*, http://www.dnzb.govt.nz accessed 22 April 2006; and M.P.K. Sorrenson, *Maori Origins and Migrations: the genesis of some Pakeha myths and legends* (Auckland 1979), 34-5.

[6] Walter Edward Gudgeon, 'The Maori People', *Journal of the Polynesian Society*, 13:51 (1904), 177-92, 177.

[7] Walter Edward Gudgeon 'The *toa taua* or warrior', *Journal of the Polynesian Society*, 13:52 (1904), 238-64, 239.

[8] *New Zealand Parliamentary Debates* [NZPD] 114 (1900): 387-426; Gudgeon, Autobiography, 25.

[9] Craig, *Destiny Well Sown*, 30, 32.

[10] E.J. Hobsbawm, *The Age of Empire, 1875-1914* (London 1987), 60.

[11] J.A. Hobson, *Imperialism: a study* (3rd edn, London 1988 [1902]), 237.

[12] Walter Edward Gudgeon, 'A journal of my residence in the South Seas and of the causes that led to that residence [1910]', in Walter Gudgeon Autobiography and Related Materials fMS-079 ATL 1. The Journal comprises 68 pages numbered 1 to 68 and lying immediately after page 73 of the Autobiography.

[13] [Edward Tregear], *The Right Hon. R.J. Seddon's Visit to Tonga, Fiji, Savage Island, and the Cook Islands, May, 1900* (Wellington 1900), 425-42; *NZPD* 114 (1900): 387-93.

[14] Seddon to Ranfurly, Memo Urging Caution, 27 December 1898, G11 70.1 Box 4 Archives New Zealand, Wellington (ANZ).

[15] Hobsbawm, *The Age of Empire*, 67.

[16] Gudgeon, Journal, 27, 62. A reference to the juggernaut character of Cecil Rhodes as portrayed fictionally in Anthony Hope [pseudonym of Sir Anthony Hope Hawkins], *The God in the Car* (London 1895).

[17] *Appendices to the Journals of the House of Representatives*, A3 (1898), 16.

[18] Gudgeon, Autobiography, 1.

[19] Gudgeon, Journal, 16.

[20] H. John Field, *Toward a Programme of Imperial Life: the British Empire at the turn of the century* (Westport, CT 1982), xii, 30.
[21] Gudgeon, Autobiography, 173.
[22] Scott 1991, 91-2.
[23] Gudgeon, Journal, 2.
[24] Gudgeon, Journal, 46-8.
[25] Gudgeon, Journal, 40-41, 45.
[26] Gudgeon, Journal 39.
[27] Allen Curnow, 'The Unhistoric Story', in idem, *Sailing or Drowning* (Wellington 1941), 20-21.
[28] Donald Denoon, 'The right to misrepresent', *The Contemporary Pacific*, 9:2 (1997): 400-18; Doug Munro, 'Who "owns" Pacific history: reflections on the insider/outsider dichotomy', *Journal of Pacific History*, 29:2 (1994): 232-37.

Chapter 16

An Accidental Biographer? On Encountering, Yet Again, the Ideas and Actions of J.W. Burton

Christine Weir

I have never set out to write a biography. I'm not sure that I know how to. But early in work on my thesis—on race, work and Christian humanitarianism in the southwest Pacific—I encountered the writing and activism of John Wear Burton (1875-1971), Methodist missionary to the Indians in Fiji, 1902-1911, and mission administrator in Sydney from the 1920s to the 1940s. My first encounter was with the Burton written about by other Pacific historians such as Ken Gillion, Brij Lal, Andrew Thornley and John Garrett: Burton the social campaigner, the whistleblower on Indian indenture in Fiji.[1] The story is well known. In 1901, the Australian Methodists upgraded their mission to the Indians, originally conducted by two lay people, John Williams and Hannah Dudley, by sending ordained European missionaries: Cyril Bavin to Lautoka and John Burton to Nausori. Initially they did not concern themselves with the indenture system; Bavin never did. Burton was rather more interested, but in 1903/4, with as yet limited experience of the conditions of indenture, he was moderately approving of the system, following the usual official and mission line:

> The whole system of Indenture is under Government control, and every effort is made to eliminate anything like abuse. On the whole the Indians are well cared for and their life here must be very much more tolerable than what they have been accustomed to in their own country.[2]

Burton's assumption that the *girmityas* were low-caste and from sordid, probably criminal, backgrounds tallied with the views of other Methodists.

However by 1909 Burton's neutral observation of indenture had turned to condemnation. There were earlier hints of a change of opinion in Mrs Deane's account of a visit to Burton's station in 1907. She went with Burton to the indentured labourers' 'lines', which she described as 'simply dreadful', to attend a service. 'I was much interested in the women', she added, 'for though they seemed happy I am told that they lead most wretched lives'. Presumably it was Burton who was doing the 'telling'.[3] By 1909 his views were clear. In a small booklet circulated within the mission in Fiji and Australia, *Our Indian Work in Fiji*, he began his chapter on indentured labourers in forthright tone:

> The life on the plantation as an indentured labourer is not of a very inviting character. The difference between this state and absolute slavery is merely in the name and the term of years. The coolies themselves ... frankly call it *(narak)* hell. The wages are low and the cost of living is comparatively high ... The accommodation appears to us very wretched ... there are some (lines) where the coolies are herded together like so many penned cattle amid the most insanitary conditions and indescribable filth.[4]

This was the most forthright condemnation of indenture ever to have come from the Methodists. Moreover, it was not a complaint that the regulations were being disregarded but a challenge to the system itself, as dehumanising and degrading.

Interestingly, there was very little adverse criticism from within church circles to the publication of the 1909 booklet. Indeed, Small, as Chairman of the Fiji District, thought it 'should do much good'[5] and the Methodist Missionary Society sent a copy of the book to every Methodist minister in Australia, recommending it for reading by study groups within churches.[6] Burton repeated his opinion in his 1910 book *Fiji of Today*, a handsome volume selling for seven shillings and sixpence. Now others recognised the criticism for what it was. The Colonial Sugar Refining Company complained to the colonial government, which in turn complained to the Methodist mission—putting the Chairman of the mission A.J. Small in a position of some embarrassment since he had written a glowing forward to Burton's book. In July 1910 Governor May wrote formally to Small, rebutting Burton's claims about the evils of the indenture system.[7] Small tried to deny involvement.[8] But Burton was impenitent and defensive, claiming that he had 'given the government credit for improvements' but that 'there is the CSR Co to contend against'.[9] Burton was passionate. The regulations introduced to ameliorate the system were not being observed, but they could not mitigate the evils of the system in any case.

Burton's criticism of the indenture system was influential in other quarters. *The Fiji of Today* was read in India and formed part of the growing call there to abolish the system. Burton's role was acknowledged by others. Before leaving India for Fiji in 1915, Gandhi's emissary, the English Anglican clergyman C.F. Andrews had read and been impressed by the book. Once it was clear that indenture was to be abolished, he wrote to Burton:

> I know what an intense joy to you it will be that the indenture system is to be utterly abolished ... I do feel very strongly that your book (the 'Fiji of Today') was the pioneer and did the pioneer work, and it is due

to that book perhaps more than to any other single cause that the whole indenture system was shown up in its proper light.[10]

In his unofficial 1916 report to the Indian government, Andrews praised the actions of Burton and Hannah Dudley, who 'saved the whole Indian community from falling to the lowest level of ignorance and vice'.[11] Pandit Totaram Sanadhya, who wrote in his memoir of his time in Fiji, also acknowledged this:

> Rev. Burton did a lot for our people. They used to flock to him and tell him their tale of woe. He would plead on their behalf to their master ... (He) was the first person in Fiji to raise his voice against the indenture system.[12]

This then is the relatively well-known heroic story: the writer who started, or at least substantially contributed to, an international campaign against a specific injustice. This is what Burton is remembered for, not his long years as mission theorist and administrator. J.W. Burton does not figure otherwise in histories of Fiji, and there is only one very short street named after him in Suva. He has no biography. His entry in the *Australian Dictionary of Biography* was written by Andrew Thornley, who has concentrated his biographical efforts on earlier missionaries within the Fiji Methodist mission.[13] As I continued with my doctoral research, however, I encountered Burton's name and opinions again and again; his role as campaigner against indenture was only the beginning of a long and interesting career. He was also a missionary (though of limited evangelistic success), photographer, writer, advocate for the League of Nations, mission administrator for nearly 30 years, newspaper columnist (mainly in the *Sydney Morning Herald*), preacher and member of the embryonic South Pacific Commission. So his was indeed a 'Pacific Life': while he lived in Fiji for only 10 years he was involved with mission and general policy in the Pacific for the rest of his life. His opinions and writings increasingly became a thread running though my own writing—yet I have never, till now, attempted to pull it all together.

With his campaign against Indian indenture, Burton seems a very suitable subject for a historian of Fiji, with an interest in missions, of liberal Christian tendencies —like myself. It seems clear that to write an effective biography one needs to have some sort of affinity with your subject. As Neil Gunson put it (this volume), the biographer should have inhabited some of the same thought world as the subject, but also have moved outside it. But of course Burton was more complex than just a social reformer and campaigner against indenture. Human beings always are. And while social justice is comprehensible and attractive to a 21st century biographer, some of Burton's attitudes are more problematic. To illustrate this, let us look more closely at *Fiji of Today*. Most of the book is actually about Fijians, and it was what he said about them rather than the comments about indenture which infuriated Burton's colleagues. There is in his comments a deeply evolutionist strand. Other missionaries, who worked with Fijians, had a deep knowledge of Fijian customs, social structures and ways of life. They identified with their Fijian converts. Burton did not—'his' people were the Indian labourers. He recognised the profound sincerity of some of the older Fijian preachers and he acknowledged that much 'progress' had been made from the pre-Christian times. But he believed that much Fijian Christianity was 'superficial'. He did not believe that Fijians 'had been changed, as if by the waving of a magic wand, from horrible blood-thirsty cannibals to saintly Christians'.[14] The early mass conversions, he thought, had led to a religious state of 'paganism tinctured with Christianity'. Burton was not enthusiastic either about the Fijian chiefly system, or the adoption by missionaries of de facto positions within it.[15] He criticised the communal system as understood and protected by Gordon, seeing it as hidebound and restrictive.

Much of Burton's analysis was based on the commonly-held belief in an evolutionary hierarchy of human groups, grounded in the assumption that modern Western European society epitomised the pinnacle of human achievement. Such assumptions ranked human societies on the rationalist criteria of the sophistication of technology, the complexity of law, and the shift from 'error' or 'superstition' to science. These assumptions Burton shared, allocating Fijians to a fairly low rung in the hierarchy. The group which interested him, his responsibility, was the Indian community, whom he saw as more advanced than Fijians. In an early *Missionary Review* article, he described revealingly an encounter between the two groups. Burton described a rather hair-raising boat trip from Suva to Navua, accompanied by an Indian catechist and young Fijian boys more enthusiastic than skilful. Eventually they made it into the calm of the Navua River:

> 'Sahib!' exclaims the hitherto terrified Catechist; 'our lives are snatched back from death. See how great dangers we meet by trusting ourselves to these dwellers in the jungle, whose minds have never been exercised by thought.'

> The Catechist evidently thinks that this is the proper place to retaliate upon the Fijians, who have been taunting him with being unable to swim.

> 'I would rather trust myself to one of these children of nature on a journey such as this,' replies the missionary, 'than to all the Persian and Sanskrit scholars of Hindustan.'[16]

The Fijians have practical skills, the Indians intellectual ones; Burton appreciated both, in their place, but the 'children of nature' comment shows where he thought the Fijians' place was.

There is considerable evidence that Burton's evolutionist beliefs changed after World War 1, during which he served as a YMCA chaplain in London. While Burton is not explicit about his own reactions, the experience, even at one remove, of the horrors of the trenches led many of his contemporaries to question the supposed superiority of European civilisation. In articles and writings from the 1920s, Burton's attitude to Fijian preachers becomes considerably more approving. In my thesis I explained his shift in attitude as caused primarily by increased personal knowledge; as Methodist General Secretary on regular visits to Papua and New Britain he saw Fijian teachers and ministers working effectively and came to know them personally. In 1926 he described the 'real winning of souls' achieved by Fijian, Tongan and Samoan pastors and teachers in Papua. There were now congregations of 300 where five years previously all had been heathen: 'it is simply marvellous to see what has been done by some of the South Sea Island teachers'.[17] But while this explanation is certainly plausible, I cannot be certain it is right, and it may very well be incomplete.

And here we encounter another problem of writing biography. How can another person be sure about a subject's motivations, changes of mind and outside influences? In Burton's case I have surprisingly little insight into some aspects of his character and motivation. This may seem an odd thing to say, for a great deal of Burton's writing exists. This consists both of published material: books on Fijian and wider Pacific mission history, study guides for congregations, sermons, numerous articles in the Methodist mission journal *Missionary Review* and the *Sydney Morning Herald*; and also unpublished letters and reports from his 30-plus years in mission administration, especially as the General Secretary of the Methodist Missionary Society. But most of this material is quite impersonal, and if biography is a balance between the individual and their context, then I feel I have much more context than individual, more letters than life.

And Burton himself encouraged this. Some time around 1956 he wrote a 200-page autobiography entitled 'The Weaver's Shuttle: memories and reflections of an octogenarian', which was never published.[18] This, he says, was 'written for my own delectation, for I have no great concern whether or not these scribblings find their way into print'. On completing it, Burton, irritatingly for any potential biographer, destroyed all his personal papers.[19] Bearing in mind Niel Gunson's reservations about autobiography (this volume), nonetheless, 'The Weaver's Shuttle' is obviously a crucial document. It also sets the terms about what Burton was, and was not, prepared to discuss in public. There is very little about his parents, marriage, children or personal relationships. We learn he migrated from Yorkshire to New Zealand with his family at the age of nine, married Florence Hadfield in 1902, had three children, the first two born in Fiji. He left Fiji in 1911 because of the ill-health of his two small daughters; Burton has little comment on how he felt about this, although one imagines it must have been a huge disappointment. I know, but not from him, that the youngest, a son also named John Wear Burton (born 1915) became famous as the head of Foreign Affairs under 'Doc' Evatt. The relationship between the two is not discussed by either. Burton tells us little more about family and friends. It is clear from other peoples' accounts that Burton was respected by his colleagues and that he had many friends. Others in the mission environment bear testimony to his influence; Robert Green, who spent 20 years as a Methodist missionary in Fiji in the 1920s and 1930s claimed Burton had inspired his interest during his visitation trips to rural Victoria in 1917.[20] But little of this personal background comes from Burton himself—and if that's how he wanted it, perhaps that's how it should be left. Any biography of Burton could only be fundamentally an intellectual biography, an examination of the public man, the administrator, campaigner and theologian.

How did Burton see his own life? His autobiography sets out his priorities. 'The major interest in my life', he wrote, 'has been Christian missions and the welfare of native races'.[21] The constant interests he saw as running through his life concern wider changes within the broader missionary movement: from exclusive denominational concern with small groups who must be converted at the peril of their souls, to an interdenominational effort which gave due consideration to indigenous perspectives—particularly the growth of the self-governing church. His other great concern was with the growing linkage, particularly in the 1920s and 1930s, between Christianity and secular endeavours for the social advancement and a willingness to consider political change for colonised people. His own representation of his life remains, as I have suggested, primarily an intellectual examination.

Burton was what we might call a theological liberal—and it is in expounding his theological ideas that he reveals most about himself. In middle age he retold the story of his 1901 commissioning as an overseas missionary. It so happened that John Paton, Presbyterian missionary for many years in the New Hebrides, attended the service in Auckland. In his sermon Burton explained his motivation for going to Fiji:

> it was not the belief that the heathen were falling into an endless hell which had impelled me to go forth, but rather the unhappy condition of people who, ignorant of the good news, were living without the happiness that Christ alone could give ... The grand old warrior [Paton] rose, shook his leonine head and ... hurled his burning indignation at the views I had expressed. "Young man," he almost roared, "do you think I would have risked my life amongst the savages and cannibals of the New Hebrides if I had not believed that every man, woman and child I met was going to hell?" The audience broke into a thunder of applause and left me feeling utterly undone.[22]

This account also gives an idea of Burton's style, and his sense of humour; he remained a noted pricker of pomposity, including his own.

Yet he maintained the rightness of this theological position, which he summarised in 1917:

> We have come to believe that there is a wideness in God's mercy like the wideness of the sea, and we have turned from the grim negative to the warm positive, from the post-mortem fortunes to the immediate needs of the human race.[23]

This he thought a 'more compelling and sustaining' motive for missionary activity than fear of hellfire—and it lasted. He was influenced by Biblical criticism and was by no means a literalist. In a radio talk in 1932 he recommended that concerns about miracles, theories and creeds be made subordinate to experiencing the love of Christ. 'I have always refused to be drawn into mere academic and theological discussion about Jesus, just as I would refuse to subject my love or those of my family circle to public analysis', he wrote—incidentally restating his view concerning personal reticence—but told young people to accept what they could of the gospels and live by that; the rest would follow.[24] His own experience of converting others was not encouraging; few Fiji Indians became Christian from his teaching even though, by his own account, he preached on street corners and in the marketplace rather than just in church.[25]

Occasionally, his words resonated: in a 1909 *Missionary Review* article entitled 'Nicodemus' he describes Gobind Das, guru to the plantation workers, who conducts an evening prayer gathering during which he follows recitations from the *Ramayana* with readings of the Beatitudes and the parable of the Prodigal Son from an old Hindi New Testament. On this occasion the guru visits the missionary by night and converts to Christianity, taking the name Nicodemus.[26] A Nicodemus appears in the Methodist preaching lists for the Nausori area in the 1910s. But such an outcome was rare; Burton's conversations with the Pandit Totaram Sanadhya in Nausori were more typical. They seem to have been good friends, regularly discussing life and death and everything in between—and both determined not to be converted by the other. Such conversations, along with a visit to India in 1906, sparked an interest in Hinduism which remained. In a 1914 sermon he encouraged new missionaries bound for India to cultivate an attitude of 'balanced sympathy' towards Hinduism and Islam, to use their religious and philosophical tenets to 'redirect the spiritual instinct of the people into new channels', towards 'a better Saviour, a better Sanctuary'.[27] At around the same time, Burton wrote articles on the Hindu revival and the Arya Samaj, and especially the poet Rabindranath Tagore, whom he saw as proto-Christian 'a forerunner—a John the Baptist, heralding the coming One'.[28] The strength of the writing got it published—but some Australian parishioners must have wondered at such topics. Certainly some others within the Methodist mission regarded him as too close to C.F. Andrews, who was in turn seen as tainted by syncretism and too influenced by Gandhi and Hinduism.[29]

Burton's tolerant and accepting attitude was also evident in his relations with other Christians. His writing is noticeably free of the anti-Catholicism common in Protestant writing of the time. His 1912 *Call of the Pacific* is unusually generous about Catholic missionary efforts in Fiji, in spite of being written only a few years after the 'Bible-burning' controversies in the Rewa delta.[30] Influenced by the Student Christian Movement from his own student days, he frequently attended and spoke at Australian and New Zealand SCM conferences, often accompanied by Presbyterian leader Frank Paton (son of his old critic).[31] His chaplaincy at the end of the First World War was under the auspices of the YMCA, membership of which led to useful links with Christian leaders all over the world. He knew and corresponded with the American ecumenist John Mott, took great interest in the growth and activities of the World Missionary Conference movement from its first meeting at Edinburgh in 1910, attended the 1921 inaugural meeting in America of the International Missionary Council, and watched these develop into the World Council of Churches.

With this view of a worldwide and inclusive Christianity necessarily involved in world affairs, Burton was not a pious figure of personal sanctity and Christian orthodoxy. Rather he tended to be criticised by more conventional colleagues for being too secular; William Slade complained to Chairman A.J. Small in 1909 that Burton advised a mission visitor to 'bring a ball dress to Fiji'. 'Our missionaries', Slade fulminated, 'lose spirituality when they mix with the irreligious spirit of parties'.[32] In many ways Burton's trajectory was typical of the more liberal wing of Christianity in the 20th century. For a biographer this raises questions of potential publisher and audience: Christian publishing outlets are usually interested in more orthodox and conservative figures, secular publishers tend to be suspicious of the 'Christian' label.

But Burton's belief that Christianity must be worked out in the world, that the Gospel was good news for human social and economic as well as spiritual wellbeing, was no mere theoretical stance. It led to his involvement not only in the campaign against indenture in Fiji in the 1910s but also his advocacy of the ideals of the League of Nations in the 1920s, his espousal of the Atlantic Charter in the 1940s and his membership of the new South Pacific Commission in the 1950s. The vocabulary used shifted with local preoccupations but the message remained the same—Christians should support political and secular attempts to improve human social conditions.

In Burton's view the greatest threat to such a improvement lay in untrammelled Western commercialism, whether by the CSR in Rewa in 1909, or plans to use indentured labour in the plantations of Mandated (former German)

New Guinea in 1921, or fears that ANGAU would overuse Papuan indentured labour for non-essential purposes in 1943. As he stated on Sydney radio in 1943:

> One of the greatest, if not the greatest, obstacles to the welfare and progress of native peoples in the past has been commercialism. Too often the commercial point of view has been that the natives are, or should be, cheap and docile labour to create profits for a superior race.[33]

But Burton had moved beyond talk of 'superior races', even if his vocabulary retained elements of paternalism. Indeed paternalism, familial imagery, are exactly how Burton did represent relationships between human groups; in 1921 he praised the Covenant of the League of Nations as:

> A daring scheme for corporate living, which transcends every other attempt in human history to provide an enduring and practical basis for human society. In looking out upon the nations of the earth it sees them as one great human family and has for its objective the promotion of true family feeling.[34]

Some members of the human family might be stronger and more capable than others, but mutual obligation and responsibility—not exploitation—should guide their relations. The exploitative relationships he feared returning in post-war PNG were rooted in 'the failure to recognize the brotherhood of man, the denial of the intrinsic value of every human being'—in other words it was a 'moral and spiritual' problem.[35]

Burton's belief in the brotherhood of man, his humanitarian impulse, was rooted in his Christianity, but interestingly he did not see such beliefs as the prerogative of Christians. He believed that missions and governments could be natural partners in 'native development', especially in education. What education existed in many Pacific countries was almost entirely provided by Christian missions, but any attempt to extend education to whole populations and establish teacher training and widespread technical training was beyond the missions' scope; only government possessed the necessary resources. While many missionaries resisted this simple truth and attempted to forestall any government move into 'their' domain, during the debates between various colonial governments and mission education bodies in the 1930s and 1940s Burton consistently welcomed greater government investment and interest. In a developed statement of his view of government's proper role in indigenous development in the Pacific, Burton wrote:

> There is a shallow view, sometimes encouraged even by missionaries, that governments are always wrong ... The truth is that, by and large, the administrative heads have been men of ability and of probity, and under them are many exceedingly well-trained and devoted officers ... though they do not take the 'spiritual' view, and often are frankly

utilitarian and realistic in their attitude, they usually have well-founded reasons for their activities, and their policy is a well-considered one.[36]

In Burton's view Christians had a right and duty to be involved in secular politics—and one of their main roles was to remind and if necessary pressure governments to take their responsibilities towards the weaker, particularly in colonial situations, seriously. In an era when the relationship between religion and politics is again under debate, Burton's views on the matter hold a new relevance.

John Burton saw the main themes of his own life as 'Christian missions and the welfare of native races'.[37] In spite of warnings about the dangers of taking a subject's judgement about what was important about a life at face value, I see little purpose in attempting to move beyond Burton's own judgement. Considering his reticence about family and personal matters, but also the nature of his public life, there seems little alternative to an intellectual biography. There are clearly elements of this life which a critical biographer would examine further, such as the evolutionism of his early years and the way it melded into a paternalism he never quite shook off. There are some major issues that need further discussion: a careful examination of his relationship with the Methodist missions in Northern Australia, his professional relationships with a number of public figures in the missions and in Australian public life with whom he had major disagreements. If I write Burton's biography, and it's a big 'if', it would be a study in the relationship between faith and action, religion and politics—which is I think the way he would have wanted it.

ENDNOTES

[1] K.L. Gillion, *Fiji's Indian Migrants: a history to the end of indenture in 1920* (Melbourne 1962); Brij V. Lal, *Broken Waves: a history of the Fiji Islands in the twentieth century* (Honolulu 1992); Andrew Thornley, 'The Methodist Mission and Fiji's Indians: 1879-1920', *New Zealand Journal of History*, 8:2 (1974); John Garrett, *To Live among the Stars: Christian origins in Oceania* (Geneva/Suva 1982).

[2] *Missionary Review*, November 1903, 6.

[3] *Missionary Review*, August 1907, 3.

[4] John W. Burton, *Our Indian Work in Fiji* (Suva 1909), 15-16. Many passages from the 1909 pamphlet are reprinted in almost identical form in John W. Burton, *The Fiji of Today* (London 1910), and the text of the pamphlet is reprinted in Brij V. Lal (ed.), *Crossing the Kali Pani: a documentary history of Indian indenture in Fiji* (Canberra/Suva 1998), 121-140.

[5] Small to Wheen, 12 May 1909, Methodist Overseas Mission archive (hereafter MOM, MMSA), box 106, Mitchell Library, Sydney. I thank the Uniting Church of Australia for permission to access and cite this material.

[6] *Missionary Review*, January 1909, 14; October 1909, 7.

[7] Gillion, *Fiji's Indian Migrants*, 167

[8] Small to Colonial Secretary, 13 August 1911, MOM 108, MMSA.

[9] Small to Danks, 28 August 1912, reporting Burton's response to Government criticism, MOM 107.

[10] *Missionary Review,* September 1916, 10; also quoted in Gillion, *Fiji's Indian Migrants*, 178.

[11] Charles Freer Andrews and William Winstanley Pearson, *Report on Indentured Labour in Fiji: an independent enquiry* (Calcutta 1916), 45.

[12] Brij V. Lal and Yogendra Yadav, 'Hinduism under indenture: Totaram Sanadhya's account of Fiji', *Journal of Pacific History*, 30: 1 (1995), 111. Totaram wrote that he planned to translate *The Fiji of Today* into Hindi (Totaram Sanadhya, *My Twenty-one Years in Fiji Islands*, trans. and ed. Jonathan Durham Kelly and Uttra Kumair Singh (Suva 1991), 78). As far as I know he did not do so.

[13] Andrew Thornley, *The Inheritance of Hope: John Hunt, apostle of Fiji* (Suva 2000); Andrew Thornley, *A Shaking of the Land: William Cross and the origins of Christianity (Na Yavalati Ni Vanua: Ko Wiliame Korosi kei na i tekitekikivu ni Lotu Vakarisito e Viti)* (Suva 2005).

[14] John W. Burton, 'The Weaver's Shuttle: memories and reflections of an octogenarian' (n.d.) 69.

[15] Burton, 'Weaver's Shuttle', 56.

[16] *Missionary Review*, August 1904, 5.

[17] John W. Burton, *Our Task in Papua* (London 1926), 78.

[18] A typescript of this memoir is lodged in the Mitchell Library, Sydney (MLMss 2899)—separately from the mission archive.

[19] Burton, 'Weaver's Shuttle', 3.

[20] Robert Green, *My Story: a record of the life and work of Robert H. Green* (Melbourne 1978), 39, 108.

[21] Burton, 'Weaver's Shuttle', 2.

[22] John W. Burton, *Modern Missions in the South Pacific* (London 1949), 12.

[23] John W. Burton, *Laymen's Missionary Lecture: some modern problems of the missionary enterprise* (Melbourne 1917), 11. Burton begins by citing a popular hymn by Frederick Edgar Faber (1862).

[24] John W. Burton, *Why I Believe in Christ* (Sydney 1932), 23.

[25] Burton, *Our Indian Work*, 23-4.

[26] This is in reference to the Jewish leader who came to talk with Jesus at night (John 3: 1-9).

[27] *Missionary Review*, September 1914, 10.

[28] *Missionary Review*, October 1915, 12. Other articles on Tagore appeared in August and September 1915.

[29] Thornley, 'The Methodist Mission and Fiji's Indians: 1879-1920'.

[30] Andrew Thornley, '"Heretics" and "Papists": Wesleyan- Roman Catholic rivalry in Fiji, 1844-1903', *Journal of Religious History*, 10 (1979).

[31] Burton, 'Weaver's Shuttle', 31-33, 90.

[32] William Slade to A.J. Small, 25-9-1909, MMSA F/3/(e), Fiji National Archives, Suva. Slade had a history of objecting to all things Indian.

[33] Broadcast address on radio 2BL, 24 October 1943, reprinted in *Missionary Review*, November 1943, 1-3.

[34] John W. Burton, *The Australian Mandate in Relation to Our Duty to Native Races* (Melbourne 1921), 3.

[35] *Missionary Review*, November 1943, 2.

[36] John W. Burton, *The Atlantic Charter and the Pacific Races* (Sydney n.d.).

[37] Burton, 'Weaver's Shuttle', 2.

Chapter 17

E.W.P. Chinnery: A Self-Made Anthropologist

Geoffrey Gray

In *South Seas in Transition*, the Australian anthropologist W.E.H. Stanner commented that a majority of 'Australians between the wars might have denied, in all innocence, even with a certain indignation, that the Commonwealth was a "Colonial Power" at all'.[1] This is, with few exceptions, all too true today, and is mirrored in the lack of scholarly investigation of the interwar period.[2] A good deal that is available focuses on Papua, which Australia administered for over 70 years, rather than New Guinea, a League of Nations mandate.[3] This paucity is to some degree due to the loss of government records. The files of the Australian administered League of Nations Mandate Territory of New Guinea were depleted first by the 1937 volcanic eruption in Rabaul and again as a result of the outbreak of war in February 1942. The National Archives of Australia explains: 'in early 1942 the Japanese invasion led to the destruction of large quantities of records ... Of the surviving eight series of records, six relate to mining in the district of Morobe; none cover the general administration of the Territory'.[4] The situation regarding the records for Papua is much better and we have, for instance, several superb histories, particularly Francis West's on J.H.P. Murray, and J.D. Legge's on Australian colonial policy. There is also some interest in the Papuan government anthropologist Francis Edgar Williams.[5]

Consequently, to develop an understanding and an appreciation of the interwar period in New Guinea, historians are largely dependent upon the private papers of colonial officials. For example, E.W.P. Chinnery's papers in the National Library of Australia are an exceptionally rich source for the workings of a colonial official in New Guinea (including Papua and the Northern Territory of Australia). His personal records are supplemented by the various government records held in Canberra and Melbourne, particularly the Central Office of the Department of Home and Territories, and the Territories Branch of the Prime Minister's Department, as well the holdings of the National Library, which has a varied collection of papers of colonial officers, especially field officials.

Chinnery's career presents an opportunity to investigate Australia's colonial involvement in all its territories, as well Australia's regional and international relations in regard to its colonial obligations and aspirations. His appointments—Government Anthropologist, Director of District Services in New Guinea, Commonwealth Advisor on Native Affairs and director of the Northern Territory Department of Native Affairs as well as his earlier service in Papua—make him one of the few colonial officials to work in the three main Australian administered territories of Papua, New Guinea and the Northern Territory.

Ernest William Pearson Chinnery (1887-1972), born in Waterloo, a Victorian country town, joined the Papuan service in 1909, rising to Acting Resident Magistrate, before leaving for England in 1917 to join the Australian Flying Corps as a navigator. After he was demobilised, he completed a diploma in anthropology at Cambridge under A.C. Haddon and W.H.R. Rivers. He returned to Papua, as the supervisor of Native labour for New Guinea Copper Mines (November 1920), and, in 1924, was appointed Government Anthropologist in New Guinea, and Director of District Services in 1932, retaining his position as Government Anthropologist. He was made Commonwealth Advisor for Native Affairs and, in April 1939, Director of the Native Affairs Branch in the Northern Territory administration. After Chinnery's resignation at the end of 1946, the Commonwealth continued to use his experience and knowledge in matters as diverse as the South Pacific Commission and the United Nations, sought his advice on the Papua New Guinea Act of 1949 and the future of the Australian School of Pacific Administration. (Chinnery had in the early 1930s represented Australia at the Permanent Mandates Commission of the League of Nations). In 1951, John Gunther, Director of Public Health in Papua New Guinea, invited Chinnery to complete a longitudinal study of depopulation in New Ireland, a project started under the German administration in 1911. Chinnery retired in 1952.

This chapter concentrates on Chinnery's work in Papua and his subsequent attendance at Cambridge in 1919, as it was in the years 1910 to 1920, I contend, that he formulated ideas about the usefulness of anthropology in the management, control and advancement of colonised peoples. In this chapter I set out what brought Chinnery to Papua, his move from a clerk to a field officer, examples of the work he undertook and the various influences on Chinnery as he developed an interest in anthropology and it uses for the governance of colonised peoples.

A Biography of Chinnery

I have been working on Chinnery since the early 1990s. Chinnery's papers were stored in the house of his eldest daughter, Sheila, and the researcher had to travel to Black Rock, a bayside suburb of Melbourne, to see them. Sheila and her late husband Larry looked after researchers well, and the atmosphere was most congenial and enjoyable. Sheila and her sisters, ever helpful to answer questions, nonetheless exercised a watchful eye over their father's legacy and encouraged researchers to concentrate on his life as a government official. As part of a larger work on Australian anthropology I wrote several articles on Chinnery and aspects of his official work.[6] After reading two of my papers on their father I was contacted and asked if I would write his biography. I discussed the proposition with various colleagues, especially Hank Nelson, and decided to start, but could give the family little by way of a completion date. I have other projects, and all research takes longer than anticipated!

My interest in Chinnery arose from my interest in the intersection between anthropology and colonial governance. In the first decades of the 20th century, anthropology was making a claim for its special relevance to the governance of colonised peoples. By the mid-1920s there was a chair of anthropology at the University of Sydney premised on the need to train colonial officials in anthropology, in order to better understand indigenous peoples and assist in their transition to modernity.

Chinnery, a colonial official trained in anthropology, had the opportunity to investigate the relationship between anthropology and colonial governance in a context wider than simply Australian colonial rule in its external territories. Such investigations also underline the international aspect of Australian colonialism. This is most explicit in regard to the administration of New Guinea, and the obligation to report to the Permanent Mandates Commission (PMC) in Geneva which put Australian rule under scrutiny. In fact when the University of Sydney's Chair of Anthropology was threatened with closure, Radcliffe-Brown turned to Lord Lugard, chair of the PMC, for support.[7]

When Chinnery joined the Papuan service, anthropology was dominated by ideas of evolution and diffusion, and ethnographers, often initially trained in biology or zoology, were interested in the origins and spread of people and culture. There was however a nascent anthropological practice developing in Britain which found expression in long-term expeditions to far-away places, such as the Torres Strait Islands and Central Australia. In some instances individuals, such as the Melbourne University biologist Baldwin Spencer, undertook what might now be considered long-term field work in Central Australia.[8] These expeditions were scientific in character and a move away from traveller tropes and mission stories of savagery, salvation and conversion. Largely as a result of colonial rule in Africa and the Pacific, a belief was developing that colonial governance could best be effected by some sort of specialised training for field officials. This was reflected in resolutions at meetings of professional associations and papers published in journals such as *Man*, the journal of the Royal Anthropological Institute of Great Britain and Ireland. For example: In 1894 the Cambridge zoologist Alfred Cort Haddon considered it was of 'urgent national importance' that colonial personnel possess some anthropological knowledge, and he approached the Royal College of Science in London 'urging that a course in General Anthropology with practical work should be provided there to meet this need, and outlining a comprehensive syllabus'.[9] Nearly 10 years later he noted that 'it can hardly be questioned that a missionary would have a better chance of success if he understood something of the aboriginal ideas which he proposes to modify or supplant'.[10] What was needed was an acceptance by universities of anthropology so that teaching could begin. In 1900 Haddon was appointed lecturer in ethnology and instituted a course of lectures in ethnology for missionaries and explorers. He was appointed Reader in Anthropology at Cambridge in 1909, a position he held until his retirement. The tripos degree in Archaeology and Anthropology was established in 1919. I mention Haddon because he trained Chinnery but there were other appointments, around the same time, such as R.R. Marett at Oxford and C.G. Seligman at the London School of Economics.

Colonial Government

Australia had some measure of responsibility for the administration of southeastern New Guinea since British annexation in 1888. From 1888 to 1902 Queensland, New South Wales and Victoria shared responsibility with Britain; from 1902 to 1905 the newly formed Federal Government of Australia replaced the three States. In 1906 Australia took full control of the territory from Britain, changed its name to Papua (it had been British New Guinea) and ruled it as a separate dependency of the Commonwealth. The foundations of policy had been laid by the British, especially Sir William MacGregor, who advocated a policy designed to protect the indigenous population in its relations with Europeans. This was a touchstone of Australian policy. J.D. Legge argues that one of the permanent themes of Australian administration of Papua was 'the benevolence of the Administration ... expressed ... in the measures designed to take control [of] the contact made ... between European and the native. More positive expressions of benevolence in the form of health services, education services, or adequate schemes for expanding native production within the framework of the village, were prohibitively expensive'.[11]

As a result, after pacification (as it was called then), much of the interaction between the administration and indigenous people was focussed on control and management, with advancement of the indigenous peoples framed within the parameters of benevolent government and near penury. Once an area was pacified, the government could concentrate on the 'civilising' and 'modernising' of the indigenous population—a government anthropologist would be able to 'help in reconciling an intelligent though very backward race to the inevitable march of civilization'.[12] J.H.P. Murray, Lt-Governor of Papua, maintained that the government had to govern and this 'automatically entailed the suppression of repugnant customs and the enforcement of certain standards of behaviour, hygiene and industry. It was irrelevant that these standards cut across traditional bases of leadership and influence, for the government had no choice but to suppress certain customary actions in the process of pacification'.[13]

A young E.W.P. Chinnery applied for a clerical position in the Papuan service. His motives are unclear but, according to his daughters, adventure was certainly one. He was attached to the Government Secretary's office in Port Moresby but it is unclear how he perceived a career in the Papuan service and whether remaining a clerk would have satisfied his yearning for adventure.[14] Francis West, in his *Australian Dictionary of Biography* entry, states that Chinnery 'seeking the prestige of field service',[15] won an appointment as a relieving patrol officer in July 1910 to Ioma in the Mambare division. The following year he took up a position of Assistant Resident Magistrate in the Kumusi division; for the next three years his work on routine patrols was said to have:

> gained the respect and the confidence of the local tribes. He was, however, not on good terms either with local Europeans or with Hubert Murray. In November 1913 Chinnery was charged with infringing the field-staff regulations and was reduced in rank. In the Rigo district in 1914, a patrol led by him clashed with tribesmen and shot seven; Murray saw the incident as probably unavoidable. By 1917 Chinnery was patrolling into new country in the central division behind Kairuku and into the Kunimaipa valley. There he discovered the source of the Waria River.[16]

Helping and Understanding

Undoubtedly Chinnery was introduced to what might be seen as a nascent anthropological method of colonial governance by Hubert Murray; in the hands of Murray it was a way of gaining a cultural and social understanding of indigenous peoples and thus enabling not only peaceful occupation of new territory but also the 'uplift' of Papuan people. Murray argued in 1912 that when certain customs are forbidden, a substitute ritual is needed to 'fill the void': when, for example, a 'native who learns for the first time' that he cannot engage in head-hunting, never collect any more heads and never fight again, he is 'likely to feel a void in his existence, for his chief occupations will be gone, and unless something is given to him which will fill the void he and his descendants will suffer'.[17] It is only later, in 1916, when Murray was negotiating for the appointment of a government anthropologist that we gain a sense of the importance of anthropology to Murray in the governance of indigenous peoples.[18]

Chinnery was convinced that anthropology was central to good governance in the colonies. He commented to the ANZAAS conference in 1955 that during his

> service as a native administration official in Papua and New Guinea between 1909 and 1938, I found it easier, after training in anthropology

and scientific methods of enquiry, to study the beliefs and practices of the people, to win and retain their confidence, and to help them through their problems, and changes due to Government, Mission and Industrial influences ... It should not be forgotten that hasty ill-advised European pressures disrupting land ownership and usages, and forcing changes in marriage systems, religious beliefs and practices, social and other observances, before people were ready to absorb them, together with irritating racial discrimination, especially in employment, have contributed largely to nativistic outbreaks damaging European and Natives alike, and holding up progress in other non-self governing Territories.[19]

The primary influence on Chinnery's anthropology and its method was Alfred Cort Haddon and W.H.R. Rivers. There is little doubt, however, that his enthusiasm for what might be now termed applied anthropology was supported by Haddon, after Rivers' death in 1922. Chinnery acknowledged the importance of Rivers for his thinking and development as anthropologist, first in his 1919 paper, 'The Application of Anthropological Methods to Tribal Development in New Guinea', and again in his 1932 ANZAAS presentation, 'Applied Anthropology in New Guinea'. But Haddon and Rivers were not the only influence on Chinnery. It was through Wilfred Beaver, a field officer at Mambare, that Chinnery became acquainted with Haddon; Beaver also encouraged Chinnery to develop his ethnography.[20] (Beaver was described as a 'man of patience and sympathy [dealing] with ... the obtuseness of Papuans'.)[21] Haddon, probably the most influential anthropologist of the time, engaged in correspondence with a number of colonial field officers and missionaries, including Beaver. This correspondence ranged over many matters but was mainly Haddon seeking specific information about customs of indigenous people. He had for example an intense interest in the prow designs of canoes.[22]

Murray developed his ideas about anthropology from discussions with anthropologists such as Seligmann and Haddon in the early years of his administration, yet he made little effort to have his officers trained in anthropology, preferring to choose field officers on the basis of character. When he did appoint a trained anthropologist to the position of assistant government anthropologist it was not his intention that the incumbent train field officers in anthropology. Chinnery, in contrast, once he was appointed Government Anthropologist in New Guinea, was eager to gain the support of the Administrator in training field officers. Chinnery supported the establishment of a chair of anthropology at the University of Sydney, as did Haddon, and planned to send field officers to undertake the course proposed by Radcliffe-Brown.[23] So did Murray, at least for a while, although he was ambivalent about the value of such a course.[24]

A Resident Magistrate was expected to undertake patrols, carry out exploration work, establish and maintain good relations with the indigenous people, and oversee modifications to their way of life and their interaction with representatives of civilisation—missionaries, traders, gold miners, and government officials. The government set about to change household and village hygiene and health, remove those customs offensive to Australian sensibilities, and introduce the rule of law.[25] Chinnery explained to the ANZAAS conference held in August 1932 that the field official

> [f]ound himself called upon to build houses, roads and bridges; to treat tropical diseases, to control epidemics, and attempt surgical relief; to make and record geographical discoveries, to pacify and control savage tribes of cannibals and head-hunters; to arrest, try and incarcerate law breakers; to perform routine departmental duties.[26]

In 1915, the year he and Wilf Beaver published a paper on the initiation ceremonies of Hunjara, the people of the Yodda Valley at the head of the Kumusi River, Chinnery was slowly grasping the nature of anthropology. As a result of this paper, a story circulated that Chinnery had been initiated. Chinnery had observed parts of the initiation ceremonies, as it was stated that 'Mr Chinnery had seen the proceedings and was to a certain degree initiated himself into the Hunjara'.[27] His formal introduction to recording aspects of indigenous life occurred in 1911, when his superior officer, Resident Magistrate Oelrichs, advised him to record 'any curiosities, any peculiarities about a person or a whole tribe'. The usefulness of drawings to record information about their way of life was stressed. This was the extent of any training he was to receive in the field. Beaver therefore was critical in Chinnery's development as an observer of native customs. Beaver had formed a relationship with Haddon some years earlier and in 1920 a book on Beaver's ethnography—that is, his experiences as government field officer—was published.[28]

Chinnery's early reports were used in the report of the Resident Magistrate.[29] In later years, Chinnery's reports were included under his own name. He collaborated with Beaver in compiling several vocabularies,[30] and it was accepted at the time that genealogical information could be adduced through such collections.[31] During his time in Papua Chinnery produced over 20 ethnographic and geographic publications, some appearing in British journals.[32]

We can infer that Chinnery's method of recording data followed Beaver's and Haddon's advice. His association with them helped him to acquire a structure in which to present his ethnographic data. In his initial correspondence with Chinnery, Haddon advised him to read Notes and Queries, especially the 1912 edition which stressed the importance of using, where possible, 'native terminology' when asking question in the field as this minimised misunderstanding between informants and investigator. The value of information freely provided was also stressed, as this was less likely to be contrived than information actively sought after.[33]

Chinnery at Cambridge

In the year he left Papua to join the Australian Flying Corp in England, Chinnery published with Haddon a paper on 'religious cults'.[34] He had shown himself to be capable of writing ethnographic reports and articles; when he was demobilised in 1919 he enrolled at Cambridge 'to undertake two years academic study in anthropology under the tutelage of A.C. Haddon and W.H.R. Rivers'.[35] Haddon had requested the Australian government assist Chinnery: he informed them that Chinnery wanted to further his theoretical and general knowledge and in particular to study the distribution and migration of cultures of Oceania.[36] His request was granted.

Critical to understanding Chinnery's enthusiastic embrace of applied anthropology is Rivers' argument as laid out in his paper on 'The government of subject peoples'.[37] This was published in a volume, edited by A.C. Seward, whose purpose was 'to demonstrate the fallacy of [the] distinction that technical education stands for efficiency and prosperity, but pure science is regarded as something apart—a purely academic subject'.[38] Hoping that 'our rulers will recognise the value of those sciences which will make our possessions more healthy and more productive', Rivers set out to show how 'anthropology can point the way to the better Government' of peoples ruled by Britain.[39] There were according to Rivers three possible lines of action when one people 'assumes the management of another': destruction, preservation or compromise. Whatever the degree of interference, 'knowledge of the culture to be modified is absolutely necessary if changes are to be made without serious injury to the moral and material welfare of the people'.[40]

Of the several tasks of the anthropologist, Rivers considered that only the collection, description and classification of the ethnographic facts had any practical value.[41] Against the stereotype of anthropologist as head-measurer and museum collector, he saw a movement away 'from physical and material towards the psychological and social aspects of the life of Mankind. [The anthropologist's] chief interest today is in just those regions of human activity with which the art of government is daily and intimately concerned'.[42] The gap between rulers' and subjects' knowledge of each other did not, according to Rivers, promote good government, nor did it 'foster a healthy sentiment of respect towards rulers'.[43] One misunderstood feature of 'lowly cultures' Rivers saw as 'the close dependence of one department of social life upon another [which] is so great that interference with any department has consequences more immediate and far reaching than in the more developed and specialized varieties of culture'.[44]

Rivers recommended that colonial governments should either employ anthropologists or sponsor research, as well as require anthropological training of their recruits.[45] Such training, however, should be concerned, not with facts, but with 'the principles which underlie the vast variety of social institutions and belief of mankind'. Nor should training be in the hands of former administrators, for this would be 'especially futile', leading only to the perpetuation of false knowledge. Finally, Rivers attempted to counter two objections: that anthropological training would lead to 'weakness and indecision on the executive side' and that time was too short. The first he saw answered by a separation of policy-makers from executives, with the latter simply feeding facts to the former; the second in that facts were collected in the normal course of administration. In short, Rivers looked to the formulation of 'policies which will reconcile the general needs of the Empire with a due regard for the moral and material welfare of the peoples to whom the Empire has so great a responsibility'.[46] This was a call which Chinnery certainly heeded once he returned to Papua in 1921. But Rivers' continued influence over Chinnery is harder to determine, not least because of his death in 1922; it was with Haddon that Chinnery maintained a correspondence until Haddon's death in 1940.

While in England Chinnery lectured to audiences of government, academic and amateur associations on colonial rule and the life and work of a colonial field officer in Papua (better known as British New Guinea).[47] It was clear that Chinnery had been cogitating on the value of anthropology as a civilising method. He gave two addresses which reflect this, the first to the Royal Geographic Society, and the other to the Royal Anthropological Institute (RAI).

To the Royal Geographic Society, Chinnery was reported as describing a clash with tribesmen in the Rigo district in 1914. The influence of Murray is apparent:

> [A] village was raided and some of its inhabitants were murdered by a hitherto unknown tribe. [Chinnery] was despatched to explore the district and capture the people responsible for the raid. He found them among the headstreams of a river draining the principal southerly spur of Mount O'Bree, one of the peaks of the central chain over 10,000 ft in height, situated to the east of Port Moresby. The valleys of these streams were inhabited by fierce peoples who had never before seen a white man or a Government party. Their villages were built on the summits or pinnacles of razor-backed ridges, generally over 4000 ft above sea level, and protected by one or two lines of stockades. The approach of Mr Chinnery's was detected at almost every case from look-out houses or platforms built on tops from within the villages. When the natives learned the purpose of his mission two or three hundred of them attacked three of the police and Mr Chinnery with spears and large stones and in the fighting which ensued six of the ringleaders of the massacre which had

given rise to the expedition were shot. The remainder fled, but afterwards accepted Mr Chinnery's offer of friendship on condition that he went into the next valley and pacified the people there, in order that inter-tribal warfare might cease. This he did under native guidance, and achieved his objective without further fighting. As a proof of their appreciation of Government intervention a good many of the natives accompanied him to the Government Station and for the first time in the history of their tribe saw the sea. Subsequently when his successor visited the district he found the native peaceful and contented under the new conditions.[48]

His address to the RAI laid out how greater efficiency could be achieved by colonial administrations when dealing with their 'responsibility to civilize' backward peoples, which resonated with the idea of a 'trusteeship', a sort of partnership between the colonised and the coloniser to uplift and advance the colonised on the ladder of civilisation, which was being discussed in such circles.[49] He pointed out that he had learnt to apply himself to the needs of primitive cultures through his work as an Assistant Resident Magistrate. His experience had given him 'a knowledge of the psychology of numerous tribes, and the application of such knowledge to general methods of administration enabled me to assist my [sic] people through their many stages of transition'. He considered the key to good government in the colonies was knowing how the minds of indigenous people work (this resonates with Murray's notion of encouraging his officers to 'think black').[50] He discussed how modifications were being made to various unacceptable elements of Papuan societies, and concluded by making the following recommendations: first, that 'general training in anthropological subjects be [given to all] District Officers and other persons holding positions of responsibility over natives'; and second, that 'publication and circulation of all existing and subsequent records of New Guinea ethnography [be provided to District Officers] for their guidance'.[51]

This progressive view of anthropology was in direct contrast to the course-work and instruction he undertook while at Cambridge. His thesis, as part of the requirement for the diploma in anthropology, was on stonework and gold mining in New Guinea.[52] In keeping with the diffusionist thrust of anthropology taught at the time, it contained many speculations and inaccuracies and shows the influence of the heliocentric school of ethnology of W.J. Perry and Grafton Elliot Smith at University College, London.[53] In fact, Perry used Chinnery's Papuan map in his Children of the Sun (1923).[54] Chinnery never lost his interest in such speculative ideas, and in 1956 and 1957 made a series of broadcasts on the ABC, in which he returned to the topics of stonework and gold mining.[55] Chinnery had opined in 1920 that 'the New Guinea objects (mortars, pestles, stone clubs, stone circles and incised stone work) appear to be similar in many aspects to objects associated with megalithic cultures in other parts of the world'.[56] These musings about origins and diffusion were elided in the practical application of anthropological knowledge to the problems of colonial government. In his work as an anthropologist we find little or no mention of these matters, nor do such theoretical interests appear to create a tension in his practical work. Certainly, he held a view that New Guineans were backward, and most likely unable to achieve their colonisers' level of civilisation. Yet, as alluded to earlier, Chinnery argued that they should be assisted to advance, and treated fairly and with due process.

Return to Papua

When Chinnery was patrolling in various parts of Papua, especially his early appointment to the Kumusi Division, one task was to arrest labourers who had deserted from rubber plantations. Native constables assisted the field officers in their policing work, while indigenous men were employed on these patrols as carriers, cooks and interpreters.[57] It was during this time that Chinnery developed an interest in labour problems, which were at the heart of the industrial project of colonial rule. Indigenous people were not skilled in working on plantations, assisting gold miners and such like. They were agricultural workers used to different rhythms and division of labour.

On his return to Papua in 1920, he was no longer an officer in the Papuan service, but was engaged as a supervisor of labour for New Guinea Copper Mines Ltd at Bootless Bay. This was not what he had anticipated when he wrote from London seeking an anthropological appointment in Murray's Papuan Administration. Murray was seeking a government anthropologist and Haddon had supported Chinnery,[58] but Murray did not want Chinnery. He wrote to his brother, Gilbert, that

> We have a man called [Chinnery] who is in England now—Haddon has a great opinion of him and wants him appointed. But he would not do at all—he is quite unreliable as to observation, collection of evidence etc—he will say any mortal thing in order to excite interest and attract attention. Not that he is a liar—but he must attract notice.[59]

It is unclear why Murray took such an attitude. To avoid any undue pressure from the Minister, Murray quickly appointed his Chief Medical Officer, Walter Mersh Strong, as government anthropologist. It has been suggested that part of Murray's dissatisfaction was with Chinnery's pursuit of heliocentric ethnology: 'attempts to link Papuan people to any romantic notions of ancient "civilizations" would have been anathema to the colonial regime'.[60] Personally, I think this is a fanciful explanation, although some years later there was an exchange between Murray and Chinnery of some of the ideas about Papua found in Perry's *Children of the Sun*.[61] Ideas such as those of Elliot Smith and Perry were academic orthodoxy at the time; rather it was functionalist theory, as promoted by anthropologists such as Malinowski, that created problems for administrators like Murray, who believed that it was a theory which supported the retention of customs despite their offensiveness, thereby keeping people in some form of cultural servitude.[62] I suspect that Chinnery's anthropology, as he had expressed in his London lectures, had the potential to question the manner in which Murray administered the colony.

While Chinnery waited for an opening in the League of Nations Mandate of New Guinea, he further enunciated the principles of an anthropologically informed administration at the Pan Pacific Science Congress of 1923. He presented a paper on native labour in which he discussed his work at the mine. He explained that an adequate supply of native labour is essential and 'as numbers in excess of those now employed may be needed ultimately, considerable thought has been given by the Company's officials as to the best means to adopt for insuring the numbers of recruits needed from time to time for any expansion of the Company's business'. He noted that 'strict observance of the provisions of the "Native Labour Ordinance", maintenance for the natives of the pre-war purchasing power of money, provision of suitable variety of foods, and the creation of conditions for insuring health and contentment of the natives, will combine to attract to our Company many boys who have refrained hitherto from entering into a contract of service, and an increased number of boys who have already worked a term with the Company'. In this connection New Guinea Copper had 'retained the services of two highly competent recruiters', and commissioned a former government official, 'long in the service of the Papuan government to make the necessary investigations and report on the future possibilities of recruiting preparatory to assuming the position of supervisor of native labour department'.[63]

Chinnery drafted the annual report on labour for New Guinea Copper, in which he stated that 'today there may be seen [Papuans] peacefully wielding the tools of industry ... who but yesterday cut off their neighbour's heads, and ate their bodies with equanimity'. He went on to explain that the company's labour policy was consistent with policies advocated by Murray who had stated that the 'preservation of native races depends on whether the energy formerly devoted to cannibalism and head hunting can be diverted into the relatively gentle activities of industrial development'. New Guinea Copper was 'actively connected with the cultural development of its savage employees, and becomes, as well as their employer, their guide and teacher through the intricate byeways [sic] leading from primitive life to the complex state know as civilization'. Once the indenture was complete, care was taken to ensure that the employee was paid off in Port Moresby 'and protected and maintained by our agents until a boat is available to take them to their homes where they are landed with their trade goods, the fruits of their labour, well content with the results of their service and the envy of their fellow villagers, who, stimulated by the example and treatment of the time expired boys will, it is hoped engage in their return'.[64]

Government Anthropologist

Chinnery saw the position as labour supervisor as a holding one. In May 1921, soon after Australian civil administration had begun in the League of Nations Mandated Territory of New Guinea,[65] Chinnery applied to the Australian government for an anthropological appointment in the territory. He informed the commonwealth government secretary that he had discussed the question of anthropology in connection with the administration of colonies with Prime Minister Billy Hughes who said he would advise Chinnery as soon as there was a suitable opening.

In his application to the Official Secretary of the Commonwealth of Australia, he described himself as a 'student [who] specialized on the ethnology of Oceania' and had 'spent three months on research in parts of the mandated territory'. Since November 1920 he had been 'studying problems of native labor [sic] for the New Guinea Copper Mines and applying the results to their organization'. To demonstrate his enthusiasm and commitment to anthropology he informed the commonwealth officer that he planned to spend 'a short time in the mountains to investigate the social organisation of one of the negrito tribes' of Papua.[66] He was eager to present himself as both the practical man and most importantly as an anthropologist, a scientist who could oversee the dramatic changes which were impacting on the indigenous population and offset the undesirable effects. His time outside the structure of government service enabled him to put into practice some of the ideas he developed while in England. Rivers played an important role in this, as it is apparent Chinnery took two strictures from him into his supervising of indigenous labour: first, to 'uphold the indigenous culture of the subject race'; and second, 'whatever the degree of interference with indigenous customs … knowledge of the culture to be modified is absolutely necessary if changes are to be made without serious injury to the moral and material culture of the people'.[67]

He no longer saw himself as merely a resident magistrate or patrol officer: he wanted to put into effect his anthropological training, which he thought could be realised by an appointment as a government anthropologist, either in Papua or the newly acquired mandated territory of New Guinea. Chinnery was both a product of colonialism and a critic of colonialism, while sensitive to the more humane ideals of the colonial enterprise. He was deeply influenced by the idealism of J.H.P. Murray's colonial philosophy which permeated his thinking and practice, as well as Haddon who served as his mentor and advisor.

Chinnery had to wait until April 1924 before he was appointed Government Anthropologist. By then he was well versed in all matters to do with an anthropology premised on assisting colonial administrations to help advance and uplift indigenous populations.

ENDNOTES

[1] W.E.H. Stanner, *The South Seas in Transition: a study of post-war rehabilitation and reconstruction in three British Pacific dependencies* (Sydney 1953), 1.

[2] See, e.g., G.W.L. Townsend, *District Officer: from untamed New Guinea to Lake Success*, 1921-1946 (Sydney 1968); J.K. McCarthy, *Patrol Into Yesterday* (Sydney 1964); Ian Downs, *The Last Mountain: a life in Papua New Guinea* (St Lucia, QLD 1986); George Stocking, 'Gatekeeper to the field: E.W.P. Chinnery and ethnography of the New Guinea Mandate', *History of Anthropology Newsletter*, 9:2 (1982), 3-12; Robin Radford, *Highlanders and Foreigners in the Upper Ramu: the Kainantu area*, 1919-1942 (Melbourne 1987); Deidre J.F. Griffiths, 'The career of F.E. Williams, government anthropologist of Papua, 1922-1943', MA thesis, Australian National University (Canberra 1977); Sarah Chinnery, *Malaguna Road: the Papua and New Guinea diaries of Sarah Chinnery*, ed. and introd. Kate Fortune (Canberra 1998); Naomi McPherson, 'Wanted: young man, must like adventure. Ian McCallum Mack, Patrol Officer', in Naomi M. McPherson (ed.), *In Colonial New Guinea: anthropological perspectives* (Pittsburgh 2001), 82-110; George Westermark, 'Anthropology and administration: colonial ethnography in the Papua New Guinea Eastern Highlands', in ibid., 45-63; cf. Maria Lepowsky, 'The Queen of Sudest: white women and colonial cultures in British New Guinea and Papua', in ibid., 125-150; Francis West, 'An Australian moving frontier', in Niel Gunson (ed.), *The Changing Pacific* (Melbourne 1978), 214-227; Bill Gammage, *The Sky Travellers: journeys in New Guinea 1938-1939* (Melbourne 1998); Francis West, 'E.W.P. Chinnery', *Australian Dictionary of Biography*, vol. 7 (Melbourne 1979) 639-640; I.C. Campbell, 'Anthropology and the professionalisation of colonial administration in Papua and New Guinea', *The Journal of Pacific History*, 33:1 (1998), 69-90; Geoffrey Gray, 'Being honest to my science: Reo Fortune and J.H.P. Murray, 1927-1930', *The Australian Journal of Anthropology*, 10: 1 (1999), 56-76. This list is by no means exhaustive.

[3] See http://www.naa.gov.au/fSheets/FS148.html

[4] Francis West, *Hubert Murray: the Australian Pro-Consul* (Melbourne 1968); J.D. Legge, *Australian Colonial Policy* (Sydney 1956).

[5] See http://www.naa.gov.au/Publications/fact_sheets/fs235.html; Michael W. Young and Julia Clark, *An Anthropologist in Papua: the photography of F.E. Williams, 1922–39* (Adelaide 2001); also Griffith, 'The career of F. E. Williams'.

[6] 'A desire to improve their conditions: E.W.P. Chinnery in New Guinea and the Northern Territory', in States and Territories, Proceedings, 1999 http://rspas.anu.edu.au/melanesia/pworkshop.htm; 'There are many difficult problems: Ernest William Pearson Chinnery—government anthropologist', *The Journal of Pacific History*, 38:3 (2003), 313-330; '"Mr Chinnery should be given the recognition he deserves": E.W.P. Chinnery in the Northern Territory', *Journal of Northern Territory History*, 15 (2004), 21-33; 'A wealthy firm like Vesteys gives us our opportunity: an attempt to reform the cattle industry', *Journal of Northern Territory History*, 16 (2005), 37-54.

[7] See Geoffrey Gray, *A Cautious Silence: the politics of Australian anthropology* (Canberra 2007), esp. ch. 3.

[8] See, e.g., Howard Morphy, 'Gillen—a man of science', in John Mulvaney, Howard Morphy and Alison Petch (eds), *My Dear Spencer: the letters of F.J. Gillen to Baldwin Spencer* (Melbourne 1997), 23-50.

[9] A.H. Quiggin, *Haddon the Headhunter: a short sketch of the life of A.C. Haddon* (Cambridge 1942), 117.

[10] Haddon, 'The Teaching of ethnology at Cambridge', *Manchester Guardian*, 5 January 1903.

[11] Legge, *Australian Colonial Policy*, 3.

[12] Murray, *Anthropology and the Government of Subject Races*, Australasian Association for the Advancement of Science (ANZAAS), vol. 15 (1921), 180. See also Murray, 'The scientific aspect of the pacification of Papua', Presidential Address, ANZAAS, 1932. The anthropologist Lucy Mair states that in many ways Murray presented an enlightened and humanitarian colonial rule but the length of his administration weakened this position, Lucy Mair, *Australia in New Guinea* (Melbourne 1970) [1948] 11-13.

[13] West, *Hubert Murray*, 173.

[14] West points out that the educational qualifications of field and office staff were not high: 'What Murray was looking for was sober, energetic and fit young men plus, for the field staff, men who could learn patience and self-control in the face of hardship or danger'. West, *Hubert Murray*, 118.

[15] Shiela Waters, in letters to me, has complained about the use of such an expression. David Lawrence suggests, without much evidence, that monetary reward attracted Chinnery to field service. 'The early ethnographic writings of E.W. Pearson Chinnery: Government Anthropologist of New Guinea', Public lecture for the National Archives of Australia, presented in Canberra, 23 March 2006, 4.

[16] West, *Hubert Murray*, 640.

[17] J.H.P. Murray, *Papua* (London 1912).

[18] West, *Hubert Murray*, 10-11. Moreover, Murray's tracts on anthropology date from 1920. His *Anthropology and the Government of Subject Races* was published in 1930.

[19] Chinnery, ANZAAS, 1955. Chinnery Papers (CP), National Library of Australia, Canberra.

[20] Haddon to Chinnery, 7 July 1915. CP.

[21] West, *Hubert Murray*, 162.

[22] A.C. Haddon and James Hornell, *Canoes of Oceania* (Honolulu 1975). (Originally three volumes, published between 1936 and 1938).

[23] Radcliffe-Brown to Gregory, 2 April 1928, Elkin Papers, Sydney University: 164/4/2/12.

[24] Gray, 'Being honest to my science' 56-76.

[25] Gray, 'Being honest to my science', 56ff.

[26] Chinnery, Applied Anthropology in New Guinea, Report of the ANZAAS, August 1932, Sydney, vol. 21 (1933), 3.

[27] E.W.P. Chinnery and W.N. Beaver, 'Notes on the initiation ceremonies of the Koko, Papua', *Man, Journal of the Royal Anthropological Institute of Great Britain and Ireland*, 45 (1915), 70.

[28] W.N. Beaver, *Unexplored New Guinea* (London 1920). Beaver was killed on the Western Front in September 1917.

[29] National Archives of Australia, Canberra (hereinafter NAA): A1, 1920/9030(b); see also Annual Report, Papua, 1911; 1914-15; 1916-17.

[30] Chinnery and Beaver, Comparative table of languages of Northern Division and vocabularies, Papua Annual Report, 1914-15, 161-7; Vocabularies—Buna Station, Kumusi Division, Papua Annual Report, 1919, 86. Chinnery, Comparative vocabulary of tribes of main range, west of Mt Albert Edward, Papua Annual Report, 1916-17, 65-7, Appendix II, III, IVa.

[31] Stocking, 'The ethnographers magic: fieldwork in British anthropology from Tylor to Malinowski', in idem, *Observers Observed: history of anthropology*, vol. 1 (Madison 1983), 91.

[32] For a list see NAA: A1, 1920/9030 (a).

[33] George Stocking, 'The ethnographer's magic', 91.

[34] Chinnery and Haddon, 'Five new religious cults in British New Guinea', *Hibbert Journal*, 1 (1917), 448-63; also Stanner, *South Seas in Transition*, 57-73.

[35] Chinnery, Applied Anthropology in New Guinea, 4.

[36] Haddon to Atlee-Hunt, 15 November 1918. NAA: A1, 1921/9820.

[37] W.H.R. Rivers, 'The government of subject peoples', in A.C. Seward (ed.), *Science and the Nation: essays by Cambridge graduates* (Cambridge 1917). 2-28.

[38] Seward, 'Preface', in idem, *Science and the Nation*.

[39] Rivers, 'The government of subject peoples', 302-3.

[40] Ibid., 305.

[41] Ibid., 305-6.

[42] Ibid., 306-7.

[43] Ibid., 309.

[44] Ibid., 311.

[45] Ibid., 321.

[46] Ibid., 325.

[47] Papua was described as the 'first grandchild of the empire'. Unattributed press cutting (London), 6 March 1920. NAA: A1/1, item 21/9820.

[48] 'At the sign of the world's cross roads: a young Australian administrator', unnamed newspaper report. NAA: A1/1, item 21/9820; also Chinnery, 'The opening of new territories in Papua', *The Geographical Journal*, June (1920), 439-459.

[49] Chinnery, 'The application of anthropological methods to tribal development in New Guinea', *Man*, 49 (1919), 36-41. For a discussion on trusteeship see Ronald Hyam, 'Bureaucracy and 'trusteeship' in the colonial empire', in Judith M. Brown and William Roger Louis, *The Twentieth Century: the Oxford history of the British Empire*, vol. 4 (Oxford 1999), 255-279.

[50] West, *Hubert Murray*, 210-11.

[51] Chinnery, 'The application of anthropological methods to tribal development', 41.

[52] It was published as, 'Stone-work and goldfields in British New Guinea', *Journal of the Royal Anthropological Institute of Great Britain and Ireland*, 49 (1919), 271-91.

[53] Among Australian anthropologists who started doctoral theses at London University under Grafton Elliot Smith and W.J. Perry were Ursula McConnel and A.P. Elkin. Tigger Wise describes Elkin's PhD, completed in 1926: 'It was a vast historical survey of burial rites, initiation rites, the making of medicine men and mythology, prefaced by 21 pages of index, studded with maps on the distribution of circumcision rites, subincison rites, the use of shell and ending with a token bow to Elliot Smith's pet hobbyhorse: the diffusion of mummification rites out of the Egyptian XXI Dynasty.' Wise, *The Self-Made Anthropologist* (Sydney 1985), 49.

[54] W.J. Perry, *The Children of the Sun: a study in the history of civilization* (London 1923), 291.

[55] NAA: A452, 1957/2232.

[56] Chinnery, 'The opening of new territories in Papua', 279.

[57] See Gammage, *The Sky Travellers*.

[58] Murray to Hunt, 21 March 1919. NAA: A1/1, item 21/9820.

[59] Murray to Gilbert Murray, 2 December 1919, in Francis West (ed.), *Selected Letters of Hubert Murray* (Melbourne 1970), 106. West deletes Chinnery's name. Murray had decided by March that there was no opening for Chinnery. Murray to Hunt, 21 March 1919. NAA: A1/1, item 21/9820. Six months earlier Murray had written to his brother that '[w]e want one and I think that I should prefer an Oxford man, though Haddon, who seems to interest himself in New Guinea more than any one else, is of course Cambridge. I wrote to Marett about it some time ago ... We could only give him about £300 a year to begin with, but we should pay his passage out and give him a sum of money for equipment'. (Murray to Gilbert, 17 July 1919, in West, *Selected Letters of Hubert Murray*, 104.)

[60] Lawrence, 'The early ethnographic writings of E.W. Pearson Chinnery', 15.

[61] Chinnery, *Man*, 27 (Nov. 1927), 214-215 and Murray's reply in *Man* 28 (Jul. 1928), 128.

[62] Gray, 'Being honest to my science'; idem, 'There are many difficult problems'.

[63] Paper presented by Chinnery to Health Section, Pan Pacific Science Congress, (Haddon chair), 1923, typescript, CP.

[64] E. Hogan Taylor, General Manager, 'General Report, The New Guinea Copper Mines Ltd.' (1921), CP.

[65] The mandate was confirmed on 17 December 1920; civil administration formally began on 9 May 1921.

[66] Chinnery to Official Secretary, Commonwealth of Australia, 27 May 1921. NAA: A518/1, R815/1 Part 1.

[67] Quoted in Chinnery, 'The application of anthropological methods to tribal development', 36.

Chapter 18

Lives Told: Australians in Papua and New Guinea

Hank Nelson

The home computer, Microsoft Word, more sophisticated programs known to younger generations, and the flourishing of family history—the practical means and the incentive—have resulted in the recent publishing of many autobiographies and biographies. That so many of the lives recorded include years spent in Papua and New Guinea reflects the fact that Australians have seen Papua New Guinea as a frontier of adventure, the beginning of the exotic and where Australians have peculiar responsibilities. Australians wanting to go 'overseas', searching for something more exciting than work in an insurance office or the daily milking of the cows and with an often unexpressed hope that they might make a name in national, church or commercial history, could get their fares to, and a job in, Papua New Guinea. It is also where Australians fought the battles of World War II closest to Australia, the theatre where most Australians went to war, and where over 8,000 Australians are named on the headstones and panels at the British Commonwealth war cemeteries at Rabaul, Lae and Port Moresby. The number of books about Australians in Papua New Guinea is also a result of the increasing enthusiasm of Australians since the late 1970s to recall and define themselves by their experiences in war.[1] While many of the books are privately published, nearly all have an ISBN number: they are produced with a consciousness that they will find readers beyond the family. The production and editorial standards of some of the privately published books—such as Betty Scarlett's *Oscar X-Ray Calling* and Paul and Eleanor Knie's *The Life Story of Ida Voss*—are as high as those of many commercial publishers.

An increase in the number of lives told is obviously an advantage to historians. On a few topics there are now several books. The growing importance of Kokoda in Australia, accelerated by the visits of Prime Minister Paul Keating when he kissed the ground in 1992, and John Howard and Sir Michael Somare in 2002 when they opened the Isurava monument, has been demonstrated in the three detailed popular histories by Peter Brune, Peter Fitzsimons and Paul Ham.[2] The autobiographies and biographies now cover most of the key players: David Horner on Vasey, Blamey and Shedden; David Day on Curtin; Gallaway on Blamey and MacArthur, Edgar on Potts; Braga on Allen; Ken Eather on his distant relative, Major General Ken Eather; and Brune on Honner. Taken with the earlier books on and by Sydney Rowell and the Americans Douglas MacArthur, Robert Eichelberger and George Kenney, and Steven Bullard's introduction to, and extension of, Japanese sources, there are few topics in Pacific history better covered than Kokoda 1942.[3] Neil McDonald's thoughtful biography of Damien Parer, the cinematographer, adds much to our understanding of how the Kokoda campaign was reported in print as well as on the screen. We now have access to much history and the making of history. And much has been written on another war photographer, Frank Hurley, who was in Papua between the wars.

The personal reminiscences tend to add detail and confirm established perceptions. Hamlyn-Harris, who first wrote his account while in hospital in 1943, described his first encounter with the Australian wounded near Myola and it 'moved [him] to the depths':

> Picking their way very carefully with expressions of solemn responsibility, came native carriers with the badly wounded. Some of these forms under their coverings were horribly mutilated and might not survive long … The natives moved softly and silently, handling the stretchers with a surprising deftness in rough places in order to save their human burden from the slightest jolt. Their homely faces were soft with pity and concern. They would carry these poor wounded along such a route as I have described, through mud and slush and morass, along the razor backs …[4]

The images and the vocabulary are familiar, and while some soldiers may have drawn on Bert Beros's popular poem, 'The Fuzzy Wuzzy Angels', others who wrote before it was published obviously did not.[5] Then and now, the carriers had the admiration of the diggers.

A few books add to published material on Kokoda. The unpretentious family history of the Hogan brothers gives a picture of the men in the prewar and follows them through their training, first impressions of Port Moresby (a 'dilapidated looking place'), combat and the postwar.[6] Two of the Hogan brothers, Tom and Nace, fought in the 3rd Battalion, a militia unit raised on the Southern Highlands of New South Wales—from Crookwell to Cooma. The militia battalions, especially those raised in country areas, were made up of men, many of whom knew one another in the prewar and who then trained together at local drill halls and at various camps. With the two Hogan boys in the 3rd Battalion were four others from Grabben Gullen who were all farewelled together. Of the six, two were killed, two wounded and the other two suffered severe illness. The worst battle for the 3rd Battalion was at Templeton's Crossing, and so within a few days in October 1942 much bad news went back to Grabben Gullen and nearby Crookwell; and it went to telephonists and ministers of religion who knew the men and their families. By providing the perspective of Bill Hogan, who stayed home, the Hogans show the interaction between home and battlefield in ways missed in much military history, and in a militia battalion that interaction was concentrated in particular communities.

Alan Hooper gives a different and more intimate account of the home and battle front through the use of the letters that passed between him and his fiancée, later wife. But Hooper also provides a detailed account of what was happening to Papua New Guineans involved in war. Having arrived in Port Moresby in a Queensland militia battalion, the 49th, before the Japanese invaded, he volunteered for service in the newly formed Papuan Infantry Battalion. In the late stages of the Kokoda and Buna-Gona battles he was on the Opi and Kumusi Rivers engaged in a complex guerrilla war. Japanese attempting to escape from battle or new troops trying to re-enforce those already there were passing through the area; survivors of crashed aircraft were struggling to make their way to safety; Papuans who had been away as indentured labourers were coming home; New Guineans who had been conscripted by the Japanese were escaping into the area; and the local Orokaiva and Binandere were disturbed by the withdrawal of much of the old system of government and mission authority, the signs of battle at sea and overhead, the armed and unarmed foreigners amongst them and the many unsettling rumours. In one incident twelve returning labourers were killed and some of Hooper's troops used their rifles to take revenge.[7] Hooper was often the only Australian with his Papuan troops, and he had had to learn Police Motu to communicate with them and the villagers. Hooper writes with the same close observation and knowledge as some of the prewar government field officers who transferred to the army, but Hooper was young and had none of the prejudices that the older officers carried with them.

The publication of John Jackson's diary and letters tells us much about the man after whom Port Moresby's airport is named, and it includes a full account of his escape after being shot down off Lae in April 1942.[8] Near Busama, he found some people 'bluffed by the Japs' and reluctant to help, other local men leading the pursuing Japanese, and two Tolai, stranded in the area, who risked everything to lead him through the Japanese to the nearest Australians. They were, Jackson wrote to his wife, 'two wonderful boys'.[9] He was flown out of Wau but killed in combat four days later.

Ken Thorpe, who served with an Independent Company (later commandos) alongside the coastwatchers on Bougainville, was another soldier dependent on Papua New Guineans. He reports using women carriers, including one who carried the heavy battery for the teleradio with her infant perched on top of the terminals. The almost casual violence of the war is apparent in his account of the Papua New Guinea police who seized two Bougainvillean 'boys', and, convinced they had been working for the Japanese, forced them to walk in front of the patrol. When the two young men made a dash for freedom, the police opened fire, killing one, but the other may have escaped into dense bush.[10] Thorpe also notes an incidental hazard of jungle fighting. Short of oil to protect his sub-machine gun, he cleaned it with pig grease, but when he fired it a stream of cockroaches and a cloud of smoke came out with the first bullet.[11] Later in the war when Thorpe was training with the 1st New Guinea Infantry Battalion, he disciplined a soldier and was later attacked by about five New Guinea soldiers when he went for a shower.[12] As on other occasions, the men in the Pacific Islands Regiment demonstrated that they had limits to the extent to which they could be pushed around. Walpole, 2/3rd Independent Company, was in the Wau-Salamuau area, but most of his book is concerned with the later campaign on Borneo. Mick Dennis, another commando, provides a report on the fighting around Wau and the 1945 Muschu Island raid, but has few reflections on the peoples and places of battle.

By contrast with those who fought in or alongside Papua New Guinean units, most of the Australians who went to Papua New Guinea during the war had brief contact with Papua New Guineans. On the Kiriwina air base Norman Medew says that children were nearly always the interpreters. A man, rarely a woman, wanting to trade might arrive with a large bunch of bananas, and it would be a young boy who would ask, 'You got bullamacow?'[13] And a swap of tinned meat for fresh bananas would be organised. Bill Marks in his uninhibited way says that he was with a group of men recently back from the Middle East. Travelling on an open truck from the Port Moresby wharf towards Rouna, they passed a group of bare-breasted women and the sudden rush to one side nearly tipped the truck over.[14] The photographs that appear in the books—particularly of those who were on the Trobriands—are evidence of the young men's at least initial interest in the grass-skirted women.[15] The more restrained John Kingsmill says they rarely saw any Papuan or New Guinean women:

> Never alone, always with her husband, the 'Mary' would be sighted, as a curiosity worth noting, walking along the side of the road as our trucks roared past, flinging up clouds of dust (or mud in the Wet). The man went several paces ahead, carrying his spear and perhaps a small child, or with the child running at his heels with the family dog. The woman walked behind her man, small and meek and heavy-laden. She looked more like his child than his wife. Suspended from a strap across her forehead was a large woven bag which she balanced on her shoulders.
>
> I never got close enough to do more than wave and they would invariably wave back and smile huge betel-nut-red smiles at us, though they probably had only the vaguest idea of what we were all doing there ... I never once saw an unfriendly face amongst them, rather it was a matter

of childlike friendliness or giggling shyness or a long frowning stare of incomprehension.[16]

Kingsmill's comments were, like most of the casual references to Papua New Guineans, well-intentioned, but indicate a superficial understanding and more than a hint of condescension.

Many of the reminiscences retain much of the language of the time, 'boong' often being used. Tom Hogan says simply says that the New Guineans were 'referred to as "Boongs"'.[17] With 'boong' are the compound terms 'boong basher' for an Angau officer and 'boong train' for a line of carriers. Lloyd Collins explained the distinction between 'coon' which he said meant a black American and 'boong' which was a Papua New Guinean. Both terms, he said, 'came to be used with much respect and endearment and were not interpreted as derogatory'.[18] Later, in the fighting out from Wau, Collins was with a group who had to carry supplies forward and they were proud to be called the 'white boongs'. It was a term of praise, Collins says, because 'every soldier in New Guinea knew [that] the word "boong" stood for service, loyalty, sacrifice and discipline'.[19] The diggers had certainly changed the old terms, for in the prewar the word 'boong' was almost unknown, and coon was commonly used for the local people in New Guinea, even appearing in the *Rabaul Times*. One of the first of the Australian troops posted to Rabaul, Jack Stebbings of the 2/22nd Battalion, wrote in a matter-of-fact way to a mate: 'the natives here are known as "Coons"', but it was not a term used in Papua.[20]

The ex-servicemen make frank comments on the Japanese. As John Holmes said, they respected the bravery of the Japanese but 'never ceased to loathe them'.[21] Several comment on the general attitude to the taking of prisoners, even if they did not record it with the brutal directness of Frank Perversi, 'We don't take fucking Jap prisoners'. Perversi says that while he heard this often, he was nearby on just the one occasion when some Australians killed a prisoner.[22] At Milne Bay the young militia soldier, James Henderson, said that after the men had seen evidence of torture of their own battalion dead, they understood that they had been ordered to take no prisoners and 'felt that what they had seen demanded it. The fury they felt would burn for decades among survivors'.[23] Near Mubo in the Morobe District, Collins recorded a digger saying 'We thought our job was to kill the bastards, not capture them'.[24] Stanton went from curiosity about prisoners, to a determination to shoot them, to sympathy for the surrendered Japanese at the end of the war. The men who had fought in the Mediterranean looked back with a 'hint of nostalgia' to campaigns that 'had a sweep and scope possible only in the open north African desert'. In New Guinea, Peter Jones said, the 'claustrophobic jungle imposed a stealth and furtiveness' and the men did not think of the Japanese as an 'honourable enemy'. The jungle war, he wrote, 'lacked mutual respect'.[25] John Bellair, who had fought in Greece and Crete, said that after 40 years 'It had not been easy to write of my brief experience in New Guinea. I thought that time had healed my memories, but I found that it was not quite so'.[26]

Perhaps the greatest value of the recent war reminiscences is the variety. Many have been written by men who were in non-combat units. Michael Pate was in a concert party and Keith Smith, radio man and comedy script writer in the postwar, was with the 15th Field Ambulance during it. Among the airmen who have recorded their experiences, Norman Medew and Arthur Gately were armourers on fighters, John Carroll and Rus Center were wireless operators and navigators on Beaufighters, Geldard was a wireless operator with 4 Army Cooperation Squadron, Derrick Rees and Laurie Edmonds were aircraft fitters, John Kingsmill and Jack Woodward were radio ground staff, John Balfe was flying transports, and William Deane-Butcher was the doctor with 75 Squadron. As a 28–year-old doctor from Sydney, Deane-Butcher went north in April 1942 equipped with a 'weighty text book about tropical medicine' and a Royal Air Force handbook which included such useful information as 'survival in the Arctic, speaking Arabic and international flags'.[27] Deane-Butcher was with 75 Squadron through the grim days from March 1942 when the 75 Squadron Kittyhawks supplied Port Moresby's main air defence against the dominant Japanese and in August 1942 the squadron operated from Gurney airstrip in the battle of Milne Bay. On his first day at the Seven Mile strip in Port Moresby, Deane-Butcher woke to terrifying din: a cook was belting a sheet of galvanised iron slung from a tree and shouting, 'Come and get it, bugger yers'.[28] With his care for the morale and physical condition of the men, Deane-Butcher's work is to be placed alongside that better known memoir of H.D. (Blue) Steward, *Recollections of a Regimental Medical Officer*. Weate's biography of the pilot Bill Newton is one of only three of at least nine Australians who won the Victoria Cross in Papua or New Guinea. Wayne Rothgeb's *New Guinea Skies* is included in the bibliography as an example of one of the memoirs of the American college boys who flew in New Guinea; but few of these are likely to surpass the earlier Edwards Park's *Nanette*. Rothgeb flew Lightings (P-38s) and Park Airacobras (P-39s) out of various New Guinea strips.

The army reminiscences include those of Bill Marks, who was a corporal cook and then in a laundry unit and of Roy Sibson, an army craftsman with skills handy when making souvenirs to sell to Americans. Jim Rudge arrived in Port Moresby in 1943, served in Angau as a Medical Assistant, and returned briefly to Australia before going back to Papua New Guinea to work in the Department of Public Health. Rudge is the only wartime medical assistant to have published an extensive account of his work. Deploying much detail, Rudge sketches people of all races, gives much ethnographic information and provides insight into the life of a medical assistant. He held posts in Kikori, Popondetta, Daru, Rigo,

Kairuku, Abau, and Bougainville. It has to be conceded that the section under the heading 'Social Life at Kikori' is short. Tarlington is one of the few who have written about the long-term impact of six years of war on the rest of his life. Polly Underwood, Australian Army Nursing Service, arrived in Port Moresby in January 1942 wearing her 'outdoor winter uniform consisting of pure wool, fully lined winter costume, jacket worn over a long-sleeve white cotton shirt with brown woollen tie, cotton stockings, brown lace-up shoes with our grey felt hats pulled well down over our eyes and our brown kid gloves clutching our neat, very small, zippered purses'.[29]

Having reached Port Moresby before the impact of battle, she saw something of the prewar Territory. On a visit to Koitaki plantation at Sogeri the nurses had their 'clothes laid out, baths drawn and ... beds made' and at meals they were attended by immaculately turned-out servants. When Moresby appeared to be under threat of invasion, the nurses were evacuated. Later in the war when Underwood was stationed at Finschhafen, the nurses were enclosed in barbed wire, guarded and not allowed out alone. The threat was said to be black Americans—and that says something about perceptions of race and gender in wartime New Guinea.[30]

Alice Bowman, another New Guinea nurse to have written an autobiography, went to New Guinea in 1939 to work in the European hospital. Choosing to stay in Rabaul after the Japanese southward assault, she was captured and interned in Japan. Her work is an account of captivity and can be placed alongside Margaret Clarence's short book on her mother, Kathleen Bignold, another civilian woman captured in Rabaul and forced to endure captivity in Japan. Peter Fenton's biography of the lively Olive Weston includes only a brief mention of her time in New Guinea.

Although we now have Alan Powell's careful unit history of Angau, the eight reminiscences of the Angau officers (Geoff Blaskett, John Cooke, Ted Fulton, Kingsley Jackson, Clarrie James, Jim Ross, Jim Rudge and Eddie Stanton) extend knowledge of the military administration of New Guinea.[31] Jackson, James, Rudge, and Stanton bring the perspective of the outsiders, the Angau officers without experience in the prewar territories. James served in a number of centres from the Highlands to Misima—including being present at the hanging of eight Islanders at Bwagaoia. James handed over Goilala station in 1946 and took up a position in Canberra that had nothing to do with Papua and New Guinea. His experience was exclusively that of the wartime *kiap*. Stanton spent most of his war in the Milne Bay Islands and in his detailed diary he displayed the racial prejudices of his time and he was equally frank about his fellow officers. By contrast Fulton first went to New Guinea in 1930, returned to run a plantation in the postwar and continued to visit Papua New Guinea after Independence. In Angau, Fulton walked the Bulldog track to Wau and just kept on going through to Bena Bena. In his revealing comments on the police, he shows an understanding of the complexities of loyalty; and his relationships with Father Schwab and other priests raise different questions about race, culture and loyalty. Both James and Rudge note that the police were carrying and demonstrating sub-machine guns on patrols among Papua New Guineans.[32] Brian McFarlane was called up to do his national service in the 1950s and stayed in the army. His is one of the few reminiscences of serving in the postwar Pacific Islands Regiment. McFarlane joined the 'black hand gang' in 1963, and was posted to Vanimo, Port Moresby and Wewak before leaving in 1965 and going on to Vietnam.

Of the four accounts of the escape from the disaster of Rabaul in 1942, Gordon Abel gives an unpretentious and moving account of the gradual reduction of his group to just two. One man, he said, committed suicide when he realised he could no longer keep up; and Abel admits the guilt of survivors who struggled on, unable to bury their dead or even record where they had died.[33] The most important, because of the key role that he played, is by Frank Holland, a timber worker, who crossed New Britain to carry news of one escaping group to the other. Included in the bibliography are books by Americans who survived as prisoners of war in Rabaul: Kepchia, McMurria and Nason were three of six American survivors from a group of 83 Allied prisoners. The only other survivor was the Australian *kiap* and coastwatcher, John Murphy. Fred Hargesheimer, another American and extraordinary survivor, is also included because he returned to New Guinea and repaid the villagers who saved his life after he crash-landed on New Britain in 1943.

Margaret Reeson in her study of those who waited and grieved during the war has shown how the thirst for knowledge among close relatives is intense and sustained.[34] And clearly the desire to know has driven the research for some sons and daughters of those caught in extraordinary circumstances and especially of those who did not survive and have no known grave. Anne McCosker has written well, not just of her mother and father and their lives on New Guinea island plantations, but of that generation and the way of life that was overwhelmed by three years of war. Margaret Henderson and Gillian Nikakis have written moving accounts of fathers they did not know and who disappeared as prisoners of the Japanese: the reader shares their obligation to chase rumours and fragments of information to understand the reaction of their mothers and to create a father with greater substance than the one existing in family lore.

Where in the past much biographical writing of peace-time Papua and New Guinea has been dominated by missionaries, government field officers and travel and adventure writers (such as James Chalmers, C.A.W. Monckton and Ion Idriess) in recent writings, apart from Kingsley Jackson, the *kiaps* and adventurers have largely abandoned publishing.[35] But there has been little change in the production rate of the male mission memoir and the book tribute to the distinguished missionary. Henry Kendall wrote his own unpretentious record of his time at the Anglican mission in Popondetta, Samarai and Dogura. Milton McFarlane was a state school teacher in Queensland who from 1961 committed himself to 17 years' teaching for the Seventh Day Adventist mission on Mussau, Bougainville and in the British Solomons. Lynette Oates has written of David Lithgow who went to the Milne Bay islands in 1964 and through the next three decades did much bible translation work. Glen O'Brien wrote a biography of Kingsley Ridgway; and Ridgway's own memories of leading the Methodist mission in the Southern Highlands in the 1960s is included within the one volume. Ian Frazer's biography of Ed Tscharke (soldier in the New Guinea Volunteer Rifles, medical assistant in Angau and Lutheran medical missionary on Karkar for nearly 40 years) is different in that Frazer is not a Lutheran and he writes with an easy journalist's style. Diane Langmore and David Wetherell provide the only outsider and scholarly studies of missionaries.

Like the war reminiscences, much of the recent writing by civilian men has broadened the range. The title of John Cooke's autobiography *Working in Papua New Guinea 1931-46* indicates what is to come—a frank narrative of someone who was, among other things, a barman, timber cutter, schooner operator, recruiter and cargo handler for Guinea Airways. Arthur John worked on the Bulolo goldfields—with a digression for sexual adventure in Japan in 1933. John says that the round trip to the near north via the China ports, Japan and the Philippines was common among the goldfields workers who had two months' leave after two years' service. Keith Buxton was a postwar medical assistant and then tour operator; Tom Cole was a crocodile shooter and coffee planter with an interest in a saw mill and a hotel; Bobby Gibbes, DSO, DFC and Bar, fought his war elsewhere, but in the postwar he operated an airline in New Guinea and owned a plantation and hotels; and Les Bell ran the Kavieng engineering works ('We repair everything from sewing machines to aeroplanes') and a plantation before serving in a radar unit in World War II. Born in England, Dennis Puffett served in the war in Europe, came to Australia and worked in the Northern Territory before being superintendent of wildlife management in Port Moresby from 1971 to 1973. Geoff Litchfield gained his initial flying experience in the services, but he was a 'fly boy' in the postwar navy and came to Papua New Guinea in 1966 as a pilot for civilian airlines. His last stint was with Air Niugini in the 1980s.

Bruce Neale gives a cheerful impression of life in bachelor quarters in early postwar Port Moresby and of later surveying roads and hydro-electricity stations for public works. Jim Allen, geologist, and Max Reynolds, vulcanologist, have written short memoirs of their work, Allen with private companies and Reynolds with the government. Phil Thomson, actor and dramatist, has provided an impressionistic account of theatrical ventures and leading a theatre company and cultural centre in Madang.

Bob Connolly's *Making 'Black Harvest'* is obviously essential reading for understanding his and Robin Anderson's prize-winning film trilogy (*First Contact, Joe Leahy's Neighbours* and *Black Harvest*) but it is more than that. Anderson kept a diary, both wrote letters written from the field. Tim Bowden taped six hours of interview with them, they took notes while filming and they had kept the film and recorded dialogue not used in the edited films. This material gives a density of evidence about what many commentators called a tragedy. As a result, Connolly has written one of the most revealing accounts of the turbulent Highlanders taking their warfare into the world of cash cropping.

One of the few of the recent books that continues an older tradition of frontier patrolling is Jim Sinclair's sympathetic and well researched life of Ivan Champion which concentrates on his exploratory patrols. Margaret Abbotts' biography of her father, Stanniforth Smith, is a family history and while it gives family context it is brief on critical incidents in Papua such as the expedition up the Kikori in 1910. The work and beliefs of Raphael Cilento, director of public health in Mandated New Guinea, has been re-assessed, but more because of his place in the history of racial attitudes and medicine in Australia, rather than for what he did in New Guinea.[36]

Before 1975, most scholars who recorded their time in Papua New Guinea wrote more in the tradition of the travel and adventure writers. Evelyn Cheesman (who was in Papua 1933-4) and Jock Marshall (New Guinea 1936) both conform to that pattern.[37] Hortense Powdermaker (New Ireland 1929-30) with her shrewd comments on the black and white societies and her discipline was an exception.[38] Of the recent books, Tim Flannery's *Throwim Way Leg* looks back—as its sub-title, *An Adventure*, makes clear—to the old tradition, but many of the others break completely with any chasing of the first, wildest and most remote.[39] Spate and Fisk write about Papua New Guinea while considering tough questions about economic development in the third world. Spate, after his second visit in 1952, decided that

> the way forward would not be by plantations, and dreams of small-scale white settlement were just that, fancy dreams. They failed to account for just about everything: the high costs of initial clearing, the almost complete lack of transport (except by air) and other infrastructure, the distance from markets.[40]

This is a long way from the last 'unknown', lost 'paradise', stone-age warriors and first contact. The intellectual problems are important, conclusions drawn from research in the rest of the third world are presented, while the exotic locations and the physical adventure have almost disappeared. In the collection edited by Brij Lal in honour of Bob Kiste, several contributors provide revealing accounts of their background and their engagement with Papua New Guinea, and while the country they encounter is different from that pictured by

Monckton or Hides, it is still exotic.[41] Ulli Beier's memoir is urban and the culture that he is concerned with is that of the Papuan New Guineans who work within the literary and visual arts appreciated in Sydney, Berlin and London. He brings comparisons with other colonies to Australians and to Papua New Guineans.

The writings of and about anthropologists have done most to expand and change scholarly biographies of foreigners in Papua New Guinea. In *Return to the High Valley*, Kenneth Read added to the base of fine writing and revelation about himself, his discipline and the people of the Asaro that he began in *The High Valley* published in 1966.[42] The extent to which he found that the Asaro had changed and the corrections that he needed to make to his original findings on basic issues such as land ownership and the hierarchies of families, enforces the need for long-term studies. The American, Michael French Smith, has written a personal account of his visits to Kragur on Kairiru Island in the East Sepik Province, the first and longest beginning in November 1975, and the later and briefer visits in 1981, 1995 and 1998. Significantly, all of Smith's visits have been to a post-independence Kragur. On his last visit he noticed that people were referring to the 'chief', both the term and position were new: in the past he had known several village bigmen who, while not equal, none was the recognised village leader. He listed other changes:

> While a mainstay of village life, Catholicism still managed to stir things up. Charismatic worship in particular gave women, the young, and the mildly rebellious opportunities to carve out new zones of freedom from established authority and hierarchy. School learning was becoming significantly more common, and its tensions with older forms of knowledge and power were becoming more pronounced. Assertive women were scandalising conservative men; youths filled with spirits of various kinds butted heads with elders; the educated young were annoying almost everyone, including each other; traditional leaders were struggling to define and assert their authority; and the gap between villagers and urban Kragurs was more apparent than ever. Some villagers found themselves divided by support of rival parliamentary candidates. The possibility of mining put an edge on concerns about land rights ...[43]

The villages remain dynamic, changing substantially within a generation, and those changes have nothing to do with Australian government—or any governments'—officers demanding or guiding change.

Margaret Mead generates comment (for example, Howard and McDowell) but no one has attempted a sustained re-evaluation of her New Guinea monographs as Derek Freeman did of *Coming of Age in Samoa*.[44] Wetherell and Carr-Gregg have written a sympathetic study of Camilla Wedgwood, and while she is an interesting character and did fieldwork on Manam Island in 1933 and engaged in important debates on education during and immediately after World War II, she was not at the forefront of a discipline or a driver of government policy. With Michael Young's work on F.E. Williams and his essays and first volume on Malinowski, scholarly biography has made a significant advance. His *Malinowski: odyssey of an anthropologist* contributes to the general history of Papua, as well as giving insights into one of the most important and complex minds to engage with the Pacific and influence the formative years of a discipline. We are indebted to the breadth of Young's research, the structure that allows easy shifts between narrative and analysis, and the lucid prose.

Since Paul Hasluck's *A Time for Building* was published in 1976, there has been no comparable exposition and defence of Australian administration; but then no other Australian minister of any department has been as willing to do the research or as able to write about policy and its implementation as Hasluck.[45] It is appropriate that Hasluck has stimulated two volumes reappraising his work (Porter and Stannage). Both Les Johnson and Rachel Cleland have given their different perceptions from government house, Port Moresby; Nott has written a biography of Charles Barnes; Peter Fox's memoir of accounting in Port Moresby and Goroka includes broader economic and political issues; Tom Leahy has recalled his time in politics before 1972; Downs has dealt briefly with his early years in the House of Assembly; Ray Whitrod has given a chapter to his time as Commissioner of Police 1969-70; but in the 30 years since independence, few of the other Australians who were actors and observers of the critical years of transition—say from 1968 to 1978—have written of their experiences in Canberra, Port Moresby or a district. If Rowley Richards aged 88 can publish his memoirs of being a prisoner of war of the Japanese, and at 89 speak eloquently about writing and memory, then there is still plenty of time.[46]

Papua and New Guinea have raised questions of definition of 'Australia' and 'Australian' for the *Australian Dictionary of Biography*. An eminent Australian citizen who worked in the Mandated Territory of New Guinea qualifies for an entry because he or she was an Australian, but German, New Zealand or American missionaries qualify only if they were thought to have worked within 'Australia' or had an impact on Australian policies. The indigenous people of the Mandated Territory and subsequently the United Nations Trust Territory were Australian protected persons, but not citizens of Australia. British New Guinea was a British possession, and the Australian colonies contributed to its revenue, but it was not Australian. Although from 1906 Papua was an Australian Territory, its indigenous inhabitants were less than citizens of Australia: they could not live on the Australian mainland, and did not qualify for Australian welfare payments. In practice, the *Dictionary* has included some foreign and indigenous inhabitants of Papua and New Guinea, but the criteria for inclusion may have been higher than for those who spent all their lives clearly within Australia. First published in 1966, the 16th volume of the *Dictionary* was published in 2002, completing the four volumes of those who died in the years 1940-1980. Those significant in Papua and New Guinea (other than those who were there because of war) in Volume 16 include: Joan Refshauge (medical practitioner and administrator), Alfred Robinson (government officer, soldier and planter), Matthias Toliman (school teacher and politician), Peter To Rot (Catholic catechist and martyr), Camilla Wedgwood (anthropologist and educationist), Eric Wright (medical practitioner), Leigh Vial (coastwatcher and patrol officer), and Yali (political and religious leader). There is also an entry on Peter Santo (indentured labourer of Espiritu Santo). The *Australian Dictionary of Biography*, a basic tool of historians of Australia, is often neglected by historians of the Pacific Islands.

When Chilla Bulbeck, Jan Roberts and Stephanie Lloyd and others put together their reminiscences of Australian women and children in Papua New Guinea, they could reasonably claim that the histories then published were histories of events in which men dominated—often apparently events in which only men were involved. Bulbeck went on to say that 'women's stories are contained in a handful of white women's memoirs and the ephemera of mission booklets'.[47] That seemed reasonable at the time; but women have been quick to exploit the ease of home publishing and recently more have had their experiences published commercially. Women live longer and as widows they may have the chance and feel an obligation to record their husbands', as well as their own, lives. Several, including Beavis, Boys, Cleland, Deasey, Kidu, Hollinshed, Maclean, Rule, Rybarz, Scarlett and Sherwood, wrote or were recorded as widows or as wives who did not share their husbands' Papua New Guinea experience.[48] Although nearly all write generously of their husbands, their accounts benefit from the absence of any personal or official constraints that the husbands might have imposed. Winsome and Ormond Speck solve the problem of wife and husband perspectives by each writing sections on their times in the eastern highlands and among the Kukukuku.

The short mission memoirs continue: Beavis, Biggs, Edwards, Freund, Gray, Scarlett, and White. They may now be more common, but the Sunday School prize market has almost disappeared and so have the old home mission societies that needed comforting reports from the field to encourage them to keep contributing funds to convert, heal and clothe the pagans. The changing audience and attitudes means fewer claims to piety, dedication and frontier adventure by the missionaries and fewer references to savages emerging from the darkness of brutality, superstition and ignorance. Betty Scarlett was the wife of a New Zealand Presbyterian minister who worked for the old London Missionary Society on the Papuan coast. The Mission had already changed its name to Papua Ekalesia and was on its way to becoming part of a Papua New Guinea United Church.

Her memoir is almost secular: she is a wife and mother in a foreign country, and the many tasks that fall to her as a minister's wife are practical.

The brief lives are more than anodyne reports: all are valuable to historians. Blanche Biggs was a doctor and coordinator of the medical services of the Anglican Mission. Her book, a collection of letters to her friends, includes reports of patrols and her work in the aftermath of the eruption of Mt Lamington in 1951. Maureen Carlon has written well of being a teacher with the Catholic mission at Kiripia in the Kaugel Valley from 1969 to 1980. (She realised she had enrolled one boy underage when a mother arrived flapping her breast to indicate it was time he was fed.) Sister Catherine O'Sullivan writes of the internment of the Rabaul Sacred Heart nurses during World War II, Dorothea Freund has an account of the evacuation of women and children in December 1942.

In many of the brief memoirs there are often points of particular interest. For example, Nancy White, a teacher with the Anglican mission from 1948 to 1967, said that at a mission conference in 1950 at Dogura the bishop announced there would be an increase in pay for white staff from 50 to 64 pounds a year. It was, she claims, the first increase the mission had ever given, and the rate of pay applied to all staff irrespective of their qualifications or position.[49] That decision said much about the poverty of the Anglican mission and the demands that it made on its staff. In October 1958, the first students from White's school at Manau at the mouth of the Mambare River sat for the examination to enter a secondary school, the Martyrs Memorial School. After the examination she sealed their papers in an envelope and two boys set out to carry it to the Martyrs School. It was three days tough walking, but, she thought, it would be good for the boys who would see their first cars and trucks, even their first road. John Waiko and his brother Bob were two of the first boys to go from Manau to the Martyrs School. John was later a professor of history at the University of Papua New Guinea and Minister for Education and Bob Dademo was a senior officer in the Papua New Guinea Defence Force.[50]

Secular women have taken up the short memoir. Anna Phillips is an able writer and has shrewd comments on memory as well as demonstrating an ability to rework them. Phillips is a daughter of Frank Tuza, a doctor who went from Hungary in the turmoil of the postwar and the Russian occupation to Australia, and after a brief course at the Australian School of Pacific Administration in 1950, to Buin in south Bougainville. By alternating her accounts with her father's, Phillips provides a rare forum for one of the refugee doctors who supplied much of the expertise in the Public Health department, and she is able to comment on the family's different memories. Phillips makes subtle comments on the position of New Guinean servants in the 1950s: 'a strange colonial amalgamation of affection, interdependence and paternalism attended by innuendo of racial superiority'. Pat Boys and Edna Maclean writing of the 1930s describe a society with clear distinctions. When she was working in Rabaul, Maclean would spend weekends at Ranau:

> There were dozens of little native girls everywhere. They pulled the punkahs in the dining room and while we were having dinner, there would be one underneath the table. We would get a smack on the leg if ever a mosquito or whatever happened to land ... On the tennis courts they would be running around getting the balls for us and throwing them back.[51]

After Margaret Wood's sister, Carol Coleman, arrived in Rabaul in the mid-1930s she worked for an accountant. He found a 'boi' for Carol, and told Carol that 'under no circumstances' was she to carry anything, not even a packet of cigarettes—that was the job of the servant who would walk a few paces behind her.[52] For many of the Australians then in Rabaul the aim was to keep the distinction between the races sharp rather than subtle.

Many of the short memoirs deserve to be more than ephemera, but more significant have been longer studies by Baranay, Deasey, Downing, Green, Golski, Kidu, Harkness, Hollinshed, Lewis, Rule, Rybarz, Sherwood and Voss. They have few male equivalents. Ida Voss, Marjorie Deasey, Doris Downing, Bessie Lewis and Joan Rule gave most of their working lives to missions. Ida Voss was born in Iowa into a family of Lutheran missionaries and travelled with her sister, Lulu, to New Guinea in 1921. A trained nurse, Ida married fellow missionary Victor Koschade in 1924. The Koschades left New Guinea in 1936, and lived in South Australia until they went north to spend five years in central Australian missions. She died in 1972.[53] Her story has been put together by her grandson, Paul Knie, and his wive Eleanor, mainly from Ida's unpublished autobiography and letters. Marjorie and Dudley Deasey went to Balimo to work among the Gogodala for the Unevangelised Fields Mission. They left in 1942, returned to Papua in 1944, retired from Balimo in 1974 and spent another ten years working for the mission—then the Evangelical Church of Papua—in Hohola. (Keith Briggs' memoir covers the extension of the Gogodala mission into Mount Bosavi. The Briggs family left in 1990.) Both Deasey and Voss reveal the church and social contexts that directed them to Papua and New Guinea, and neither the Australian Baptist nor the American Lutheran background is readily available to most historians of Papua New Guinea.

Both books have much interesting detail. Marjorie Deasey almost provides a history of the Gogodala. On her arrival, they were a people lightly touched by the outside world, still living in longhouses and nobody baptised. When she left 35 years later the Gogodala were within months of being citizens in an independent nation. Her perspective as a woman is evident in the broad issues and the trivial. (A man might not note when the Gogodala women first began clothing their babies in nappies—it was 1953-1954.)[54] In writing of her sister,

Doris Downing, Joyce is able to fill in the background that gave rise to the dedicated teacher, but unfortunately many of her letters from 1929-1941 written while at the Anglican station of Boianai have been lost. There is much more detail on her earlier life in the Carpentaria mission and on her return to Papua from 1944 to 1946.

Joan Rule, who spent 40 years in the Southern Highlands, is strongest on the problems of learning a language and producing written material in the new language. She and her husband did not leave Kutubu and Mendi until 1991, but she has only brief comments on the impact of gas and oil production. In her reminiscence of nursing at Anguganak in the West Sepik from 1965 to 1981, Bessie Lewis gives a thoughtful account of the medical work of the Christian Missions in Many Lands. Judith Green's *These were my children* recalls the four years that she and Barney Green spent at Bundi in the early 1960s. That was the year that August Kituai started Standard 1 as a nine-year old boarder under the care of 'Masta and Misis Green'. They did, he said, 'wonderful work'.[55]

Carol Kidu's book is a frank account of a romance; her marriage in 1969 to the Papuan lawyer and later judge, Buri Kidu; married life in Papua New Guinea from 1969; and, after Buri's death in 1994, her election to parliament in 1997.[56] She allows the reader a level of intimacy that brings understanding to race relations, cross-cultural marriage and politics. None of the Australian men who have married Papua New Guinean women have written a book of their experiences; and Tom Leahy is one of the few to have given an account of contesting elections and life in the House of Assembly, but his experience was before independence and only a handful of copies of his book were printed.[57]

In her 10 years in Papua New Guinea from 1951, Beverley Rybarz had a rollicking, emotional time. Having arrived in Lae as the bride of a pilot, she soon separated, and in 1957 married Stanislau Rybarz. Rybarz was contracting for major road and bridge projects—such as the Kumusi Bridge—and Beverley was sometimes with him and sometimes working elsewhere. She admits to being caught with a bare bum more often than anyone in other confessional memoirs. Her life is in sharp contrast to that of the moral rectitude maintained by most of her mission sisters. Barbara Sherwood arrived in Manus in 1946 when it was still strewn with the debris of war, and American troops were still present. A lecturer in biology at the University of New England before her marriage to Bill, a doctor and linguist, she was also a talented artist. Her memories of Manus, Samarai, Mapamoiwa, Rabaul and Port Moresby are gentle, perceptive and illustrated with her own line drawings and wash paintings.

The books by Harkness, Hollinshed, Carlon, Golski and Baranay make a Highlands sequence. Chris Harkness was in Mount Hagen working for the administration from 1965 to 1968 and her book is a detailed evocation of the lives of the expatriates at the height of their influence and when Tom Ellis, as

District Commissioner, was 'the greatest of men'.[58] This would be a better book at half the length, but it must be conceded that some of its value lies in its detail. Hollinshed arrived in the Western Highlands nearly a decade earlier in 1956 and she records the struggle to establish the coffee plantations, the flourishing of the plantations, and the deterioration resulting from crime and resurgent tribal fighting. She suffered personal assault and as a reporter for the *Post-Courier* wrote of the warfare through the Nebilyer Valley in the 1970s: thousands of coffee trees and many houses were destroyed, at least 15 people killed and some 'of the injured died, others were too afraid to go to hospital and some lived maimed for the rest of their lives'.[59]

Judith Hollinshed and her husband left Papua New Guinea at the end of the 1980s and she returned to bury his ashes at Verona plantation in 2000 to see 'bleak evidence of lawlessness'.[60] Maureen Carlon arrived at Kiripia mission station in 1969 and taught there until 1980. With Mount Giluwe in the distance, Carlon was living in an area more isolated from the obvious changes and violence; and she has chosen to say little of any disturbing reverberations that came into the valley. Inez Baranay and Kathy Golski were in the Highlands well after independence, Golski at Rulna out of Mount Hagen in 1981 and Baranay at Wabag in 1992. Neither had a position of authority over Papua New Guineans—and did not expect one. In fact, one of Baranay's problems was the assertiveness of her Papuan New Guinean boss. Both women have a sense of being guests in another country, and of having to tolerate inconvenience and negotiate for much that they would have liked to have taken for granted. Both are articulate, have absorbed much about gender, colonialism and third world aid, and both accept that no culture has a monopoly on virtue or evil. In memories and judgments they are further from the women of the Territory than the passing of 20 or 30 years would suggest. The changing perceptions of place and roles are apparent, but less extreme, in the deft impressions recorded by Jean Bourke and others in *Our Time But Not Our Place*.

Before 1975, the government field officers, the mission patriarchs and the independent adventurers were writing their books within a context of easily measured progress. For the government officers there were increasing numbers of peoples being contacted and brought under control. New sub-districts and patrol posts were being opened, peace imposed, and obviously repugnant practices such as cannibalism, payback killings and infanticide suppressed. With a few injections and a wider range of foods the people were healthier. People were concentrated into better built and cleaner villages, and tracks between villages were cut and maintained. The police, village officials and *dokta bois*—under the direction of government officers who eliminated the few backsliders—were efficient and loyal. The planters cleared the jungle, tended the orderly tree crops and provided the revenue that paid for government. Their labourers returned home taller, stronger, knowing the ways of the cash economy and equipped with a lingua franca.

The missionaries saw themselves coming among peoples living in fear, ignorance and dirt. They gave them literacy in their own languages, freed them from superstition and malign sorcery, provided them with modern health services, and brought them the intellectual, spiritual and institutional benefits of a world religion and a promise of a life beyond death. All had ready self-images and metaphors: they were explorers, pioneers on an untamed frontier, manning outposts of empire, civilisers, and peace-makers. They replaced stone with steel; they were the bringers of light into the earth's last dark corners; and in the end they were the makers of a democratic and Christian nation. Even if the biographers avoided triumphalism, and conceded that they went to the Territory to do good for themselves, they had still worked within a greater scheme of progress. They had, as it was sometimes said, 'done good while doing well'.

Those who have written reminiscences since 1980, and certainly since 1990, have written either as builders of institutions that have failed, decayed or been replaced, or they have gone to a foreign country with obligations to abide by local laws and customs and work within institutions where power is held by Papua New Guineans. Missionaries, particularly those from the old missions—the Catholic, Lutheran, Anglican, Methodist, and London Missionary Society—must now face the facts that they might suffer assault; and that, in areas where they were once dominant and in the towns, charismatic movements have captured the enthusiasm, and collection money, of many Papua New Guineans. But the institutional strength of the Catholic, Lutheran and Seventh Day Adventist churches has remained important, and where the state has not been able to meet the needs of its citizens, the missions may have increased in importance. The crowds greeting visiting hot-gospellers, the numbers of people claiming to be 'born-again', and the assertions of their faith by leaders indicate that Papua New Guinea's belief systems have been strongly influenced by over 130 years of missionary endeavour.

The government officers who brought peace now read of resurgent tribal fighting, a 10-year low-level war on Bougainville and that razor wire is standard on houses in the towns. Those who took 'government' to villages know that now no government services reach many of those villages. *Kiap* government was for many an interlude, not a transformation. The miners have seen the destruction of one of the world's great mines on Bougainville, the transfer of ownership of Ok Tedi, the ravaging of the alluvial field at Mount Kare and the fluctuations on the oil and gas fields between riches and corruption and violence. Elizabeth Thurston, the daughter of a planter and later the wife and partner of a planter, wrote of their unlocked plantation house in the 1960s: 'None of us could have believed that in the next decade or so this presumption of innocence and enduring stability would be replaced by fear, uncertainty, a sense of anarchy and a groundswell of political pressure and change'.[61]

That shift in the context in which biographies have been written in the last twenty or so years could be expected to change them—in tone, in reflection on what might have been done better, and in assessing the legacy. In practice, the impact has varied. The government field officers have largely stopped writing. Perhaps they are inhibited because those ready images of the outpost of empire, the boys' own adventure on the frontier and bringing the benefits of civilization to ignorant tribesmen have so passed from fashion their resurrection seems impossible. Perhaps, too, some are conscious that Bill Gammage in his writing on Jim Taylor and John Black and the Hagen-Sepik patrol has introduced a level of frankness and complexity that they could not, and may not want to, reach.[62] But it may also be because they would have to write defensively—to explain why their peace was for many an interruption, not a legacy. The silence of the field officers is unfortunate: we need to know more about what they were doing when they were not on patrol. We need to hear their own tough self-evaluation of trying to set up local government councils, conduct national elections, introduce the first Papua New Guinean patrol officers and specialists into their districts, and maintain peace when their authority was shifting to others. The continuing reluctance of most of the bureaucrats in Canberra and Port Moresby to write memoirs means that social scientists and historians have no equivalent to Paul Hasluck's *Time for Building* to help them interpret government files.

Resources for administrative and political histories may be thin, but the possibilities of other sorts of histories have increased. Now there are the memoirs of film-makers, dramatists, literature and art teachers, geologists, self-taught mechanical engineers, mine workers, recruiters, accountants, school teachers, anthropologists, wildlife managers, hydro-electricity plant planners, Pacific Islands Regiment officers, planters and civilian pilots.

The missionaries have continued to write, and the range of writers has widened to include the lay workers and subordinates who will not have mission colleges and scholarships named after them. In their lives there is an emphasis on achievement, and it is undoubtedly justified. For little material reward and often putting up with physical hardship, they taught, healed and gave people the first printed texts in their own languages. A few still have the piety, fervour and faith of the prewar mission books: these are lives fulfilling a greater design. But in many in the last few pages there is now a brief summary of crime and corruption and competing beliefs. Seven years after leaving Papua New Guinea in 1971, Betty Scarlett and her daughters returned to the house in Port Moresby used by transiting missionaries. She said, 'Our welcome in this wholly expatriate establishment was cool. They seemed to have interest only in *Faith Missions*, not those like our United Church ...'[63]

Many mission biographies also now include a defence against charges of suppressing benign and creative elements in local cultures. The excesses, they claim, were often carried out by converts, not by overseas missionaries. Marjorie Deasey comes closest to admitting to a 'life of failure' after more than 30 years among the Gogodala. Having faced accusations about destroying Gogodala culture and being caught up in local politics, Marjorie and Dudley Deasey flew out of Balimo with no farewell. They recovered in Port Moresby where their house was a second home to the Gogodala, and after Dudley died Marjorie was feted on her return to Balimo. Marjorie Deasey's self-assessment of the dedicated missionary allows glimpses of opposing arguments, the possibility of failure and the personal anguish that would follow. In the end, the Deaseys could claim success, but it is not triumphant.

What is common to the great diversity of lives now recorded is that by going to Papua New Guinea they claim to have had their lives enriched. Even those who were in Papua New Guinea for just two or three years, regard Papua New Guinea as having been important in who they became and what they remember. Seen in this way, the biographers are not claiming to have done good, but almost incidentally to have had good done to them.

The most obvious change that has taken place has been the increase in the number of women writers. Whether church or secular, or from pre- or post-independence Papua New Guinea, in the last 25 years women have been more ready to record their lives. They have had less immediate responsibility for policies, and less responsibility for their implementation, so they have been free of the restraints that may have inhibited some men. Also, women who have been aware of the feminist movement and have changed their roles or aspirations in the workforce and in their relationships with men may be more ready to adapt to the changes that came with the transition from 'territory' to 'colony' to foreign country. Whatever the reason, many women have been ready to accept the present and concentrate on the immediate task—whether that was running a health clinic in the West Sepik, opening a school in the Highlands, or trying to introduce a literacy program for womens' groups. Often the most engaging and revealing moments are not incidents of great drama—they are the memories of nights spent on pitching small boats, clinging to small children, chucking up over the side, and accepting the impossibility of using the only toilet, a bucket; or noticing that the school children had placed the long buds of the red flowers of the tulip tree on their desks—they contained water and were used to clean their slates; or trying to explain to a 16-year-old son why he could not ride a motor bike exuberantly in front of a group of Highlanders who once would have been entertained but were now enraged because this was an arrogant display of what they did not have and could not do in their own country.

The men obviously vary widely from the fundamentalist missionaries to the knockabout labourers, but the women reveal a wider range of attitudes. No man writes with Kidu's commitment to a Papua New Guinean community, or with Baranay's distance and criticism of contemporary Highlands. The diversity of the women is most obvious in their vocabularies. While some women can write of having to 'slosh along in pig shit', ask 'What the fuck do I want?', or recall having a 'hot fanny', for other women such terms—and implicit values—are as alien as an iceberg in Moresby Harbour.

The servicemen and women who were 'in the islands' during World War II have had much encouragement to write. The increasing crowds at Anzac Day ceremonies, the repeated public appearances of prime ministers at battle sites and war graves, the affirmation of the values of a nation displayed and reaffirmed in war, and the many celebrations of the 50th and the 60th anniversaries have increased consciousness of war service. The emphasis has been on particular battles, theatres and experiences: the prisoners of war of the Japanese and the battles in Papua New Guinea, particularly Kokoda. This has been consistent with the desire to bring the symbols of nationhood closer to home, to diminish distant and empire service, and to make central the battles in immediate defence of Australia and without moral ambiguity. The soldiers did not aim to convert, rule or make money out of Papua New Guineans. Their memories are set against the 'special relationship', their dependence on the carriers and the carriers' generous response. The servicemen and women therefore can exempt themselves from any of the sins of commission and omission of colonial masters and nation builders, and they write to record experiences seen as critical in the making of their own nation. And it is not only men who were in battle who write, but many of the support troops.

Social scientists now, and historians now and in the future, have a mass of memoirs to exploit. Where the archival records of governments, missions and companies are largely written by men, the memoirs are being taken over by women. The division between male political and economic history and female social history seems to be widening. In this two-stream world of enquiry, the value of those few who bridge the streams—such as Carol Kidu who is as revealing on politics as she is on social history—are all the more important.[64]

Bibliography
A selection of books published since 1980 primarily by or about Australians who went to Papua New Guinea

Abbotts, Margaret, *One Man's Life: Staniforth Smith*, Books and Stuff, Welshpool, 1994.

Abel, Gordon, *To War and Back: a young soldier's journey through the terrors and boredoms of World War Two*, privately published, 1999.

Allen, Jim, *Goodbye to the Territory: no ken kam bek!* privately published, 1999.

Australian Dictionary of Biography, Vols 1-16, Melbourne University Press, Melbourne, 1966-2.

Balfe, John, *... And Far From Home: flying RAAF transports in the Pacific War and after*, Macmillan, Melbourne, 1985.

Baranay, Inez, *Rascal Rain: a year in Papua New Guinea*, Angus and Robertson, Sydney, 1994.

Barnes, Robert, *Village Ministry Breakthrough*, privately published, 1983.

Black, Geoff, *Against All Odds: the survival of Australian Z-Special Unit Commando 'Mick' Dennis behind enemy lines*, privately published, 2004.

Bloomfield, David, *Rabaul Diary: escaping captivity in 1942*, Australian Military History Publications, Loftus, 2001.

Beavis, A. Halliday, *My Life in Papua 1929-1967*, privately published,1994.

Beier, Ulli, *Decolonising the Mind: the impact of the University on culture and identity in Papua New Guinea, 1971-74*, Pandanus Books, Canberra, 2005.

Bell, Less and Gillian Shadbolt, *New Guinea Engineer,* Rosenberg Publishing, Dural, 2002.

Bellair, John, *Amateur Soldier: an Australian machine gunner's memories of World War II*, Spectrum, Melbourne, 1984.

Blaskett, Geoffrey, *Islands and Mountains*, privately published, no date (1990?).

Bice, Raymond, *A Victoria Cross on Bougainville 24 July 1945*, privately published, 1999(?).

Biggs, Blanche, *From Papua with Love,* Australian Board of Missions, Sydney, 1987(?).

Boehm, Ken, *Rabaul Erupts: my experiences at Sonoma Care Centre during the Rabaul volcanic eruptions*, H and R Dixon, Morisset, 1999.

Bourke, M. Jean, et al, *Our Time but not Our Place: voices of expatriate women in Papua New Guinea*, Melbourne University Press, Melbourne, 1993.

Bowman, Alice, *Not Now Tomorrow: ima nai ishita*, privately published, 1996.

Boys, Pat, *Coconuts and Tearooms*, privately published, 1993.

Brennan, Niall, *Damien Parer: cameraman*, Melbourne University Press, Melbourne, 1994.

Braga, Stuart, *Kokoda Commander: a life of Major-General 'Tubby' Allen*, Oxford University Press, Melbourne, 2004.

Briggs, Keith, *Potato Milkshakes and Other Aspects of Pioneer Missionary Life*, Asia Pacific Christian Mission, Melbourne, 1995(?).

Brown, Rodger, *Talatala: Kath and Rodger Brown's life in pre- and post-war PNG and their escape from the Japanese*, privately published, 2001

Brune, Peter, *We Band of Brothers: a biography of Ralph Honner, soldier and statesman*, Allen and Unwin, Sydney, 2000.

Burke, Gail, *Meeting the Challenge – Australian teachers in Papua New Guinea, Pre-Independence 1955-1975*, privately published, 2005.

Bywater, Ern, *No Names – No Pack Drill*, Royal Australian Army Resources and Reproduction Unit, Puckapunyal, 1989(?).

Buxton, Keith, *Papua New Guinea: the golden years*, Privately published, No Date.

Carlon, Maureen, *Taim long Kiripia: my time at Kiripia 1969-1980*, Killabakh, NSW, 2000.

Carroll, John, *Good Fortune Flew with Me: memoirs of John W. Carroll's tours of operational duty during World War II*, privately published, 2002.

Center, Rus, *An Armchair Ride*, Seaview Press, Adelaide, 1997.

Chinnery, Sarah, *Malaguna Road: the Papua and New Guinea Diaries of Sarah Chinnery*, National Library of Australia, Canberra, 1998.

Clarence, Margaret, *Yield Not to the Wind*, privately published, 1982.

Cleland, Dame Rachel, *Papua New Guinea: pathways to Independence official and family life 1951-1975*, Artlook Books, Perth, 1983.

Cole, Tom, *The Last Paradise*, Random House, Sydney, 1990.

Collins, Lloyd, *New Guinea Narrative 1942-1943: incorporating the wartime diary of a cipher operator*, privately published, 2001.

Connolly, Bob, *Making 'Black Harvest': warfare, film-making and living dangerously in the Highlands of Papua New Guinea*, ABC Books, Sydney, 2005.

Cooke, John, *Working in Papua-New Guinea 1931-1946*, Lara Publications, Mt Gravatt, 1983.

Coombes, David, *Morshead: hero of Tobruk and El Alamein*, Oxford University Press, Melbourne, 2001.

Damman, Sheila, *The Lieutenant and Her Tin Trunk*, privately published, 1999(?).

Day, David, *John Curtin: a life*, HarperCollins, Sydney, 1999.

Deane-Butcher, William, *Fighter Squadron Doctor: 75 Squadron Royal Australian Air Force New Guinea 1942*, privately published, 1990.

Deasey, Marjorie, *Never Say I Can't*, privately published, 2004.

Dixon, Jonathan, *Papuan Islands Pilgrimage*, privately published, 1988(?).

Down, Goldie, *When Father Disappeared*, Eben Publishers, Mt Colah (?), 1994(?).

Downing, Doris, *The Bridle Path: Doris Downing, her life and letters,* ed. by her sister Joyce, privately published, 1991.

Downs, Ian, *The Last Mountain: a life in Papua New Guinea*, University of Queensland Press, Brisbane, 1986.

Eather, Steve, *Desert Sands, Jungle Lands: a biography of Major General Ken Eather, CB, CBE, DSO, DSC*, Allen and Unwin, Sydney, 2003.

Edgar, Bill, *Warrior of Kokoda: a biography of Brigadier Arnold Potts,* Allen & Unwin, Sydney, 1999.

Edmonds, Laurie, *Down Through the years: the story of my life*, privately published, 1996.

Edwards, Doreen, *Woman of Vision: Sister Catherine O'Sullivan Daughter of our Lady of the Sacred Heart also known as Mother Flavia and 'The Little Flower of Rabaul'*, privately published, no date.

Ennis, Helen, *Man with a Camera: Frank Hurley overseas*, National Library of Australia, Canberra, 2002.

Epstein, T. Scarlett, *Swimming Upstream: a Jewish woman from Vienna,* Valentine Mitchell, London, 2005.

Farquhar, Murray, *Derrick, V.C.*, Rigby, Adelaide, 1982.

Fenton, Peter, *Olive Weston: the heroic life of a World War II nurse,* HarperCollins, Sydney, 2003.

Fisher, Fedora, *Raphael Cilento: a biography*, University of Queensland Press Brisbane, 1994.

Fisk, E.K., *Hardly Ever a Dull Moment*, National Centre for Development Studies, History of Development Studies 5, Australian National University, Canberra, 1995.

Fowke, John, *Kundi Dan,* University of Queensland Press, Brisbane, 1995.

Fox, Peter, *Stephenson called Peter: a life, Peter Fox*, Crawford House, Bathurst, 1995.

Flannery, Tim, *Throwim Way Leg: an adventure*, Text, Melbourne, 1998.

Frazer, Ian, *God's Maverick,* Albatross Books, Sydney, 1992.

Freund, A.P.H., *Missionary Turns Spy,* Lutheran Homes, Adelaide, 1989.

Freund, Dorothea, *I Will Uphold You: the memoirs of Dorothea M. Freund, nee Ey,* Lutheran Publishing, Adelaide, 1985.

Fulton, E.T.W., *No Turning Back: a memoir,* Pandanus Books, Canberra, 2005.

Gallaway, Jack, *The Odd Couple: Blamey and MacArthur at war,* University of Queensland Press, Brisbane, 2000.

Gately, Arthur, *A Call to Arms: war service with the RAAF 1942-1946, diary notes and memoirs of Arthur Gately,* Aerospace Centre, RAAF Base, Fairbairn, 2003.

Geldard, Wal, *Forked Lightning,* privately published, 1998.

Gibbes, Bobby, *You Live But Once: an autobiography,* privately published, 1994.

Glinster, O.E., *Forgotten Hero,* privately published, 1995,

Golski, Kathy, *Watched by Ancestors: an Australian family in Papua New Guinea,* Sceptre, Sydney, 1998.

Gomme, Brian, *A Gunner's Eye View,* privately published, 1997.

Gray, Laurel, *Sinabada Woman among Warriors: a biography of the Rev. Sue Rankin,* Joint Board of Christian Education, Melbourne, 1988.

Graham, Vincent, *At Scarlet Beach: the story of a soldier,* privately published, 1995(?).

Green, Judith, *These were my children,* Landin Press, Adelaide, 1989.

Green, Olwyn, *The Name's Still Charlie,* University of Queensland Press, Brisbane, 1993.

Hamlyn-Harris, Geoffrey, *Through Mud and Blood to Victory,* Wild & Woolley, Sydney, 1993.

Hand, David, *Modawa: Papua New Guinea and me 1946-2002,* Port Moresby, 2002.

Hargesheimer, Fred, *The School that Fell from the Sky,* eBookstand Books, Auburn, 2002.

Harkness, Chris, *New Guinea: the Wahgi impact,* Robert Brown, Cooparoo, 1994.

Harle, Charles, *A Rising Son of Empire,* Mostly Unsung Military History, Melbourne, 1993.

Henderson, James, *Onward Boy Soldiers: the battle for Milne Bay,* University of Western Australia Press, Perth, 1992.

Henderson, Margaret, *Yours Sincerely, Tom: a lost child of empire,* privately published, 2000.

Henderson, Margaret, *Yours Sincerely, Tom, Revisited,* Seaview Press, Adelaide, 2005.

Hoe, Susanna, *At Home in Paradise: a house and garden in Papua New Guinea,* Women's History Press, Oxford, 2003.

Hollinshed, Judith, *Innocence to Independence: life in the Papua New Guinea Highlands 1956-1980,* Pandanus Books, Canberra, 2004.

Holmes, John, *Smiles of Fortune: a memoir of the war against Japan 1943-45,* Kangaroo Press, Sydney, 2001.

Hogan, Tom, Nace and Bill, *From Grabben Gullen to Kokoda,* privately published, 1992.

Hogbin, H. Ian, *Conversations with Ian Hogbin/Jeremy Beckett,* Oceania Monographs, 35, University of Sydney, Sydney, 1989.

Hooper, Alan, *Love War & Letters PNG 1940-45: an autobiography 1940-1945,* Robert Brown, Coorparoo, 1994.

Horner, David, *General Vasey's War,* Melbourne University Press, Melbourne, 1992.

Horner, David, *Blamey: the Commander-in-Chief,* Allen & Unwin, Sydney, 1998.

Horner, David, *Defence Supremo: Sir Frederick Shedden and the making of Australian defence policy,* Allen and Unwin, Sydney, 2000.

Howard, Jane, *Margaret Mead: a life,* Simon and Schuster, New York, 1984.

Hungerford, T.A.G., *A Knockabout with a Slouch Hat: an autobiographical collection 1942-1951,* Fremantle Arts Centre Press, Fremantle, 1985.

Jackson, Kingsley, *Not Always Wise,* privately published, 2004.

Jackson, Patricia and Arthur Jackson, eds, *'A Lot to Fight For': the war diaries and letters of S/Ldr J.F.Jackson, DFC,* privately published, 1996.

James, Clarrie, *ANGAU One Man Law,* Australian Military History Publications, Loftus, 1999.

John, Arthur, *Fortune Favoured Me,* privately published, 1999.

Johnson, L.W., *Colonial Sunset: Australia and Papua New Guinea 1970-74,* University of Queensland Press, Brisbane, 1983.

Jones, Peter, *The Reluctant Volunteer in Service with the Ninth Division 1940-1945,* Australian Military History Publications, Loftus, 1997.

Kendall, Henry, *Not Forever in Green Pastures: the personal memoirs of the Rt Revd H.T.A.Kendall MA*, Diocese of North Queensland, Townsville, 1988.

Kepchia, John, *M.I.A. over Rabaul*, privately published, 1986.

Kidu, Carol, *A Remarkable Journey,* Longman, Sydney, 2002.

Kingsmill, John, *No Hero: memoirs of a raw recruit in World War II*, Hale & Iremonger, Sydney, 1994.

Klitzman, Robert, *The Trembling Mountain: a personal account of kuru, cannibals, and mad cow disease*, Plenum Press, New York, 1998.

Knie, Paul and Eleanor, *To the Ends of the Earth: the life story of Ida Voss*, privately published, 2004.

Kuelinad, Marlon, *My Memories of Life in the Forest: images of a forest village in the Gogol Valley*, Pearson Education, Melbourne, 2004.

Lal, Brij, ed., *Pacific Places, Pacific Histories: essays in honor of Robert C. Kiste*, University of Hawai'i Press, Honolulu, 2004.

Langmore, Diane, *Missionary Lives: Papua, 1874-1914*, University of Hawai'i Press, Honolulu, 1989.

Laughton, Valerie, *From Housework to Adventure*, privately published, 1978.

Leahy, Tom, *Markham Tom: memoirs of an Australian pioneer in Papua New Guinea,* edited by Chris Ashton, Crawford House, Adelaide, 2002.

Lewis, Bessie, *Nupela Misis: an Australian nurse in Papua New Guinea,* Lowden Publishing, Melbourne, 2002.

Litchfield, Geoff, *Fly Boy*, privately published, 2002.

Lloyd, Stephanie, Marlena Jeffery and Jenny Hearn, *Taim Bilong Misis Bilong Armi: memories of wives of Australian servicemen in Papua New Guinea 1951-1975*, Pandanus Books, Canberra, 2001.

Lock, Lester, *Locks that Opened Doors*, Signs Publishing, Warburton, No Date.

McDonald, A.K., *War Memories of A.K.McDonald: a Bougainville non-combatant remembers*, privately published, 1994.

McDonald, Neil, *War Cameraman: the story of Damien Parer*, Lothian, Melbourne, 1994.

McDowell, Nancy, *The Mundugumor: from the field notes of Margaret Mead and Reo Fortune*, Smithsonian Institution Press, Washington, 1991.

McFarlane, Brian, *We band of Brothers: a true Australian adventure story*, privately published, 2000.

McFarlane, Milton, *What God Did with my Life*, Dixon, Morisset, 1999(?).

McGregor, Alasdair, *Frank Hurley: a photographer's life*, Viking, Melbourne, 2004

Mackie, Ronald, *Prelude to Battle of Wau*, privately published, 1990.

Maclean, Edna, *My Loves and Hates*, privately published, 1990.

McCosker, Anne, *Masked Eden: a history of the Australians in New Guinea*, privately published, 1998.

McMurria, James, *Trial and Triumph*, privately published, 1991.

Marks, Bill, *The Fall of the Dice*, Fremantle Arts Centre Press, Fremantle, 1991.

Marne, Jack, *The World around the Corner*, Seaview Press, Adelaide, 2001.

Masters, Peter, *Born Lucky*, Seaview Press, Adelaide, 1998

Medew, Norman, *Up North in Fortythree: the story of a spitfire squadron in the Island War*, privately published, 1989.

Mennis, Mary, *Ferdy: The story of Father Ferdinand Parer O.F.M., 1910-1997*, Lalong Enterprises, Aspley, 2003.

Mitchell, Rob, *One Bloke's Story, 1937 to 1946, Henry Mitchell's MM escape from Rabaul*, privately published, 1998.

Morris, Harry, *Memories of New Guinea: Rabaul 1937-1942*, privately published, no date.

Nason, Joseph and Robert Holt, *Horio You Next Die*, Pacific Rim Press, Carlsbad, 1987.

Nelson, Hank ed., *The War Diaries of Eddie Allan Stanton: Papua 1942-45, New Guinea 1945-6*, Allen and Unwin, Sydney, 1996.

Neale, Bruce, *Nine Lives Had I*, privately published, 1991(?).

Nikakis, Gillian, *He's Not Coming Home: a story of love, loss* and *discovery in Rabaul during World War 2*, Lothian, Melbourne, 2005.

Nott, Lorraine, *CEB: Exploits of an Uncommon Man*, Pioneer Press, Warwick, 1989.

Oates, Lynette, *Not in the Common Mould: the life of Dr David Lithgow*, Wycliffe Bible Translators, Kangaroo Ground, 1997.

O'Brien, Glen, *Kingsley Ridgway: pioneer with a passion, his life and legacy*, Wesleyan Methodist Church of Australia, Melbourne, 1996. (The second half of this book is an autobiography by Kingsley Ridgway.)

Olson, William, *The Years Away*, Wordspec, Canberra, 1993.

Pate, Michael, *An Entertaining War*, Dreamweaver Books, Sydney, 1986.

Park, Edwards, *Nanette*, Andre Deutsch, London, 1978 (Norton, 1977)

Pearson, Arthur, *Brothers Battlers and Bastards*, Boolarong Press, Maroochydore, 1995.

Pearce, Lionel, *Feathers of a Snow Angel, Memories of a child in exile*, Fremantle Arts Centre Press, Fremantle, 2002.

Perversi, Frank, *From Tobruk to Borneo: memoirs of an Italian-Aussie volunteer*, Rosenberg, Sydney, 2002.

Phillips, Anna, *As the Catalina Flies: a Hungarian girl growing up in Bougainville*, Butterfly Books, Springwood, 1993.

Phillips, Norman, *My Highway of Life*, privately published, 1995.

Pinney, Peter, *The Barbarians: a soldier's New Guinea diary*, University of Queensland Press, Brisbane, 1988.

Pinney, Peter, *The Glass Cannon: a Bougainville diary 1944-45*, University of Queensland Press, Brisbane, 1990.

Pinney, Peter, *The Devils' Garden: Solomon Islands war diary, 1945*, University of Queensland Press, Brisbane, 1992.

Porter, Robert, *Paul Hasluck: a political biography*, University of Western Australia Press, Perth, 1993.

Puffett, Dennis, *With a Bit of Luck*, Charles Darwin University Press, Darwin, 2004.

Pybus, Cassandra, *The Devil and James McAuley*, University of Queensland Press, Brisbane, 2001.

Raggett, Sidney, *All About Sid: the story of a gunner in World War II*, privately published, 1991.

Ralph, Len, *The Ramblings of a Wandering Radar-Man*, privately published, 2004.

Read, Kenneth, *Return to the High Valley: coming full circle*, University of California Press, Berkeley, 1986.

Rees, Derrick, *By Then I was Thirteen*, Lexington Avenue, Sydney, 1999.

Reynolds, Max, *Experiences in Vulcanology & Life in the Territory of Papua New Guinea 1953-1957*, privately published, no date.

Rolleston, Frank, *Not a Conquering Hero: the Siege of Tobruk, Battles of Milne Bay, Buna, Shaggy Ridge*, Pacific Rim Press, Currimundi, 1984.

Ross, James (Jim), *My First Seventy Years*, privately published, 1991.

Rothgeb, Wayne, *New Guinea Skies: a fighter pilot's view of World War II*, Iowa State University Press, Ames, 1992.

Rudge, G.A., *A Medast's Way Part 1 1943-46*, privately published, 1987.

Rudge, G.A., *Halfway to the Sun*, privately published, 1989.

Rule, *Beyond the Limestone Barrier*, DSAMC Education, Tamworth, 2001.

Rybarz, Beverley, *The Bridge Builder*, Wakefield Press, Kent Town, 2005.

Sandell, Arthur, *Dicing with Death: an airman's account of his training and operations against Japan*, Aerospace Centre, RAAF Base, Fairbairn, 2001.

Scarlett, Betty, *Oscar X-Ray Calling: the story of the Scarlett family in Papua New Guinea 1962-1971*, privately published, 2005.

Schacht, Tod, *My War on Bougainville: war under the Southern Cross*, Australian Military History Publications, Loftus, 1999.

Sibson, Roy, *My Life As I Saw It: boots 'n' all*, privately published, 1997.

Sinclair, James, *Last Frontiers: the explorations of Ivan Champion of Papua*, Pacific Press, Gold Coast, 1988.

Sherwood, Barbara, *Too Long in the Tropicals: a tale of the Papua New Guinea in the fifteen years after World War Two*, Parker Pattinson Publishing, Douglas Park, 2003.

Smith, Michael French, *Village on the Edge: changing times in Papua New Guinea*, University of Hawai'i, Honolulu, 2002

Spate, Oskar, *On the Margins of History: from the Punjab to Fiji*, National Centre for Development Studies, History of Development Studies, 3, Australian National University, Canberra, 1991.

Keith Smith, *World War II Wasn't All Hell*, Hutchinson, Sydney, 1988.

Speck, Winsome and Ormond, *Into the Unknown: featuring a life-time of adventures, anecdotes and evidences of God's hand in the period 1948-1998*, privately published, 1999.

Stannage, Tom, Kay Saunders and Richard Nile, *Paul Hasluck in Australian History: civic personality and public life,* University of Queensland Press, Brisbane, 1998.

Stubbings, Leon, *Command Wisely: the biography of Lieutenant Colonel Lee William Fargher*, privately published, 1996.

Steward, H.D., *Recollections of Regimental Medical Officer*, Melbourne University Press, Melbourne, 1983.

Stone, John, ed., *El Tigre: Frank Holland, M.B.E. – Commando, Coastwatcher*, Oceans Enterprises, Yarram, 1999.

Tarlington, George, *Shifting Sands & Savage Jungle: the memoirs of a frontline infantryman*, Australian Military History Publications, Loftus, 1994.

Thomson, Phil, *Whitefella Wandering*, Fremantle Arts Centre Press, Fremantle, 2001.

Thorpe, Ken, *My Wartime Story*, Brolga Press, Gundaroo, 1996.

Underwood, Polly, *The Reflections of an Old Grey Mare: a salute to those who served*, privately published, no date.

Veale, Lionel, *Wewak Mission: coastwatchers at war in New Guinea*, privately published, 1996. And see his novel, *And then there were two ... A New Guinea saga of life before and during the war against Japan*, Privately published, 2000.

Wallace, Doug, *You Asked! Remember?* Privately published, 2000(?).

Walpole, Brian, *My War: life is for living*, ABC Books, Sydney, 2004

Weate, Mark, *Bill Newton V.C.: the short life of a RAAF hero*, Australian Military History Publications, Loftus, 1999.

Wetherell, David, ed., *The New Guinea Diaries of Philip Strong 1936-1945*, Macmillan, Melbourne, 1981.

Wetherell, David and C. Carr-Gregg, *Camilla C. H. Wedgwood 1901-1955: a life*, New South Wales University Press, Sydney, 1990.

Wetherell, David, *Charles Abel and the Kwato Mission of Papua New Guinea 1891-1975*, Melbourne University Press, Melbourne, 1996.

White, Nancy, *Sharing the Climb,* Oxford University Press, Melbourne, 1991.

Whitelock, Ian, *Missionary Memories (and Mishaps): family missionary life in Papua New Guinea 1960-1971*, privately published, 2005.

Whitrod, Ray, *Before I Sleep: memoirs of a modern police commissioner*, University of Queensland Press, Brisbane, 2001.

Woodward, Jack, *Under it Down Under: surviving in slit trenches*, privately published, 1996.

Woodward, Jack, *Singing for the Unsung: WW2 New Guinea,* privately published, 2000.

Young, Michael and Julia Clark, *An Anthropologist in Papua: the photography of F.E. Williams 1922-39*, Crawford House, Adelaide, 2001.

Young, Michael, *Malinowski: odyssey of an anthropologist 1884-1920*, Yale University Press, London, 2004.

Zigas, Vincent, *Laughing Death: the untold story of Kuru*, Humana Press, Clifton NJ, 1990.

Of those listed, I have not seen: Barnes, Boehm, Bywater, Damman, Dixon, Down, Glinster, Graham, Hoe, Jackson, K., Kueland, McDonald A.K., Mennis, Pearce, Ralph, Stubbings, Wallace, Whitelock.

Hank Nelson (December 2005)

Biographies Published since December 2005

Chalmers, Gloria, *Kundus, Cannibals and Cargo Cults*, privately published, 2006.

Genty, Owen, *The Planter*, privately published, 2006.

Guntner, Mary W., *Doctor in Paradise: challenges and rewards in medical service New Guinea 1958-1970*, Crawford House, Adelaide, 2006.

Hurrell, A. Lloyd, *Hurrell's Way: an autobiography*, Crawford House, Adelaide, 2006.

Huxley, Jim, *New Guinea Experience: gold, war & peace*, Australian Military History Publications, Loftus, 2007.

Jephcott, Barbara, *Bombs to Beef: development of Dumpu Cattle Station, Papua New Guinea*, privately published, 2007.

Murray, John, *The Minnows of Triton: policing, politics, crime and corruption in the South Pacific Islands*, privately published, 2005.

Smith, Chris Viner, *Australia's Forgotten Frontline: the unsung police who held our PNG front line*, privately published, 2007.

Sturt, John, *Loving Life: one physician's journey*, DayStar Publications, Auckland, 2006.

ENDNOTES

[1] With one or two exceptions, all books listed have been published since 1980.

[2] Peter Brune, *A Bastard of a Place: the Australians in Papua* (Sydney 2003); Peter Fitzsimons, *Kokoda* (Sydney 2004); and Paul Ham, *Kokoda* (Sydney 2004).

[3] Sydney Rowell, *Full Circle* (Melbourne 1974); Lieutenant General Robert Eichelberger, *Jungle Road to Tokyo* (London 1951); George Kenny, *General Kenny Reports: a personal history of the Pacific War* (New York 1949); Clayton James, *The Years of MacArthur: 1941-1945*, vol. 2, (Boston 1975) remains one of the best on MacArthur in the Pacific; Steven Bullard, '"The Great enemy of humanity": malaria and the Japanese medical corps in Papua, 1942-43', *Journal of Pacific History*, 39:2 (2004), 203-20.

[4] Geoffrey Hamlyn-Harris, *Through Mud and Blood to Victory* (Sydney 1993), 50-1.

[5] Beros says it was written on 14 October 1942, *The Fuzzy Wuzzy Angels and Other Verses* (Sydney n. d.). The poem was in the *Courier Mail* and the *Women's Weekly* before it appeared in the book. It was certainly published in Australia before the end of 1942.

[6] Tom Hogan, Nace and Bill, *From Grabben Gullen to Kokoda*, privately published (1992), 106.

[7] Alan Hooper, *Love War & Letters PNG 1940-45: an autobiography 1940-1945* (Coorparoo 1994), 142.

[8] Also quoted in David Wilson, *The Decisive Factor: 75 & 76 Squadrons—Port Moresby and Milne Bay 1942* (Melbourne 1991), 46-50.

[9] Patricia and Arthur Jackson (eds), *'A Lot to Fight For': the war diaries and letters of S/Ldr J.F. Jackson, DFC*, privately published (1996), 230.

[10] Ken Thorpe, *My Wartime Story* (Gundaroo 1996), 37.

[11] Ibid., 33.
[12] Ibid., 64.
[13] Norman Medew, *Up North in Fortythree: the story of a spitfire squadron in the Island War*, privately published (1989), 31. Carroll also comments on the peoples of Goodenough and Kiriwina.
[14] Bill Marks, *The Fall of the Dice* (Fremantle 1991), 113.
[15] John Carroll, *Good Fortune Flew with Me: memoirs of John W. Carroll's tours of operational duty during World War II*, privately published (2002), has several good photographs—of more than Papuan women.
[16] John Kingsmill, *No Hero: memoirs of a raw recruit in World War II* (Sydney 1994), 160.
[17] Hogan, *From Grabben Gullen to Kokoda*, 121.
[18] Lloyd Collins, *New Guinea Narrative 1942-1943: incorporating the wartime diary of a cipher operator*, privately published (2001), 6.
[19] Ibid., 102.
[20] Jack Stebbings to Bert Collinson (n.d.), letter collection in Salvation Army Heritage Centre, Bourke St, Melbourne.
[21] John Holmes, *Smiles of Fortune: a memoir of the war against Japan 1943-45* (Sydney 2001), 81.
[22] Frank Perversi, *From Tobruk to Borneo: memoirs of an Italian-Aussie volunteer* (Sydney 2002), 131.
[23] James Henderson, *Onward Boy Soldiers: the battle for Milne Bay* (Perth 1992), 161.
[24] Collins, *New Guinea Narrative*, 112 and 95.
[25] Peter Jones, *The Reluctant Volunteer in Service with the Ninth Division 1940-1945* (Loftus 1997), 161.
[26] John Bellair, *Amateur Soldier: an Australian machine gunner's memories of World War II* (Melbourne 1984), viii.
[27] William Deane-Butcher, *Fighter Squadron Doctor: 75 Squadron Royal Australian Air Force New Guinea 1942*, privately published (1990), 18.
[28] Ibid., 27.
[29] Polly Underwood, *The Reflections of an Old Grey Mare: a salute to those who served*, privately published (n. d.), 14.
[30] Ibid., 42.
[31] Alan Powell, *The Third Force: ANGAU's New Guinea War* (Melbourne 2003). Also, Frazer has written of Ed Tscharke, a medical assistant in Angau.
[32] Clarrie James, *ANGAU: one man law* (Loftus 1999), 81; G.A. Rudge, *A Medast's Way*, Part 1: *1943-46*, privately published (1987), 37.
[33] Gordon Abel, *To War and Back: a young soldier's journey through the terrors and boredoms of World War Two*, privately published (1999), 29.
[34] Margaret Reeson, *A Very Long War: the families who waited* (Melbourne 2000). See also Carolyn Newman (ed.), *Legacies of our Father: World War II prisoners of the Japanese—their sons and daughters tell their stories* (Melbourne 2005).
[35] Philip Fitzpatrick, *Bamahuta: leaving Papua* (Canberra 2005), has been omitted because a 'number of characters are fictitious and one or two things didn't quite happen in the way I've described' (preface). Similarly I have left out E.I. Symons, *Beyond the Reef*, privately published (1985), who has written a novel, but the section on the war in New Guinea is he says, the story of his own platoon and 'as true as my memory will allow', 173.
[36] See, e.g., Warwick Anderson, *The Cultivation of Whiteness: science, health and racial destiny in Australia* (Melbourne 2002).
[37] Evelyn Cheesman, *Things Worth While* (London 1958), brings together her travels. A.J. Marshall, *The Men and Birds of Paradise: journeys through equatorial New Guinea* (London 1938).
[38] Hortense Powdermaker, *Stranger and Friend: the way of an anthropologist* (London 1967).
[39] The *Age*, 22 March 1998, headed its review 'Boy's own story'—and Flannery writes sharp clear narrative.
[40] Oskar Spate, *On the Margins of History: from the Punjab to Fiji* (Canberra 1991), 91.
[41] Brij V. Lal (ed.), *Pacific Places, Pacific Histories* (Honolulu 2004).
[42] Kenneth Read, *The High Valley* (London 1966).
[43] Michael French Smith, *Village on the Edge: changing times in Papua New Guinea* (Honolulu 2002), 168.

44 Derek Freeman, *Margaret Mead and Samoa: the making and unmaking of an anthropological myth* (Canberra 1983).
45 Paul Hasluck, *A Time for Building: Australian administration in Papua and New Guinea 1951-1963* (Melbourne 1976).
46 Rowley Richards, *A Doctor's War* (Sydney 2005).
47 Chilla Bulbeck, *Australian women in Papua New Guinea: colonial passages 1920-1960* (Melbourne : 1992), 2.
48 I have used 'Boys' but she is the daughter of Margaret Woods, and it is Woods who lived in New Guinea. Several of the other women noted earlier also wrote as widows, e.g. Bowman, Epstein, and Green.
49 Nancy White, *Sharing the Climb* (Melbourne 1991), 34.
50 Ibid., 81.
51 Edna Maclean, *My Loves and Hates*, privately published (1990), 30.
52 Pat Boys, *Coconuts and Tearooms*, privately published (1993), 107.
53 Contrary to most of the women noted here, Ida Voss was outlived by her husband by some nine years.
54 Marjorie Deasey, *Never Say I Can't*, privately published (2004), 188.
55 August Kituai in a letter to Hank Nelson, 1 December 2005. It is interesting that the primary teachers of the two historians, John Waiko and August Kituai, have both written reminiscences.
56 Carol Kidu, *A Remarkable Journey* (South Melbourne 2002).
57 There is no copy in the National Library of Australia. As noted earlier, Ian Downs has a little of his own involvement in politics.
58 Chris Harkness, *New Guinea: the Wahgi impact* (Cooparoo 1994), 274. A biography of Ellis is included in an appendix.
59 Judith Hollinshed, *Innocence to Independence: life in the Papua New Guinea Highlands 1956-1980* (Canberra 2004), 204.
60 Hollinshed, *Innocence to Independence*, 3.
61 E.T.W. Fulton, *No Turning Back: a memoir* (Canberra 2005), 284.
62 Bill Gammage, *The Sky Travellers: journeys in New Guinea 1938-1939* (Melbourne 1998).
63 Betty Scarlett, *Oscar X-Ray Calling: the story of the Scarlett family in Papua New Guinea 1962-1971*, privately published (2005), 170.
64 Kidu, *A Remarkable Journey*.

Chapter 19

Biography of a Nation: Compiling a Historical Dictionary of the Solomon Islands

Clive Moore

I have been conducting research in the Solomon Islands since the 1970s, but must admit my intensity varied during the 1980s and 1990s, when I continued to visit my adopted family[1] but concentrated on other historical projects elsewhere. Then in the early 1990s, I conceived the idea of writing a history of Malaita Province from the time the British administration began on the island in 1909 and started working slowly, through the files in the National Archives in Honiara. At the beginning, this meant a few weeks each year or two, typing everything into my laptop as there was no photocopying facility available. I came to respect the huge amount of material in the archives and despaired that I would never get through it all. During the crisis years, 1998-2003, my attention to events in the contemporary Solomon Islands intensified and eventually I decided to write an account of the years, which appeared in 2004 as *Happy Isles in Crisis: the historical causes for a failing state in Solomon Islands, 1998-2004*.[2] At the same time, I applied for Australian Research Council funding to write a history of Malaita, and received a large grant over 2005-2007.

In writing *Happy Isles in Crisis*, I became aware of just how difficult it is to gather even basic biographical information on the leaders of the nation, or to get reliable information on everything from the oil palm plantations to churches and other organisations. I now know I got some things slightly wrong, and a few things quite wrong. I even slighted a Prime Minister, Francis Billy Hilly, in a short biographical piece, by omitting to mention that he had once been Premier of Western Province. These frustrations led me to think about how this situation could be rectified, both for myself in the future, and for other researchers. In my speech when the book was launched in Honiara in August 2005, I began to formulate a plan to create a historical dictionary of the Solomon Islands. During 2005, I had a full-time research assistant, and the funds to buy microfilm. I used it to complete the necessary Malaita research, but at the same time gathered a wider source base that will enable me to work on the whole history of the Solomon Islands, and to create a historical dictionary for the nation.

The Solomon Islands is the second largest nation in the Pacific in land area, and has a population of over half a million. Yet it is poorly served in historical literature. There is a substantial bibliography of published sources on the Solomon Islands to 1980, by Sally Edridge, which is something of a bible for all Solomons scholars.[3] There is a large literature on the Solomon Islands, some of it scientific, relating to geology, agriculture and marine studies, but most of it is social science monographs, chapters and journal articles that are not easily accessible to Solomon Islanders. There are two excellent general histories, *Wealth of the Solomons* and *Pacific Forest* by Judith Bennett, church histories such as those by David Hilliard for the Anglicans, Hugh Laracy and Claire O'Brien on the Catholics, and Dennis Steley on the Seventh-Day Adventists, labour trade histories by Corris and Moore, and a substantial body of Second World War writings, but overall the Solomons has not been well served by general texts.[4] There is also Graham Goldens' *The Early European Settlers of the Solomon Islands* (1993), which is of indifferent quality, and a large collection of autobiographical reminiscences by missionaries, planters, traders, government officials, and anthropologists, mainly written since the 1920s.

My proposal is to create a historical dictionary of the Solomon Islands which will contain a dictionary of biography and a historical encyclopaedia of events for the Solomon Islands, arranged alphabetically. The models for the project are Jackson Rannells' *PNG: a fact book on modern Papua New Guinea*,[5] and to a greater extent Ann Turner's *Historical Dictionary of Papua New Guinea*.[6] This Solomons' historical project will be in two volumes, one covering the period from first foreign contact to Independence in 1978, concentrating on the 1893-1978 British Solomon Islands Protectorate years, written or edited by Clive Moore. The second would cover the period from Independence to the present day. The overall aim of the project is to foster national consciousness in the Solomon Islands and to provide easily accessible information for use by government departments, churches, civil society organisations, the tourist industry, students, teachers, and the interested general public.

Based on the Scarecrow Press model that has worked successfully for Papua New Guinea and dozens of other countries, the two books would contain:

- A chronology
- A historical dictionary of biography on leading citizens of the British Solomon Islands Protectorate (BSIP) to 1978; and of the modern nation since 1978
- A historical encyclopaedia of information on important events and places
- A short bibliography of easily available sources on the Solomon Islands.

There are differences between this and the Scarecrow Press model: Scarecrow uses only one volume for each nation. My concept has two volumes, and the research base for each volume will be different. Scarecrow Press usually contracts single authors to write each volume. This would probably be the case for volume one, but not for volume two of the Solomons project.

Volume One

Volume One will depend mainly on existing materials already published by the BSIP government, private newspapers, secondary sources, and hopefully the assistance of colleagues and the Solomons general public, both as critics and to supplement areas where my information is too meagre. I have gathered large amounts of material on a variety of topics from the National Archives in Honiara and from the Western Pacific High Commission Archives now situated in Auckland, which will form part of the basic entries. This will be supplemented by newspaper sources. The Government Information Service began a roneoed *News Sheet* in 1955, and each District also had its own local version. The Pacific Manuscripts Bureau has copied the main *News Sheet* and intends to copy the District *News Sheets* in the near future. In Malaita District, for instance, the local *News Sheet* began in 1954, continued until the mid-1980s, then staggered on until 1991. The Honiara-based BSIP *News Sheet* continued until 1975 when it turned into a weekly newspaper called *Solomons News Drum*. The first private newspaper was *The Kakamora Reporter*, published between 1970 and 1975, set up as an alternative to the government-controlled press. This was followed by *Solomons Toktok*, which began in 1977 (originally published as the *Melanesian Nius* and the *Kiokio Nius*), and continued publication until 1992. The *Toktok* was the first Solomons tabloid newspaper with its own version of sensationalist reporting. It came out in competition with the government-owned *Solomons News Drum* and was intended to have more popular appeal. The *Solomons News Drum* was privatised in mid-1982, taken over by Solomon Islander shareholders, and renamed the *Solomon Star*. It remains the main newspaper today, with five issues a week.[7] Other newspapers have also come and gone. At present, the lesser rivals to the *Solomon Star* are the *National Express* and various church papers.

As in all newspapers, the quality of the reporting varies, but collectively the Solomons papers are an enormous resource that has been little tapped by historians. The print media from the 1950s and 1960s contained many biographical pieces on the nation's first educated and politically conscious citizens. It is possible to build up biographies and other items of interest by compiling them from a run of sources. Young future leaders such as Peter Kenilorea, Baddeley Devesi, Mariano Kelesi or Lilly Ogatina Poznanski start to appear through snippets in newspapers, and in government records bit-by-bit as they attended school, progressed through the public service or entered politics. Older famous citizens such as Jacob Vuza, Jonathan Fifi'i, 'Elota, Fred Osifelo, Lloyd Maepeza Gina, Belshazzar Gina, Gideon Zoleveke and Dominiko Alebua have written autobiographies or had books or chapters written about them,[8] and they can also be followed in the media. Although newspapers are an invaluable aid, later in this paper I will give some examples of why newspapers should not be trusted as sole sources of information.

So far I have prepared a 50,000 word draft of 186 biographical entries and 184 general entries for Volume One, which vary in length from a few lines to 2,500 words for the Diocese of Melanesia (the Melanesian Mission). There are many entries for non-Solomon Islanders who have served the Solomon Islands in some way. The Resident Commissioners, some District Officers, planters and bishops all deserve entries, as do some of the quite remarkable lesser clergy. How could I leave out Sister Mary Joseph, or Mother Superior Marie Irene, or the Reverend Charles Fox? Sister Mary Joseph, an Australian, joined the Catholic Mission in 1941. In 1944 she was sent to the Makogai Leprosarium in Fiji for two years, to specialise in the care of those suffering from Hansen's disease. She arrived in the Protectorate in 1946 and became sister-in-charge of the Government Leprosarium at Tetere in 1949, where she remained, improving and extending the hospital. A 1950s World Health Organisation survey found that two-thirds of the lepers in the Protectorate were being treated at Tetere and the Mission leprosariums, using DDS (Diphenyl-dimena-sulphone), an effective cure for most cases, rendering the patients non-contagious. She was awarded an MBE in 1957. Although Sister Mary Joseph was much loved by Solomon Islanders, John Roughan, a long-time resident of the Solomons, has a memory of her as being quite ferocious to any patient who did not take their medication at the correct time, and as having an interesting hobby. She was a good shot and loved going crocodile hunting. They bred tough nuns in the Solomon Islands.[9]

Sister Marie Irene was the first Catholic nun to become a missionary in the Solomon Islands in 1904. Born in France in 1878, for nearly 40 years she directed the work of the Mission's Sisters throughout the Protectorate. First based at Rua Sura, Guadalcanal, where she educated women, she next served at Tangarare, opening the first girls' school there. Based at the Visale headquarters when the Japanese invaded, she escaped with other Mission staff to Tangarere, where she was picked up on a government boat and taken to Lunga to travel by American Liberty ship to Nouméa. Returning to the Protectorate in 1946, she was again stationed at Visale, this time as Mother Superior. After retirement, she continued to train local Sisters at Visale. Awarded an MBE in 1959, she died on 23 September 1965. She gave over 60 years service to the Solomon Islands, her few years in Nouméa the only absence.[10] There are many other clergy who similarly spent many decades in the Protectorate.

While Mother Superior Marie Irene's stay was quite remarkable, she was eclipsed by Charles Elliot Fox, an Anglican priest and Brother who gave 65 years of his long life to the Protectorate. Born in 1878 in Dorset, England, Charles Fox holds the record as the longest-serving expatriate member of any religious order in the Solomon Islands. Son of Canon John Elliot Fox and Emma L. F. (née Phillips), he was educated at Napier Boys High School, the College of St John the Evangelist, Auckland and at the University of New Zealand (Auckland College) where he obtained BA and MA degrees (1899-1901). After a short spell teaching science in New Zealand, he became a member of the Melanesian Mission on Norfolk Island in 1902, and was ordained in 1903. He taught for a short time at the Norfolk school, where there were 240 boys, 160 of them from the Solomon Islands, which was the beginning of his interest in the Protectorate. After a few months on Mota Island in the New Hebrides, Fox began his Solomon years as a missionary at Pamua on San Cristoval. In 1905 he returned to teach at Norfolk Island, before returning to San Cristoval in 1908, where he remained for the next 10 years. In 1911 he opened the first boarding school in the Solomon Islands, St Michael's at Pauma, for boys from San Cristoval, Ulawa and Malaita. In its early years the school had to post guards to prevent attacks from marauding bushmen. In 1922, the Melanesian Mission's main school on Norfolk was moved to Pawa on Ugi Ne Masi Island, near San Cristoval, and between 1924 and 1932 Fox became principal of All Hallows School, Pawa, which in the 1920s was the finest school in the Protectorate. In 1932 he declined the Melanesian bishopric, becoming a member of the Melanesian Brotherhood on Guadalcanal (1933-44), and at Fiu, Malaita (1944-50).

During the war, then well over 60, he spent some time as a coastwatcher on Malaita, before moving to Nggela as a guest of the American Seebee Construction Corps. In 1950 he became principal of the Catechists school, and in 1952 chaplain at diocesan headquarters, before two years (1952-54) as Head Brother of the Melanesian Brotherhood at the headquarter school at Tabalia. In 1956 he was made Canon of Melanesia, and finally (1968-70) was based as chaplain at Taroaniara. He retired to New Zealand in 1973. Also known as 'Takibaina', this was an exchange name given to him during his early years on San Cristoval, when he gave his name, house and possessions to a local man in a swap of identity. Author of a dozen books on the Solomon Islands, his major publications include *Introduction to the Study of Oceanic Languages* (1910), *Threshold of the Pacific* (1924), *Lord of the Solomon Islands* (1958), his memoirs *Kakamora* (1961), and dictionaries of the Nggela, Lau and Arosi languages. Fox received a Doctor of Literature from the University of New Zealand in 1922, an MBE in 1952 and a CBE in 1974. He died in 1977, one year short of 100.[11]

What is clear from these three European biographical entries is that the detail on expatriates is usually better than on Solomon Islanders in this period, but I have also tried to include as many indigenous entries as possible. Two will serve as examples. In 1851 William Didi was the first Solomon Islander to be baptised by the Melanesian Mission. Born on San Cristoval, he was taken from the island in 1850 by the Captain of the HMS *Havannah* and sent to St John's College in New Zealand where he spent 1850-51. Then he joined a vessel as crew, which took him to China and around the Pacific. Returning to St John's in 1858, Didi helped Bishop George Selwyn translate the Lord's Prayer into the Arosi language.[12] Another very different Christian convert was Monilaws Soga, the last great chief of Isobel Island. Soga, son of the great fighting chief Bera, was a chief at the time when head-hunting raids from New Georgia were causing havoc. He lived at Pirihandi in the Bugotu area and was personally responsible for a great deal of the upheaval. In the 1890s it was said that Soga had earlier destroyed many of the coastal communities, and he had entirely wiped out the people of St George's (Maumolu Naunitu) Island. He was baptised in 1889 after an 1886 influenza epidemic, when he was nursed back to health by Bishop John Selwyn. Charles Fox described him as a 'tall, lean, powerful man' who always travelled with an armed bodyguard.[13] Bishop Wilson described Soga as 'a very remarkable man', 'with a face and bearing of one greater than all his neighbours'.[14] Easily able to raise an army of 200 men, after baptism he was as fervent a Christian as he had ever been a warrior, and used his power to befriend the New Georgia raiders and his enemies on Isabel. Through his great influence, peace was achieved and the Melanesian Mission was able to spread Christianity through the island. In later life he lived at Sepi village and when he died in 1898, the cross on his grave bore the inscription *Ke vonungia na dotho* (He was filled with love).[15]

There are many other such individuals of note, and the art will be in achieving a balance between foreigners and Solomon Islanders, and between the biographical and historical events and places sections. At the moment, Honiara has the longest place entry, and my favourite entry is on the *Kakamora*, the legendry midget humans of San Cristoval, Guadalcanal, Malaita and the Banks Group, believed to be about two feet to four feet tall with long black hair and long finger nails. On South Malaita they are called *Mumu*. They are said to hide in the mountains, living in caves and eating wild bush foods, never using fire. They have a reputation as mischievous, and were said to become aggressive when cornered.[16] Charles Fox seemed to believe they existed when he wrote about them in his book *The Threshold of the Pacific* (1924), and used the name as the title for his autobiography, in which he said '[t]hey build no houses, have no tools, make no fires, but they are strong and live in holes or caves'.[17] They may be like fairies and goblins of European mythology, but since the early 2000s archaeological discovery that a small, pre-modern human-related race once lived on Flores Island in Indonesia, the myth has regained some validity. Whatever the truth, how could I leave them out?

Volume Two

The plan for Volume Two takes an altogether different approach. Because of its time-period, it will consist primarily of entries on citizens of the Solomon Islands and would be written mainly by Solomon Islanders. The problem is how to gather the material. The various newspapers since 1978 will still be a basic resource, but the second volume is intended as a people's history, gathered largely through public cooperation and as a nation-building exercise. Its level of success will depend both on local support and on obtaining funding.

Gathering a new set of biographical pieces, provided by the citizens of today, along with support from foreign academics, clergy and others who work or have worked in the Solomon Islands, will be a crucial part of the project. Although some entries will be about the rich, famous, illustrious, dreaded, or in some other way well known, many of the entries for Volume Two would not be about national Bigmen and Bigwomen. Along with the national personalities, a regional/provincial focus will be necessary, as would be a fairly proportioned emphasis on women's entries. Medical Dressers, Native Medical Practitioners, District Headmen, teachers, nurses, clergy, and traditional leaders of all sorts have made the nation what it is today and deserve fair mention. My suggestion of a way to achieve this balance and spread has three essentials: local autonomy; local involvement and agency; and incorporation of and assistance from the local media.

Committee

There needs to be a local committee to oversee the process. I suggest that the committee should be chaired by the University of the South Pacific (USP) Centre Director or his nominee. The committee would be responsible for organising the local collection of material, and ensuring standards and accuracy of the pieces that are published in the *Solomon Star* or aired over the radio. The committee would include representatives of USP, the Solomon Islands College of Higher Education, churches, some NGOs, the national government, all provinces, as well as the *Solomon Star* and the Solomon Islands Broadcasting Corporation (SIBC). This would not be a paid committee, and I am presuming that all members would be Honiara-based, which would allow easy communication. Much of the minor communication could be via email. Members would take on the task for love of their nation, not love of money.

Solomon Star and SIBC

The cooperation of the *Solomon Star* and the government radio stations will be a crucial part of the project. At the beginning, to get the project rolling, public interest could be gained by publishing a weekly column in the *Solomon Star* that included draft entries from Volume One. This would enable trialling of the entries and correction of any errors through public responses. Then, I envisage a national competition, the best material from which would be published in the *Solomon Star*. Each week for a year or two, a biographical or historical place or event entry could be published in the paper in a regular column. These would vary in size from 200 to 700 words, depending of the importance of the subject.

Once the Volume Two series has begun, there would be a prize offered for each new entry published, probably of about SI$150 to SI$300, as it has to be worth winning, but not so large as to be too expensive for donors. Fifty historical columns paid for at SI$300 each would cost SI$15,000, which is less than A$3,000 for a year, or A$6,000 for two years. Publishing about 50-100 pieces in the *Solomon Star* would generate many more, which might not be of sufficient standard to publish, but would also contain valuable historical information which could be followed up to make other entries. Perhaps the committee would end up with 500 entries, of various standards, which would all be deposited in the National Library as a record for the future. The committee and the newspaper would have the final veto over publication of any entry, to ensure standards are met and defamation avoided. The *Solomon Star* would benefit from free copy every week, and presumably through sales.

At the same time, a wider coverage could be achieved by using the SIBC. The newspapers really only reach the urban areas, but the medium wave and short wave radio stations reach out to all parts of Solomon Islands. There are also FM stations, which can be heard over quite surprising distances (the east coast of Malaita, for instance), but generally the SIBC and commercial FM stations only tap the urban population. Radio is the premier media in the Pacific and would need to be used to supplement the newspaper.

National Competition

Hopefully, these first pieces would generate the interest of the newspaper's readers, and prepare them for a bigger, national competition. The Committee could offer different types of prizes for entries on national, provincial, area council, business, church leaders, village and customary leaders, and teachers and health workers etc. Women's biographies would be a special, lucrative category to encourage as many entries as possible. There could also be a section for places and events: cathedrals and major church buildings, sports, institutions, towns, companies, schools, and industries etc. The committee could offer prizes in many different categories, making sure that all provinces are covered and that as many women as possible are included. The prizes could vary in size: SI$1,000 for the best entry; SI$500 for the next 10 best, down to SI$200 for worthy entries. SI$20,000 worth of prizes would only cost A$4,000.

Funding

So far, the suggested costs are no more than A$10,000. The Committee could approach the various High Commissions and Embassies for supporting funds to an initial level of about A$25,000, which should be easy to obtain for a nation-building exercise that has spin-offs for education. One problem will be that that many of the entries will be handwritten, not typed. The *Solomon Star* and the SIBC are going to need their material typed up and on computer disk, and there will be expenses involved in this. All entries should be typed up for posterity and possible use in the Historical Dictionary. The Committee would have to decide on the level of funding necessary. Permanent secretarial staff are not envisaged in the early stages, but this would become a cost in final preparation stages.

Publication and Editing

Through its Institute for Pacific Studies, the University of the South Pacific has produced an extensive set of publications from its member countries. Although the nature of IPS has changed in recent years, I see the USP as the natural home for the publication, both as a book and in electronic form. The involvement of the Honiara USP Centre is crucial in planning, as the conduit back to the main campus, and with present plans to upgrade the Honiara campus into a central part of the USP hub, this project could become a focus of community outreach. At a later stage, the Committee would have to choose an editor/editors for Volume Two, and negotiate with the USP over methods of publication. Outside referees would ensure that standards were maintained.

Referees and Overseas Contributors

There is a large group of academics, church and NGO leaders, and tertiary educated Solomon Islanders who have material that can be used. Any anthropologists could easily provide several entries on traditional leaders and institutions, and historians, geographers and political scientists can also be asked to participate. A refereeing practice would be followed, using knowledgeable Solomon Islanders at home and abroad, and other experts. The bibliography for Volumes Two can be compiled with co-operation from the National Library, but essentially it will probably be an extended version of the one prepared for Volume One.

National Library

All of the project materials would be deposited in the National Library for long-term storage, preferably in digital and paper format. Photographs could also be gathered and copied at the same time. Digital cameras and computers now make copying much easier than back in the days of negative film. An accompanying part of the project could be to ask permission from institutions with photographic collections on the Solomon Islands, copies of many of which are held by the National Museum and Library, to allow these ethnographic and historical photographs to be made easily accessible on a webpage. The speed at which the electronic world is developing may make this quite easy within the next five years or so, and although I am not as naive as to envisage villagers using solar electricity and laptops to access this material, the resources could easily be made available in all towns and to many schools.

The Pitfalls of Writing Entries

Finally, let me discuss the pitfalls of writing entries. Writing entries for historical dictionaries of Pacific nations is fraught and an excellent test for the skills of any historian. I have become quite fascinated with the art of writing concise, accurate but interesting entries, and have been on a steep learning-curve when it comes to balancing entries and chasing contacts. The example of the major Christian denominations is the best. The Anglican Church of Melanesia produced a rich secondary literature during the colonial years, far better than that available on the Catholics, the South Seas Evangelical Mission, the Seventh Day Adventists or the United Church. There will be criticisms if the Anglicans dominate Volume One, but at the moment this certainly is the case. But sources have to be reasonably readily available, and I am not planning to brush up my school-boy French and head off to the Vatican archives to improve the Catholic entries. There are often no supporting rite of passage documents such as the birth, marriage and death certificates, on which other similar projects such as the *Australian Dictionary of Biography* or the *Dictionary of New Zealand Biography* rely. In the end, Volume One may have some flaws that can be improved upon in a second edition. There will be a fine line between delaying because there is not enough material, and going ahead, knowing there are still some problems with balance.

And as any historian knows, information in the public record can be misleading, even downright wrong. A good example would be any entry I began to write on Petero Ara'iasi, a traditional *ramo* (warrior and bounty-hunter) at Tarapaina in the 'Are'are language area, Hauvarivari Passage, Small Malaita. His age can only be estimated, based on the first written references to him when he was in his 20s. We can presume that he was born in the mid-1880s, the time when Malaita was the chief source of indentured labour for Queensland and Fiji sugar plantations.

When he died in died on 11 February 1963, at about 80 years of age, the *British Solomon Islands News Sheet* granted him a paragraph obituary, which is how he first caught my eye.[18] In it there is a claim that in his youth he had killed 80 men while a *ramo*, which I must admit rather impressed me. The *News Sheet* said that Ara'iasi first met Father Jean Coicaud, a long-serving Catholic priest in the Solomon Islands, when Ara'iasi was exiled to Marau, Guadalcanal, and the two became friends. Ara'iasi is supposed to have invited the Catholic priest to return with him to begin missionary work at Tarapaina. Claire O'Brien believed this story, which she dated at 1911.[19] Soon after Ara'iasi teamed up with Father Jean Coicaud, Ara'iasi is supposed to have killed a man from Rokera, was hunted by the police and captured but managed to escape. The *News Sheet* said that Coicaud made a deal with District Officer William Bell that he would hold Ara'iasi as his personal prisoner for at least 10 years, to which Bell supposedly agreed, but impounded Ara'iasi's large collection of shell money and kept it at Auki as security. After some years, Ara'iasi was said to have captured a South Malaitan who had escaped from Tulagi, and was rewarded with release from detention, returning to Tarapaina, where he became a Christian. Not able to stop his old *ramo* ways, he murdered another man, but as he was now a Christian, he went to Auki to report his crime. At the same time he brought with him another man who had shot his own sister, after which Ara'iasi was supposedly pardoned. The *News Sheet* also said that after the death of Bell at Sinerango in 1927, Ara'iasi was appointed Headman of Tarapaina for three years, and thereafter lived a Christian life, much respected as a hereditary chief and ex-*ramo*.

My further explorations have not confirmed this tale, which had obviously been gleaned from Catholic sources on Malaita when Ara'iasi died. He was the son of a *ramo*, and was also the spokesman for Iava'o, the hereditary *araha* (paramount chief) for the area. Hugh Laracy, using church sources, records that in 1909 Ara'iasi was offended by Florence Young, founder of the SSEM, who wanted to establish a base in 'Are'are, but he and Iava'o recognised that there were benefits from having a missionary presence, and invited the Marists to begin a station. The Catholics chose Tarapaina as the site in 1910, but due to poor soils, moved to Rohinari in 1912, where Ara'iasi had arranged a contact with the local *ramo* Aris'imae.[20] Catholic records contain the following explanation by Father Raucaz:

> The old man-eater had already met him [Aris'imae] at Marau. But he wanted details about his generosity: the quality of tobacco, pipes and matches that he would bring with him. Religion was of no account to him; he would not touch it at any price; what would his spirits think of such an idea? He therefore questioned the crew and also Ara'iasi, his rival from the south isle. The report must have been favourable, for the old bandit immediately agreed to sell the small isle of Rohinari with a good portion of ground on the mainland.[21]

Father Bertreux purchased the Tarapaina land in 1910. Florence Young made another attempt to establish the SSEM in the area in 1911, but once more managed to insult the local people. Certainly, a relationship of mutual benefit developed between the Bigmen and the Catholic mission: Ara'iasi extended his power through access to medical aid and European goods and the missionaries received protection. In 1916 Ara'iasi was accused of another murder and was paroled for four years to Rohinari and Visale on Guadalcanal, where he was baptised in 1922. Aris'imae was less beholden to the mission, but was also baptised on his deathbed in 1947.[22]

Another complication is working out which Father Coicaud one is talking about? There were two brothers from Le Regrippiere, Loire Infoieure, France, in the Marist order on Malaita, Jean-Baptiste (born 1878) and Donatien Joseph Pierre (born 1881), both bearded, and both worked on Malaita. It would be very easy for memories of the brothers to get mixed up over decades. Father Jean Coicaud was in BSIP from at least 1902 and stationed at Marau, Guadalcanal from 1905.[23] He arrived at Tarapaiana in 1911, after the second SSEM fiasco. His older brother, Father Donatien, came to the Pacific from France in 1910 and was first appointed to New Caledonia. In 1912 he was transferred to BSIP, first posted to Rua Sura and Visale on Guadalcanal. One 1913 record suggests that he was sent to Rohinari Mission on Malaita, but all other evidence suggests that this was his brother Jean. That year the Coicaud surname appeared in a list of the 32 foreigners on Malaita, and there is another unnamed Marist priest as well, which presumably means both brothers were present.[24] In 1914 Donatien was posted to Buma mission station on the west coast of Malaita where he remained until the time of his death on 11 January 1957. From 1914 until the early 1930s, Father Donatien made frequent journeys along the Malaita coast, north of Buma in the Mission ketch *Hambia*, and later on a smaller vessel. He established a reputation for his medical work and for his knowledge of Malaitan custom and languages. In 1918 he was in Auki, trying to obtain a lease on land at the mouth of the Kwareuna River in north Malaita. In 1917 'Jean-Baptiste Coicaud' was at Auki, the headquarters for Malaita District, wanting to purchase land at Bira River, at the head of Su'u Harbour, for the site of a mission. They were certainly both on the island in 1918 when a census of foreign residents was held: a 'Jean-Marie Coicaud' was at Rohinari and 'Donatiey Joseph Pierre Coicaud' was living at a mission base in Langalanga Lagoon [Buma].[25] Donatien Coicaud spent 39 years in BSIP, broken only by four years in Australia during the war. Jean Coicaud remained at Rohinara from 1912 to 1942.[26]

The BSIP officers on Malaita had been trying to curb Ara'iasi's murderous ways for many years. William Bell said that at the time when the SSEM had first tried to establish a mission post a Tarapaina (when Florence Young insulted Ara'iasi), Ara'iasi had taken part in the murder of two men and maimed a woman at Pau. This was before there was a government station on Malaita, and although the SSEM's Dr Northcoat Deck had informed Resident Commissioner Woodford, the government as unable to do anything. At about this stage, probably in 1905, Ara'iasi turned against the SSEM mission and invited the Catholics to take their place.

In about March 1916, Manihuot was killed at Nusi by Ahau and Hoa from the inland village of Weisiala'ala, and the Administration thought that Ara'iasi was behind it all. Manihout was from the same village as Ara'iasi, and in late 1915 he was accused of using sorcery to kill a man and his son, which caused him in mid-1916 to seek protection at the Catholic Mission at Tarapaina. While there he had an affair with a woman, which caused Ara'iasi to demand compensation from the man's relatives, who refused to pay and gave Ara'iasi permission to kill Manihout. In fact they helped catch him and gave him to Ara'iasi, who told Ahau and Hoa to take him away in a canoe and kill him at Nusi. When the murder of Manihout occurred, Bell was on leave and F. M. Campbell and the Native Police went to Tarapaina to arrest Ara'iasi, but he eluded them. At the time Father Jean Coicaud just 'spread out his hands and shrugged his shoulders', which Bell believed indicated that he thought it was the government's problem and that Ara'iasi was welcome to continue to live at the mission. In 1918 Bell had been talking to the other Coicaud, Father Donatien, who was in charge of Buma mission. Father Donatien indicated that Araiasa had been involved in at least 10 other murders.[27]

In 1918 District Officer William Bell was still trying to get control of Ara'iasi. He reported to the acting Resident Commissioner:

> On this occasion [1916] I passed through the Maramasike Passage at night with the police. We surrounded the house of Alaiasi before daybreak and demanded the surrender of Alaiasi, Kope and Lamamatawa. Two men from the house broke through the police to the bush. On my instructions the police broke in the doors and we entered the house and detained the people in it. We searched the house and collected the property above-stated, and also a Snider rifle, some native weapons which were destroyed, and some cooking utensils, which were handed back shortly after on the same day. The same day Lamamatawa was brought in by two natives and the people detained were released with the exception of a man named Kope. Later I found out that the Kope I had in custody was not the Kope I wanted. The man wanted is Kope (Pipiala). The people who saw the shooting at Pau told me that one of the men who did the shooting was Kope a piccaninny of Alaiasi. Kope Pipiala was adopted by Alaiasi when a child and brought up by Alaiasi at Tarapaina, which accounts for the natives considering him also as a piccaninny of Alaiasi. Since he has grown up I am informed Kope Pipiala has lived most of his time at Tarapaina and sometimes at Iorailamu. Alaiasi is not really a chief but he has acquired power through his murderous habits. The Tarapaina and the Iorailamu people are practically one and the same community. In my efforts to arrest the murderers of Hiruaru'se and Laokeni I have been handicapped by the natives being afraid to give information and other assistance, and the man they say they are most afraid of is Alaiasi of Tarapaina, not Ala'aiasi of Iorailamu.

In the process Bell and his police confiscated a large amount of property: 48 strings of red money, 127 porpoise teeth, two cane knives, one sheath-knife and sheath, one *davi*, and 28 sticks of trade twist tobacco. These were held in pawn until Kope Pipiala was surrendered for the murder of Hiruatu'e and Laokeni, and Ara'iasi was charged with being an accessory to the murder of Manihout in 1916. This seems to be the origin of the story that Bell confiscated Ara'iasi's wealth. However, the police appear to have been over-diligent in their seizures and had taken more than Bell knew. Constable Bera had a new waistcoat, Constable Abanakona had purloined a singlet and a pair of knickerbockers, and a complete case of trade tobacco belonging to Father Jean Coicaud had also gone missing from Ara'iasi's house. The police also insisted that Ara'iasi feed the patrol and had consumed about two hundredweight of yams.

Three weeks after his raid, Bell was back in Tarapaina, and reported to acting Resident Commissioner Workman that Ara'iasi had laid traps around his house at the mission—slanted bamboo stakes buried in the ground in hidden ditches. Workman advised Bell to pay for Ara'iasi's yams at the current price and to continue to pursue him.[28] My investigation is continuing, but at the least I have learnt not to put to much faith into obituaries written 50 years after the events being described.

Conclusion

This project is underway, but is a long way off completion. I sometimes think I am very foolhardy to even consider beginning it. But it seems to me that this method of creating a historical dictionary of the Solomon Islands holds lessons and implications for the history of other Pacific nations. As historians we have a responsibility to try to get away from monograph myopia, as Kerry Howe once advised. In recent years there have been several new general histories of the Pacific, and the Lal and Fortune encyclopaedia,[29] but we need more reference works that go in-depth into the history of individuals and events in Pacific nations. There have been other major biographical projects, such as the Papua New Guinea Dictionary of Contemporary Biography, and Stewart Firth and Daryl Tarte's edited book on 20th century Fiji.[30] In past decades the USP produced the first national histories of many Pacific nations. Now we need to think about reference works, and perhaps a set of historical dictionaries for all Pacific Islands nations. Changes in publishing styles and finances, and the growth of electronic media may well mean a different approach from the old way of producing hardcover, expensive books. Any projects need to consider all of the possibilities, but I believe that we need to try.

ENDNOTES

[1] Clive Moore, 'Rakwane', in Brij V. Lal (ed.), *Pacific Places, Pacific Histories: essays in honour of Robert C. Kiste* (Honolulu 2004), 242-266.

[2] Published by Asia Pacific Press, Canberra.

[3] Sally Edridge, *Solomon Islands Bibliography to 1980* (Suva, Wellington, and Honiara 1985).

[4] Judith A. Bennett, *Wealth of the Solomons: a history of a Pacific archipelago, 1800-1978* (Honolulu 1987); Bennett, *Pacific Forest: a history of resource control and contest in Solomon Islands, c. 1800-1997* (Cambridge 2000); David Hilliard, *God's Gentleman: a history of the Melanesian Mission, 1849-1942* (St Lucia QLD 1978); Hugh M. Laracy, *Marists and Melanesians: a history of the Catholic Missions in the*

Solomon Islands (Canberra 1976); Claire O'Brien, *A Greater Than Solomon Here: a story of Catholic Church in Solomon Islands, 1567-1967* (Honiara 1995); Dennis Steley, 'Juapa Rane, 1914-1942', MA thesis, University of Auckland (Auckland 1983); Peter Corris, *Passage, Port and Plantation: a history of Solomon Islands labour migration, 1870-1914* (Melbourne 1973); Clive Moore, *Kanaka: a history of Melanesian Mackay* (Port Moresby 1985).

[5] Jackson Rannells, *PNG: a fact book on modern Papua New Guinea* (Melbourne 1990).

[6] Ann Turner, *Historical Dictionary of Papua New Guinea* (Lanham, Maryland & London 2006).

[7] Much of description comes from the PAMBU catalogue, which in turn comes from Dr Ian Frazer at Otago University, whose collection of Solomon newspapers is unsurpassed.

[8] Jonathon Fifi'i, *From Pig-Theft to Parliament: my life between two worlds*, trans. and ed. Roger M. Keesing (Honiara and Suva 1989); Roger M. Keesing, *'Elota's Story: the life and times of a Solomon Islands big man* (Brisbane 1978); Frederick Osifelo, *Kanaka Boy: an autobiography* (Suva 1985); Lloyd Maepeza Gina, *Journeys in a Small Canoe: the life and times of a Solomon Islander*, ed. Judith A. Bennett and Khyla J. Russell (Suva and Canberra 2003); George G. Carter, *Yours in His Service: a reflection on the life and times of Reverend Belshazzar Gina of Solomon Islands*, ed. Esa Tuza (Honiara 1990); Gideon Zoleveke, *Zoleveke: a man from Choiseul / an autobiography by Gideon A.P. Zoleveke*, ed. John Chick (Suva 1980); Tarcisius Tara Kabutaulaka, *Footprints in the Tasimauri Sea: a biography of Dominiko Alebua* (Suva 2002).

[9] British Solomon Islands Protectorate News Sheet (BSIPNS), January 1957; October 1957; email, John Roughan, 24 November 2005.

[10] BSIPNS, May 1959; 30 September 1965.

[11] Biographical Summaries of the Anglican Clergy; *Pacific Islands Monthly*, May 1952; July 1956; BSIPNS, March 1962; Charles E. Fox, *Lord of the Southern Isles: being the story of the Anglican Mission in Melanesia, 1849-1949* (London 1958); Charles E. Fox, *Kakamora* (London 1962).

[12] Fox, *Lord of the Southern Isles*, 159.

[13] Fox, *Lord of the Southern Isles*, 198, and 31, 196.

[14] Cecil Wilson, *The Wake of the Southern Cross: work and adventures in the South Seas* (London 1932), 228-31.

[15] Henry H. Montgomery, *The Light of Melanesia: a record of thirty-five years mission work in the South Seas*, (London 1904), [1896 edition], ch. 21.

[16] *Pacific Islands Monthly*, February, March 1950; D.C. Horton, *The Happy Isles: a diary of the Solomons* (London 1966), 25.

[17] Fox, *Kakamora*, 22-23.

[18] BSIPNS, 15 March 1963.

[19] O'Brien, *A Greater Than Solomon Here*, 176.

[20] Laracy, *Marists and Melanesians*, 48.

[21] O'Brien, *A Greater Than Solomon Here*, 177.

[22] Laracy, *Marists and Melanesian*, 48-49; BSIPNS, 15 March 1963.

[23] Laracy, *Marists and Melanesians*, 76.

[24] Solomon Islands National Archives (SINA) BSIP 14/41, 15 April 1913, District Officer T.W. Edge-Partington to Resident Commissioner Charles M. Woodford.

[25] SINA BSIP 14/45, 26 August 1917, District Officer W.R. Bell to acting Resident Commissioner; BSIP 14/46, 25 February 1918, District Officer W. R. Bell to Acting Resident Commissioner Charles Workman.

[26] SINA BSIP, 1, 22 January 1917; BSIP 14/46, 5 January 1918, District Officer W. R. Bell to Acting Resident Commissioner Charles Workman.

[27] SINA BSIP 14/44, 11 September 1916, District Officer W.R. Bell to Acting Resident Commissioner F.J. Barnett.

[28] SINA BSIP 14/46, 23 September 1918, District Officer W.R. Bell to acting Resident Commissioner Charles Workman; 14/12, 10 October 1918, Acting Resident Commissioner Charles Workman to District Officer, W. R. Bell.

[29] Brij V. Lal and Kate Fortune (eds), *The Pacific Islands: an encyclopaedia* (Honolulu 2000).

[30] The Papua New Guinea Dictionary of Contemporary Biography was begun by James Griffin in the 1980s when a considerable number of entries were generated. Refer to Sam Kaima, 'Papua New Guinea Dictionary of Contemporary Biography', (paper written for but not presented at) 'Telling Pacific Lives' Workshop, Division of Pacific and Asian History, RSPAS, Australian National University, 5-7 December

2005, Appendix Two for a list of the entries; Stewart Firth and Daryl Tarte (eds), *20th Century Fiji: people who shaped this nation* (Suva 2001).

Notes on Contributors

Pauline McKenzie Aucoin completed her doctorate in anthropology at the University of Toronto, and currently teaches at the University of Ottawa.

Lucy de Bruce completed her graduate studies at the University of Technology Sydney and is currently a freelance scholar.

Michael Goddard teaches anthropology at the University of Newcastle, NSW.

Michael Goldsmith teaches anthropology in the Department of Societies and Cultures at the University of Waikato.

Geoffrey Gray is a Research Fellow at the Australian Institute for Aboriginal and Torres Strait Islander Studies and Honorary Research Associate in the School of History, Monash University.

Niel Gunson is a Visiting Fellow in the Division of Pacific and Asian History at The Australian National University.

David Hanlon is the Director of the Center for Pacific Islands Studies at the University of Hawai'i at Manoa.

Christina Houen is a doctoral student at Curtin University, in the School of Media, Society and Culture, and a research assistant in the Australia Research Institute at Curtin.

Wolfgang Kempf is a lecturer and researcher at the Institute of Cultural and Social Anthropology, University of Göttingen.

Brij V. Lal is Professor of Pacific and Asian History in the Research School of Pacific and Asian Studies, The Australian National University.

Vicki Luker is Executive Editor of *The Journal of Pacific History* in the Division of Pacific and Asian History, The Australian National University.

Clive Moore is Professor Pacific and Australian History at the University of Queensland.

Doug Munro is an Adjunct Professor in the School of History at Victoria University of Wellington.

Hank Nelson is an Emeritus Professor in the Division of Pacific and Asian History, Research School of Pacific and Asian Studies, The Australian National University.

Andrew Robson teaches English at the University of Wisconsin, Oshkosh.

Sr Alaima Talu is currently pursuing graduate studies at the University of the South Pacific.

Deborah van Heekeren is an anthropologist in the School of Humanities at the University of Newcastle.

Christine Weir teaches history at the University of the South Pacific, Suva.

Graeme Whimp is a graduate of the Pacific Studies Programme, Va'amanū Pasifika, Victoria University of Wellington.

Elizabeth Wood-Ellem is the author of *Queen Salote of Tonga: the story of an era 1900-1965*, editor of *Songs and Poems of Queen Salote* and of *Tonga and the Tongans: heritage and identity*. She is an honorary senior fellow in the School of Historical Studies at the University of Melbourne.

Index

Abaijah, Josephine 46
Abanakona, Const 289
Abbotts, Margaret 252
Abel, Gordon 250
Ahau 288
Ahuia Ova, 40ff
Aikman, Colin 155
Alebua, Dominiko 279
Alesana, Enoka 118
Alesana, Usoali'i 118
Allen, Jim 251
Amaraich, Andohn 173
Amery, Julian 187
Anderson, Robin 252
Andrews, CF 216-217, 222
Ara'iasi, Petero 286-7, 288-90
Aris'imae 287
Avinashnanda, Swami 191
Backscheider, Paula 159
Bain, Kenneth 184
Baker, Ray 185
Baker, Shirley Waldermar 6-8
Balfe, John 248
Ballard, Chris 3
Banks, Charles W 208
Baranay, Inez 257, 258, 259
Barley, Jack Charles 104
Barnes, Charles 254
Barsden, Joseph 4
Baudrillard, Jean 71, 77
Bavin, Cyril 215
Baxter, George 5
Bay, Max 184
Beaver, Wilfred 232, 233
Beavis, AH 255
Bebe, Ratu Taitusi 99
Becke, Louis 10
Begley, Sr Ursula 125
Beier, Ulli 253
Bell, Les 251
Bell, William 286-7, 288-290
Bellair, John 247-8
Bennett, Judith 278
Bera, Const 290
Beros, Bert 242
Bertreux, Fr 287
Besnier, Niko 108, 114
Biggs, B 255, 256
Bignold, Kathleen 267
Bingham, Rev. Hiram, 117
Binner, George 197
Black, John 261
Blanc, Bishop 141
Blaskett, Geoff 249
Bose, Subhash Chandra 190
Bougainville, Louis Antoine de 9
Bourke, Jean 259
Bowden, Tim 252
Bowman, Alice 249
Boyd, Mary 155
Boys, P 255, 256
Braga, S 243
Brennan, Geoffrey, QC 182-183
Briggs, Keith 257
Brodie, Fawn 8
Bower, Dr Isaac 201
Bruce, William Henry clan 97ff
Brune, Peter 243
Buasi 37
Bulbeck, Chilla 255
Bullard, Steven 244
Bullen, Frank 10
Burkitt, Ian 114
Burton, JW 215-224
Burton, JW (Jr) 220
Buxton, Keith 251
Byatt, AS 70-71, 81
Cakobau, Ratu George 187
Cakobau, Seru 196, 197, 199-200
Caldwell, 208
Calvert, James 200, 201
Campbell, Ian 7
Campbell, John Dr 5
Capps, Lisa 91
Carlon, Maureen 256, 258, 259
Carlyle, Thomas 11
Carr-Gregg, C 253
Carroll, John 248
Catholic nuns, Kiribati 126ff
Center, Gus 266
Certeau, Michel de 76, 81
Chalmers, James 9, 250
Chalmers, NS 182
Champion, Ivan 252
Cheesman, Evelyn 252
Chinnery, EWP 227ff
Churchwood, William 141
Cilento, Raphael 252
Clarence, Margaret 249
Clark, Sr Christine 127
Claxton, Sr Berness 130, 131, 136
Cleland, Rachel 254, 255

Clifford, James 20
Coicaud, Fr Donatien Joseph Pierre 288
Coicaud, Fr Jean-Baptiste 286, 287-8, 290
Cole, Tom 251
Coleman, Carol 257
Collins, Lloyd 247
Connolly, Bob 252
Cook, Captain James 4, 9
Cooke, John 249, 251
Cooper, Frederick 205, 206
Corris, P 278
Coward, Noel 147
Cummins, Geoff 6
Curnow, Allen 211
Dademo, Bob 256
Dagora, Kevau 41ff
Damien, Fr De Veuster 5, 9
Dampier, William 9
Das, Gobind 221
Davidson, George 159
Davidson, Jim (JW) 8, 9, 11, 149ff
Davidson, Mabel 159
Davidson, Ruth 154-155, 156
Daws, Gavan 6
Day, David 243
Deakin, Alfred 8
Deane, Mrs 215
Deane-Butcher, William 248
Deasey, Dudley 257, 262
Deasey, Marjorie 255, 257, 262
Deck, Dr Northcoat 288
Defoe, Daniel 159
Deleuze, Gilles 69ff
Dening, Greg 196
Denison, Sir William 197
Denning, Lord 182, 192, 193
Dennis, Mick 246
Denoon, Donald 211
Derrick, Ronald 202
Devesi, Baddeley 279
Didi, William 281
Dillon, Peter 9
Dirks, Nicholas B 205
Doi, Takeo 76
Donnelly, Sr John Bosco 126, 131, 132
Douglas, Norman 8
Downing, Doris 257, 258
Downs, Ian 254
Dudley, Hannal 215, 216
Dunmore, John 11
Eather, Major General Ken 243
Edridge, Sally 278

Edwards, D 255
Eichelberger, Robert 244
Elekana 107ff
Ellis, Tom 258
Ellis, Henry 208
'Elota 56, 279
Eve, Sir Malcolm Trustram 182
Exham, Richard 209
Fairbairn, Ian 154
Falcam, Leo 172
Falvey, John 183, 188, 199
Farrer, TH 201
Fekitetele 4
Fenton, Peter 249
Fielakepa 141
Field, H John 208
Field, Norma 80
Fifi'i, Jonathan 279
Finau 4
Finau, Bishop 141
Firth, Sir Raymond 153
Firth, Stewart 252
Fisk, EK 252
Fitzgerald, Scott 122, 123
Fitzsimons, Peter 243
Fitzpatrick, Brian 153
Flannery, Tim 252
Flynn, Sr Callistus 125
Forster, EM 139
Fortune, K 290
Foster, Sir Robert 189
Foster, Stephen 151
Foucault, Michel 113
Fox, Rev. Charles Elliott 280-1, 282
Fox, Emma L 281
France, Peter 180
Frank, George 122
Frazer, Ian 251
Freeman, Derek 1, 253
Freud, Sigmund 69ff
Freund, Dorothea 255, 256
Fujitsubo 79
Fujiwara, Kaneie 78
Fulton, Ted, 249-50
Furbank, Nick 139
Fusipala, Princess 145ff
Gaigo, Bobby 44ff
Gammage, Bill 261
Gandhi, Mahatma 121, 122
Ganilau, Ratu Penaia 187
Garnier 208
Garrett, John 215

Gately, Arthur 248
Gauguin 9
Gebauer, G 52
Geldard, W 248
Gelling 208
Gerre Rupa, 32
Gibbes, Bobby 251
Gibson, Walter Murray 6
Gill, William, 11
Gina, Belshazzar 279
Gina, Loyd Maepeza 279
Glover, Ellen Fanny 200
Glynn, Sr Oliva 126, 133
Goldens, Graham 278
Goodwin, Frederick 209
Golski, Kathy 257, 258, 259
Gormley, Sr Mary 132
Gosset, Ralph 209
Graham, Sheila (Lily Sheil) 122ff
Gray, L 255
Green, B 258
Green, J 257, 258
Greenwood, Caroline 158
Greenwood, Cecilia (Pips) 158
Greenwood, Miles 158
Grey, Sir George 207
Grimble, Arthur 10
Grin, Henri Louis 10
Guattarri, Felix 69ff
Gudgeon, Walter Edward 205ff
Guichet, Bishop Peter 132
Gulati 39
Gunther, John 228
Gure Gure 22ff
Gure Kila 27
Gure Velapo 22
Haddon, AC 228, 229, 230, 232, 233, 234, 235
Hadfield, Florence 219
Hair, Paul 155
Hall, Harold 188
Ham, Paul 243
Hamlyn-Harris, G 244
Hancock, Sir Keith 9, 153
Hanlon, David 151
Hanrahan, Sr Nora 132
Hargesheimer, Fred 250
Harkness, Chris 257, 258
Harris-Hamlyn 262
Hasluck, Paul 254, 261
Hatab, LJ 36
Hau'ofa, Barbara 144
Hau'ofa, Epeli 144

Heian Japanese women 69ff
Hempenstall, Peter 10
Henderson, James 247
Henderson, Margaret 250
Hennings, Frederick 201
Henry, Betwel 173
Hilliard, David 278
Hilly, Francis Billy 277
Hirsch, Fr 128
Hoa 288
Hobsbawn, Eric 207
Hobson, JA 207
Hogan, Bill 263
Hogan, Nace 244
Hogan, Tom 244, 247
Holland, DC 51
Holland, Frank 250
Hollinshed, Judith 255, 257, 258, 259
Hollis, Sr Veronica 132, 135
Holmes, Richard 150
Hooper, Alan 245
Horner, David 243
Howard, Catherine 133
Howe, Kerry 290
Hurley, Frank 244
Hughes, Billy 239
Iava'o 287
Idriess, Ion 250
Iga, Wala 20
Igawai, Kila Kaile 27ff
Ihlein, Anne 133
Iieshi, Ambilos 173
Irene, Mother Sup Marie 280
Jackson, John 245
Jackson, Kingsley 249, 250, 186, 187, 188
Jakeway, Sir Derek 185, 187, 188, 189
James, Clarrie 249, 250
John, Arthur 251
Johnson, Les 254
Jones, Mary Harris (Mother) 122ff
Jones, Peter 247
Joseph, Sr Mary 280
Kabua, Amata 166, 171
Kailoma 93ff
Kalawa Walo 21, 24ff
Kamehameha 9
Kana Vali 18
Kearsley, Richard 189
Keating, Paul 243
Kee, Ioanna Ben Kum 130
Keesing, Roger 62
Kelesi, Mariano 279

Kendall, Henry 251
Kenilorea, Peter 279
Kenney, George 244
Kennedy, DG 109ff
Kenona, Marica 99
Kidu, Buri 258
Kidu, Carol 255, 257, 258, 263
Kikang, John 51ff
Kila Kawa Igawai 25
Kila Wari Lui Rupa 19
Kilawari stories 15ff
Kingsmill, John 246-7, 248
Kiste, Robert 252
Kituai, August 258
Knie, Paul and Eleanor 243, 257
Koch, Klaus-Friederich 114
Konio 38ff
Kopi Kila Kana 18
Kori Taboro 41ff
Koschade, Victor 257
Koya, Siddiq 182, 186, 190
Krämer, Augustin 3
Krishnamurthy 188
Kwamala Wari 18
La Nauz, John 8
La Pérouse, Comte de 9
La'a 25
Lacan, Jacques 69ff
Lal, Brij 215, 252, 290
Langdon, Robert 11
Langmore, Diane 7, 9, 259
Laracy, Hugh 12, 278, 287
Large 209
Laval, Father 6
Lawes, WG 41
Le Carré, John 149
Leahy, Tom 254, 258
Lee, Helen Morton 145
Leehardt, Maurice 39-40
Legge, JD 227, 230
Leonardo, Micaela di 87
Lévi-Strauss, Claude 69ff
Lewis, Bessie 257, 258
Lifuka, Neli 108ff
Lilburn, Douglas 158-159
Lindt, JW 23
Linnekin, Jocelyn 113
Litchfield, Geoff 251
Lloyd, Stephanie 255
Lono 22
Lugard, Lord 229
Luomala, Katherine 2

Ma'afu 200, 203
MacArthur, Douglas 244
Macdonald, Barrie 6
Macdonald, PD 183
MacGregor, William 45, 230, E 255, 256-7
Maclean, Edna 255, 256-7
Maddocks, Sir Kenneth 181
Mailefihi, Tungi 142
Malapasina 3-4
Malinowski, B 16, 40, 238
Mangafel, John 173
Manihout 288-290
Mara, Ratu 182, 183, 187-188
Marett, RR 230
Mariner, Will 9
Marks, Bill 246, 248
Marshall, Jock 252
Massumi, Brian 71
Mata'afa 199
Maude, Harry 5, 152
Maui 2-3
Maxwell, Dale 133
May, Governor 216
McArthur, Piera 5
McCosker, Anne 250
McDonald, Niel 244
McDowell, Nancy 253
McFarlane, Brian 250
McFarlane, Milton 251
Mea Gure 22ff
Mea, Paul 132
Mead, Margaret 253
Medew, Norman 246, 248
Mega Velapo 22
Melberg, Arne 66
Melville, Herman 6, 9
Merivale, Herman 196
'Michitsuna, mother of' 77
Mihalic, Francis 61
Mihter 181
Miller, Perry 8
Monckton, CAW 250, 253
Moore, Clive 278
Moore, William 214
Moresby, John 49
Morris, Ivan 78
Moss, Frederick Joseph 219, 222
Motu-Koita 35ff
Moulton, JE 6
Mückler, Hermann Dr 198
Munro, Doug 107, 109, 211
Murasaki Shikibu, 72ff

Murphy, John 250
Murray, AW 11
Murray, Gilbert 252
Murray, JHP 40, 227, 230, 231, 232, 235, 237
Murray, Sir James 201
Naite, Nakesa Luisa 104
Nakayama, Tosiwo 165ff
Nakayama, Sydiniha 165
Nakayama, Masami 165
Nakayama, Mihter 171
Naniseni, Maheu 137
Natusch, Guy 158
Natusch, Sheila 158
Neale, Bruce 251
Nelson, Hank 229
Newton, Bill 248
Ngiraked, John 172
Nicholas, Henry 208
Nightingale, Florence 9
Nikakis, Gillian 250
Noser, Adolph Alexander 55
Nott, Henry 197
Nott, L 254
Numa Name Gure 27ff
Oates, Lynette 251
O'Brien, Claire 278, 286
O'Brien, Glen 251
O'Reilly, Father Patrick 11
O'Shea, Sr Dennis 126
O'Sullivan, Catherine 256
Ochs, E 91
Okada, Richard 73
Olter, Bailey 173
Omai Ongka 57
Oram, Nigel 18, 23
Orsmond, John Muggridge 9
Osifelo Sir Frederick 123, 279
Palmer, Bryan 152
Park, Edward 248
Parula Wari 25ff
Pasifika, Frank 108ff
Pate, Michael 248
Patel, AD 177ff
Patel, Leela & family 178-192
Paton, John 220, 222
Peacock, JL 51
Perry, WJ 236
Perversi, Frank 247
Phillips, Anna 256
Poitier, Sidney 121 ff
Pomare 209-210
Pompallier, Bishop 5

Porter, Andrew 196
Powdermaker, Hortense 252
Powell, Alan 249
Powell, Graeme 156
Porter, R 254
Poyer, Lin 113
Poznanski, Lilly Ogatina 279
Prakash, Gyan 205, 206
Pritchard, George 202
Pritchard, Patisepa 199-200
Pritchard, William 195ff
Puffett, Dennis 251
Pulusi, Tafaoata 118
Rabuka, Sitiveni 10
Radcliffe-Brown, AR 229, 232
Ralston, Caroline 7
Ramrakha, Karam 182
Ramirez, Guadalupe 200
Rannells, Jackson 278
Raucaz, Fr 287
Read, Kenneth 253
Rees, Derrick 248
Reeson, Margaret 250
Refalopei, Kalisto 172
Refshauge, Joan 255
Reid, AC 185
Remelik, Haruo 172
Reynolds, Max 251
Richards, Audrey 153
Richards, Rowley 254
Richards, Thomas 205
Riessman, CK 87-88
Rivers WHR 228, 232, 234, 235
Roberts, Jan 255
Robinson, Alfred 255
Roger, Gordon 184, 185
Rogers, Sir Frederic 195-196, 202
Roimata 3, 12
Ross, Jim 249
Rothgeb, Wayne 248
Rotia, Sr 137
Rougemont, Louise de 10
Rowell, Sydney 244
Rudge, Jim, 248, 249, 250
Rudrananda, Swami 185, 191
Rule, Joan 255, 257, 258
Rutherford, Noel 6
Rybarz, Beverley 255, 257, 258
Rybarz, Stanslau 258
Sahlins, Marshall 113
Said, Edward 195, 201
Salamasina 3

Sali, Lazarus 1173
Salote, Queen 9, 149ff
Samson, Jane 196, 202
Sanadhya, Pandit Totaram 217, 221
Sanders, Robert 182
Sanneh, Lamin 197
Santo, Peter 255
Saussure, Ferdinand de 69ff
Scarlett, Betty 243, 255-256, 261
Scarr, Deryck 9, 11
Schoeffel-Meleisea, Penny 3
Schwab, Fr 250
Searson, Anne 133, 134
Seddon, Richard 207
Seemann, Berthold 190, 202, 203
Seidensticker, Edward G 72
Seligman, CG 40, 230, 232
Sellers, Peter 3
Selwyn, George 197, 282
Selwyn, John 282
Senimili, Adi 99
Seward AC 234
Seymour, Commodore 199, 214
Shepperson, George 155, 156
Sherman, Thos 208, 209
Sherwood, Barbara 277
Sherwood, Bill 258
Short, Lillian M 16
Sibson, Roy 248
Silsoe, Lord 182
Sinaitakala 4
Sinclair, Jim 252
Singh, Ram Dayal 178
Singh, James Shankar 186
Singh, Vijay R 182
Sitas, Ari 90
Skinner, Sr Rita Mary 132
Slade, William 222
Small, AJ 216, 222
Small, Cathy 145
Smith, Barry 9
Smith, Grafton Elliot 236
Smith, Keith 248
Smith, Michael French 253
Smith, Stanniforth 252
Smith, Trafford 183, 187, 188, 189
Smythe, Colonel 197, 200, 201, 203
Soga, Monilaws 282
Somare, Sir Michael 46, 243
Spate, Oskar 7, 9, 157, 252
Speck, Ormond & Winsome 255
Spencer, Baldwin 229

Stanley, GAV 41
Stanley, Owen 45
Stannage, T 254
Stanner, WEH 227
Stanton, Eddie 247, 249
Stebbings, Jack 247
Steley, Dennis 278
Stevenson, Robert Louise 6, 9
Steward, HD 248
Stewart, Richard 6
Stoler, Ann Laura 205, 206
Strathern, Andrew 56
Strong, Walter Mersh 237
Sukuna, Ratu Sir Lala 9, 177
Sura 89
Ta'emoemimi 3-4
Tabuanaba, Viane 118
Tabuanaba, Taeaniti, 124
Tabuanaba, Ioane, 124
Tabuana, Teresa 124
Tagore, Rabindranath 221
Takau, 'Queen' Makea 209
Tarte, D 290
Taukoriri, Takenrerei 130
Taunga 10
Tawita, Witake 133
Taylor, Jim 261
Tebwebwe, Bwebwenteiti 130
Teuo, Taulu 118
Tefolaha 124
Thaman, Konai Helu 113
Thomas, John 109
Thomas, Nicholas 205
Thompson, EP 152
Thomson, Phil 251
Thomson, Sir Basil 7
Thornley, Andrew 215
Thorpe, Ken 245
Thurston, Elizabeth 260
Thurston, Sir JB 9
Te Pou, Jimmy 207
Timbs, Sr Marie 133
Tmetuchl, Roman 173
To Rot, Peter 255
Toliman, Matthias 255
Tongilava, Sione Filipe 152
Tora, Apisai 190
Tscharke, Ed, 251
Tu'i Tonga Fefine 3-4
Tun, Petrus 173
Tupou, King George 195
Tupou IV, King 146

Tupou Moheofo 4
Turner, Ann 278
Turner, WY 42
Tuza, Frank, 256
Tyler, Royall 72, 77
Underwood, Malcolm 152
Underwood, Polly 249
Usher, Leonard 183-185
Vainu'upo, Malietoa 198, 203
Vairuarangi, Panapa 209
Vakatani, Makea Daniela 208
Varghese, Margaret 151
Vial, Lee 255
Vivekananda, Swami 191
Voss, Ida 243, 257
Vuza, Jacob 279
Waiko, John 256
Waiko, Bob 256
Wala Iga 17
Waley, Arthur 72
Walo Kalawa 21, 24
Wari Lui Kila Rupa 19ff
Warinumani Lui 18
Washington, Captain John 196
Waterhouse, Rev John 5
Watkins, Rev JB 142
Weate, M, 248
Wedgewood, Camilla 253, 255
Wendt, Albert 198
Wesley, John 8
West, Francis 227, 231
Weston, Olive 249
Weston, QVL 192-193
Wetherell, David 251, 253
White, Eireen 188
Whitlam, Gough 139
Whitrod, Ray 254
Whitty, Albert 209
Williams, FE 40ff, 227, 254
Williams, Henry 5
Williams, John 5, 6, 9, 198, 215
Wilson, Bp 282
Wolff, Michael 155, 156, 160
Wood, Margaret 257
Wood-Ellem, Elizabeth 9
Woodburn, Susan 152
Woodford, Comm. 288
Woodhouse, Jena 72
Woodward, Jack 248
Workman, Res. Comm. 290
Wright, Eric 255
Wulf, Charles 52

Yali 255
Young, Florence 287, 288
Young, Michael 254
Zoleveke, Gideon 279

www.ingramcontent.com/pod-product-compliance
Lightning Source LLC
Chambersburg PA
CBHW040935240426
43671CB00028B/2981